What they said about '77 *Sulphate Strip*:

If Nick Cohn's *Awopbopaloobop Alopbamboom* is Ye Olde Testament of Rock, the New (Wave) Testament being Jon Savage's *England's Dreaming*, then Barry Cain's '77 *Sulphate Strip* is surely the Dead Sea Scrolls.
Dave Collins, DJ and writer

A substantial addition to the period's literature.
Jon Savage, author, England's Dreaming

Barry first interviewed John Lydon when the Sex Pistols signed to EMI and went on to cover various Pistols shows through 1977. JohnLydon.com heartily recommends you check out '77 *Sulphate Strip*. We guarantee you'll find a truly unique 30+ page interview with Mr Rotten. A heady mix of cantankerous mischief and content, laced with revelations you won't read elsewhere.
JohnLydon.com

'77 *Sulphate Strip* stands as a brilliant collection of interviews and reviews. Then and now, Barry Cain writes with such intensity, clarity of feeling and precision of expression that it's almost heart-breaking... Joe Strummer once called him 'the most original writer in the music press'. Read this book and you'll see why. You could call it a triumph of style over substance abuse. And if music has ever meant the world to you, go out now and get a copy.
Claudia Elliot, music journalist

'77 *Sulphate Strip* is, quite simply, the most entertaining delve into the infamous punk era that you could take. Barry Cain still knows how to write and has delivered a belter.
Distorted magazine

Barry was a talented writer, noted as such not just by myself and Joe Strummer, but also people like Rat Scabies and John Lydon. What makes this book truly great is how it connects the past to the present.
Phil Chevron, The Pogues (2008)

Finally a real book about punk from someone who was there and not the post punk wannabes and their scrappy tatty interviews. If you young puppies want a true incite into 1977 buy this book. If you are an old git like me buy the book!
www.punkfm.com

'77 Sulphate Strip is a marvellous first-hand account of the year music exploded and it's hard to put his book down.
Strangled Magazine

A genuinely compelling bit of work, s   a
heart fluttering quantity of drugs and
Richard Porter, www.sniffpetrol.com

Text © Barry Cain 2007–2016
This second edition © Red Planet Books Ltd 2016

Publisher: Mark Neeter
Editors: Hazel Orme and Matt Milton
Photography: Rex Features (except where indicated)

ISBN: 978 1 9059 5992 1

Printed in the UK

77
SULPHATE
STRIP

AN EYEWITNESS ACCOUNT OF THE YEAR THAT CHANGED EVERYTHING

red
planet

Foreword

Punk may have started in '76 but it mattered in '77. Those '76 trombones morphed into an orchestra.

I wrote this book because 1977 mattered to me. Oh, and also because I wanted to make a shitload of money and become famous. One out of three ain't bad I guess. Yep, 1977 still matters.

It appears enough people over the last decade bought '77 Sulphate Strip to warrant this reprint, yet not enough to make me rich and famous. This publishing malarkey is a shitter. Anyway, this new and improved edition is pretty much the same old song but with no different meaning. I'm still waiting for life to teach me something conclusive – get back to you on that.

The new book does, however, feature a brand new interview with Paul Weller, sadly elusive in the first version, who turns out not to be the old bastard I was convinced he'd become.

Oh, and my sincere gratitude goes out to everyone who purchased this book. Very much obliged. And if you actually have the first version and still bought this one, well, I take my hat off to you. You're either stupid or rich or more likely both (apologies if you're neither) but thank you, thank you, thank you...

So, I'll just say goodbye to love and leave it at that...

Goodbye to love and leave it at that.

Boom, boom.

Meanwhile, a long time ago in a dancehall far, far away...

6

Contents

I saw Buddy Holly at Hammersmith Odeon in 1959 with my mum when I was six. My Aunt Jessie was an usherette and got comps for us in the third row of the circle. I remember the pineapple Mivvi my aunt gave me as I sat down. I remember Gary Miller singing 'Garden Of Eden'. I remember seeing Buddy on stage in front of the Crickets. I remember his big glasses and tight suit. I remember 'Everyday'.

I bet Don McLean can't say that.

Introduction

JOHN, PAUL, GEORGE AND FRANK
New Year's Eve 1968, Streatham Locarno

I guess it really did start with a kiss. A skinhead's kiss. Bridge of the nose. Perfect. In the bowels of the Streatham Locarno that heaved with Motown and reeked of speed. The first hour of '69. I'd dropped 15 pills. The world was twisted.

Frank's face came out of the gloom. All I saw were his eyes penetrating my forehead. "Ave some of that, you cunt.'

As I went down, blood on my mohair, pain in my heart, I laughed.

I knew right away.

There and then.

I'd never touch speed again.

Ever...

'I Heard It Through The Grapevine' eased its way off the dancefloor.

It slithered up the stairs and along the red-carpeted foyer towards the entrance, like a snake on Mandrax, then wrapped itself round me as the bouncer ran his hand up my inside trouser leg. 'Okay pal,' he said. 'In you go.'

I was always clean. We all were except John and nobody ever searched him. He was too big and too mean and too fuck-you, so he carried for everyone and dished them out in the toilet along with the dexies. Streatham Locarno was a long way from home on New Year's Eve and you had to be tooled up, just in case.

Frank and John both had chivs, Paul – John's younger brother – always put a penknife in his sock and George had a Stanley knife. All I could muster was a ladies' steel comb with a sharpened handle but it had done the business once, in the toilets at the Manor House, when Frank ripped it out of my hand as I touched up my number three and stabbed a Greek – who had just called him a flash bastard – twice in the leg. The Greek cried like a baby and screamed, '*Pesevengis, pesevengis!*' over and over again. We didn't know what he was saying but it sounded offensive enough to Frank to warrant a further two thrusts deep into the same wounds.

The divvying up of the tools was a ritual I always got a kick out of, but I knew the comb, like the obligatory packet of three I carried beneath the red silk handkerchief in my top pocket, would never be used – not by me anyway. I was there strictly for the music and a possible brief encounter with a ruby red female tongue.

George, Paul and I downed some dexies. Frank and John never touched drugs then. Frank frowned on it and John was always on a natural high.

Frank was the main man. He looked like Long John Baldry without the sideburns and stuttered like a freak but he was number one, no question. Blond and cool, he ruled the roost. When he walked towards you his shoulders swayed and his legs bent at the knee, like there wasn't enough room between his head and the sky, and he'd sing 'Heatwave' somewhere deep inside and then he'd come right up to you, right in your face, and smile. If he looked you in the eyes you were okay. If he looked you in the nose he'd nut it.

Not surprisingly, most people weren't comfortable with the idea of Frank walking towards them. But John, Paul, George and me were his Vandellas. We called him Mr Moonlight because it was his favourite Beatles track and he sang it at least ten times a day.

Frank never knew his limitations and none of us could compete with the steely confidence such ignorance spawned. He lived on the bad side of sane but always pretty close to town.

Frank's stutter vanished when he sang, which was why he sang a lot. He knew the entire Stax/Volt catalogue – Sam and Dave, Carla Thomas, and Otis, naturally – and most of Motown. He thought Spector lacked soul and would only tolerate the Ronettes when he was pissed.

A few weeks earlier I'd been standing outside a bathroom at a party in Loretta C's flat while her parents were away, third in a queue of three waiting to shaft Sheila the Feeler who was coming across with the goods to Frank on the toilet floor. John and George were ahead of me and we were all on a promise.

I was 16 and a virgin but nobody knew. Frank told us Sheila was game that night and everybody knew she loved it. She had an amazing pair of tits and when she laughed you could hear her on the tenth floor. She flashed 'a step inside love' look guaranteed to put a smile on your face and a few extra inches in your Winfield Y fronts.

But that night I guess she was a little more pissed than usual.

So we're standing there, John and George laughing and joking, me shitting my pants, when Frank, behind the door, starts singing the Ronettes "Be My Baby' – and then comes his load.

'Get in there, me sons,' he said, as he came out making a big point of zipping up his fly. I can't speak for John and George but I certainly didn't get in there. I shot in my beige Sta-Prest before I got anywhere near her and she called me a stupid bastard and then started laughing, like a hyena on sulphate, and everyone downstairs could hear her – even though 'Baby Come Back' was blasting out of the Pye Black Box.

'Why was she laughing P-P-Prof?' asked Frank, when I finally plucked up the courage to venture down. He called me 'Prof' because I was the only guy he knew who was still at school.

'I couldn't find the hole, Frank,' I whispered.

''Ere, you 'ear that?' he yelled. 'The P-P-Prof couldn't f-f-f-find the f-f-f-fuckin' 'ole,' and everyone in the room – and we're talking 50 people at least – creased up. Fortunately, at that moment Stevie S bottled Harry D and the place exploded. That was the night Lenny F bled all over the white carpet in Loretta's bedroom after Frank shoved Paul's penknife up his arse (funny how he never used his own weapon to inflict the deadliest blows) while John, Paul and George held him down.

He got away with it. Nobody dared grass Frank up and nobody

liked Lenny F, especially after he was caught with his hand up the dress of a seven-year-old girl in a lift.

They got Frank eventually, but that was another Mr Moonlight. The one with more lysergic acid diethylamide coursing through his veins than blood. The one who liked Donovan better than Eddie Floyd. The one who rode newspaper taxis instead of stolen Cortinas.

'I f-f-f-feel like a f-f-f-fuck tonight,' Frank shouted, as we walked up the stairs that led to the gallery bar. When it came to pulling, Frank was about as subtle as an H-bomb. His sex life consisted entirely of line-ups and Marilyn C, known locally as the Last Resort, who'd do anything for a couple of port-and-lemons and a Sobranie Black Russian.

Frank could sniff out the ones who'd come across, only they never wanted to come across with him. The poor sod couldn't help the odd gob with his stuttering, and you wouldn't believe the amount of girls out there who didn't appreciate his saliva sliding down their cheeks when he was a couple of feet away uttering a sentence with too many Fs in it.

He could only pull girls who didn't let him get a word in edgeways either because they didn't give a toss for anyone but themselves or because they were romantically sympathetic to his affliction and attempted to spare him the shame by dominating the conversation. That narrowed down the field considerably – one, maybe two girls might fit the bill out of the 500 or so who shimmied down the velvet-clad stairs leading to the dance-floor in a blaze of nylon that turned the brass banisters into electrical fields.

Of course he was looking for the sympathetic one first because she'd most likely let him have something – a feel up, or even a finger. But they were rarer than a 1933 penny so he had to be content with the garrulous, synthetic ones. And they never let anyone near them until they'd been going out for six months.

I needed the protection that half a dozen light-and-bitters and the anonymity that Dream Time could afford when I made small-talk in darkness that was occasionally illuminated by an ad for footwear on the giant screen suspended above the dance-floor. All I ever got was a snog and a noseful of heavily lacquered hair, but for me, that was enough.

It was all about the music. That dancehall music. And the drugs...

I mixed with the Fantastic Four because I lived on the same estate. Every estate had its own identity, its pulse. The graffiti were different, the shit in the chute had a different smell, the kids had a different feel – they weren't from your home even though they lived just a quarter of a mile away and went to the same school.

I was an only child and they became my brothers. I was dead and they became my life.

It was the end of 1968 and everything was groovy...

The two most important years of my life, key years that supplanted the imbroglio and revealed alternatives, were 1968 and 1977. The first helped me to a better understanding of the second, thanks largely to cool haircuts, coruscating drugs and sublime music. It laid the foundation for snort heaven, which was 1977. In 1968 the pills made Motown slower; in '77 the powder made punk faster.

Both years were laced with anarchy and uncertainty. In 1968 a decaying socialist government looked on helplessly as people took to the streets and rioted in their thousands against everything from the war in Vietnam to Enoch Powell's 'rivers of blood' speech. Grosvenor Square became a battleground as the American Embassy was besieged. France, rocked by student demos, ground to a halt. And all against a soundtrack of tippy-toe dance music from the streets of Detroit.

In 1977 a decaying socialist government looked on helplessly as unemployment spiralled out of control. Across the UK anti-fascist clashed with National Front disciple that culminated in a huge riot in Lewisham against a soundtrack of hard, driving music stripped of all black influences.

Adolescence is one part pubic hair and two parts anarchy. Throw drugs, unemployment and racial tension into the mix and you get music that matters.

The Beatles never made it to those '68 dancehall turntables. It was strictly Motown and the occasional impersonator because that was what made you dance. Motown gave you room on the dance floor... John didn't need to wait for Dream Time to pull. There were three records guaranteed to awaken the soul in his shoes – 'This Old Heart Of Mine', 'I Can't Help Myself' and 'Baby, Now That I've Found You' – and the moment one hit the deck he hit the floor with a vengeance. Johnny Tillitson got it right – 'Poetry In Motion'. John lived next door to Frank on the sixth floor. They were born on the same day in the same hospital. John was six foot three, a ringer for Solomon King without the chins and the main reason why Frank, who had more enemies than Idi Amin, stayed alive. John was known locally as the Chiv King on account of the huge cutthroat razor he carried. He once carved a 30-year-old local heavy from the top of his arse to the back of his neck in one brutally elegant stroke.

Girls were attracted to him. Paul and George thought it was the Kirk Douglas cleft in his chin they went for but I put it down to the fact that he could dance better than anyone I'd ever seen. Shit, I could have fucked him myself the night I saw him in the spasmodic piebald glory of a strobe light, defying gravity to Juicy Lucy's 'Who Do You Love?'.

The big man possessed a style that transcended the ten inches of razor-sharp steel motionless in a sheath beneath his sweat-soaked Ben Sherman. He eschewed the formalities and never asked a girl to dance – they always asked him.

Sure enough, the Four Tops descended from heaven and John couldn't help himself. He steamed on to the floor and was soon entangled in a web of sticky-sweet stares spun by creamy girls. His mesmerising movements, fuelled by an ocean of Double Diamond, again seemed to defy gravity.

Paul didn't need to move away from the bar before he pulled. He was as sharp as the crease on a brand new pair of Sta-Prest, and when he spoke you listened. He looked like Barry Ryan, made everything that ever happened to him sound spectacularly interesting, and you loved him for it. A few months later when Paul started dropping acid he began to listen, really listen, to what you had to say, every fucking syllable, like he was starving for sound, trying desperately to make sense of everything. It was a little disconcerting and Frank hated it, dismissing Paul as a 'weirdo' at every opportunity.

That night we'd driven down to the Locarno in a Morris Oxford that George had nicked in Upper Street and dumped round the corner. We had to find another motor to get home because the car would already have been reported missing. There were no buses or tubes, a cab was out of the question and it was a good nine-mile walk through Brixton, where five were not enough.

George was the only one of us who could drive so we needed him and his huge set of keys, which could open any car, anywhere, anytime. They jangled in his pocket like a mass of tosheroons and you could hear him walking from the other side of our estate.

Frank told me to keep an eye on him which, in Frankspeak, meant, don't let him out of your f-f-f-fucking sight or else you're f-f-f-fucked.

I watched George as he darted among the wallflowers searching for the eye that told the right tale, the open-legged tale of desertion and despondency that guaranteed a greasy screw and a fake telephone number. George rarely saw his conquests again. Tonight I had to stop that tongue slip-sliding away. He was half Greek and had a fearsome crop that made him look a little like John Cassavetes in 'The Dirty Dozen'. When he wasn't nicking cars he was screwing birds left, right and centre. He must have caught the clap a dozen times. He was the eldest in a family of ten and he was the only one of us who didn't live on the estate. He slept in a bedroom with an indeterminate number of brothers and sisters on the top floor of a tenement off Pentonville Road where at least 25 people shared the basement toilet and the bathroom was the front room on a Friday night in a tin tub by the fire.

But he always looked the part: you never saw George without a three-piece mohair suit, even when the sun was so hot it melted dog shit on the pavement. It was always two-tone – blue, grey, green, beige – and the jacket had to be tailored with a single 12-inch vent revealing the merest hint of Ben Sherman. He held his trousers up with bizarre patterned braces that Frank could never resist snapping on the rare occasion George removed his jacket. He was Mr Immaculate, a style victim who funded his indulgence with stolen eight-track players stuffed with Andy Williams cartridges. 'I've got an eye that knows and a cock that crows,' he told me one Friday night, in the Sportsman on City Road, before sliding 'Wichita Lineman' on the jukebox. Neat.

I watched George make his move – shit, he was smooth.

She was standing with a couple of friends; pretty, a virgin. To me, every girl was a virgin – that was why I never got to screw any. My experience with Sheila the Feeler had fucked me up big-time. Now I was content with a kiss and a slow dance to a cool song. To George, every girl was a ten-minute trip into oblivion.

He walked up to her, one hand clutching the keys in his side pocket so they wouldn't jangle, the other swinging by his side like he owned the place. He bought all three girls a drink, that was his style, and after five minutes, when it became clear who he was after, the other two drifted into the blur.

I clocked the time – 11.45. He'd pulled. It was a quarter to midnight on New Year's Eve and I had to stop George having his first screw of 1969.

I edged through the mohair tribe until I reached his back, which I tapped – nervously. In one movement he turned, wrapped a glistening grey arm round my shimmering blue shoulder, turned me about and pressed his mouth fiercely to my ear. 'This better be fucking good.'

I knew it had to be. 'It's gonna be off outside,' I lied.

'Who with?'

'Some geezers who took the piss out of Moonlight while he was trying to chat up a bird.'

'So? ʼIm and John can sort that one out. Can't you see I'm on a promise?'

'There's too many of them. They said they were gonna jump Frank.'

'Shit.'

George was like me – he didn't like bother and I was no street-fighting man. I didn't need to be, with Frank, John and Paul around. George could handle himself, but the words 'too many of them' made him think frantically of a way out without losing a red badge. Both of us knew it didn't exist.

'Well, let me get a bit of tit off this bird when the clock strikes 12. I'll come and find you.'

I still tailed him, of course. George's cock would get in the way of anything. I watched him walk her on to the dance-floor.

It was the same format every year, whether it was the Locarno or the Lyceum or the Tottenham Royal. Motown followed by 'Auld Lang Syne', followed by the 'Hokey Cokey', followed by 'Maybe It's Because I'm A Londoner', followed by the flavour of the month – which, this year, was the get-back-in-the-groove 'Dance To the Music'. The girls would lose their inhibitions and snog everyone in sight, but even though they were blind, stinking drunk they still moved your hand off their tit – well, my hand, anyway, and you could tread on the toes of the meanest-looking dude this side of Broadmoor and he'd shake your hand and the whole world felt good and juicy and reeked of love and hope and unbridled joy.

It was the most wonderful 15 minutes of the year.

And I'm standing on the edge of heaven surrounded by goofy nerds who couldn't pull a fucking cracker, watching George feeling up a bird with amazing tits. I might as well have stayed at home and watched Andy Stewart do Elvis impressions in a kilt while singing 'Donald Where's Yer Troosers?'

It was cold outside, too cold to walk nine miles. George was our heat home.

A Motown medley was in full swing when I tapped his shoulder again. 'George.'

'If I remember correctly I said I'd find you.'

'We've got to go, George.'

It was then I realised I didn't know where the others were. I checked out the faces around me like a searchlight dancing on prison walls. The dexies were still hitting and 'I'm Gonna Make You Love Me' spilled its sticky smooch juice over the dance-floor when my panic beam fell on her. She was about 20 feet away, dancing with a guy. He hugged her and she looked a little uncomfortable. She was the most beautiful girl I'd ever set eyes on and moved like a field of wheat in a summer breeze. I liked to dress up my hard-ons.

I needed to hear her voice. The dying 'yes, I will' embers of the song drilled holes into the floor, blocking my way. I could see she didn't want to dance with Slowhand again. I had to make a move. I had to hear her voice.

'You're All I Need To Get By' crept in. It gave me strength.

'Would you like to dance?'

She was alone. Slowhand had outstayed his welcome.

'Yes.'

I liked the way she said, 'Yes,' and not 'Yeah'. I liked the way she looked at me – like I was more than Joe Schmuck, like I was someone with something I never knew I had.

The fire burned in her eyes. Oh, baby.

My leg slid instinctively between hers as we held each other. The music soared through my head and gave me such unfettered confidence that I couldn't help myself. 'I need to kiss you.' I'd never said that to anyone before. Blame it on Marvin.

'I'm glad you said that,' she whispered. They were the most wonderful words I'd ever heard.

Her smile enveloped me, 'And with love and determination' we melted into each other's arms. As a car insurance ad played above our heads we kissed and our tongues danced in a tunnel of love…

Shit! George!

I pulled out of the tunnel and looked around. He was gone. He knew that, whatever happened, he'd be able to talk himself out of it, so he didn't give a toss about leaving us high and dry. He'd find a car, the smartest car on the street, and knock her off her feet. He'd drive around for a while and get inside her head before he got inside her knickers. Then he'd take her home and drive back to the Angel, cock, presumably, still crowing.

Shit.

Suddenly I felt a sharp pain in my ribs. 'Prof. Where's G-G-G-George?'

John and Paul flanked him.

'I just this second lost him, Frank. He was with a bird one minute, the next he was gone. You know what he's like.'

'Yeah, I know what 'e's f-f-f-fucking like and that's why I told you to f-f-f-fucking keep an eye on 'im.' He looked me in the nose and I knew what was coming. 'Now 'ow are we supposed to get 'ome? 'Ave some of that, you cunt.'

The head-butt was hard, but not hard enough to knock me out. Frank's head had been responsible for a lot of unconsciousness in Islington so I knew he'd held back. But he still busted my nose. The blood spurted out as the blow connected and sparkled as it ran down the front of my white Ben Sherman and on to my midnight blue mohair waistcoat.

John pulled me up and led me off the dance-floor. I turned. She was standing there with blood on her face. My blood. It was the most intimate moment of my life.

Obviously, it was time to stuff my speed habit into a bag of Waddington games and 'Classics Illustrated', shove it under the bed and concentrate on my A levels.

Frank, John, Paul and I walked all the way home to the Angel on 1 January 1969. My nose ached like fuck and I sang 'You're All I Need To Get By' over and over again to myself.

The music got me home. It always did.

I never saw my Tammi Terrell again.

I did things like that at 16. On a Saturday night Motown made me feel glad to be alive and taught me about love and sorrow and how to move and how to slow-dance a smiling girl.

I'd been reared on Berlin, Porter, Gershwin and Carmichael, songs of love that poured on to piano keys in pubs and parties. As a result I craved melody in my music. I craved love.

What the fuck was punk to me?

In my teenage years I found, in abundance, melody and love in the music of the Beatles, the Beach Boys, the Small Faces, Simon and Garfunkel, the Isley Brothers, the Four Tops, Stevie Wonder, the Ronettes, Otis and Sam and Dave. I even had a sneaky liking for 'Love Grows Where My Rosemary Goes'.

What the fuck was punk to me?

In East End pubs, and dancehalls from Hammersmith Palais to the Strand Lyceum, I wanted Motown. I still wanted Motown through glitter, through mid-Seventies disco pap, through The Rubettes. I wanted Motown to smooth the wrinkles in my tortured brow.

What the *fuck* was punk to me?

Little did I realise that those years had prepared me for 1977. Cavemen were fighting in the dancehalls in '68 and '77. It was just a different turntable jive.

Speed made you feel good and Motown made you feel better. Speed made you feel fast and punk made you feel faster. I saw vicious, blood-soaked fights at music venues in both years – the same frustration that danced round Smokey Robinson clung to The Clash like a leech. These were the years of change, of questioning. The years of the young born outside war. The years of having a good time.

But the good times wouldn't last for ever.

Frank was murdered after ten guys had beaten him to a pulp with steel milk crates. John got life for disembowelling a Turk who'd spent all the proceeds of an armed robbery they pulled off together while John was inside taking the rap. Paul became a cab driver and George ended up doing seven years for dealing in smack.

Me? I became a music writer.

MUSIC JOURNALIST
Late 1976

In the early Seventies I guess Chris Welch of 'Melody Maker' was the first music writer I ever really got into. He made me laugh when I read him and I'd never experienced that before. Later, Charles Shaar Murray of 'New Musical Express' was a revelation and I bought the mag for him alone.

And here I was, a writer on a genuine weekly music paper. It was my goal, ever since I'd been told by a careers officer at school that I could aspire only to the dizzy heights of bank clerk.

Fuck me.

I wanted to be a journalist and mentioned it meekly. The careers officer looked at my mock O-level results and almost sneered as he said, 'bank clerk.'

Fuck you.

I got to be a journalist and then I got to be a music writer. Dream sorted.

When I joined 'Record Mirror' at the tail end of 1976 it was a pop paper in a comfortable, colourful coma. Tina Charles was on the cover, 'Save Your Kisses For Me' was voted single of the year, and the mag sold more than 150,000 copies a week even though you had to be a 13 year-old girl or a chart buff to derive any kind of pleasure from reading it.

I'd never read a copy in my life.

I hit 24 in the middle of 1976. I sported a closely cropped beard, long hair and flared jeans. I was an only child and lived with my mum and dad in a two-bedroom council flat on the second floor of a block just off Pentonville Road. I relied on women asking me back to their place when they were too pissed to care. I relied in vain.

My first four interviews were two face-to-faces with John Miles and, wait for it, Bert Weedon, and two telephone chats with Barry Biggs in Jamaica and Bill Nelson of Be Bop De Luxe in New York for the start of his US tour. Drivel for dribblers.

The *Hotel California* album seemed always to be playing in the office. We'd have a few beers at lunchtime, wander back, put the Eagles on the turntable and, well, fuck about. It was pleasant but it had no edge, just a bunch of drunken memories.

The foxiest night out I had was with Tony Parsons from 'NME' when, after a Nazareth gig in Hamburg – my very first 'business' trip abroad – we strolled round the honey-pot part of the city, astounded by the number of juicy women feigning blow-jobs from the shadows of shop doorways.

The music was dull, but the drink was free.

I used to write my questions on the back of the record-company biog on the tube train if I was interviewing someone in town. It was that easy. But I couldn't resist searching for the angle – sadly elusive when it came to a Detroit Spinner.

I started to wonder where all this was leading.

My first line of speed made me wonder no more.

Suddenly I was back in Motown, my hometown, cruising the streets with the hood down and the sound up.

I'd forgotten just how good speed was and snorting it – shit! Pills were never like that. The rush was phenomenal and, best of all, one hit and I could stay up all night long, no need for top-ups. The promise I'd made to myself in the Locarno went straight up my nose.

And if that wasn't enough, enter the bollocks…

'Anarchy In The UK' was the most perfect slice of pop music I'd ever heard.

'New Rose' was the 'She Loves You' of punk.

'Peaches' startled.

'White Riot' gripped.

'In The City' slapped punk into a Sixties suit and asked it to dance.

And 'God Save the Queen' accepted.

I was 16 again, my tongue down the throat of a teenage girl under the Locarno spotlight.

All the new bands were from London and its suburbs. It was big-city rock and it was my city. The bands became my passion. I'd lost that lovin' feelin' a long while back and they found it for me.

They were my heroes – n-n-n-19 year-olds with big fat ejaculations of sound in a bleach-white, sexual explosion. Imagine the shockwaves if Elvis, moving his hips on the Ed Sullivan Show in the Fifties, had said, in that inimitable Elvis way, 'America is a shithole.' That was punk.

'Record Mirror' changed. Its readership changed. I changed. That was punk's sexy little secret. I looked at people in a different way. I looked at myself in a different way. I listened to music in a different way.

For the second time in my life, I felt glad to be alive.

1977 was the year I realised nostrils were meant for a lot more than picking – and I inhaled more speed than fucking air. It was the only way to listen to punk because 90 per cent of it was shit.

But, oh, that ten per cent. That sublime ten per cent, that ten per cent that took its rightful residence in music heaven. Of course it was unstable. It had to be. But it was cheap, and promoters saved hundreds by booking punk bands that attracted as many punters as pub-rock groups that commanded much higher fees. Consequently punk spread across the UK like the bubonic plague.

Punk as a movement perished over three sweltering '77 August days in a bullring on the French-Spanish border – the venue for the Mont de Marsan punk festival.

It died because The Clash decided to stare out the audience before they broke into one of their worst ever sets – akin to a shit footballer wearing gold boots.

It died because the Jam refused to play and walked off in an ever-changing Woking mood.

And it died when I saw four of the longest lines of coke being delivered to Dr Feelgood's dressing room by two roadies, lines that stretched the length of the hall mirror they were carrying. For me, the Feelgoods were a prototype punk band with R&B haircuts and they were selling out. It was all about speed, not £65-a-gram coke – a week's wages then – carried around in solid silver containers.

I felt cheated.

The speed being hawked around at the festival was cut with bleach and, like the brown acid at Woodstock, to be avoided. I snorted a bucketful of that French powder and it killed 99 per cent of everything up my nose.

Dead.

In Mont de Marsan I saw bands, who once really did hope they'd die before they got old, embrace the glitz. It had got to them. It had to. They were revered by a generation of dissolute nonconformists and disingenuous record companies. Over those few days they became bands in their own right, boys to men, in control of their own destiny and able to wriggle free from the manacles of punk. They didn't need a movement any more; they needed recognition.

There was a brief revival when the Sex Pistols ripped up the drugstore cowboys of downhome America as 1977 spun off the road into a '78 ditch. They were the talk of the town but they went down, all guns blazing, leaving a trail of death and self-destruction. A fitting, wonderful finale.

During those glorious months, punk replaced the Motown in my soul. Such innovation was irresistible. This was the most exciting year in pop history – full of East End promise and teenage swank. It guaranteed the world and delivered an allotment. What more could a poor boy want?

As a style, punk was a cross between souped-up skinhead and drug-crazed hippie – the most outlandish fashion of the twentieth century that put the fear of God into an army of average Joes, tit-fed Val Doonican and Roger Whittaker. Punk as music bordered at times on miraculous, and when the key players of '77 got it right live, they took my breath away.

This is the story of that year and how I remember it. It's also the way Johnny Rotten, Hugh Cornwell, Rat Scabies and Alan Edwards remember it.

I'm not that stupid.

But before we walk hand in hand down a '77 Memory Lane, let me tell you about a little meeting I had as the candle went out on '76.

I met Johnny Rotten for the first time at the EMI offices in Manchester Square at the end of November 1976, the day before the infamous Bill Grundy interview on ITV's 'Today' show. I'd started working on 'Record Mirror' a few weeks earlier.

The Sex Pistols had just been signed and 'Anarchy In The UK' was about to be released. They were the hottest pop property in Britain, due as much to Malcolm McLaren's astuteness as Johnny Rotten's image.

I was sceptical. The whole thing stank of hype and I was determined to expose it for what it was – uncouth shit from loudmouths. 'Anarchy In The UK' my arse.

What the fuck was punk to me?

JOHNNY ROTTEN: EMI, LONDON
30 November, 1976

Johnny sits on the floor, back up against the wall, as I walk into EMI's press office.

I hadn't known what to expect, except that it wouldn't be The Rubettes. I had seen genuine fear in the face of a reporter also waiting to interview the band. I like Johnny's smile. It's genuine. There's a flash of honesty about him. We were both raised in the Desolation Row that was Sixties' Islington so he knows my life and I know his, and that gets the biographical shit out of the way. Yes, he looks mean, but for a mean fucker he sure spews diamonds. He doesn't hold back, he doesn't care. It's one big verbal blow-job.

Johnny knows where he's coming from.

His vitriol is meticulous but strangely melodious, something I've never encountered before. His vocabulary is extensive – music to the ears of someone who had sexed up his interview technique on transatlantic phone interviews with big US soul acts from some Midwest town who talked a lot about God.

I always take shorthand notes and I'm fast but I have to hang on to Johnny's coat-tails as he whistles down the wind because I don't want to lose a single precious word. He has 'star' written right through him, like a stick of Brighton punk rock. His words are sexy and sassy, strong and genuine, untutored, nourishing. I must catch every one, every aching syllable. I feel liberated and lubricated at the same time, like a tunnel ride in a water park.

'Groups like The Who and the Stones are revolting. They have nothing to offer the kids any-more. All they're good for is making money.

'You just read their balance sheets – life's really become safe for them. They're just so pathetic.'

Every so often his eyes open wide and he lifts his lips into a smile with invisible strings, and for a moment I wonder if he's a conman, but it doesn't matter because I'm conman enough for both of us.

'They try to ruin you from the start.

'They take away your soul.

'They destroy you.'

And all the time Johnny's eyes are staring into my forehead like Frank's in the Locarno. He speaks like he sings, violently but truthfully, and it's sweet soul music to my dying ears.

"Be a bank clerk' or 'Join the army' is what they give you at school. And if you do what they say you'll end up like the moron they want you to be...'

Exactly! A fucking bank clerk!

'You have no future, nothing. You are made unequal.

'I don't believe in marriage, mortgage or a house in the country.

'It's awful.

'It's disgusting.

'All these creeps who've crawled out of their little suburban huts. The only constructive thing left for them to do is to fucking kill themselves. You've met one, you've met them all. Their personality is governed by what they do and they do nothing worth talking about. They don't like people having notions because they accept the way they live.

'If I hadn't joined the Sex Pistols I would have been locked up, put quietly away, classified insane. Difference is, I know I'm not mad. Can you say that?'

Rat-a-tat-tat. Every sentence an emblem, every syllable a grudge.

'There hasn't been a very white thing in dance music for years.

'But it's all so easy when the music is done by someone else – and it's done by blacks for whites. I hate disco.'

It's true. Yes. We sway to a black tango that beguiles and we've swayed for a long time.

'At 30 it's too late. Most people are clapped out with beer guts – look at Mick Jagger.

'We're just doing our bit to punch the rest of 1976 away. Our songs are ideas. Spend one night in London and you'll become fucked off with the old ways – you're bound to get ideas from that.

'Soon this whole country will be just one city.

'What will happen then…?'

The following day at Thames Television a three-minute chat changed the world for ever.

It went something like this:

Bill Grundy: 'Safety pins? Chains round the neck? And that's just it fellas, yeah yeah. I mean, it's just the fellas – yeah. They're punk rockers, the new craze they tell me. Their heroes?'

Steve Jones: 'Not the nice clean Rolling Stones.'

Bill: 'Not the nice clean Rolling Stones – you see, they are as drunk as I am. They're clean by comparison. They're a group called the Sex Pistols and I'm surrounded now by all of them!'

Steve: 'In action!'

Bill: 'Just let us see the Sex Pistols – in action! Come on, chicks! I'm told that the group have received £40,000 from a record company. Doesn't that seem slightly opposed to their anti-materialistic way of life?'

Glen Matlock: 'No, the more the merrier.'

Bill: 'Really?'

Glen: 'Oh yeah.'

Bill: 'Well, tell me more then.'

Steve: 'We've fucking spent it, ain't we?'

Bill: 'I don't know, have you?'

Glen: 'Yep, it's all gone down the boozer.'

Bill: 'Really? Good Lord.'

Glen: 'Golly gosh.'

Bill: 'Now I want to know one thing.'

Glen: 'What?'

Bill: 'Are you serious or are you just making things up?'

Glen: 'No, it's —'

Bill: 'Really?'

Glen: 'Yeah.'

Bill: 'But I mean about what you're doing?'

Glen: 'Oh, yeah.'

Bill: 'You are serious?'

Glen: 'Mmm.'

Bill: 'Beethoven, Mozart, Bach and Brahms have all died.'

Johnny Rotten: 'Oh God, they're heroes of ours, ain't they.'

Bill: 'Really? What? What are you saying, sir?'

Johnny: 'They're such wonderful people.'

Bill: 'Are they?'

Johnny: 'Oh, yes! They really turn us on.'

Bill: 'Well, suppose they turn other people on.'

Johnny: (quietly) 'That's just their tough shit.'

Bill: 'It's what?'

Johnny: 'Nothing, a rude word – next question.'

Bill: 'No, no. What was the rude word?'

Johnny: 'Shit.'

Bill: 'Was it really? Good God, you frighten me to death.'

Johnny: 'Oh all right, Siegfried.'

Bill: 'What about you girls behind?'

Glen: 'He's like yer dad, ain't he this geezer?'

Bill: 'Are you worried or just enjoying yourself?'

Glen: 'Or yer granddad.'

Siouxsie Sioux: 'Enjoying myself.'

Bill: 'Are you?'

Siouxsie: 'Yeah.'

Bill: 'That's what I thought you were doing.'

Siouxsie: 'I always wanted to meet you.'

Bill: 'Did you, really?

Siouxsie: 'Yeah.'

Bill: 'We'll meet afterwards, then, shall we?'

Steve: 'You dirty sod! You dirty old man!'

Bill: 'Well, keep going, chief, keep going. Go on, you've got another five seconds, say something outrageous.'

Steve: 'You dirty bastard!'

Bill: 'Go on, again.'

Steve: 'You dirty fucker!'

Bill: 'What a clever boy!'

Steve: 'What a fucking rotter!'

Bill: 'Well, that's it for tonight. The other rocker Eamonn.'

Glen: 'Eamonn!'

Bill: 'I'm saying nothing else about him, will be back tomorrow. I'll be seeing you soon – I hope I'll not be seeing you (to the Pistols) again. From me, though, good night.'

THE BRITISH LIBRARY
Colindale, 2007

The branch of the British Library that keeps back issues of music magazines lies in sunny Colindale, handily not too far away from my humble north-London abode.

I rang and was put swiftly through to Victor, a man who patently knew his stuff. This was good old-fashioned phone hospitality, a million miles away from Bombay call centres and electronic voices offering six options with yours always the last.

Victor loved punk but loved Hawkwind more. Yes – I could feel him smiling – of course they had those particular back issues of 'Record Mirror'. When would I like to come in and see them? When I do, just ask for him and he'll sort me out.

His words brought a tear to my eye. This was service above and beyond the call of duty. Victor's the man.

Two days later I pulled into the ultra-convenient car park at the library. The building reminded me of my old grammar school at the Angel. Maybe it was because I knew it was full of books.

'Hi, Victor.'

'Hullo, Mr Cain.'

'Oh, please, call me Barry.'

'Well, I've got the books out for you, Barry. They're at the desk.'

I walked towards the desk, where a rather stern-looking attendant looked me straight in the eye. 'Er, 'Record Mirror', 1977?' I asked.

'There you are.'

Suddenly he was Michael Aspel and 'This Was My Life'. These beautiful leather volumes, each containing 26 issues, stirred my soul. The blue leather felt old and comfortable and had that sweet dying-paper smell.

This was home to all those thousands upon thousands of words I'd written 30 years ago. Naively enthusiastic words, rough-and-tumble words, oddly used words, shit words, ugly words, wrong words, words that made me cringe with embarrassment. But, like my three kids, they're mine and there's fuck-all I can do about it.

I placed the books on a nearby desk, sat down and opened the first one: Jan-Jun '77.

The rest is history…

1977

JANUARY

Top ten singles
beginning of January

1. When A Child Is Born – Johnny Mathis
2. Under The Moon Of Love – Showaddywaddy
3. Money Money Money – Abba
4. Somebody To Love – Queen
5. Portsmouth – Mike Oldfield
6. Living Thing – ELO
7. Love Me – Yvonne Elliman
8. Dr Love – Tina Charles
9. Living Next Door To Alice – Smokie
10. Bionic Santa – Chris Hill

Top ten albums
beginning of January

1. A Day At The Races – Queen
2. 20 Golden Greats – Glen Campbell
3. Arrival – Abba
4. Greatest Hits – Showaddywaddy
5. Disco Rocket – Various
6. Greatest Hits – Abba
7. Hotel California – the Eagles
8. Songs in The Key Of Life – Stevie Wonder
9. 22 Golden Guitar Greats – Bert Weedon
10. Greatest Hits – Frankie Valli and The Four Seasons

The fallout from the Grundy interview begins to bite. The Stranglers are banned from appearing on Thames TV's 'Magpie' after they'd been booked to perform their début single 'Grip' on 21 January.

'There are many groups in existence who are genuinely trying to make their way in the music jungle,' says a Thames spokesman.

'Normally we would try and reflect these groups' interests on 'Magpie'. But while the image of new-wave groups seems to be lumped with the punk-rock Sex Pistols scene, 'Magpie' has to guard its image and refrain from featuring any bands who have any links with the Pistols, however tenuous.

'Hopefully when the ballyhoo has died down the programme can return to its normal job of reflecting what is new and interesting on the pop scene.'

When I start on 'Record Mirror', I'm dating a blonde Californian singer called Colette who shares a flat in west London with a friend of Dr Feelgood's legendary wide-eyed and leggy guitarist Wilko Johnson. On the couple of occasions he visits the flat I bump into him and he eventually agrees to do a surprisingly revealing exclusive interview, which appears in the 6 January edition under the dodgy headline 'Wilko and Out'.

In many ways, the Feelgoods are the harbingers of British punk. Their stripped-down, wiped-out style of R&B disavows the dalliance and foreplay that had crept furtively into Seventies music and heads straight for the unlubricated fanny. You feel dirty and defiled after hearing it but a nation of dirty and defiled record-buyers put the band's live album 'Stupidity' at number one.

Wilko is something of a recluse and does very few interviews. I get lucky.

WILKO JOHNSON
Kilburn, north-west London

Just a song at twilight.

Wilko Johnson bounces into the room like a spot that needs scratching. His face is a skull with just one layer of skin and his hair looks drippy, but it works. He's a handsome rock beast who is erudite and honest.

He also travels around the stage like an angel on heat. I've never seen anyone move like Wilko Johnson.

of exhaust hypes…

'It was the last gig of the tour that established the Feelgoods – Hammersmith Odeon about a year ago. I really didn't know where I was or what I was supposed to be doing. All I remember is standing out front and thinking, This is a big place, it must be important! I had geared myself into the two-nights-a-week set-up at the smaller venues.

'The night before the concert we had had this big party at the Kursaal and all the tension went. So I had nothing more to give.

'I guess I just misjudged things. See, the rest of the band worry a bit less than me. They were knackered, all right, but not as bad as I was. All the music press were at the Odeon that night. We were terrible and they knew it.

'After the show I just went home and stayed in bed for three days. I wanted to kill myself. I felt like apologising personally to everyone who went along. That's why we played two nights in London before going to America – to make up for it.

'The only way of showing that you do care is to give all you've got. I learned a lot from that episode.'

His shadow laughs at him from behind. The white wall is alive with Wilko wriggling from one position to another. His hands speak for themselves.

of matters invincible…

'Everyone doing this job is sometimes bound to think, to hell with it. It's such a crazy life. As a kid, I remember reading interviews with rock stars saying how hard the whole thing was and used to think, wow, that's ridiculous. But now I know. It's hard work physically. People are judging you all the time, and that's probably the hardest part – the competition.

'When you're on the way up – that's the best time. But it's so difficult to realise afterwards you're in a place you thought was reserved for other people.

'But I'd rather feel that I'm giving every ounce now than saving it up for my old age. Better to believe you're living as much as you can in the present. If you start worrying about your health and being sensible then you've got one foot in the grave. You've got to believe you're invincible.

'I never stop and think – I jump in and see where I end up.'

of emergency exits…

'On stage is where it all makes sense. All the travelling, all the hotel rooms, it gets very depressing.

'But in an emergency people will discover parts of themselves they never knew existed. And going on stage is like an emergency every time. It's so charged. When I come off I can't talk to anyone.

'That makes me uneasy. The life I lead is making me behave in ways that I would never have done previously. It's just a way of survival. Life on the road is 90 per cent boredom – airports, cars, trains, hotels, dressing rooms. You're forever waiting for something to happen.

'So I just live for walking on that stage. To me that's rock'n'roll.'

The top button of his black shirt looks like it's strangling him. He sits on the back of the sofa, then slides down to the arm.

of obscure fame…

'The Feelgoods are in a funny position. We're not famous like famous groups are famous. We're not hit names. The people who are into us are very into us. They can think, justifiably, that they've made a little discovery for themselves, and I guarantee that none of their mums has ever heard of us.

'The lady who lives next door has known me since I was a little boy. She knows I'm playing in a group, but she doesn't think I'm like 'that'. I can travel on the bus and tube and I know no one will recognise me.

'It's like a ridiculously well-known secret.

'When this is all over it's going to hit me quite hard. There are not many scenes where you can travel round the world and get money for doing something you really love. If four years ago, someone had told me I'd be doing this now I would have laughed. And I haven't the faintest idea what I'll be doing four years from now.

'The Feelgoods can expect to keep going for as long as anybody. It's just so silly to count on anything. Logic tells you that eventually something will happen to the band.'

of things Indian…

'My old man was in the army on the North West Frontier and told stories about it that fascinated me. I'd vowed I'd go there just before we formed the band, so four years ago I took off. I lived on the street with the beggars, who were very interested in my wristwatch. But at the same time they look at things very logically, very relatively.

'It enabled me to see how greedy we are in the West. I realised then the troubles with world shortages are because so-called civilised people simply eat too much. When your address is a street corner in Bombay and your home is a blanket that's true poverty.'

Wilko contracted hepatitis in India. Now he doesn't drink. Well, you can't have everything.

of 'are you really like that?' and assorted love songs…

'Are you really like that? is the question people always ask when we're introduced. It's such a joke. Up to a year ago none of the band thought of themselves as musicians. The whole thing seemed like such an accident. I was teaching English when I bumped into Lee Brilleaux on the street and we decided to form a band.

'Now we're riding in limos through New York. I'm just an ordinary bloke that this has happened to but yes – now I do think of myself purely and simply as a musician.

'At university I was always well known as an extrovert. Now I get everything out on stage, which makes me more withdrawn.

of Wilkommen…

'My father died when I was 16. That's the time most kids want to kill their old man because he's the person restraining you. As a result, I had these guilt feelings after his death for all the bad things I'd thought about him. Then I had to start living my own life.

'I didn't turn out the way my mother had hoped. Although in the end she wasn't ashamed of me, she would still have liked me to be a quantity surveyor or something. She died when I was a teacher and probably thought I'd settled down at last to something sensible.

'My dad got very ill during the time of the Canvey Island floods because he worked in the water laying gas pipes. He badly damaged his lungs and finally died – six months before my mum was due to have qualified for a widow's pension from the company. And what really sickens me about the whole thing is that for a long time after his death the same firm he worked so many years for still sent us bills in his name. They didn't even know he was dead.

'When my mum died it upset me greatly because she was really beginning to enjoy herself. She'd just started work and had saved up some money for the first holiday of her life. Then suddenly she got cancer and within three months she was dead. She'd done such a lot for me and it seemed so unfair. But I don't get all D. H. Lawrencey about it. It seems to me you always get the rough end of things.

'I come from the working class and feel most at ease with working class people. But at the same time I'm not working class because I've never ever done a day's work in my life.'

of clichéd questions and bands on the run...

'Let's just set the record straight – I think it's fucking good that punk has happened. And the Feelgoods can justifiably take a bit of credit for the whole thing. We showed the record companies you don't need to look at established rock musicians to make music. It can come from anywhere.

'And now the tables have turned. They're looking everywhere for new acts because they constantly have money on their minds so they sign rubbish. OK, so we might take the piss. But I also take the piss out of the working class because I feel close enough to it to laugh. That way I'm laughing at myself as well.

'Punk is back to the fundamentals, the basics of music, the musicians themselves. What frightens me are the headlines in the 'Sun' and the 'Daily Mirror'. If the establishment takes over the music it will make it a part of itself and ultimately destroy it.

'The political side of punk is another matter. I think you can make more effective political statements just by laying your own emotions on the table. Overt political comments are easy to deflate. Look at the mid-Sixties – those heavy revolutionary songs have been castrated. Ninety per cent of them sound so embarrassing now because it all came to nothing.

'The Feelgoods don't set out to do anything. When I write songs I write about the things I know and understand, not about rolling down some freeway in a truck. When the Pistols sing about anarchy I don't know what they mean – I'm not sure they do either. But good luck to them.'

His voice bears the customary Cockney accent and it's hard to detect whether or not it's false, like so many other acquired tones in rock. His replies are very precise and roll out with the speed of a charging snail.

of Punch and Moody shows…

'Violence at punk gigs – at any gigs – is a complete waste of time. What's the point of tearing into each other when the guys who should be getting a punch in the mouth are sitting on the side raking in all the money? This whole idea of violence as being the great unleashing of a revolutionary power is shit because when you get down to it a punch in the kisser hurts – you want to avoid it.

'Sure, I've been involved in fights. I hurt someone real bad once, and now I'm ashamed even to think of it. There were a lot of harder geezers than me on Canvey Island and the only injury I used to get was jaw-ache from trying to talk my way out of tight spots.

'In the band there's a lot of heaviness. Friction reaches a head in the dressing room. But it soon clears. I can honestly say there has never been any physical violence within the Feelgoods. We've had our heavy moments – but if something like that happened it would be the end.

'There are several different personalities within the band. Lee is the kind of guy who will suddenly explode when things go wrong.

Me, I get very moody and sulk in a similar situation. Sparko is a laconic while the Big Figure is very calm and such a nice guy. We never argue about the stage act, although we've been getting some criticism recently. It does change – but not much. We know how we get off on playing.

'We've never planned the act and never will. Let's face it – we've only done two tours of this country, and on the last one there were a lot of people who wanted to see just the same as before. Perhaps next time we will do something a bit different. Our kangaroo suits are nearly finished! At the moment we're taking our first real break. Towards the end of this month we'll go into the studio to record some new material, then think about going back to the States.'

of heirs and graces…

'The only responsibility I have towards my son is simply to look after him and to give him the benefit of such wisdom as I have acquired. By the time he's old enough, he'll think I'm a silly old bastard. While I'm crashed out on the floor, stoned out of my head, he'll probably dash out to catch the 8.20 into town in his suit, carrying a briefcase, and I shall say 'I don't understand the younger generation,' and fall back over in a stupor.

'cos in the end everybody's a fucking idiot.'

Three months after that interview Wilko Johnson will quit Dr Feelgood. The Feelgoods will never be the same again and Wilko drifts through the decades. He has immense style but when I interview him I can't help thinking he looks all out of focus and all out of fun.

The band appear to be drowning in the new wave and Wilko leaves in acrimonious circumstances. Lead singer Lee Brilleaux manfully flies the Feelgoods flag for another 17 years until his untimely death from cancer in 1994 at the age of 41. Wilko forms a band called the Solid Senders who get a deal with Virgin. In 1979 he joins Ian Dury's Blockheads but leaves a year later. Wilko still tours, 35 years after he and Brilleaux created the Feelgood's dream.

Who says rock'n' roll is dead?

HUGH CORNWELL
The Nashville, Dingwalls, Speakeasy

'What I really want to do is melt down Led Zeppelin and reinforce all the church roofs in England,' whispers Hugh Cornwell in the depths of Dingwalls.

My first Stranglers interview: a night on the town with Mr Cornwell. I'm picked up outside my flat by a chauffeur-driven Granada provided by the record company with Hugh sitting in the back. As I walk out of the entrance to the block my mum and dad bang on our second floor window and wave at me.

'Is that your parents?' asks Hugh, who is smoking a joint, which he duly offers me and which I duly accept. I've met him on several occasions before, but never like this.

'Yes.'

'Do you live there?'

'Yes.'

'With them?'

'Yes.'

'Cool.'

'Old ladies are being mugged on their way to churches and it's a shame,' he says, as we motor across town to the Nashville. 'Things won't change by violence. There'll be a silent revolution. A lot of very intelligent people around today are fed up with our constitution. They're slowly increasing in number and something's going to happen soon.'

Hugh is an articulate member of an articulate band – musically, the Stranglers are streets ahead of their contemporaries, and comparisons with the Doors are frequent. He is the gaunt-faced, Byronesque, gob-from-the-depths front man who spurts songs awash with decadence and degradation.

'A majority of people have come to the conclusion that the government has no credibility,' says Hugh, as we sit down to a couple

of beers in the bar at the Nashville, my favourite pub music venue. 'I
see my role as someone trying to make the country understand that
all these 60-and 70-year-old politicians have absolutely no contact
with the public. They start off with good intentions but after years of
crawling they become meaningless. Like Denis Squealy, they don't
want to lose what they've got.'

We climb back into the Granada, which is waiting for us outside,
and head off to Dingwalls. Some speed appears magically from a guy
in the front seat and disappears magically up my nose.

'I'd like to make enough money to buy a huge mansion and put all
the politicians in separate rooms so they can play with themselves,'
says Hugh. 'What we need desperately is a Robin Hood character. I
used to know this bank robber who shot someone once. I asked him
about it and he said, 'Look, if someone's stupid enough to get in the
way then I'm gonna stop them.' And he's right because the only one
who's gonna lose out if he gets away with it is the bank. All it would
mean is that someone, somewhere, will have one ounce of caviar
less a week.

'People have got this weird idea that if they see a thief they've got
to stop him. What they should do is try to help him escape. The thief
will spend the money and spread it around. This country isn't poor. If
people can spend fifty-grand on a flat we can't be broke.

'I couldn't be a bank robber, though. I don't like being on the run.'

Hugh embraces the outrage. The Clash shoot from the heart, the
Stranglers from the hip. It's what makes them special.

Dingwalls is packed out. The club is slap-bang in the middle of
Camden Lock and overlooks the canal. When it's heaving there's no
other place you want to be. Hugh and I stand at the bar and drink
draught Stella.

'I take all the music papers with a large pinch of salt. I find them
far too heavily opinionated and style has become more important
than content. They're dealing with music which is an escape clause
from the con tricks of life. The papers exist in their own ivory towers.
They don't have to search for stories because they're always there.

'Melody Maker's' got no humour and takes itself far too seriously. 'NME' is the direct opposite but just as bad – I've had a few shit experiences with them and I think you can distil the whole thing down to one reporter. The rest are probably old hippies. 'Sounds' treats new bands and established bands in the same way, which is pretty good.

'I find 'Record Mirror' quite refreshing because it contains articles on totally different things and that's healthy.'

He knows how to sweet talk a guy.

'The papers don't always cite the truth and I reckon stories are far too heavily tampered with between writing and printing.'

Paul Cook wanders by and the two, who hadn't met before, have a brief conversation – Hugh congratulates him on the Bill Grundy débácle, Paul nods and wanders off.

'If music leads to violence it's not music any more,' he continues. 'The function of the artist is to reflect the environment. A band should demonstrate to people that they're well within their rights to hold a certain view. There's no point in making things up, the artist has got to be true to his experiences. Music's function is not to create. It isn't a spark in a fuse. It's a separate entity. And the great thing about punk is that the guy singing on stage has the same problems as those watching.

'I'm fed up with those little schmucks,' [glitzy rock stars] 'who live, breathe and have the same bodily functions as everyone else yet strive to be inaccessible. Even Rod Stewart gets diarrhoea. Punk could be the first step towards Utopia.'

After several more pints we leave and cruise over the dope to the Speakeasy round the back of Oxford Street, which is just about the best music-biz club in town and where everyone knows your name.

'I studied biochemistry at university which comes in very useful, especially when applied to narcotics,' says Hugh, as we sit down to a beer. 'I know everything there is to know about drugs. I'm into decadence – you've got to enjoy it because it comes only from warped, privileged minds. My definition of decadence is having a huge table covered with grapes and instead of taking one at a time you leap onto the table and indulge yourself in the juice of the squashed fruit.

'Indulge yourself, get completely wiped out. Forget your problems. You can OD on acid, start smoking dope, get a rush in your head and take off like a rocket.'

I've already done that and jettisoned two modules.

So, what does Hugh make of the rest of the bands on the saliva circuit?

'The Sex Pistols opened the floodgates and must be credited with that. The Damned are a bit lightweight but they've got a couple of really good numbers. And Eddie and the Hotrods are even more lightweight than The Damned. The Feelgoods are very good at what they do but they've got to come up with some new material quick. And The Clash are really exciting. I saw Queen on TV at Christmas and they were crap. Give the Pistols their equipment and they could come across with the goods.'

We end up at his friend's flat in Kensington where Hugh is crashing on the sofa and where we smoke dope until dawn – well, maybe not dawn but it's pretty late and maybe it's just the one joint between four. But I feel sufficiently decadent and stoned.

FEBRUARY 1977

Top ten singles
beginning of February

1. Don't Give Up On Us – David Soul
2. Don't Cry For Me Argentina – Julie Covington
3. Sideshow – Barry Biggs
4. Isn't She Lovely – David Parton
5. When I Need You – Leo Sayer
6. Daddy Cool – Boney M
7. You're More Than A Number – The Drifters
8. Things We Do For Love – 10cc
9. Suspicion – Elvis Presley
10. Car Wash – Rose Royce

Top ten albums
beginning of February

1. Red River Valley – Slim Whitman
2. Low – David Bowie
3. David Soul – David Soul
4. Songs in The Key Of Life – Stevie Wonder
5. Arrival – Abba
6. Evita – Various
7. Greatest Hits – Showaddywaddy
8. Hotel California – the Eagles
9. Greatest Hits – Abba
10. Wings Over America – Wings

'Record Mirror' Annual Poll
(published in the first issue of the month)

Male Singer – Rod Stewart
Group – Queen
Best Dressed – Noel Edmonds
Bore of the Year – Punk rock
Songwriter – Freddie Mercury
Female Singer – Kiki Dee
Album – Frampton Comes Alive
Single – Somebody To Love
TV Show – 'Top of the Pops'
Radio Show – 'Noel Edmonds Breakfast Show'
Brightest Hope for '77 – Eddie and the Hot Rods
DJ – Noel Edmonds
Live Group – Queen

Cute, huh? And what about Mr Edmonds? He was only topped by Queen in number of awards won. Punk might have been Bore of theYear but it generates more mail in 'Record Mirror' than anything else – with the possible exception of Queen. I don't remember Noel Edmonds ever being mentioned.

'To the Sex Pistols

The first thing I would do to you cretins is line you up in a crowded street, pull your trousers down and birch you.

Then I would haul you off to a labour camp and work you so hard you would have no reason for being bored.

The second thing I would do is take you under guard to places where the most important people work (doctors etc) and ask you the question: 'With so much to be done in the world, how can you say you're bored?'

You four are so mentally deficient you haven't got the intelligence to think of doing sensible things. I suppose you pathetic apologies for Homo sapiens consider it normal to stick pins through your nostrils, carve people up with sharp weapons and smash heads with beer bottles – what a waste of alcohol!

Then you have the cheek to criticise the government. I would love to meet you four and show you where I would stuff your opinion.

A dedicated Sex Pistols' hater'

'Over the past ten years I have been a fan of the Rolling Stones, but over the past few weeks I have been following the press reports on the activities of the Sex Pistols and I actually agree with 90 per cent of what they are trying to do.

It's true that from the day we are born we are brainwashed into accepting set roles, and for too long the majority have followed hypocritical routines without question. At school we are taught to be honest but when we are they don't approve so we learn to do and say only what is expected.

Why?

The real problem is that for generations people have been brainwashed into being shocked by the truth.

In the Sixties, the Stones sang 'Let's Spend The Night Together' and 'I Can't Get No Satisfaction' and the majority disapproved. Now they sing far more explicit lyrics – witness 'Star Star' and 'Hot Stuff' – and they are accepted. It's not the group that's changed, it's just that people have grown to expect it. In a few years time the Pistols will be classed as boring for performing more outrageous things than they are doing now.

Can you imagine the reaction of the general public if Marie Osmond included the line 'Stick it up ooh, can't get enough' in her next single? It would be banned and probably make the front page of the Sun. She may think it but she can't sing it!

Yes, I am in favour of anything that may change this hypocritical society. What I don't like is the Pistols' music and unnecessary violence. Musically, I prefer Patti Smith, Hawkwind and the Stones. The swear words used by the Pistols are not offensive. The only obscene four-letter word is KILL.

G. Clarke, Whitwick, Leics.'

Punk is the antithesis of Queen. Queen is about what you have, punk is about what you want. The one thing they have in common is adroit showmanship.

Each significant band will have its trademark move – the Stranglers have the Jean-Jacques Burnel duckwalk; the Jam have The Who mid-air kickbox; The Clash, the Joe Strummer pound; the Pistols Johnny Rotten and Sid Vicious; The Damned... er, The Damned.

The Damned are early trailblazers in the Famous Five. They're the first to release an album and the first UK punk band to tour the States.

I'd met Captain Sensible – real name Ray Burns – on a couple of occasions. One sunny morning, he strolls into the Benwell Road 'Record Mirror' office accompanied by a press officer from Stiff, The Damned's record company. I'm speaking to my mother on the phone as he wanders past my desk.

'Hullo Bazza. How's it going? Who you speaking to?'

'My mum.'

'Can I say hullo to her?'

Ray is one of the most outrageously eccentric people I've ever met but I chance it and hand him the phone.

'Hullo, is that Barry's mum? Do you want to suck my cock?'

My immediate reaction is to reach for the sharpened steel comb in my top pocket. But I don't have a top pocket any-more and my comb's plastic because that doesn't cause static in my long, fine hair. So I laugh and grab the phone out of his hand.

'What did he say?' asks my mum.

'Oh, he's going to Bangkok or something. Gotta go.'

I call him a bastard and laugh again. It's funny, and I figure that any guy who dyes his hair Monroe blond, wears a tutu on stage and gets covered from head to foot in phlegmy gob six times a week could be forgiven for asking my mum for a blow-job.

It's the least I can do.

DAMNED, DAMNED, DAMNED
Album review

Ladies and gentlemen, welcome to the world's first 78 r.p.m. album. At last, a record that gives credence to the claim that punk does have a place in the hierarchal structure of contemporary music. Sorry, change that to hieranarchical.

Damned Damned Damned lifts punk out of the dole queue and gives it a position in the logical progression of rock. Just listen to 'Feel The Pain' and then tell me that The Damned and their ilk are simply purveyors of frantic, hollow fabrications. Just listen to 'New Rose' and then tell me that punk lacks humour. Just listen to 'One Of The Two' and tell me this music has no guts. Like the guy says, 'I was born to kill!' – they're dancing on the grave of the Seventies.

Stiff is going places.

The album review and subsequent interview go down so well that I'm invited along when The Damned fly over to New York in April to do a week at CBGB's. Strangely enough, my mum isn't on the guest list.

Between the punk fixes I inhabit a mundane world of music in brown paper packages tied up with string.

'Record Mirror' shares its Holloway editorial office with 'Sounds', which is much hipper – hipper words, hipper staff, hipper pot *en masse*. But it can never pip the hip of 'NME' no matter how hard it tries, and that leads to its ultimate downfall. We, that's the 'Record Mirror' staff, are looked upon by the black leather-jacketed bunch across the room as being faintly ridiculous inhabitants of a popolicious world where the Bay City Rollers and David Soul reign supreme.

And they're not far wrong. I mean, Bonnie Tyler on the cover? Lost in fucking France or what? We certainly know how to fill the droid void.

Still, the perks aren't too shabby.

I go to Zurich to see Chicago – the music's shit but the surroundings are tasty. I stay in the baroque Golderkrand Hotel and wait for the band to arrive in the German president's private train, which ferries them from town to town and costs a fortune to hire.

I also go on the road with the Steve Gibbons Band and interview The Rubettes. Surreal, huh?

In a darkened Park Lane hotel room Nils Lofgren tells me, 'The night I saw Jimi Hendrix I knew what I had to do. My environment hadn't been conducive to being a rock'n'roll artist.

'Man, could you believe I had sleepless nights worrying that God was going to send his full wrath against me because I'd forgotten myself and sworn once? That's how bad it had become.

'When I was a kid I thought I was strange. I wasn't sure where I'd come from and became more and more convinced it wasn't from this planet – like I was going through this big room and not knowing why and trying to find a door out.'

Spooky...

THE DAMNED
Stiff Records office, London

'We recorded it in under 30 hours and that included the mixing,' says Captain Sensible, of his band's debut album, *Damned Damned Damned*.

We, that's The Damned and me, sit in what seems like a front room at Stiff Records. This is the third major punk interview to appear in 'Record Mirror'. I am now officially the punk correspondent mainly, I think, because I'm the only one who can identify with it.

The music press is essentially middle class with the odd oik thrown in for good measure. The chic-slingers among them are so up their own arses you can see their heads every time they open their mouths. But they can write, and write well. And that's all that matters.

'The album was taken live and we had some real fun doing it,' continues the Captain. 'We were slightly apprehensive about it at first, but the record gave us a chance to really listen to our work and we realised that some of the things we play on stage were all wrong. The album has certainly tightened up our whole approach.'

'We've been very surprised at the reaction the album has received,' says Brian James, the band's pulse and pin-up. 'Did you see us on Supersonic? Cliff Richard was on the show and he refused to introduce us.'

Rat Scabies, the Artful Dodger: 'I always knew we were gonna be big. We're about to tour with Marc Bolan. How good the fuck is that? And we'll have room to move on stage, to breathe. It'll be like moving out of a council house into a mansion.'

Rat looks like he's just come out of prison and wouldn't mind going straight back in.

'I've always been a great fan of Bolan's,' says the Captain, 'but I'm a much better performer than he is.

'The audiences are so good up north. When they like you they really like you. In London you get too many poseurs.'

The Captain, bleach-blond, shades, square-jawed, looks like something straight out of 'Thunderbirds'.

'The Roxy's an awful place to play. And we ain't the coolest band in town either. Robert Plant checked us out at the Roxy the other night. He's a good geezer – well, I'd buy him a pint. His long hair and the different culture didn't matter.'

'I hate the word 'punk,' says Brian. 'It conjures up visions of safety-pins and dumb kids. The definition should be someone who really gets off on stage.'

Brian James looks the part, talks the part and writes the part. He's a natural.

'Look, no matter what a lot of people may think,' says Rat, 'The Damned ain't out to change the world. The other bands like The Clash and the Pistols might have such ambitions but that doesn't mean we come from different backgrounds. We're all working class and have been on the dole, and now the money's coming in we're just about breaking even.

'What got me really annoyed about the Pistols was that when they released 'Anarchy In The UK' they were staying in fucking flash Holiday Inn hotels while we checked into two-quid-a-night rooms.'

When I hear that I laugh long and loud inside. For me, staying in flash Holiday Inn Hotels while singing 'Anarchy In The UK' is *exactly* what punk is all about.

'Then they wanted to charge us a grand to stick all our gear on their special coach and there was loads of fucking room on it.'

'Status Quo, Yes, Pink Floyd – we're as good as that but we've got more to prove, and that's healthy,' says Dave Vanian. Slick showman on stage, quiet as a mouse off. 'There's no violence usually but if there is a fight it's not started by punks but by hippies that don't understand.'

'Everything happens in a seven-year cycle,' says Rat. 'Music progresses but attitudes remain the same. There was Liszt, then this geezer Wagner bowls up with something a lot heavier and he gets slagged off. I just hope we can do something constructive for the kids years from now. I'd like to open a club and put on the kind of music that won't be acceptable then, like punk is now. That's something bands like the Stones and The Who have never done with all their millions. I like to think we give people their money's worth. The fans know they can come and see us and do what they like. It's a party.

'We don't want to influence, just make people feel a bit freer.'

That is sheer Sixties hippie-spiel. You can almost see Rat's bollocks flapping – as if he's dancing naked to Sly and the Family Stone at

Woodstock. But he's sincere because, deep down, he probably is a Sixties hippie, with balls.

The Damned are a great punk band, they just aren't *truly* great on vinyl. But they have a good time being just great.

Marc Bolan says of his forthcoming tour with The Damned, 'I'm more punkoid than any of these new-wave bands. My first group, John's Children, was probably the first British punk band ever. I'm looking forward to playing with The Damned.'

As February fades my soul starts to itch. This music's getting to me. This hard, cold, contemptuous music is *really* starting to get to me. Up till now I've only seen the Stranglers and The Damned live but, fuck, they're good, and totally different from each other. The Stranglers ooze a brazen style, an alluring combination of impeccable musicianship and hard-core porn. The Damned are sheer vaudeville, a bunch of irreverent Max Millers who break the sound barrier every time they play.

Surely it can't get any better.

February, however, goes out on a sour note. My girlfriend dumps me. I've been going out with Dina, a Greek Cypriot, for a month although I've known her for five years; it's a long story. The Californian girl, Colette, faded from view after she went on tour with her band around Europe.

By the way, Dina is the love of my life, but it's been turbulent.

And she finally dumps me as a result of a Uriah Heep concert.

The heavy-metal band are playing the Odeon in Birmingham and their record company, Bronze, hires a couple of train carriages crammed with food and booze and makes the awful mistake of inviting aboard a shitload of journalists and their mates, and a smattering of photographers. I, like a schmuck, invite Dina. It's a recipe for disaster. She's as straight as a die. There's not a trace of rock'n'roll in her soul.

The train pulls out of Euston and we all sit round tables that have been immaculately laid out – silver service, bottles of wine, flowers, the works. They're soon covered by an abundance of food that lasts all the way to Birmingham. So far so good.

When we finally get to the Odeon we have a few more drinks in the bar during the support band then go for the big one, Uriah Heep. I make sure I sit at the end of an aisle so we can sneak out undetected after the first song.

I sweep Dina through the foyer and out into the Bullring where I'm confronted by a number of my fellow matadors who also can't stand Uriah Heep. We retire to a local pub, have a few more drinks, then creep back into the cinema for the after-show party, where we have a few more drinks, by which time everyone is pissed and starting to create a little havoc. Then it's back on the train where we have, yes, a few more drinks. Top rock photographer Chalkie Davies sits opposite Dina and me, and she hasn't touched a drop of alcohol all night.

I bet him he can't eat his wine glass – as you do – and he proceeds to wrap it in his napkin, tap it until it smashes, then puts a piece into his mouth, grinds it up in his teeth, swallows and starts on another. Someone throws a sandwich, I throw one back – and it's carnage. We wreck the carriage like football hooligans. It just feels right, like we're doing our bit, doing it for anarchy. We're white punks on dope between Birmingham New Street and Euston and it feels good.

Doesn't feel so right the next morning when I wake up to a kiss-off note from a disgusted Dina and a Hammer Horror of a hangover.

MARCH 1977

Top ten singles
beginning of March

1. When I Need You – Leo Sayer
2. Boogie Nights – Heatwave
3. Chanson D'Amour – Manhattan Transfer
4. Romeo - Mr. Big
5. Don't Cry For Me Argentina – Julie Covington
6. Don't Give Up On Us – David Soul
7. Don't Leave Me This Way – Harold Melvin & The Bluenotes
8. Sing Me – The Brothers
9. Jack In The Box – Moments
10. What Can I Say? – Boz Scaggs

Top ten albums
beginning of March

1. 20 Golden Greats – the Shadows
2. Animals – Pink Floyd
3. Heartbreakers – Various
4. Endless Flight – Leo Sayer
5. Evita – Various
6. Dance To The Music – Various
7. Rumours – Fleetwood Mac
8. Songs in The Key Of Life – Stevie Wonder
9. Arrival – Abba
10. Motorvatin' – Chuck Berry

As March opens its legs I go to Bath with 'Living Next Door To Alice' boys Smokie, who drink inordinate amounts of Scotch and laugh 'till dawn.

Another new band appears on the scene…

The Vibrators aren't wonderful, but they can play properly. I'd seen them live a few months earlier at the Rock Garden in Covent Garden – good band but shit songs. They manage to land a deal with ultra-smart multi-millionaire pop star turned music entrepreneur, Mickie Most, owner of RAK Records.

I meet him, along with the band – shabby bassist Pat Collier, eyebrowless guitarist John Ellis, disenchanted drummer John Edwards, guitarist with bruised knees Knox – at RAK's Mayfair offices.

THE VIBRATORS
RAK Records, Mayfair

Knox – 'We're not going to get a hardcore Pistols or Clash audience. We're much more acceptable than The Clash. Like in Germany we just sold out a thousand-seater and one rock paper there called us the best band to come out of England for ten years. I think the name's helped.

Most – 'OK, rock'n'roll is about sexuality, but we have to give the radio stations your name. Is it preposterous for me to want them to think of you as a band and not a sex aid? Oh, well, there's nothing we can do about the band's name now.

'One of the things that interests me about this band is that they're prolific writers. Let's face it, they ain't no Carole King, Albert Hammond or Neil Sedaka but they'll do.

'You see, punk to me isn't a new thing – the Heavy Metal Kids are in a class of their own, as far as punk is concerned. They were into the seedier side of rock before any of the new bands on the scene and they're better musicians. The Vibrators don't even look like punks. I don't know what punk is but I do know about records that sell or don't sell. I've been a record producer for 20 years trying to re-create the sound of Eddie Cochran. The trouble with English people is that they have a hang-up about the past and that's why I want to put out 'Jumpin' Jack Flash' as The Vibrators' next single.

Knox – 'Who makes these rules?'

Most – 'If we cut it and it went up the charts you'd be as happy as sandboys. I don't think my relationship with the record-buying public has improved – they're very unimpressed with me producing your records. To them I'm part of the establishment, a capitalist in cashmere who dishes out marks on a TV talent show while you look like fugitives from a squat, with your emaciated faces and torn T-shirts. But I bet you 500 quid they'd rather be me than you.

'I've been involved with a lot of bands and they all think like you – they want success and when it comes they're the biggest fucking cop-out going. They even start making support acts pay for the privilege of appearing on the same bill as them.

'I'd much rather be on a beach in Nassau than in a recording studio, which is just about the worst place in the world. It's no great highlight of my life to go in the studio and listen to you tell me, who's sold over 250 million records, how to make records. Even if Elvis was in there performing I'd still rather be at home because I've done it.

'You need a buzz. Going to bed with a girl isn't a buzz unless she can make love well. Chris Spedding got very involved with the Pistols last year and cut tracks with them at our studios. He asked me to listen to them and I wasn't that impressed but I discussed a deal with their manager, Malcolm McLaren, which fell through.

'I'm glad I wasn't involved. I hope I'd never have to resort to those kinds of amateur dramatics to sell a group. So the Stones shock, so The Who shock, but the Pistols just OD'd. The manager planned it, and good luck to him, but it's dated. If The Vibrators did anything I didn't like I'd drop them right away.'

Most, who discovered The Animals and produced, amongst others, Donovan, Hot Chocolate, Lulu, Herman's Hermits and Suzi Quatro, once said, 'I wouldn't know cocaine or heroin if I got run over by it.' Mind you, he also said, 'I've never read a book in my life.' He finds fame again, as a Simon Cowell-style critic on New Faces in the Seventies and will eventually sell RAK to EMI in 1983 to concentrate on managing his lucrative publishing copyrights and other enterprises. Those prosper to such an extent that, by the mid-Nineties, he makes it into the Sunday Times Rich List.

A keep-fit fanatic, he will die of cancer at a comparatively young 60. I still get goosebumps when I hear the chorus to 'No Doubt About It' and the opening verse of 'So You Win Again" and for that, Mr Most, I thank you.

THE CLASH
Harlesden

Somewhere west of Karachi.

Oh yeah, I forgot about the fuzz. Must be a dozen sitting in that wagon outside the flick palace. Haste disposal unit. Checking, just checking.

Routine.

They don't come much stranger, venues that is. A Pakistani cinema in Harlesden, west London, hired for the night to enhance the reputations of the Slits, Subway Sect, the Buzzcocks and The Clash, the last hailed as the kings of the current wildfire. The fuss is justified.

'This is a Pakistani exercise,' yells Sabu Joe Strummer, at the start. 'Who pulled my cord out?' he enquires in the middle, when the band is plagued by technical phantoms.

'The weekend starts here!' he screams at the end.

Think of John Lennon 15 years ago with St Vitus' dance. That's

Joe. Quickfire guitarist, cutthroat vocalist – 'London's Burning' and debut single 'White Riot'.

Sahib Mick Jones is the definitive new-wave guitarist – a chimera sculpting influences like Wilko Johnson and Brian Connolly into his own likeness. Breathtaking, bitter, biting, cheat cheat cheat.

Cobra Paul Simonon, a bassist who looks like a front man. Bullet bass sound that fits nicely into the Colt chamber formed by the rest of the band. Just pull the trigger – you'll see what I mean.

Turban Terry Chimes – oh-so-serious drummer with the Mount Rushmore face.

And as the 400 punkers file out a kung-fu film somersaults across the screen.

And a 'White Riot' checks out into a NW10 night.

The Old Bill needn't have bothered.

A few days after that review appears I find myself standing behind Joe Strummer outside an after show party for The Kinks. We're both trying to blag our way in, without success. When I say my name to the doorman Joe turns around. 'You the bloke who wrote the review in 'Record Mirror'?'

Shit, he looks tough in his black-leather jacket, black bondage trousers and punk quiff. He obviously hated what I'd written. I knew it was crap the minute I'd finished writing it. Why didn't I just do a straight review? Is he going to bottle me? Why the fuck am I here? Why did I smoke that grass earlier? Why did I call him Sabu?

'It was really good man.' That's all he says before he wanders off into the night.

Official, Joe Strummer is a nice guy – in my book, anyway. He didn't think I was crap and that does wonders for the complexion.

Still can't get into the Kinks' party though, even if I wait all day and all of the night.

The following night I go along to the Roxy for the launch of Marc Bolan's new album *Dandy in the Underworld*. The guests include forgotten man Donovan, Mike Mansfield, Lionel Bart,

Harry Nilsson, and punks a-plenty including Johnny Rotten.

Johnny's not around when Steve Jones, Paul Cook and Sid Vicious are involved in a brawl at the Speakeasy a few days later. In the resulting mêlée, 'Old Grey Whistle Test' presenter Bob Harris and studio recording engineer George Nicholson are hurt. Nicholson has 14 stitches in his head while Harris suffers cuts and bruises.

Official: the Pistols can mix it with anyone.

The Pistols finally sign a deal with A&M outside Buckingham Palace to mark the release of their new single 'God Save The Queen'.

The following week A&M, in the face of public condemnation for having signed the Pistols, issue a statement: 'A&M Records wishes to announce that its recording agreement with the Sex Pistols has been terminated with immediate effect. The company therefore will not be releasing any product from the group and there is no further association with them.'

The band receive a cool seventy-five grand for the termination.

Meanwhile, Johnny Rotten makes an appearance of a different nature when he turns up on a drugs charge at Marlborough Street Magistrates' Court. He admits possession of amphetamine sulphate and is fined £40.

The court hears that Johnny earns £25 a week and gives his mother £15. His defence counsel claims his client does not take drugs and that the amphetamines had been given to him by a fan after a rehearsal session. Counsel also says that Johnny isn't interested in drugs. 'He prefers going to a pub and having a few drinks rather than taking drugs.'

Then the big one – Sid's first ever gig with the Pistols.

The band play a secret, one-off gig at a church hall in Leicester Square in front of just 50 people, to be filmed by NBC TV for screening in the US. I keep my gleaming nous antennae close to the ground. I get in. I'm the only journalist in the house.

Fuck.

THE SEX PISTOLS
Notre Dame Hall, Leicester Square

A multicoloured mob, rainsoaked, restless, devouring a West End side-street. In conflict; storm the church-hall doors or bide their time?

The doors open and the red flashing-light reflection from a nightclub opposite is replaced by a spiky-topped head, like a shadow hand mimicking a hen. Fifty people fall out, looking for all the world like survivors from the raid on Entebbe. Some are greeted by friends.

The doors close.

So, what's it all about?

A church-hall hijack?

A rabid priest – it was Catholic, after all – holding his flock to ransom?

The devil himself?

Even – no, surely not that – the great Boy Scout Massacre?

Flashback. Mid-afternoon, a smoky pub opposite. A stealthy whisper: 'Bleep bleep church hall. The bleep bleeps. Better get there early, there's a war on.'

Bleeps on the horizon at 7.30 sir. Ready, aim.

The cab pulls up outside the hall, which is sandwiched between two clubs, at 6.30 pm. Already a small queue of suspenders, plastic macs and green hair – oh, and Danny. How do I know it's Danny? He's got a smashed-up nose, he's spitting blood on the wall and writing his name in it, silly.

The hall has been newly decorated with shimmering plastic stars on the walls and cardboard angels dancing from the ceiling. There are exactly 50 chairs in neat rows starting a few feet from the stage.

Silence. I feel like I'm waiting for a school nativity play to begin.

And on walk the Sex Pistols.

Straight into 'God Save The Queen', the doomed single in solitary confinement

God Save The Queen

It's a fascist regime.

Johnny Rotten, that's the mark-two version with the black tail, sonic-booming over Steve Jones crashing guitar.

No fewchar for me.

Rumour has it there are 20,000 copies of the single, abandoned and weeping in some A&M ossuary.

A word of explanation. NBC, that glorious American TV company, has a crew in this country filming the earthquake rulers on London's current rock scene. They already had in the can live footage of The Damned and the Hot Rods but they desperately wanted the Pistols. The band, however, are banned throughout the UK. Dilemma.

Enter a saviour in a dog-collar.

A Roman Catholic priest, who wishes to remain anonymous, agreed to let NBC and the Pistols use the hall. Conditions? Only 50 people were to be allowed in, first come, first served, and the whole operation would last just a couple of hours.

Meanwhile, back at the gig, it's 'I Wanna Be Me' time.

Rotten, torn red T-shirt and black bondage trousers, a malevolent marionette with no strings attached. The seated audience, overcome by the wild strangeness of it all, remain seated. 'It's not worth it,' says Rotten at the end of the number. 'Why bother?' Then into 'I'm A Lazy Sod'.

See my face, not a trace, no reality.

Sid Vicious, who replaced bassist Glen Matlock just before the ill-fated A&M signing, is uncharacteristically quiet. He's concentrating on getting the notes dead right, watching his fingers, watching his weight. Finally, he breaks the silence at the end of 'Lazy Sod'...

'Get the fuck up!'

'This is really very funny,' says a venomous Rotten. 'In one year nothing's changed.'

A girl jumps to the front – 'C'mon, everybody, get up' – and around 20 oblige, leaping, kicking, crashing into each other's sweat-soaked bodies.

After every number a guy walks onstage, cracks a clapperboard in front of the cameras and walks off.

Steve Jones makes it a split-level leap about. Looking more cocksure than ever, grappling with elusive identity in his plain white T-shirt and winning, his guitar scorching, lashing the solid shore sound provided by Paul Cook's drumming on 20-foot breakers. 'Pretty Vacant' and stranger on the shore Vicious blending like a Kenwood. Then the killer – 'EMI', about money and freedom and hypocrisy and a brilliant last line:
Goodbye EMI, hullo A&M.

Rotten – 'Maybe it was a good thing, us being banned from this country. Looking at you lot, it seems like it anyway.'

'This is from our next LP,' says Vicious, and 'Problems' follows.

For a band who haven't played in public for some months, and with the added burden of a brand new bassist, the Pistols are piss-good with a bollock-kick in every note. The arrogance hasn't been suffocated by the indecent exposure.

'Problems' segues into 'No Feelings', then a pause before the anthemic 'Anarchy In The UK' that turns out to be a total anti-climax with no heart and no fun. Rotten, realising, cuts it short. Exit.

Forty minutes. Eleven songs. For Chrissakes, somebody with some sense out there, sign them up. You won't regret it.

Outside, the natives grow restless. As the 50 file out, some guys in the crowd hurl abuse and garbage. But it's all too late.

It was only the early birds that caught the worms.

A few days after that gig I drive out to Aylesbury to watch original punk Iggy Pop accompanied on keyboards by a pre-*Low* David Bowie. The performance is tepid in comparison with the Pistols, rather like tasting a korma after a lifetime of vindaloo.

On the last day of the month I interview a charming Lynsey de

Paul and discover we share the same birthday. She even remembers to send me a card when I hit 25 that year, the little sweetheart.

March had come in like a lamb with a Vibrator up its arse. We're in for a good, cobweb-shattering shit, hosed down by some hefty April golden showers that really will bloom in May, if that makes any sense.

I miss Dina but won't ring her. A man has his pride...

APRIL 1977

Top ten singles
beginning of April

1. Knowing Me Knowing You – Abba
2. Going In With My Eyes Open – David Soul
3. Chanson D'Amour – Manhattan Transfer
4. When – Showaddywaddy
5. Sound & Vision – David Bowie
6. Moody Blue – Elvis Presley
7. Sunny – Boney M
8. I Don't Want To Put A Hold On You – Berni Flint
9. Torn Between Two Lovers – Mary MacGregor
10. Boogie Nights – Heatwave

Top ten albums
beginning of April

1. Portrait Of Sinatra – Frank Sinatra
2. 20 Golden Greats – the Shadows
3. Arrival – Abba
4. Heartbreakers – Various
5. Hollies Live Hits
6. Endless Flight – Leo Sayer
7. Animals – Pink Floyd
8. Every Face Tells A Story – Cliff Richard
9. Live – Status Quo
10. Rumours – Fleetwood Mac

And down in the cellar at the Hope and Anchor something big is brewing...

THE JAM
Hope & Anchor

Obvious band for the slag-off merchants, this.

'A Who rip-off? Nothing new.'

Think again, Batman!

Throw nine years off your backs, and you're smouldering in those two-tone days of college ties, three-piece blue mohair, light-and-bitter and the local Palais. What music could you identify with then, kiddo?

You might as well throw most of the Seventies in, too. The fact is, you 16 year-olds don't realise how lucky you are to have bands around to hang onto. The Jam are just such a band. Easy to read too much importance into the current set-up but there is something.

When I was 16 what band could I look at, really look at, and say, 'That's me! That's me up there singing, performing, saying exactly what I want to say'? Sure, there were bands I loved, adored even, but they weren't me. They were performing at me, providing music as a pleasure to dance to, to sit in my bedroom and listen to, but never ultimately to be me.

Since the love-in Sixties kicked-in, pop music in the UK has been aimed largely at that burgeoning breakaway group from the working classes who realised the only way out was to borrow. The HP generation, the popped-in, sold-out, music-to-prosper-to generation.

There was nothing remotely working class about the music – from the Beatles to the Stones to Pink Floyd. 'All The Young Dudes' was a decent stab in the dark, but I'm not convinced Bowie really did wanna relate to me. The Stones are a US band with about as much relevance to a working-class kid as Sunday tea at Fortnum & Mason.

Punk reeks of working class, of shit and piss and fucked-up estates, of quickfire love, concrete playgrounds and taking a punch now and then.

The Clash, the Pistols, The Damned, even the Stranglers in their exotic Fortnum & Mason kind of way, are white soul bands telling it like it is. And you can dance to some of it too.

You can dance to all of the Jam.

Anyway, there's Paul Weller, lead guitar and vocals, Bruce Foxton, bass, and Rick Buckler, drums, dancing with songs like 'I've Changed My Address', 'Bricks and Mortar' and the debut single 'In The City'. Weller in his Sixties suit, white shirt and the tiny Sixties knot in his tie, crumpling each song up and hurling it into the audience. 'Ride Your Pony', 'Slow Down', 'Heatwave', 'Batman', 'Much Too Much', the last two immortalised by the Who. So it may be turning back the clock, but the clock was slow anyway.

And the Jam are a wind-up in the nicest way.

The thing about 'Record Mirror' reviews, and most of the interviews, is that they're ten cents a dance when compared to the epic, bone-crunching pyrotechnics favoured by the heavier mags.

We have to be short and sweet because, number one, 'Record Mirror' doesn't generate as much advertising as the other titles on the market so our pagination is curtailed and, number two, our younger readers are perceived as having a shorter attention span.

Writers on 'NME' and 'Melody Maker' can flex their quills and spread their thoughts across five A3 pages, if they think the subject warrants it. We have to make do with a snappy intro, a snappy middle and a snappier finale. We are the Ramones of music writing, and old habits die hard. But die they eventually do.

THE CLASH
Camden Town

The Clash use a rehearsal studio in the aptly named Rehearsal Rehearsals. It's on the first floor of a warehouse just inside the gates of the British Rail yard in Chalk Farm Road. A tumbleweed connection stuffed with bravado.

That's the venue for my interview and, notebook in hand, I sit in front of Mick Jones, Joe Strummer, Paul Simonon and Nicky 'Topper' Headon in a corner of the cavernous studio.

They pass round a gun, probably of the air variety, during the first part of the interview in what I perceive to be an attempt at intimidation. It is kind of disconcerting, especially as the joint I'd smoked earlier had put me into tilt mode.

But The Clash turn out to be some of life's good guys.

They have to be. It's their nature. They're the first skinhead hippie band and they play fast and loose with my heart.

In the beginning

Rain in the city, sliding down the monolithic offices, seeking out concrete crevices.

Spews in the mews. Macs in the cul-de-sacs. Fleets in the streets. Metropolis mirages on each droplet. The distorted face of Joe Strummer peering out of the top-deck window of a number 19 bus in Cambridge Circus inhabits a globule. He's with a girl. 'You ought to be a guitarist,' she says.

He ignores her, 19 and nebulous. 'She's a slag anyway.'

Couple of drug-taking years follow. Boring. Then he remembers her voice…

In south London, Mick Jones – five O levels and a degree of uncertainty – buys records by the score. That's what working for Social Security can do to you.

It's dream-time down the Streatham Locarno, and Paul Simonon, after a hard day on the terraces, unwinds to the sweet soul music.

And in the gutters the tyre-splashed debris of the day gurgles like a baby.

Incarnation

Like three neon cave-dwellers who have just learned the dark secret of fire, The Clash dispel any puritanical doubts with the ultimate weapon: sincerity. Not the Hughie Green sweaty-palm brand, but the kind found scrawled on tenancy walls – 'JL is a grass and he's gonna get his legs cut off.'

They send shivers down my spine when they get it right, and they get it right nearly all the time. 'Janie Jones' hits a spot I never knew I had.

'We wanted to do something,' says Mick. 'And, like most others, we haven't given up half-way. It comes out good and it goes through rubbish again. But it can all be overblown. There are so many useless bands around. It's taken a long time to break out of the love-song syndrome.'

Mick Jones is currently being hailed as the new Keith Richards. He's got the hair and he's got the stare, but does he have the dare? He keeps stopping mid-way through sentences, throws looks at the other two, smiles, and continues. 'There's still the deaf-aid of rock'n'roll. It takes a lot to overcome it, like ten years ago in America when comfortable college kids were coming home from Vietnam in wooden boxes. People like Phil Ochs started singing about it. Everyone took LSD. People who are frightened of us will take what we sing about as major political statements. All I know is what we're in, what we understand. We still have the code of the street.'

Their début single 'White Riot' climbed 60 places in the chart last week and their album has phenomenal advance sales.

The Clash have arrived.

'A lot of people feel very angry about us because they cannot identify with what we play,' says Mick. 'Some guys followed us home after a gig and threw a brick through our window. Things like that are always happening. That's just because they don't know what's going on. But I think they'll hear it soon. 'White Riot' is a good rock'n'roll record. There are a lot of good rock'n'roll records with terrible words – like 'Happy Jack'. And it's never worried us that they might not hear our words.'

Another piercing glance. Another smile. He's articulate and he knows it, and I'm starting to love him for it.

'Young white guys need an identity. We're talking to kids like us who don't have anything. Those who remember 1955 were lucky. They had their own music.

'We ain't looking for swastikas, just rock'n'roll. Before, it was only authors who made important statements.

'Music has always spoken to me. The only difference between us and the music of the Sixties and Seventies is that now we're saying it plainer, more coherently. I'm selling most of the records I ever bought because listening to them now is a waste of time.

'The Clash work on a purely emotional level.'

Mick looks like he doesn't suffer fools gladly. In fact, every 'punk' of any note I've met has that same contemptuous look, which ultimately eases when comprehension sets in.

'We recorded our album in a few weeks. It took ELP two years to do their last one. Wow, they must be wondering what on earth's happened now.

'All we're saying is, question what you're doing and if the answer doesn't satisfy you, then fucking do what you want. It's not preaching, I fucking hate that. It's just encouragement.'

Strummer's bombsite soliloquy

'The fact that 'White Riot' has jumped so much is good – but it's not good enough. I want more. I want a number one. It's not getting any radio plays because the people in control of the airwaves are so fucking against us. They want to stamp us out. They feel threatened. They are Nazis. We ain't, but we want to persecute, to fucking wipe them off the face of the earth.

'I've found you can only really think when you're completely alone. It's impossible when other people are around. That's why I only live late at night because that's when I can do strange things. A lot of the time I get molested by the police because they want to know what I'm up to. It's dark and getting darker.

'I foresee restrictions, not just for individuals but for entire governments, cities, nations. I foresee the return of conscription. I foresee less personal freedom and the introduction of identity cards. I see numbers.

'I can feel it

'The government wants ultimate control and if they don't get it they lose. So it stands to reason they're going to do everything in their fucking power to obtain that control. But I don't think that's frightening. If I did, I couldn't live. I know I'm never gonna be able to beat them so I don't believe in other people. Other people are fucking morons – they must be to stand for all this.

'And when the government get ultimate control all I can see is bombsites and a handful of survivors. Roll the credits – end. You'll soon know when that control comes – things will start booming. Industry will thrive, unemployment will come down, people will march through the streets waving banners proclaiming their willingness to die for Queen and country.

'And I'll get my head kicked in.

'The Clash can't change people – we can only create an atmosphere. If people want to change they will.

'I have a great time banging guitars and shouting. People can read too much into that and it makes me sick. They're stupid creeps. All this talking about how people can gain from what we do makes me puke.

'Lawrence of Arabia was my only hero 'cos I thought it was real smooth him just coming out of England and leading the Arabs.

'I find myself in a void, and it's a good void. I've always known what to do and always known what I'm doing it for. I'm smart. I'm lucky and luck is a dominant factor in life. You make your own luck by grabbing opportunities, and I grab opportunities by following the Cherokee Indian way. When they have to make a decision they always choose the most reckless course of action. I always like to have my hands on the steering-wheel.

'I suppose I'm like this because people have walked all over me in the past. When they do that I'm interested. I want to know why so they won't do it again. When I was nine I went to a boarding-school. On the first day I was surrounded by a bunch of boys who frogmarched me to the bathroom where I was confronted by a bath full of used toilet paper, a smear of shit on each fucking sheet. They said I had to get in. If I refused they'd beat me up.

'I got fucking beaten up.'

The Clash will fuck up big-time. They should have been U2 with knobs on but they fuck up. They even crack America for a few glorious months with 'Rock The Casbah' but they still manage to fuck up. They deprive me of a future full of their glorious music and I despise them for it.

After the interview, Joe and I jump a tube to Leicester Square on the way to the Marquee. As we walk to the club in Wardour Street he hands some money to a beggar. I feel a little guilty, but not guilty enough to put my own hand in my pocket. Years of being accosted by drunken Scotsmen in Kings Cross demanding 'two bob for a cup of tea' have beaten the good Samaritan out of me.

Tony Parsons congratulates me on the interview when I bump into him at a Damned gig in the Roundhouse the following week. That's rare for music writers. Suddenly Tony's up there with Strummer in my estimation.

A week after The Clash interview during an after-show party for Southside Johnny backstage at the Rainbow, I spot Joe Strummer talking to Johnny Rotten in a corner. At the end of a frenetic conversation, he casually picks up a floral arrangement and starts to eat it. Naturally.

I've never met anyone quite like Johnny Thunders.

He's fugitive from a chain gang meets 'West Side Story' and he can play rock'n'roll like he's got just 24 hours to live. Unfortunately, most nights he plays like he died 24 hours earlier. So many drugs, so little time.

Spawned by the New York Dolls, Johnny's band, The Heartbreakers – which includes guitarist-with-movie-star-looks, the sublime Walter Lure – are gaining more success in dear old Blighty with their flick-knife, Times Square hooker set pieces like 'Chinese Rocks' and 'Born To Loose' than amongst the skyscraper streets of their native lost world.

The band's only album *LAMF* – Like A Motherfucker – is shot through with classic shoot-up slappers of songs, ruined by a production more tragic than 'Othello'. I shed a tear when I hear *LAMF* for the first time but still give it a five-star review. I have to – I figure I owe it to Johnny for letting me into his secrets.

I meet Johnny and Walter for an interview and dinner in, appropriately, the New York-themed Covent Garden restaurant Joe Allen's where I first tasted raw beef and Caesar salad.

Before dinner Johnny, Walter and I knock back a few Heartbreaker cocktails – cranberry juice, vodka, sloe gin and a cherry. During dinner the three of us get through six bottles of champagne. After dinner we each have a few large Cognacs.

JOHNNY THUNDERS AND WALTER LURE
Joe Allen restaurant, Covent Garden

Walter: 'Cocktails before dinner, champagne during, Cognac after and mixed drinks to go to sleep with.'

Johnny: 'You sleep with who you want.'

They're both pissed but coherent. Perfect interview fodder. Out comes the trusty notebook. I try to forget my drunkenness for a while. So do they. In fact, they aren't pissed at all. Turns out they can drink like Manhattan camels.

Johnny: 'We were in the toilet when we first came over here. The New York Dolls had a bad reputation. We never listened to what anyone told us, just did what we wanted, and that made people dislike us. But now we've paid our dues and I just want to work.'

Walter: 'We all come from New York gangs. Each gang is made up of lower-middle-class kids who think they're in a band or something. There are street-corner fights all the time. It was something to do, y'know. Sure, we used weapons. Zip guns. Car aerials – whip someone in the face with one of them, boy, and he's scarred for life. Rumbles start real easy. But I never broke nobody's neck. The lower-class kids aren't in the gangs because, there, it was every man for himself. They just have to survive each day. So there we were, getting drunk and having fights. But when you're 17 and you're into music, you move to Manhattan.'

Johnny: 'I played in school bands.'

Walter: 'That's because you couldn't play anything else.'

Johnny: 'When we started to play rock'n'roll it was a way of life. You can't play it legitimately if you're Black Sabbath. Even the Stones don't play legit. They used to until Ron Wood joined. Now they got no roots. And the new bands are too political. We ain't political at all. The only politics we wanna sell is the changing of the drug laws. And you know what? If you were arrested in New York for being drunk, like you are here, there would be a lot of cops with broken heads. You should hear the news there. 'This guy got killed, this guy got murdered, this guy got tortured.'

'There are more clowns than good guys in music. British bands don't play as well as American bands. Rock'n'roll is simply an attitude – you don't have to play the greatest guitar. It makes me laugh when people acclaim our musicianship and technical brilliance.'

Walter: 'People used to try and play like Yes and Clapton. But who needs it?'

Johnny: 'The Dolls proved you don't need to be technically far ahead of anyone else to be accepted. We know our five chords. I was once gonna play in a band with Iggy Pop and y'know something? David Bowie's like a sponge soaking everything up that he hears. I wouldn't let him near me with a ten-foot pole. He's just an old English beatnik. Iggy never asked him into his world – Bowie dragged him into his. That's it, I've finally decided I wanna change our name to the Junkies because it shows we're a no holds-barred band.'

Walter: 'It shows you're a fucking don't-care-about-anything band.'

Johnny: 'I don't like 'The Heartbreakers'. I wanna sell more than music. I wanna sell art. Rock'n'roll is cheap.'

Walter: 'No, it ain't. I'm not trying to make everyone a punk. 'Junkies' is a name that'll cause controversy. 'Heartbreakers' doesn't.'

Johnny: 'We've hit the punks, the kids who've seen it all. All the new bands think they're gonna change the fucking world – but all they're gonna change is their nappies. Johnny Rotten is Dr Jekyll and Mrs Hyde. He tries too hard to live up to his image and he comes across like a pussycat. On his own, he's a nice guy. Steve and Paul are okay, but John and Sid Vicious are dolls. Now he tries to be more disgusting, but they know nothing about life. Sid and John are about as legitimate as Cherry Vanilla.'

THE CLASH
Album review

Start at the deep end. This is the best debut album any British band has ever produced. Forget the sociological quagmire predictably promoted by crawling confederates. Forget the patronising 'whatever they lack in musical ability they more than make up for in sheer gut political energy.' Forget all the new-wave regalia that haunts every toilet-paper periodical like computer data. The Clash pull the chain on all the crap that's preceded them with a stunningly conceived record. If you've got ears the message is, 'We'll smash your face in soon enough but don't be impatient. Just savour the rest of the deal because it's straight from the top of the pack.'

There's no such thing as a highlight on this album. Every track has an identity, a concrete and clay beauty. Strummer and Jones have written all the songs, except Junior Murvin's 'Police & Thieves'. Reggae? The Clash? White boys don't sing reggae. But they do if they make it white-boy reggae decked with white-boy aggression and white-boy attitude. Its inclusion is genius. At a masterstroke they've punched their way out of the punkweight division, successfully taking the *h* out of Clash and replacing it with an *s*.

I never knew phasers could be so effective – 'Cheat' is a track that actually needs the often superfluous Frampton device. There's also a remix of 'White Riot' and it sounds far superior to the single. The production is sometimes a little oblique but Strummer's heavy-artillery voice, Jones's maniacal/disciplined guitar and Paul Simonon's all-embracing bass blast criticism into kingdom come.

Oh, and 'Janie Jones' is a work of art.

So here I am, leaving on a jet plane from Heathrow to JFK, on my first-ever trip to America, courtesy of Island Records and The Damned. The weak speed I snorted in the toilets at Heathrow is already wearing off in the clouds but the complimentary bourbon is still mysterious. The drugs don't work. But you can have a great time trying to fix them.

I'm the only journo to tag along on this historic trip – The Damned are the first British punk band to cross the Atlantic to tour, starting with a four-night spot at New York's renowned CBGB's, home of Patti Smith and Yankee black chic.

Suddenly I feel lucky, like I could take on the world and win. I'm heading for the Wild West on a freebie and I want a window seat every inch of the way. I've hit heaven full on.

'So, which hotel are we staying in, Don?' I ask the doughty record company PR, as we cruise over the dishevelled clouds that slash the skies above Greenland.

'We're, er, not exactly staying at an hotel.' I hear the words 'friend' and 'nice flat' and 'sofa' mentioned in the same sentence, and my fate is sealed. I'm to be put up on a sofa for seven days in a downtown Manhattan apartment.

And that means no room service, no breakfast, no free phone calls home. I have to spend MY OWN MONEY!

I'm unprepared. I need funds. Badly.

Enter the hero of the hour, Rat Scabies, the ginger Ninja. I get Rat alone and tell him I'm going to hold a raffle among the passengers on the plane. I'll ask each one to guess the exact time the wheels of our plane touch down at JFK airport. They have to write it down on a piece of paper together with their first name and hand it to me with a dollar bill. The nearest time will win the pot. I tell him it's well worth entering, and wink.

He smiles. He knows it, and I know he knows it. I guess we just fucking know it.

Not everyone participates; some may even smell a rat. But I'm back on board that Birmingham express, speeding up the anarchy line, and it feels right again. I collect enough – even the air hostesses want a piece of the action – and the time is announced over the loudspeaker by the pilot himself as we land.

Rat wins. What a coincidence. We pocket about fifty quid each.

You can take the boy out of the Angel but you can never take the Angel out of the boy.

Forgive me.

THE DAMNED
CBGB's, New York

The Taking of CBGB's, Day One

A long narrow hall on the worst side of town, corner of Bleeker Street and the Bowery where only drunks dare wander at night. Inside, a calculated shabbiness, dim, slightly off-key and get this: you've got to book tables. The ol' New York kitsch nightclub syndrome spills on to the drunken Bowery.

Where there's tables there's sedation. The whole set-up reeks of a late-Sixties London folk club. I sidle up to the bar and ask for bourbon on the rocks. I always dreamed that one day I'd order bourbon on the rocks in a New York bar. The shock of realising a dream galvanises me into ordering several more, failing to notice how much bourbon they put into the glasses.

On stage, the Dead Boys. First impressions: Stiv Bators, the lead singer, is a Johnny Rotten rip off. Innocuous songs, indifferent musicians – Cheetah Chrome and Jimmy Zero on guitars, Johnny Glitz on drums. Get the picture? 'God!' says Rat, as the Fantastic Four walk in. 'Just what we feared, only worse. This looks like a job for the Thing.'

A waitress keels in horror – 'Oh no! It's hideous! I've heard of the Thing but I never dreamed it could look this terrible.'

'Easy, honey,' says Rat. 'I haven't even changed yet.'

Enter Sensible, the Human Torch...

FLAME ON! *Whoooosh!* Straight into 'Feel Alright', the old Stooges number. Sensible sucks the mike like he's giving head, burns up the stage and falls over. Never mind, he's up again.

And Vanian starts to sing, and, yeah, here it comes...

His hand begins to stretch right to the very end of the club and grabs the poseurs' attentions. But it's not quite there. Sensible's plug keeps falling out of his guitar, his flame burned out completely. Dave's elongated arm is twisted with cramp. There are pauses between each number. That ain't The Damned. The second set is an improvement, but it's only pulled out of mediocrity when the Torch jumps into the audience and drags a fat blonde on to the stage where he nearly has his wicked way with her.

'Would you have done it with him?' someone asks, when she returns.

'Yeah, I felt like it, but I don't know – after all, I am a virgin.' A virgin? In CBGB's? Oh, and there's a few pies thrown around by some topless girls, courtesy of the Rolling Stones, in town for a recording session – they sent them especially for the occasion.

After the gig Brian James makes himself invisible and Rat, who still hasn't reverted to orange-skin powerhouse guise, complains bitterly about the CBGB people.

Meanwhile, like a bridge over troubled water, Art Garfunkel plays on the pinball machine out front, oblivious to punk in all its guises.

The Taking of CBGB's, Day Two

I wake up on the sofa in the downtown Manhattan apartment, which is, actually, not too shabby. But, shit, I feel ill and throw up a zillion times, watching morning game shows on the state-of-the-art TV. But this is New York and recovery times are speedier.

I eat my first hamburger, with all the trimmings, in a café round the corner and sober up after a few beers. Then I take the walk of my life down Himalayan streets that grab me by the bollocks and toss me into moon river avenues wider than a mile. I feel like Flash Gordon. All I need is my Dale.

The Dead Boys are getting better. Each number is gradually taking on an identity of its own.

'Playing with The Damned was the best thing that ever happened to us,' says Cheetah. Oh, and The Damned flop – again.

The Captain takes the blame. He just forgets sometimes that he's got a, y'know, guitar in his hand so the cord tends to get tangled round his rubbery legs and he falls over and rips the plug out of the amp. Silence. But he keeps on falling over until he busts the guitar. They play on in treble splendour, then break for ten minutes to patch things up, but all impetus is lost and the finale, 'Stab Your Back' and 'All Messed Up', verges on pathetic.

Again, the second set is an improvement – anything would have been – but it's still plagued by technical problems that even Sensible's nurse's uniform can't cure.

The Taking of CBGB's, Day Three

I get accosted day and night by hookers from Broadway to 42nd Street via a Times Square riddled with sex booths and dildo shops and, yep, more hookers. I climb to the top of the Empire State Building and look down upon the acid-wriggling yellow carpet of cabs.

It feels like I'm in Gomorrah.

I'm now convinced the Dead Boys are one of the best new bands on the New York scene. Bators is good enough to be a star – wafer-thin face, cloak-and-dagger smile, shades, a wasted Graham Parker, if that's possible.

The Damned are cooking tonight. Scabies is in fine insulting form coercing the audience into some kind of response, however minimal. Someone throws a bottle – that's something.

'All right, we're fed up with all you poseurs. We're English. Get up.'

No takers. Some people actually think he's menacing. Damned gullible, these Yanks. The band play the same set every night but this is the first time they've hit it on the head. Everything's working. The Captain's more restrained – he only falls over once.

'You guys are so terrible I love you,' screams an ageing bearded hippie at the back.

America isn't ready for The Damned. There are one or two clued-in punters among the hairy audience and they appreciate just how good they are. But the rest...

'This has been the most exciting period of my life,' says the Captain, in the cupboard that doubles as a dressing room.

Some American guy asks who I am. 'He's the Nick Kent of pop journalism,' says Rat. Don't know whether to feel pissed-off or honoured.

At the start of the Dead Boys second set The Damned join them on stage for an impromptu version of 'Anarchy In The UK', a big favourite with the CBGB's bang gang.

The Taking of CBGB's, Day Four

It's three a.m. and I'm on Broadway, alone. They say the neon lights are bright there but not bright enough to attract the usual moth-like cabs. I continue to walk in the general direction of the apartment – a good ten blocks away – and turn into an ocean of a street without the merest trace of life.

After walking for five, maybe ten minutes without seeing a human, a car or a piece of paper trembling in the breeze, I notice a group of people in the distance heading towards me. As they get nearer I can make out six of them. Guys. Hooded.

What do I do? Cross the road? It's pretty wide and maybe that'd be the signal for them to pounce. Or, in the immortal words of Val Doonican, *walk tall, walk straight and look the world right in the eye.* At this moment I kind of wish I was knee high again, listening to my mother's advice and a lifetime away from this certain death.

I don't stray from my path, which is just about dead centre of the pack. I feel like a Dam buster. Tonight I'm going to die, but I'll go down fighting.

I'm a few feet away when my bottle goes completely, and I veer to my left in a hopeless attempt at making it to the kerb and across the street. I lose my balance and fall into the arms of the big guy at the end. I prepare my throat for slashing and wish I could have tasted Dina's lips one more time.

'Hey man, you okay?' His voice was deeper than the Grand Canyon.

Er, yes. Thanks.

'Hey, guys, this dude's English.' They all smile at me and carry on walking.

'You should get a cab, man. It's ain't too safe around here,' is my angel's parting shot.

I've never been so scared and I've never been more full of hope.

This is it. The Big One.

From 'Stab Your Back' to 'Feel The Pain' they have never performed better. Without once coming up for air they play 'Feel Alright', 'See

Her Tonight', 'Help', 'Neat Neat Neat' and 'So Messed Up' in the menacing, meathead way British audiences have come to expect, but the Yanks don't and it knocks them out.

The Brian James songbook is bound in gold tonight. Collar turned up, eyes locked in a pre-ejaculation clench, his guitar a perfect distance from his lean body; Brian is the archetypal teen dream, and the predominantly Patti Smith audience – she's appearing after The Damned – is converted in a moment. But only a moment. The Damned's homespun delights are a little too rich.

Well, that's it. Mission accomplished. Or is it? The Damned have had the first bite of the Big Apple with little success. It was a merely a reconnaissance expedition. UK punk has started to blaze the trail west.

I stay on for the Patti Smith gig which is of reverential nature. Nobody speaks while she sings so it's with particular lip-smacking relish that I enjoy the moment during the slow build-up to 'Horses' when the hairy hippie at the back yells, 'Bring back the fucking Damned!'

A local record company says of The Damned CBGB's stint, 'They are the presidential visitors of tomorrow.'

Hmm.

Much as I adore New York, the Manhattan lights are somewhat dimmed by the spectre of Dina. I haven't seen her for about six weeks and I really miss her. The intensity of the skyscrapers, like frozen tornadoes, generates a real need for human touch. On my sofa at night I ache, but that might be because it's only four-foot-six long.

On the trip I snort my first line of coke in a top-of-the-range apartment on Riverside Drive, belonging to a well-known session guitarist. Four of us sit waiting for his Man, which I'd thought was a bit of a myth but, sure enough, this guy turns up carrying a special case laden with every drug known to Man, each in its own compartment and each clearly labelled. He looks unnervingly like a tax inspector in a flowery shirt.

Out comes the coke and it's duly sliced into five lines. I don't know the correct etiquette so I hope and pray he passes it to his right instead of to his immediate left, which is where I'm sitting, so I can observe how all the others do it.

'So, you're a journalist from England, huh?' says the Man. 'Shit, be my guest, man,' and he hands me a rolled-up $100 bill, which I stick at the bottom of a line and snort up, up and away. I pass it to my left and watch, in total embarrassment, as everyone blocks a nostril then snorts with the other. Not only that but some venture half-way up their line, reverse fingers and snort the rest up the other nostril. I sniffed cocaine like I sniffed speed – straight up one nostril with my finger anywhere but on the other side of my nose. They must think I'm barbaric. I feel foolish, unhip, bearded.

The Man turns to me and smiles. I get the picture. Still, there is one consolation – at least this white stuff doesn't bring tears to your eyes.

The next night, after a tip-off from a very sexy waitress friend of a record company PR I meet at CBGB's, I get the chance to try it again, at some length, in a Manhattan recording studio. Lisa, who 'just adores' my accent, knows a guy who runs the studio at the midnight hour and he told her the Stones are recording that night. She's dressed to the nines in a gold lamé catsuit, I kid you not, when she takes me down to the studio in her red Ford Mustang. My notebook throbs in my jeans as we wait but after two hours the erection finally subsides. The band don't show.

The studio guy, a big, smooth black dude, is very apologetic. To numb the pain, he produces from his inside pocket a small bag of coke. Four fat lines each later, I couldn't give a toss about the Stones. I'm hot and horny and fancy the pants off Lisa. I could have danced all night and I want to Watusi with her and her alone. We finally leave the studio at around three and she drives me back to the apartment where I'm staying.

We sit outside in the car and talk for an hour about life, the universe and James Stewart movies. It's the most wonderful conversation I've ever had with a woman and it's not only because she's wearing a catsuit, looks a lot like a dirtier version of Elizabeth Montgomery and I've just snorted half a gram of class-one coke.

I want desperately to invite her up, but how can I? Luke, the sweet guy who owns it, sleeps in the one bedroom and is probably still up anyway. We can't go to hers because she shares an apartment with her sister and brother-in-law.

For only the second time in my life I say, 'I need to kiss you,' and for the second time it works. Her tongue lights up the Dinaless dark for what seems like a gold lamé eternity.

I wave as she drives off and catch the elevator to the fifth-floor apartment. On the kitchen table I find the following (suicide) note: 'Out all night, back tomorrow around lunchtime. The flat is yours tonight Barry.'

My coke-stiffened hand reaches for my notebook.

THE STRANGLERS
Rattus Norvegicus IV album review

How three blind-mice musicians are led Indian-file style into a drainy abyss by the 'loneliness-is-such-a-drag' voice of Hugh Cornwell, the long-distance runner.

Hot Rats.

The Stranglers have this cold-cream foundation of sound with Cornwell's storm-trooper tones pushing up through the mass like a running sore. He's a street-corner spiv with a suitcase, whispering in your ear, 'I've got something here that might interest you,' namely 'Peaches', the first great package-holiday song since 'Uno Paloma Blanca'.

But what really sets them apart from the other new-rave bands is Dave Greenfield's undiluted keyboard work, especially on 'Sometimes', 'Goodbye Toulouse' with its Pink Floyd 'Welcome To The Machine' fade-out and 'Grip', the single. Hence the Velvet-Underground-with-balls tag, an understatement, incidentally. Bassist Jean-Jacques Burnel sings the shit out of 'London Lady'.

Cornwell's guitar work occasionally sounds like Television's Tom Verlaine – check out 'Princess Of The Streets', the best track on an initial hearing, and 'Hanging Around', and that can't be bad. Criticism, shoddy production on one or two tracks. But I can live with that.

What had been little more than a '76 fashion statement is, in 1977, turning into a full-blooded musical movement. Punk rock is becoming a great deal more than the sum of its parts. It is now a phrase on the tongues of a nation.

Meanwhile, the return of the prodigal sons.

THE DAMNED

The Roundhouse

Good? Of course they're good. It takes a lot more than a Stateside sojourn to fillet these fugitives from a sane gang.

There aren't many bands around who can whip up a Roundhouse frenzy barely 12 hours after flying in from LA. But it is the Captain's birthday.

A paint-daubed-sheet backdrop screams, 'Tax exiles return!' and the Captain appears in a Margot Fonteyn, which is too, too much. It soon comes off, leaving him in black tights. And what's this? They're removed for the first encore leaving him stark bollock naked.

How apt.

Pies are thrown, beer is spilled as the Rat is let out of the bag along with pounds of talc, which he duly sprinkles over the crowd out front. Lovely stuff. Okay, they recycle the album and play 'Neat Neat Neat' twice. It would have been nice to hear at least one new number.

Just one.

But the crowds who cram into the Roundhouse want to get off on what they know, what their blistered feet can identify with.

A handful of songs and two encores later the DJ says it all: 'That's the most outrageous show the Roundhouse has ever seen.'

The key word there is 'show'. That's exactly what The Damned are all about.

MAY 1977

Top ten singles
beginning of May

1. Free – Deniece Williams
2. Sir Duke – Stevie Wonder
3. Red Light Spells Danger – Billy Ocean
4. I Don't Want To Talk About It – Rod Stewart
5. Who Done It? – Tavares
6. Have I The Right? – Dead End Kids
7. Knowing Me Knowing You – Abba
8. Pearl's A Singer – Elkie Brooks
9. I Don't Want To Put A Hold On You – Berni Flint
10. How Much Love? – Leo Sayer

Top ten albums
beginning of May

1. Arrival – Abba
2. 20 Golden Greats – the Shadows
3. Hotel California – the Eagles
4. Rattus Norvegicus VI – The Stranglers
5. Portrait Of Sinatra – Frank Sinatra
6. Greatest Hits – Abba
7. Endless Flight – Leo Sayer
8. A Star Is Born – Soundtrack
9. Greatest Hits – Smokie
10. Rumours – Fleetwood Mac

I love Paris in the springtime. Especially when the champagne is Bollinger…

THE CLASH
Palais de Glace, Paris

Jet. Charles De Gaulle airport. Mercedes. Hotel. Mercedes. The house
of flicks. Outside the Palais de Glace, an ageing Parisian cinema in
downtown Paris, Algerian pickpockets discuss fashion trends and
the distinct lack of orifices to excite their educated fingers.

As I push my way through the crowd that has gathered outside
the venue, I look down and spot a hand carefully removing a
fifty-franc note from my jeans pocket. When I grab it back a
considerable number of Algerian guys surround me and it's
starting to look ugly, until one of the doormen pushes through and
ushers me into the foyer.

Lucky for them, huh?

The dustmen are on strike, soon to be joined by public-transport
workers and the power men. The streets stink of dodgy onions and
rotting garlic and stale baguettes 'turn cartwheels 'cross the floor'.

The occasional gendarme holsters past.

Police and thieves on the streets. The punters are more pink than
punk – leather bombers and jeans and, wait for it, berets in aerial
formation across the balcony.

On stage Subway Sect are a blazing inertia, only hands showing
any sign of life. Singer Vic Goddard reads the lyrics from scraps of
paper in a vaguely mocking style, and when they leave the stage
after a 30-minute set there are one or two Frenchmen in a state of
Mon Dieu.

The cinema is narrow, seats 800 and there's about 500 inside.
It's got surprisingly good sound. The backdrop is a picture of the
Notting Hill riots last year – the one on the reverse of The Clash
album. The stage is both roomy and rheumy. The audience is
vociferous. The dominant colour is grey, tinged with black. The cost
of a ticket is 25 francs; £3.20.

Then The Clash walk on.

I feel like a 13-year-old Bay City Rollers fan just before her heroes appear, a skip-a-beat, pre-show-trauma python wrapped round her neck in the shape of a tartan scarf.

Nothing flash, just a casual stroll on and straight into 'Londres Est En Flammes' wherein Paul Simonon breaks a string on his bass.

The light show is limited but effective. Strummer's 3000cc voice is encased in soft green, red and white body shells. He slams on the brakes at the penultimate second of the song and introduces the band, 'We are Les Clash.' While Paul fixes the string, Strummer continues, 'So you are *les punks de* Paris. You look like a bunch of fucking hippies to me.' His shoulders flap Cagney-style as he walks, and his voice has a kinda John Wayne intonation. We're in for a Strummer summer.

'1977' is next up.

Mick Jones sandwiches every slice of meat that right-on axemen have dished up through the years, from a Marriott criss-cross walk to a Townsend leap. But he covers it in his own unique Rockfort dressing. He's the antithesis of Strummer's on-the-spot throbbing, burning up every inch of the stage, slipping and a-sliding on his own sweat. At times he and Paul look like a pair of grossly distorted Chinese bookends

'Toots Chute Sepressurisée' is a strange choice, which succeeds mainly because of Paul's thunderous bassline. Then there's 'Je M'en Fous Telement De l'USA'. Hey, I've just remembered – they've got a new drummer, again, haven't they? Of course. Ol' wassisname, again, Nicky Headon. That's a tribute. It's taken me 45 minutes to realise there's a different drummer in their midst. He's blending well, like he's been with them for years. But he looks so ill.

'Haine Et Guerre' has Mick at the mike. The Frenchman in the next seat nudges me in the ribs. 'They are good musicians but they are not playing music.' Shut up and stop breathing garlic over me. I flash a friendly smile. After all, the guy could be another fucking pickpocket.

After 'Tricheur' we're treated to 'Flics et Voleurs', only the second time the Junior Murvin song from the album has been performed live. It's a slightly different version from the record and it works like a dream. 'This is a song for the intelligentsia, *les* intellectuals,' says Joe.

Holes are dug in the music of The Clash, holes scratched deep by fingernails into which words are poured by Strummer. In the years that follow they'll dry into bone-hard relics of a frustrated generation.

'48 Heures' and then one for the girls, if there are any, 'Dis Moi Non' and new song 'Radio Capitale', included on a special EP about the famous London radio station, which, folly upon folly, has already banned it.

'Controle De Loin' and 'Opportunité De Carrière' are fired in quick succession and a big cheer for the anthem 'Emeute Des Blancs' with Strummer screaming, '1968!' before tearing into the hit single. Favourite for the next single, 'Janie Jones', the most insanely commercial song from the album, is given the all important pole position in the finale.

Two encores – 'Band de Garage' and a re-blast of 'Emeute' first, '1977' and 'Londres Est En Flammes' second. The band are treating this gig, and, indeed, all others in this short European tour, as a warm-up for the all important nationwide stint, which kicked off in Guildford last Sunday. If this is a warm-up I want an Eiffel of their hot nights because they'll be unbelievable.

The overwhelming success the gods have in store for The Clash will be totally justified. In the recording studio and live, there are very few bands around that are anywhere near them.

And down in the dark streets where the prostitutes scream, Mick Jones and Strummer meet up with a certain Captain Sensible and Rat Scabies, who have been known to play musical instruments. And what's this? The four actually jamming together before a handful of people on the stage of an incredibly depressing disco on a dirty boulevard in a grubby part of town on the wrong side of shit. They play 'Louie Louie' and 'White Riot' and embrace like football players.

The speed makes me feel horny and in a corner of the disco Clash manager Bernie Rhodes advises me to find a nice little punkette to bed down with for the night. But I don't speak French and Dina is the only *vin* for my *coq*.

You get to meet all sorts when you hang out with The Clash.

Then there's Shaar-Murray, my music-writing hero, who looks like a character from a black and white Fifties Italian movie. He's on edge throughout, like he's testing himself and the people around him and always coming up short.

In the cab on the way back to London, Charles suggests we go to his place for a farewell coffee. Turns out he lives with his girlfriend in a flat on Pentonville Road, my hometown. She's locked herself in the bedroom and refuses to come out, despite Charles's pleas. He makes some coffee, we drink it sharply and as we leave we say, 'Cheerio', to the bedroom door and the bedroom door says, 'Cheerio', back.

Meanwhile, I can't get enough of the Jam

THE JAM
Royal College of Art, London

It's a godawful small affair…

Stage as long as Platform six at Victoria station. Baggageless porters the Jam 40 feet apart and monitorless. Full house. Lights! The Tyla Gang before and the Cimarrons after.

An artless audience at the Royal College of Art show their appreciation of the white-soul boys up there on the stage with the huge Union Jack backdrop depicting the three moods the Jam take you through at a gig – red hot expanding into white heat, contracting into teenage blue.

In case you've forgotten, guitarist Paul Weller, bassist Bruce Foxton and drummer Rick Buckler are the Jam. They are not, I repeat *not*, a recycled Who. They write concise, contemporary songs like 'In The City', 'Bricks & Mortar' and 'I've Changed My Address' enhancing the overall effect with a shrewd selection of old material – 'Batman', 'So Sad About Us' and 'Midnight Hour'. The result? A well-equipped show, incisive, dynamic, piebald. Black suits, white lights, black ties, white shirts, black thoughts, white rock. They won't blow it now.

The Jam always come across as much younger than other bands, like Brian Kidd in a team of Bobby Charltons. They have the pace and the sneer – Paul Weller could hardly be described as 'this smiling man'. He drinks but refuses to take drugs, on the grounds that they are immoral, debilitating and, well, uncool. Drug-induced confidence is unnecessary for the cool dude that's Paul Weller. But he gets more hangovers that way.

Paul is cool because he's a man with a genuine talent who hasn't quite realised it yet. And that's when the good stuff comes.

Three sides of the coin
Billy Idol, Chris Glenn and Demis Roussos talk about money, money, money

BILLY IDOL

Money in pocket at time of interview: '£5. That's a lot. I've got this much 'cos I have to buy some guitar strings today.' [Shit, no wonder he sneers all the time].

Lifestyle: 'I can't buy new clothes so I make my own. I had a job driving a van a little while ago but I had to give it up if I was gonna make any serious attempt at making music. I've sold some guitars and my record collection is dwindling rapidly as I continue to look for more sources to raise cash but it doesn't bother me at the moment 'cos I'm playing my own music. I can't afford to drink much – that's a luxury. When I do it can only be beer – it's cheaper and it lasts longer.

'I live at home and my parents think I'm totally cracked. I've conned them into thinking I make enough to live on but I'm hardly ever there anyway. I rely a lot on friends to put me up when I need a roof over my head. I don't know where I'll be staying tonight but I'm sure I'll end up somewhere.'

Time in business: 'I've been in Generation X for six months. I went straight into a band from the front of a mirror where I posed rock'n'roll star style.'

Money making: 'Any money I get, I get from my manager – the amount depends on the prestige the band have in any particular area. For example, at Leicester University where they never have any punk bands we played a gig recently and £150 was taken at the door but it cost us that in travelling expenses and roadies.

'All we ever seem to do is break even or lose money. When we played in Wales it cost us 200 quid. I reckon average receipts are well below one hundred. In other words, we're stony broke. But I trust the guy who looks after us – you have to. I don't want to have to rely on other people all the time.

'At the moment, there's no way I'm gonna make any money out of all this. But I can't ever see myself doing anything else.'

CHRIS GLENN
(SENSATIONAL ALEX HARVEY BAND)

Money in pocket: '£40. That's really only beer money. I always carry that sort of sum around with me.'

Lifestyle: 'Most of the things I want are about as far away as a telephone call. If I have to pay a bill, it's paid for me. I can't say I want X amount of money and get it because we work on tabs. When a management company is involved they deal with everything on the financial side and debit it to the band's accounts. SAHB are a working band. If it wasn't I'd probably be more into material things.

'Sure, I've got a house in London and a Ford car. The only reason I've got a car is because my wife needs it. What's the point of me owning a really flash motor if I'm hardly ever there to take advantage of it?

'I spend money on crazy things like gadgets. I've got a television with 16 tapes on remote control and a push button-telephone, among other things. That really does cost a lot.

'I don't know how much money I've got or how much money I haven't got. And I don't want to know.'

Time in the business: 'Eight years. The main reason you join a band is because you're a poseur – you like chicks looking at you. The reason our drummer took up music was because he found he could pull more birds.'

Money making: 'The minute you call yourself a band you're in debt. When we played four Christmas shows in London and three in Glasgow we knew before even walking on to the stage we were losing money. It was just as well they were sell-outs, otherwise we'd have been in real trouble.

'Take the Rainbow – 3,000 people pay four and a half grand at the door. The theatre takes five per cent, the ticket office rakes off another ten. The hire of the hall is a grand. Then there's the cost of the PA – £500 a night for a good one – the lights, the guys who work the lights. If there's a promoter, there goes another 15 to 20 per cent. So you ain't left with much.

'Record companies spend more money on the drinks for a reception than on a PA. Same with records. The hire of a recording studio is about £1 a minute. And even if you make a really successful album it's a long time before you see any money out of it. A hit single doesn't bring in much either.

'We lost 40 grand on our debut American tour. When we first started out things got so difficult, money wise, that we were on the verge of breaking up. I think it's easier for new bands now. There's things available that weren't before. I used to get everything on HP and that put my old man into hock for the rest of his life.'

DEMIS ROUSSOS

Money in pocket: 'Nothing. I don't need it. If I want something I just get it. Everyone knows who I am. They know where to send the bill.'

Lifestyle: 'I earn two million dollars a year. I sell five million albums a year in 50 countries. I tour seven months a year and make more than 250 performances. I receive 200 letters a day from my fans all over the world. I am unique because I bridge the gap between fans of the Rolling Stones and fans of Liberace.

'I'm not a miser – and I don't like to spend money needlessly either. I believe that in life when we want something we must take the opportunity. I have a lot of money, I spend a lot of money. I pay a lot of taxes. In my time I've bought a lot of nice things with money I've worked for, not that I've found. So I can do what I like with it. I have golden taps in my bathroom. I have a mansion in France and a mansion in Los Angeles. I have my own cinema in one of them.

'I buy things after calculating. I'm not impulsive. Life is the best school. Sometimes when I wake up in the morning I eat six eggs. It all depends how hungry I am. Then I have meetings, then I eat in a restaurant.

'I like to have a lot of time with my wife and kids, and from now on I shall spend six months in Europe and six months in America each year.

'I used to have my own jet but I sold it. I have two Rolls-Royces because that's the most economical car. It never breaks down.

'Twenty families live off me. I invest in wine, diamonds and gold. Last year I bought mineral water and we had a very hot summer so I made a killing.'

Time in the business: 'Fifteen years. I was the son of a very rich man who lived in Egypt. Then the Arabs took all his money and we became broke. I was 15 when that happened and we had to move to a very small apartment in Athens.

I had to help my family by working and the only thing I could do was play music. I worked for £1 a night at first and moved slowly up. Seven years later along came Aphrodite's Child and three years after that I started my solo career. So I didn't become a star just like that.'

Money making: You said it.

HUGH CORNWELL
Douai, France

'Pssst, I've got something here that might interest you.'

Never drop acid with a Strangler.

I'm in a country lane just outside Dunkirk with Hugh Cornwell and a fresh-faced photographer and I've just taken some acid. It gets a little weird, from 'Alice In Wonderland' to a fatal car crash, as we try to capture the whole trip in the form of a colour photo story entitled 'Go Body Go'.

The night before the band were due to play a village hall in Douai but were double-booked with a yoga class and only 30 people turn up. 'We ain't playing!' they yell and drive off into the night to their hotel. The following morning, Hugh oversleeps and by the time he gets downstairs the rest of the band, tired of waiting, have already set off for Paris.

Paris is 153 kilometres away and the skies darken with steamy rain clouds. With nothing but a few random thoughts and a five-franc piece for comfort, Hugh embarks on his solitary way. He wanders through the damp French villages like a First World War hero on his way to slice a loaf of Hovis. It's four in the afternoon when he sees it, the biggest, whitest rat in France with a gold watch and chain around its neck. Hugh is convinced the rat is saying, 'I'm late, I'm late.'

He pursues the rodent as it disappears into sewer. Down, down he falls and lands on a mound of shit.

Hugh gets up, brushes himself down and looks around. The rat is nowhere in sight. 'Fill you up, sir?' says a multi-coloured petrol pump-attendant.

'Yeah,' says Hugh. 'Five-star, please.' The petrol has a profound effect. He shrinks. 'Try the four-star, sir. You're pinking.'

It has the reverse effect and Hugh grows and grows until he's able to crawl back out of the sewer. I must get a grip on myself, he thinks. I've got to get to Paris in one piece.

Time is getting on and hitchhiker Hugh is at a low ebb. Time for a spot of praying. Luckily he stumbles across a beautiful church of Cornwellian orthodoxy by the side of the road.

'Oh, please, dear Ford, I don't ask much – just the occasional hit record and sell-out concert but, see, I'm in this dilemma and Ford knows how I'm gonna get out of it. Could you see your way clear to help me just this once?'

Suddenly a huge Ford Zodiac flashes across the sky uttering the immortal words, 'Drop thy strides, Hugh.' And Hugh obeys.

'Try this for size,' and, like a miracle, his lack of French dressing has the desired effect. A pillar-box red Citroën flashes past, then screeches to a halt.

'*Bonjour*,' says Daniel, a psychoanalyst on his way to Paris to meet some friends for a meal in the Latin quarter.

'*Bonjour*. I'm going to Paris,' says Hugh.

'*Venez avec moi*,' says Daniel, and Hugh climbs inside.

Daniel smokes vast quantities of untipped Gauloises and often speaks of the English climate.

'*Je joue la guitare dans la groupe de pop Les Étrangleurs*,' says Hugh, and Daniel looks suitably impressed.

'I, er, like you, Hugh. You very funny.'

Hugh smiles.

Night falls as the little car speeds through a tiny village on the outskirts of Paris.

'We are, er, nearly at the city,' says Daniel.

Hugh is excited. It won't be long before I see the other guys now, he thinks. I can't wait. We'll have a great night out in Paris.

He nods off, never to wake again. A heavy fog engulfs the village and at that moment a drunken peasant wanders aimlessly across the road, ignorant of the pillar-box red Citroën hurtling towards him.

Daniel sees the old man too late, hits him, and spins out of control. The car crashes into a tree and bursts into flames.

And that's how the Stranglers never get to play in Paris. A tragedy, yes, but that's the only way Hugh would have wanted it – on the road. I recall the words of Rupert Brooke: 'If I should die think only this of me, that there's some corner of a foreign field that is forever England.'

The Stranglers will continue as a trio.

The strangest thing. The photos we take in France of Hugh in the make-believe car smash – fake blood, the works – don't come out. I arrange hastily to meet him and the photographer at the back of York Way in Kings Cross, the home of the car-wreck yard. The guys who work there recognise Hugh, and let us use one of the wrecks for a real full-on car-crash shot. They even find us a pillar-box red Citroën.

Hugh's a natural in front of the camera. All the bands know how to pose, the off-the-shoulder fuck you look is a prerequisite, although some, like Hugh, can pull it off better than others.

He looks totally dead: wild, staring eyes, fake blood streaming from his mouth as he flops his head out of the shattered car windscreen. Paul takes loads of shots. They don't come out either. Paul is devastated. Hugh is freaked and laughs. I write the feature and fall over.

Back home, I catch a train to Sheffield to see New Zealand bizarros Split Enz with record-company PR Joe, who has a reputation with women that I envy. When he first met my Californian blonde ex-girlfriend Colette she was standing a few feet away with her back to us, watching Talking Heads at their UK début gig downstairs at the Rock Garden. 'I'd love to fuck the arse off that,' he shouted in my ear, as we were standing near the speakers, blissfully unaware that she was with me. I didn't know whether to take it as a compliment or an insult. I decided on the former. 'I have done,' I replied. 'She's my girlfriend.'

Joe went down on his knees and begged forgiveness.

And then it happens. The Pistols sign another record deal. It's Virgin, and this time it looks like for keeps, judging by Virgin's admirably aggressive attitude.

Check it out: 'However other record companies might protest, they would all like to have signed the Sex Pistols,' says a Virgin representative. 'Their reluctance was not because of strong disapproval but fear of what others, the press, their American offices, their own artists, might think. The Sex Pistols have thrown a successful spanner into the rock works. Thanks to them, many new-wave bands have been able to emerge. They have problems getting live gigs, the BBC will not play their records and the press has refused to accept their advertising, but the Sex Pistols, while being the most hated, must be potentially the most successful group around.'

THE JAM
Carnaby Street

At last.

The Jam.

In Carnaby Street.

Red, white and blue jackets. Attitude, youth and soul. Paul Weller writes sublime punk pop, sings like a white Otis and manages to tell it like it is.

During the interview he's shy but forthcoming, a neat contradiction. Bruce and Rick provide the back-up. It's a job they do well.

The photo session will go on to be the most famous the band ever did. The Union Jack image sticks with them for a while and, although it becomes a small monkey no bigger than a marmoset on their bony backs, makes them a little more famous a little more quickly. Oh, and the music helps a bit.

Woking-class heroes with Union J-J-Jack tenacity. The J-J-Jam.

'The Jam are about rock'n'roll.' Paul Weller, 18, singer, guitarist.

'The Jam create today's music for today's kids.' Bruce Foxton, 21, bassist, singer.

'The Jam are just a band you shouldn't miss out on. I often wish I was in the audience so I could watch us.' Rick Buckler, 21, drummer.

They're all from council-house Surrey with the fringe on top. Upbringing an inconclusive gesture purporting to represent the best our dear nation can offer.

Occasionally such indoctrination doesn't have the desired effect and the J-J-Jam are formed. Working-men's clubs, social gatherings, youth clubs, WHAMMO! Big record company, hit single, hit album, stars.

Old story? Yes. Fact is, the book hasn't been opened for more than ten years. It's been gathering dust on a woodwormy shelf in a room full of cobwebs at the back of a house somewhere. Then, like a go-ahead council, 1977 comes along and pulls the whole thing down.

It's a ready-steady-go afternoon.

Wet, cold Monday in Carnaby Street. Bruce tries on his newly made Union J-J-Jacket, laughs and turns milky. 'Maybe it wasn't such a good idea, after all,' he says.

The three walk out of the tailor's shop along a narrow alleyway and fall in beneath 'Carnaby Street Welcomes the World'. Their white strides hang immaculately above winkle-pickered feet. Photo-session number one begins.

'Are they a punk-rock group?' asks a policeman, as they pose. 'Well, how long are you going to be? This is a busy street, you know. Make it quick.'

Before the swinging Sixties Carnaby Street was j-j-just another West End grimeroad, it's only claim to fame a nightclub with the laughable name the Blue Lagoon. Max Bygraves and Tommy Cooper both got their breaks there.

J-j-just like that the session ends. Into cabs and on to the Mall. More photos. Next stop Westminster Bridge. 'My Generation' stance beneath Big Ben. Home, J-J-James.

The weekend ends here.

Change of clothes, though not of sentiments, a quick freshen-up, couple of drinks and we're into the interview.

'Everything is misconstrued,' says Paul. 'When I said I'd vote Tory everyone jumped on my back. All I meant was when the Tories are in power people have more money in their pockets. Nobody can deny that.'

Red trousers, black j-j-jacket, dishevelled hair. Like a cat on the morning doorstep after a shooting-star night.

'Heavy weekend. See, things have been getting out of hand. Instead of writing songs that mean something, all that's dished up is a lot of mindless crap. Now we're getting a natural revolution. It's like going against what your mum and dad say, like at school with all its rules. I'd just like to break down all that. Make your own rules. And it's just the same with music.'

Bruce and Rick sit apart from Paul. Bruce of the perpetual smile, Rick of the thinking face.

'It's a case of every generation having its own cult and refusing what's gone before,' says Paul.

'Right,' adds Rick. 'It's all been underground and Led Zeppelin up until now.'

'Kids should make their mark on this generation otherwise it's going to be too late,' says Paul. 'Youth was real important in the Fifties and Sixties but now it ain't. Maybe the kids have seen all the cults which have come to nothing and ain't bothered.'

'There are so many different people around now, the leftovers from all the previous cults,' says Rick. 'But it's a good thing to be what you want to be.'

'Everything goes in cycles,' Paul insists. 'The present set-up won't go on for ever. It's, like, I can't imagine how anyone can go on stage at the age of 32 and sing 'My Generation' and still be a force. The Sixties were so potent and when they passed it left such a void. Everyone has been out of breath for a long time.'

Three schoolboys in Woking. Dinner-time music sessions. Four-hour stints at local clubs during their 'Blue Moon' period. 'We're more musically mature than most of the other bands around now. We don't abide by their stupid little punk rules,' says Paul.

'We don't sit around and think of what we're going to rebel against next,' says Bruce.

For the Rickenbacker kids 'reality's so hard'. But that's not gonna stop them clearing up. The single 'In The City' is getting chart action and an album of the same name released last week is already at number 43 and pushing a lot of copies.

They've been supporting The Clash on a nationwide tour and are about to embark on their own first major headline tour. Brocks would be proud of their on-stage antics, which are as far away from posing as Mick J-J-Jagger is from his fans.

At the moment Weller emerges as the mainman wonder. He writes all the home-grown material, mono-sings and dances the night away. 'I take it as a compliment to be regarded as the new Who,' he says, 'but it's very funny 'cos none of us has ever seen them. But we're intent on becoming stars. Okay, I hate Rod Stewart, I hate Mick Jagger, but I want to be a star.' He pauses. 'Star is such a horrible word. But, look, I took a lot of stick at school from the teachers about how thick I was and how I wasn't gonna get anywhere. That made me determined to get on. I want to go back and rub it in their faces – 'Look what I've become.'

'In places like Birmingham and Glasgow a lot of kids have very little hope of getting a job when they leave school or even joining a rock band. We all come from working-class backgrounds but to many people our council houses, surrounded by a few trees and a bit of grass, probably seem like a lower-middle-class set-up.

'Most of the new-wave bands are all trying too hard to be stars and get money in their pockets. I don't think they can identify with the kids.

''My Generation' was the most socially significant song ever written. All I write about is youth and hate. Hatred of teachers who spend all their time telling you how they won the war instead of asking you what *you've* been doing – I left school with a big chip on my shoulder. Hatred of greedy people – and there are a lot of them around. Hatred of groups like the National Front – I sincerely hope our dress and national pride doesn't make people think we're involved with them. Bands have got a certain duty to their fans and I hate to see them wearing swastikas on stage.

'I want to see whites and blacks working together, trying to solve problems instead of creating them.'

Paul admits he isn't a prolific songwriter. Anyone who tells you he is, is either a liar or a useless writer. 'I get a week of sudden inspiration and then don't write another song for a couple of months. One thing that really got to me was when I read about a guy called Liddle Towers who got beaten up outside a disco by six coppers and eventually died. His rancour was channelled into 'Time For Truth'.

'Coppers have now got the right to kill you,' Paul continues. 'We're heading for a police state. More and more laws are being made for the police to carry out. That's what happens when the population increases.'

Bruce doesn't involve himself in political discussions. 'I'd rather just leave it.'

And then there's the J-J-Jubilee.

'We like the Queen,' says Paul. 'I don't see the point of putting her down. And for those that do it's just their mohair suits – their stab at being fashionable. All the other new bands refuse to talk politics with us 'cos we're always right.'

'Politics and pop is taken too far,' interrupts Bruce. 'Like the other night a guy came up to me after the show and said Joe Strummer's his favourite politician. The Clash are only interested in rock'n'roll and that's a fact.'

What of the short series of J-J-Jubilee gigs? 'We just wanted to contribute something,' says Paul. 'Instead of sitting back knocking the country, people should do something constructive.'

So, the Jam are playing three Jubilee shows for nothing – Chelsea Football Ground for Hammersmith Council, 12 June, Poplar Civic Hall for Tower Hamlets Council, 18 June and Battersea Town Hall for Wandsworth Council, 27 June.

'When you've got no money in your pocket and you're out of a job, it's then you know what politics means,' says Paul

So young for slogans. So tired about us.

TOM VERLAINE
Glasgow

I think I'm going to be a little out of my depth with Tom Verlaine. Shit, that's the second time this month I've felt out of my depth. I'm drowning here.

I'm convinced the Television frontman, responsible for the epic *Marquee Moon*, is going to be one of those smart-alec New York dolls with wit like a whiplash and an innate intellectual rapacity. New Yorkers scare me: they seem infinitely more sophisticated and intelligent and, well, superior in every way. The true master race. Verlaine is the antithesis of Johnny Thunders. There's not an intellectual bone in Johnny's three-star body, just an ounce of five-star smack. He's bound to pink some time.

Five floors above the deranged contours of Glasgow a dismembered light in the three a.m. thickness. Pretty metaphysical, huh? Especially when the denizen of this particular eight-by-eight chamber just happens to be Ol' Glue Eyes himself, Tom Verlaine – midnight rambler and word conductor of Television.

The opening night of his short British tour is already a five-hours-old statue. Over. A stunning confirmation of a piercing talent, maybe, but Newcastle next. The world will follow. So now on this fading tight-toy night, Tom sits on a wooden chair by the side of his bed and smiles. He is the man who put the 'wan' in 'wanderer', a pasty poet-faced searcher for truth and the un-American way.

He's a thinking smiler, a million years away from the 'baulking egomania' stance ascribed to him by one journalist.

'There's a lot of irresponsibility in journalism – and everything else,' he says. 'It simply depends on whether you like what you're doing. With I-don't-care attitudes there's absolutely nothing you can do. Sometimes that attitude can also leave someone with a feeling of superiority. See, there are times when you've got to say, 'I don't give a toss."

What times?

'Like landing up in a hole-in-the-wall hotel that's the only one in town. Sure, it's an easy way out.'

Do you ever get that 'I-don't-give-a-toss' attitude when it comes to Television?

'I care about what we do completely. It's no big deal when you realise that everyone has a certain spirit which is almost taken for granted. A vitality. It's just being unconsciously aware that there's intelligence in life. It's up to you how much of it you choose to use.'

Unfortunately Television (that's Verlaine, lead vocals and guitar, Richard Lloyd, guitar, Fred Smith, bass and Billy Ficca, drums) have been sucked into the new-wave whirlpool created by the uninitiated. Maybe it's the inherent anguish on their album. Maybe it's the ripped-up New York tag. Anyway, it's crap because compared to other Big Apple bands, Television are on another wavelength. They are the most important American band to have emerged in a long time.

'The current set-up in Britain with the new bands just couldn't happen in the States,' he says. 'America is so blasé, so comfort-oriented. The vitality and response is not what it should be. Just look at the kind of records that sell. Over here some people really are wasted, you don't get that back home. Class structure in the States is what's on people's minds – but it's more of an intelligence structure. Regardless of what kind of background you come from, people can gravitate upwards. What I've gleaned from this country is, if you don't make money you really don't make money.

'The attitude to music here now just wouldn't be accepted in the States. There's nobody around who seems to want a committed sound – they want the wallpaper, not the wall. People wouldn't lump us with other new-wave bands if we came from New Orleans.'

Television began in 1974 in New York. Richard Hell was in the original line-up but was replaced a year later by ex-Blondie bassist Fred Smith. They played all the city's joints like Max's and CBGB's and attracted a large following. Fame spread straight from the fridge, and after the relative success of a bootleg single – 'Little Johnny Jewel' – they were signed.

The *Marquee Moon* album has been hailed as being both innovative and ingenious.

'I'm not saying that our album is perfect. Our best reception has come from New York and England – your home is where your heart is. It also doesn't strike me as being so fantastically different from anything else. It's all a question of style – and I was satisfied with that.'

Are your songs of a transitory nature? (That sounded sufficiently intellectual. That'll impress Tom. Shit, I feel like Jerry.)

'I guess my desire to do more stuff is greater than my desire to perfect less-recent stuff. That doesn't mean my songs are off the cuff. They're particular memories in a lifetime. For example, I like London. When I first got there I didn't do any writing for three days, then I started. It's funny how people have this impression of me as being a very literary person. I seldom get past the first two pages of a book. All I read is Lorca and Nerval, a French author who strung himself up on a lamp-post in 1870. I also like Persian writers who are always talking about wine. They have a certain grace. Marc Bolan puts references to novelists in his songs. I don't.'

I confess to finding the New York music scene a trifle overrated.

'Oh, I've always been disappointed with it – that's why I never hang out there. We all try to keep away from the centre. Besides, journalists make scenes more than anything else.'

But of course...

'By the time clubs get their reputations in England they've already peaked. CBGB's just happened to have a stage and a liberal owner. To develop as a band in New York you have to play the Top 40 and please the drinking customers.'

Time tiptoes by. The darkness doubles.

'It's funny when I read about the band in all these papers and the cult-figure stuff. I always seem to forget it. Okay, it's nice to read good stuff about yourself when you've worked on something very hard but it concerns me more when people write lies. Inaccuracy is depressing.

'Music is something special and when someone is over exposed to it, be it a journalist or DJ, he becomes jaded. He actually stops responding.'

Sorry? What?

Complete change of subject. Why did you change your name from Miller?

'It's a way of disassociating yourself from yourself. I used to write poems under my last name.' He laughs. 'It was just something to do, I guess. Most people who change their name do it for something to do.'

The connotations of that remark are pretty frightening, if the notion was intended. Why the need to disassociate? Does that make you a loner?

'I'm not a loner. You've just got to know who your friends are. Everyone has their own crowd. Birds of a feather. I number Patti Smith and John Cale among my New York friends.

'But there are certain things you should do on your own. There are certain movies you should see alone. There are certain places you should go to alone. When you find yourself alone you find that you're not. I don't have a telephone because people's lives are centred around them.'

Time for the hurl-old-quotes-at-them-and-see-the-reaction one-two…: *'The standard of musicianship is higher here – you expect that in New York.'*

'If a guy is a good musician over there he can make $2,000 a week on sessions, so why should he bother to get a band together? What you've got left are guys like me who only just learned how to play. We make the bands. In England all the musicians seem to start forming bands.'

Okay – what about *'I'm not into theatre at all'*?

'I'm not into pre-meditated shock efforts like blood capsules. I like variety in the music. Anyone I've ever admired has always changed his style – Bowie and Dylan are classic examples.'

It seems appropriate to leave.

Tom will sleep light on these shores tonight.

Television will not deliver another album to match the might and the magic of Marquee Moon. They will prove to be the new-wave version of Love, capturing a moment before pissing off into obscurity. Still, Tom Verlaine is a clever clogs who manages to shine like a crazy diamond.

I do a phone interview with Kenny Rogers in the same week, just to keep my hand in. I ask him about punk: he's only aware of the word as an integral part of James Cagney's rich vocabulary – 'Johnny Rotten? Sid Vicious? Aren't they characters from a Dickens novel?'

JUNE 1977

Top ten singles
beginning of June

1. I Don't Want To Talk About It – Rod Stewart
2. Lucille – Kenny Rogers
3. Ain't Gonna Bump No More – Joe Tex
4. A Star Is Born (Evergreen) – Barbra Streisand
5. The Shuffle – Van McCoy
6. Good Morning Judge – 10cc
7. Got To Give It Up – Marvin Gaye
8. Half Way Down The Stairs – The Muppets
9. Mah Na Mah Na – Piero Umiliani
10. Okay – Rock Follies

Top ten albums
beginning of June

1. Arrival – Abba
2. Hotel California – the Eagles
3. Deceptive Bends – 10cc
4. A Star Is Born – Soundtrack
5. The Beatles At The Hollywood Bowl
6. Sheer Magic – Acker Bilk
7. Rattus Norvegicus VI – the Stranglers
8. Rumours – Fleetwood Mac
9. Time Loves A Hero – Little Feat
10. All To Yourself – Jack Jones

The Heartbreakers are arrested in Birmingham on suspicion of theft. They're staying in the city's New Victoria Hotel when a payphone is broken into. The band and their entourage are woken and taken to the local police station where they are held for three hours. A fingerprint check proves that none of them had had anything to do with the theft. Johnny is later held up by an armed intruder who claims he's from the SAS on a mission to protect the band.

A month of parties. Record companies are awash with money and receptions are ever more lavish, often involving huge indoor swimming-pools, suckling pigs and there always seems to be an endless supply of drugs.

Meanwhile, in the real world...

'DAILY MIRROR' LEADER COMMENT

'It's not much fun to be young today. If you think otherwise take a look at yesterday's jobless figures. In a single month 104,000 school leavers have gone straight from their classrooms to an idle and purposeless life on the dole. That's equal to the entire population of a city the size of York.

'Is it any wonder youngsters feel disillusioned and betrayed? Is it any wonder they turn to anarchistic heroes like Johnny Rotten, the punk rock singer slashed in the face with a razor the other day? Punk rock is tailor-made for youngsters who think they only have a punk future.

'Some gain places on government work-experience schemes where they are paid to watch others working. It's better than nothing but demoralising just the same. Others plan to stay at school to better their qualifications and job prospects but hard-up parents cannot keep them and they drift on to the dole to help meet inflated family grocery bills.

'Those who work hard and pass their exams, those who train to be teachers are just as likely to be denied work as those who do not. And the plight of the young Britons is beginning to reap the bitter harvest of inflation. A brave new generation of talent and purpose is turning sour before our very eyes.'

TELEVISION AND BLONDIE
Hammersmith Odeon

Aah, the Watusi. Fickle freckle girls used to do it in those implausible discos found in carefree college campus movies and on the sets of long-running US TV series like 'Peyton Place'. Sandra Dee used to Watusi. Debbie Harry does now. So she wears hot-pants and black tights and sings in a band but she still bears all the hallmarks of a thoroughbred, mid-Sixties all-American blonde. Dagwood would be proud.

They're a pop-at-the-hop band and only in that context have they become acceptable. At Hammersmith Odeon a week of taut UK touring has so obviously peeled off the gloss. When I saw them in Glasgow on their opening night Blondie were embarrassing and clumsy – too much too soon. But six days, six rays of hope. Fey at first, but now almost assured of a long run. Only 'almost', though. The world may not be ready for the Watusi wake just yet.

Ice-skaters at the gates of dawn, Television need the Verlaine rink of confidence. They get more than their fair share of barracking by the Hammersmith backroom boys throughout their set, which, with its plethora of painful pauses, is particularly susceptible to the turkeys.

Television don't actually *do* anything on stage but play. There's an effective frozen light show, sure, but for the most part the band are immobile allowing the music to do the work. Verlaine and Richard Lloyd together weave a complex pattern of chords on the fine cloth provided by Fred Smith and Billy Ficca.

Tortuously efficient, dead eyes in midnight alleyways, Television are an important band and at Hammersmith they show why.

A malady in these highly charged Brands Hatch days.

Gig follows lig follows gig follows lig. I'm a six-year-old kid again, spinning round and round the post at school and adoring the intoxication of being out of control and realizing early on that there was more to life than just breath and heartbeats and Santa Claus. Like someone crept inside you, stole your soul, crept out and waved it around in the air for the whole world to see.

But, shit, I like Brighton...

THE STRANGLERS
Top Rank, Brighton

We shall fight them on the peaches...

Five days after this gig Jean-Jacques Burnel will leap to the rescue of a fan being beaten up in a back-street by celibate Canterbury students screaming for the death of punk.

Queen fans.

And at nearly every show girls and boys are plucked from the front with the breath screwed out of them. The Stranglers have broken all the rules – and rule breaking is what it's all about. Just ask the kids who rate the band as the best in the country – there's plenty of them about.

Right, so what do we get? A Top Rank stained carpet skirting a Pledge polished floor, chocolate bars with beer taps, Bernie the Bolt bouncers and Marks & Sparks fashion parades. Don't knock it. They've always served a purpose, probably more so in the boot-through-the-glass-door ballroom days of the late Sixties when Desmond Dekker compared West Indian poets to those of the early

Israelites. Now it's the turn of the Stranglers to compare the plight of many British kids to, well, other British kids.

Their music is immaculate, luxurious, arrangements severe enough to hurt/court fevered brows.

Mr Lascivious Legs Hugh Cornwell wraps his broken-bottle larynx around 'Sometimes', 'Straightaway', 'I Feel Like a Wog', 'about victimisation in this country', 'Dagenham Dave', 'about a friend of ours who committed suicide in London', 'Peasant In The Big Shitty', 'Family Favourites', 'for all the school children everywhere', 'Peaches', 'No More Heroes', 'there ain't no more heroes, and you should be your own one anyway', 'Hanging Around', 'London Lady' with Jean-Jacques' controlled rabid voice, and, finally, 'Down In The Sewer'. Encore 'Something Better Change', 'Go Buddy Go' with Jimmy Page Cornwell antics. Last encore, 'Ugly'.

And then someone nicks the DJ's records.

The Sex Pistols' 'God Save The Queen' has sold 150,000 copies even though it's now been banned from all television and radio. The BBC has put a blanket ban on the single – the decision was taken personally by the head of programming Charles McLelland, 46, who considers it to be in gross bad taste.

'We don't feel the single is suitable to be played on Radio 1 or 2,' says a BBC spokesman. 'It's unfortunate because we would really like to play everything that's popular with the record-buying public, but despite its popularity we can't reconsider our decision.

'Many more people listen to the radio than buy records and many of them are quite likely to be offended by this single. Ten million people listen to Radios 1 and 2 – from schoolchildren up to middle-aged housewives – and we feel they listen primarily to be entertained. There are specialist programmes like John Peel of course but they're a different matter. We don't set public standards, we reflect them. However, in this case the single has even been banned on John Peel's show.'

In the words of the spokesman the ban is across the board.

Following the BBC's lead the Independent Broadcasting Authority announce that they have advised all independent stations not to play the single. Says a spokesman, 'The IBA has to comply with an Act of Parliament, which applies to all independent broadcasting. It states that it shall be the duty of the authority to see that as far as possible nothing should be included in a programme which offends against good taste or decency.

'This is the section which we feel applies to the Sex Pistols single. Although the wording of the statement is advice, it is effectively a total ban. When we ask the stations not to play something we expect them to comply. As far as we know, no station has gone against our advice. It would be purely conjectural to comment on what would happen if one of the stations went ahead and played the single. We have asked them not to include it in normal programming, but it can be played in exceptional editorial circumstances where it's used as a point of discussion.

'The single became number one on the Capital Radio hitline in which listeners vote for their current favourite records. It was not played during the hitline show but was included in the Open Line discussion show.'

Colin MacDonald, spokesman for Glasgow's Radio Clyde, says, 'Personally, I think the Sex Pistols have brought the whole of the music business into disrepute. Anyway, the single never was a turntable hit. It became a hit because of all the exposure it's had in the media. It will be interesting to see what happens if it gets to number one. I suppose we can hardly have a three-minute silence on the show.'

Cathal McCabe, deputy programme controller on Belfast Downtown Radio, says, 'In my view punk rock is media-inspired rather than musically inspired. I am well aware that anything connected with sex, excrement or destruction makes good copy for a certain type of magazine or newspaper.'

Al Clark, from Virgin, says, 'It's curious that at a time when Britain is flaunting its democracy the most popular record in the country should be banned simply because it doesn't fit in with the usual jubilee sentiments.'

And the Pistols, in an interview with 'Record Mirror' this week, say, 'It's the public that counts in the end. I know the record companies have a lot to do with what goes into the charts but this time the public's done it. We don't take any of this seriously. You can slag us off, it just doesn't matter any more.'

I meet the boys again, under the headline 'Enemies of the World'. Can't miss it, a block away from a *Rock Follies* feature and just around the corner from a Kermit the Frog interview.

THE SEX PISTOLS
West End park

Pssst. Wanna know a secret?

Wanna know a saucerful of secrets?

Right.

Before the coffer of cognisance is opened though there are one or two things you've got to envisage.

Like the Sex Pistols. Don't fall into the trap of simply imagining the various connotations of the name. That's the English way. Just think of a band that happens to make stunning pop rockers.

Got that? Good.

Now think of the BBC and the music business. I know that may be difficult for you as it ain't a pretty thought. If it's too hard, just think of arsehole breeding-grounds. Okay?

Just one more. The British public. Think of that as being manufactured by the last two institutions.

Now shut your eyes playschool style – y'know, jelly tight. Mix all dem thoughts up good and thick. All right? Open them and you're in a playground somewhere in the West End. Empty. Except for Fun, Fun, Fun – Johnny Rotten, Steve Jones, Paul Cook. But that don't last long.

'Get out!' screams a fat lady attendant, with roundabout hips and monkey-bar legs. They sneer but, like naughty schoolboys, wander out to a nearby bench used as a club by the local pigeons.

'Rats with wings,' says Johnny, and opens a bottle of Pils.

A pigeon bowls over and kicks him in the leg. 'Any more wemarks like that me ol' cockspawwa an I'll 'ave to wing up the boys down at Trafalgar Square. And you wouldn't like that, would ya, Johnny boy?'

I guess this is just as good a point as any to open the rusty-hinged coffer.

'We enjoy life,' says Johnny, rubbing his bruised leg. 'It's a laugh and music's a relief, to get away from the pressures. Now, you get a band like The Clash. Very military in their attitudes. Even wear the same clothes. They're too depressing. I don't care about them at all.'

'Joe Strummer used to sing in the 101'ers,' says Steve. 'They were a country-and-western band. Now he sings about being on the dole.'

'We've been on the dole,' says Johnny. 'Big deal. We haven't written one single song about how depressing it is to be on the dole. Getting money for nothing ain't that depressing. We only say there's nothing to do in this country. Like we can't get a drink now 'cos it's five past three.'

'Everywhere closes at two in the morning,' says Paul.

'Promotion of opinion shouldn't cause aggravation,' says Johnny. 'It's what you respect. Essentially it's what you believe in that counts. People should be able to work things out for themselves. I despise those that are too lazy and complacent to do that. That's ignorance.'

'We never let things carry on without saying something. We're totally honest with each other.' That was Steve.

Fact: the Pistols have been spat upon and shat upon by just about every slimy sliver of negative thinking you could possibly conceive.

They did you no wrong.

Paul: 'We ain't interested in politics.'

John: 'And we most definitely ain't fascist. If you just listen to the first verse of the single you'll realise that fact immediately. Calling us fascists is just a cheap excuse to get rid of us. We have a lot of enemies. Sure, the National Front would love to be a part of us. But I'm not that stupid. I don't like what they're doing. They're ridiculous. They're élitist. People are voting for them simply because they're fed up with the other parties. They want something to do and I doubt if anyone seriously wants them in. If you could see what they'd do when they get in well, it wouldn't be very pleasant. You should be allowed to live where you like when you like. They're creating civil war. Still, the Socialists are probably even worse.'

Fact: The Pistols have made the two best rock'n'roll singles ever released in this country – 'Anarchy In The UK' and 'God Save The Queen'. Both have been banned by the BBC.

Paul: 'The music business is filth. It just wants to see the colour of your money. None of the people in it have an opinion. They change when someone else says so. Soon as anything starts selling, record companies turn round and say, 'Right, we'd better get ourselves a punk band.' Virgin wanted us ages ago. When 'Anarchy' was banned they wanted us to buy out all the copies.'

Sidetrack: Glen Matlock. Rumour has it he was called in to help remix 'The Queen'.

John: 'That's another load of crap. We get this every day of the week. It's just rubbish. He doesn't even play on 'God Save The Queen'. He's only saying that to promote his new band – and he needs it badly, knowing what that band's gonna be like. We kicked him out. He was unbearable. Him and his snotty middle-class ideals.'

Steve: 'He had some ideas for songs but they just didn't come out right. He hates all the things we've ever done. D'you know what? His mum rang me up while he was in the band and accused us of corrupting him. His mum used to tell him how to do things. Once your family start interfering like that you have to split.'

In Malcolm McLaren's office Matlock's face is blacked out of every old photo of the band on the wall.

Sid Vicious is due to appear in court this morning on an offensive-weapon charge, relating to last September at the 100 Club punk débácle.

John: 'Sid's always been around, right from the early gigs. He always came along.'

Paul: 'Sid doesn't take it seriously. He's like us.'

Fact: the Pistols have been subjected to all manner of lies slobbering off the presses of newspapers around the world.

John: 'We don't take any of this press shit. You could slag us off – it just doesn't matter any more. We'll never consent to do what anyone wants us to do. It's always been what *we* want. And if nobody likes that idea they can all get fucked. But nobody has really lost. The single is at number 11. It's a piece of history.'

Paul: 'It's good to know that people are out there buying your records and supporting you. What we started was right and it made the BBC and the Top Thirty redundant. Our record has only been played five times on Radio 1. So it shows you what kind of force that has in this country.'

John: 'EMI stopped 'Anarchy' because they were frightened of it. They were worried that it was gonna make the charts. It was sabotage.'

Paul: 'But what do they care?' They've always got Cliff Richard.'

Steve: 'It's the public that counts in the end. I know the record companies have a lot to do with what goes in the charts – but this time it's the public that's done it. Sir John Reid, head of EMI, goes to dinner with the Queen. He didn't want to be associated with us when he sat down with her – so he got rid of us.'

Paul: 'People on the shop floor supported us.'

John: 'Then CBS intimated an interest. But suddenly they shied off. Then A&M came along and gave us a load of bollocks about the single. I don't know what happened with A&M. So you have a fight. But what's a fight got to do with selling records? Sure, Sid was involved in a bundle with Bob Harris and his mate. But if a fight's got to do with records, how come we had to take the brunt of the blame and not the DJ?'

Steve: 'A lot of other DJ's gave A&M an ultimatum. They told them if they didn't get rid of us they'd never play any more of the company's records. And with all these Peter Frampton and Rick

Wakeman get-rid-of-them-or-else rumours, I dunno. I reckon the whole thing was a bit of publicity for A&M.'

Paul: 'Then there was that earlier business at the airport on our way to Amsterdam. What was it we were supposed to have done? Spit and vomit over passengers? That whole set-up was just the final excuse to get rid of us. Some people flew over simply to trump up the charges.'

John: 'And there was never any witnesses to that. Lots of nameless bystanders but nothing concrete. That whole thing was planned. They just wanted us out of the country.'

Then there's that little question of 'Today' with Bill okay-we've-got-a-minute-say-what-you-want Grundy.

John: 'If you see it a second time it's so obvious how he really provoked us. It was a would-you-let-your-daughter-marry-this set-up. They shoved us into a box and said, 'You sit here until we drag you out.''

Paul: 'There was no bar.'

Steve: 'We never spoke to him once before we appeared.'

John: 'And then there was that lorry driver who smashed his telly in as a result of the show. Now what a fine example of British manhood he was.'

Steve: 'His kids probably laughed at him more than the programme.'

John: 'People are gullible to the media. That's the British way. We've all been brought up to be like that.'

Steve: 'There's no way we'll ever regret what we've done.'

John: 'You should never regret anything. That's a regressive attitude. People like Cliff Richard are the only ones who can regret their past. Besides, it's worked out better saying we don't give a fuck. We don't give a damn whether anyone chucks us off a record label or not.'

Steve: 'We don't ever see people from Virgin. They're not as big as, say, A&M, so they ain't got any responsibility to live up to. If Queen got banned throughout the country they've still got their own record outlets. Why should we sign to a small label? We want the best for our records and as many people as possible should be allowed to listen to them.'

Trouble at mill. Printers are refusing to have anything to do with their current advertising campaign, depicting the smiling face of Elizabeth R.

John: 'It gives the printers something to live for, whether they like the ad or not. And it made 'Sounds' look ridiculous leaving out part of it. They should either have used it all or none of it.'

Paul: 'People will use anything as a cheap excuse for a strike. Same with factories. They'll do it when they fancy a few days off. Any excuse will do. I know, I used to work in one.'

John: 'What about the music papers? There's too much of a pseudo-intellectual approach. The music press should be fun. It's just got too serious. The papers make music seem decrepit. What they don't seem to understand is music should have as many attitudes as possible. It should also have different forms. Take 'Sounds'. It's becoming all punk. It's drivel. 'NME' writes the same kind of tripe, but it's not as offensive because they take the piss. But they're still half serious about their piss-taking.'

Paul: 'Melody Maker' is by far the most boring. In fact, I don't know why we ever did that interview with them. It just takes itself too seriously.'

John: "Record Mirror',' Gulp! 'Well, it's a different kind of paper.'

Steve: 'You don't want to change your policy. It's great.'

It's just like I always suspected. The Pistols are a nice *discerning* bunch of geezers.

John: 'And the fanzines are just as bad. I haven't read a good one yet. The funniest ones are those that are unintentionally funny.'

Paul: 'Sniffin' Glue is laughable. To them everything new-wave is great. They just don't slag it.'

John: 'I mean, they don't say the truth – like the Stranglers are nothing more than bandwagoneers.'

Paul: 'Yeah, they're :worse than Chris Spedding. They're what the over-thirties feel safe about getting into. They say how decadent and debauched they are. Never in a million years. They couldn't strangle anything except their own vocals. See, we know we're not gonna be sucked into the music whirlpool. But I suppose people think we have been already. I don't worry about things like that. I just don't believe anything anyone tells me any more.'

John: 'It's an accepted fact that we're gonna end up like Rod Stewart. The only people who managed to get over that hurdle in the past are Marc Bolan and Gary Glitter, who enjoyed the whole star trip because they were always taking the piss out of it. They turned it into a joke. I respect that. They made some highly enjoyable records – if not great. It's a case of not listening to a word your record company tells you. From now on they work for us, not the other way round. Once the other new bands sign for record labels it's their downfall.'

'God Save The Queen'. Publicity stunt?

John: 'The single was written six months ago. We played it on the 'Anarchy' tour. It's just a coincidence that it happens to be Jubilee year. If we were still on EMI it would have been released ages ago. It was gonna be released on A&M and they wouldn't even give us a copy of the disc.

'Half of the CBS distributors had a copy of it. Even one of The Clash had a copy of it. But we didn't. The Jubilee is ridiculous. It's a bandwagon. Everyone is so patriotic, but come Christmas, she'll be slagged off for her speech by those same people.'

Steve: 'If a bomb dropped tomorrow you'd never see her again. She'd be well out of it. She's a million miles away from me – and she means nothing.'

Paul: 'The Jubilee's just a cheap excuse for a piss-up. What slayed me the other day was the geezer who organised the whole thing. He died.'

John: 'In my area they've taken money out of the National Health to make the celebrations go with more of a swing, That's absolutely appalling. What's more important? Health or a load of old cronies getting drunk? Why is it that people are proud to be British only in jubilee year?'

Paul: 'Because Liverpool won the European Cup. That's why.'

John: 'Everything's done in the name of the Queen. You must make up your own minds. When things start becoming controlled and contrived, that's wrong.'

Steve: 'And there's nothing wrong with telling someone what you think of them.'

Paul: 'People in this country are too scared to say what they think of other people.'

John: 'British people don't question anything. If you feel something, say it. But no, they're content going out and buying their tins of beans. Closing their minds. Ninety per cent of the population are slowly being destroyed.'

Steve: 'Do you know there are vast stores of food kept below Buckingham Palace that are thrown away every year just in case there's a war? If we die the Queen should die with us. I wouldn't miss her. She just helps to sell us overseas.'

John: 'It's all a classic form of hypocrisy. Her speeches are written by someone else. There's no feeling or expression in her voice. She's a plastic person.'

Rumour One: Dave Vanian of The Damned was beaten up by Johnny Rotten at The Heartbreakers gig recently...

John: 'Crap. He had a go at my brother because he happens to have long hair. I had nothing to do with it.'

Rumour Two: the Pistols get their concerts banned on purpose for more publicity.

John: 'What possible reason could we have for doing that? Do you think we need the publicity? That's just typically British. The truth is always scary for them. Every council in the country has banned us.'

Steve: 'If you got four boot boys in a pub smashing it up, nothing more is said about it. But everybody's up in arms if it happens to be us. We don't set out to be obnoxious.'

John: 'What people don't seem to realise is that the Pistols are giving them a form of entertainment. We are, above all things, a dance band.'

They're all dance bands and they make me want to shout.

And talking of dance bands...

THE JAM
Barbarellas, Birmingham

1, 2, 3, 4…The Jam begin their first headlining nationwide tour.

Now, there are some sumptuous scribes around who want to coax you into believing that the band are just not ready for it. Misconception time. If your album's a hit, you're ready to headline. Embryonic stage, my arse. The Jam cut it.

Those guileless souls who would have you think otherwise are conditioned by years of top-heavy technology manifested into worthless/priceless on-stage equipment used by the likes of Zep and ELP. Sure, that may be okay for a while but it ends up leaving a sour taste in your mouth, not to mention shitty hearing.

Anyway, tonight The Jam regally declare the tour open at Barbarellas. Barbarellas I like – it's a disco in every sense of the word haunted by pre-'Ballroom Blitz' Sweet tunes and Jonathan King's illegitimate love songs. Natch, it's garish, but it's not difficult to get a drink.

It's jubilee night and the band come on stage wearing black suits and singing 'Art School' and then try to get the most immobile crowd to scratch a toe for the next five numbers – 'Change My Address', 'Modern World', a new song with more than a passing interest in 'Pictures Of Lily', 'Slow Down' and 'Carnaby Street'. No dice.

Then 'In The City' and the Brum amoebae multiply. The song is already a classic and announces the birth of another unique sound garnered from a million influences and tied up with string.

You can tell the crowd has livened up – 'This is a song called 'London Girls',' says Paul, in his flat, diffident way.

'Get 'em off!' screams a girl at the back.

Rock'n'roll rejoices with 'Sound of the Streets', 'Time For Truth', 'In The Midnight Hour' and 'Away From The Numbers' – still my personal album pop-picker. The last song particularly reveals the harmonic incisiveness between Paul and bassist Bruce Foxton.

The band are in top form but after the two encores – a reprise of 'In The City', 'Batman' and the Who's 'So Sad About Us' they troop off-stage completely knackered. There's a long road ahead but the Jam will make it. No sweat.

It's those who think they won't I feel sorry for.

LIVE AT THE ROXY, VARIOUS ARTISTS
Album review

Tension + creativity = slags.

A formula to bear in mind when considering the last six months. The Roxy phenomenon began on 14 December when the two-storey West End disco opened its doors to banned music. Generation X played that night to a very empty house. Seven days later The Heartbreakers met with better success, and between 1 January and 23 April, shiny new bands featured every night.

This album was recorded over four nights on a 24-track mobile, which means good reproduction. Microphones were hidden in every part of the club – yeah, even the toilets – and, as the press handout that accompanies the album points out, the net result of all this care was that music was played and people behaved as they would any night of the week.

So, what have we got? Eight bands, 12 songs, authentic chat. Unfortunately much of that authentic chat is inaudible. Snippets. It appears that most of these new-wave bands are full of nice, well-spoken chaps – 'Do you come here often? It's really nice, it's a really nice atmosphere'; 'I wanna riot'; 'Are you on the guest list?'

Bands – Slaughter and the Dogs, the Unwanted, Wire, the Adverts, Johnny Moped, Eater, X Ray Spex, Buzzcocks.

The Buzzcocks impress: two numbers, 'Breakdown' and 'Love Battery', indicate a future. Slaughter and the Dogs just make it, the

Adverts border, Eater have seen better days – and when you're 16 that's really saying something. The Unwanted are awful, but it was their début gig, and the rest are indifferent.

But this isn't an album to review on a purely musical basis. It's about reviewing a feel, and that brings me back to my original formula. See, tense situations have a habit of producing creative people – history bears that out – and that in turn throws up a lot of no-good arseholes too shallow to be original themselves but shamming dreams by catching the regular bandwagon out of platform two.

The contemporary word for just such an animal is 'poseur' and the Roxy eventually excluded everyone but their kind. This album is full of empty statements – 'I Wanna Riot' after a few lagers at 75p a pint? – and breathless indecision, 'You ain't hip if you pose at the Roxy anymore,' says the guy from Eater and adds, though it's taken out of context, 'Everybody knows that you're just a bunch of fakes.'

The new-wave milieu is essentially a rough, inharmonious thing and this album is an attempt to smooth the edges and make it a digestible, marketable product. Mikes in the toilets? But give it a whirl. Personal choice is what it's about after all.

Over the weekend the anti-punk rock/anti-Sex Pistols movement takes a nasty and disturbing turn. On Saturday night Johnny Rotten is ambushed by six or eight attackers armed with knives outside a London pub, the Pegasus in Highbury. With Rotten are recording studio engineer Bill Price and record producer Chris Thomas. Both receive minor injuries as they try to fend off the attack. Rotten is taken to hospital where he had two stitches in his arm. The injuries would have been more severe if he'd not been wearing a heavy coat.

On Sunday night Pistols drummer Paul Cook is attacked by six people outside Shepherds Bush underground station. He's hit on the back of the head with an iron bar. The injury requires 15 stitches and Cook is allowed home after treatment. 'Britain is not the place to be if you want to speak your mind,' says Virgin spokesman Al Clark. 'It looks as if punk rockers are in for a hard time.'

Meanwhile, the Sex Pistols are planning to make a film written by Johnny Speight and produced by Russ Meyer. 'There are certain plans in that direction but I'm not going to tell you any more at this stage,' says a Virgin spokesman. Johnny Rotten is quoted in a national newspaper describing Johnny Speight's house as 'like some museum in Eastbourne'.

The Pistols' forthcoming album has neither a release date nor a title as yet. A new single is likely to be put out first and it will not be taken from the album as the band do not believe in issuing singles as trailers for albums.

'The album is not going to be called 'Another Load of Old Bollocks From The Sex Pistols',' Clark confirms. 'It's more likely to be called 'Olivia Newton John's Greatest Hits'. Clark also dismisses reports in the 'Sun' that the Pistols are to appear at Stonehenge to coincide with the Druid's Festival.

'The likelihood of the Pistols appearing at Stonehenge is comparable to that of Vince Hill doing a season at CBGB's,' says Clark, everybody's favourite press officer.

Going on the road with a band always involves lots of drugs and alcohol, seven a.m. calls and hangover drives to airports. I love walking into hotel rooms; some of them are huge with two double beds and a bar, others you can't swing a fucking hamster. But for a night or two they're mine. Well, mine and the swinging hamster's. Hotel rooms make me feel incredibly randy and I always, but always, fantasise about the maid and the sneaky blow-job in the middle of the night.

Dinner, usually in the hotel, beckons. Then the gig, the drink in the backstage bar, a club, the hotel. And none of this costs me a brass farthing. This is legitimate blagging and it's wonderful.

I also get expenses.

Nevertheless, I continue to live at home with my mum and dad – my bedroom, as fleeting as the hotel rooms, is still shot through with love and the odd egg and bacon sandwich with brown sauce and a piping hot cup of tea served to me in bed by my mum at weekends. I live in the middle of London. I work in the middle of London. I'm an only child. It makes sense.

My dad has two talents. He can talk to anyone for hours on end and he can play the piano like an angel. He once played in a few pubs on the manor and was often invited to parties where I'd watch him churn out tune after tune from an upright in the corner till the blood from the broken blisters on his fingers splattered across the ivories. He always started with the same song, 'She's Funny That Way':

He refuses to accept that he has a drop of the Irish in him despite his red hair, freckles, a Catholic upbringing and that he answers to the name of Pat. He's the consummate old school misanthropist who yearns for the Brylcreem days when coppers cuffed ears and people poured into Collins' Music Hall in Islington Green on a Saturday night. He saw the street he was born in suddenly turn into Nicosia overnight and it scared the shit out of him. He hates to see his London sink into a 'sweet and sour kebab vindaloo' and wonders if Enoch Powell had the right idea.

Betting shops are his passion; it goes with the music. When the side-street bookies in nearby Chapel Market disappeared after off-course gambling became legit, he revelled in the sheltered comfort, live commentary and pinned-up race cards.

He got the nickname 'Sherpa' after Tenzing because he always stood on top of the biggest pile of torn betting slips in the shop. He frittered away a fortune on Yankees and each-way accumulators and was always one horse away from retirement.

He did win big once. In 1963 he collected nearly three grand from an accumulator bet at William Hill in the Angel. He came home and threw all of it up in the air during 'Blue Peter'. After that I associated Valerie Singleton with £20 notes.

He blew the lot in the bookies. We could've bought a house in Islington outright and my mum, Betty, never forgave him.

She didn't care for pubs, cinemas or parties, preferring instead the company of a thick, fruity historical romance. She left school at 11 and became an evacuee in 1940, shipped down to a dark, dingy house in Cambridge surrounded by fallen apples and dead leaves. She lasted just six weeks before my Nan took her back to the Westway to dodge the bombs.

The feeling of isolation she experienced after being torn from her home awakened the poet in her soul. She often talks of that autumn and the pain of separation – in between the books. She ploughs through four 400-page plus novels a month, sometimes more. She can answer correctly at least ten questions on each edition of 'University Challenge'.

Not long after she returned to London to face the Blitz my mum was attacked from behind by a maniac as she walked home alone along the Westway. He hit her over the head with an iron bar and fractured her skull. During the eight weeks she spent in hospital she contracted rheumatic fever and had to stay for a year. She knows all about the pain of separation. It's the one thing she has in common with my dad. When he was 17 he was knocked into oblivion by a motorbike while hop-picking in Kent and spent nine months in hospital. They share their separations. It keeps them together.

'Nobody will ever love you like your mother,' my dad tells me, in a pub off Essex Road. His ginger hair – he prefers 'auburn' – has been replaced with gleaming grey flecked with Vitalis. He drinks only brandy and water. I've never seen him with a beer in his hand.

'I know she moans all the time,' he says, his freckled face flushed with Courvoisier, 'but she's a class act, make no mistake.'

If it wasn't for the washable vinyl wallpaper we had in the living room, the walls would have been peppered with gravy stains from the dinners she threw at him on Sundays when he was late back from the pub. He started taking me with him when I was 15 because he knew my mum wouldn't be so angry if I was beside him when he was late. I was his perpetual Sunday alibi. By taking me he freed himself from one of his many guilts.

For all his charm and wisecracking my dad carries a lot of guilt. He's a gregarious man who thrives in company, but he's married to a semi-recluse and that makes him feel guilty. He can't shake off the aura of spivishness that snaps at his heels and that makes him feel guilty. He works all night cooking dinners for taxi-drivers in a cab shelter at the Temple and sleeps all day and that makes him feel guilty. He smokes 30 Peter Stuyvesant a day and that makes him feel guilty. He always manages to dodge the plates hurled at him by his irate wife and even *that* makes him feel guilty.

But every week the guilt evaporates after the second brandy and the third song.

Each Sunday the pubs are packed out with stallholders and spivs, all braces and trilbies and silk top handkerchiefs and cheap King Edwards acquired from some Yank army base up the line and shit-hot schmutter and short, sharp sentences laced with gold; their wives swimming in shoals through rivers of Max Factor' and port and lemon, only surfacing, like plump, shimmering salmon, to join in with the chorus of 'It Had To Be You' or 'Strangers In The Night'.

In 1977 there are a couple of sharpshooters in two local pubs – Jacky Appleton and Joey Burns. Dad and I go to see them on alternate Sundays.

Each pianist has a trademark intro. Joey begins, 'Good afternoon, gents and gentesses,' and then sings, in classic Cockney music-hall style:

Why should I be poor
When me mother's on the game?
Why should I be poor
When me sister is the same?
Me dad's a bit of a tea leaf,
Me aunt's a five to four,

And I'm a bit of a ponce meself
So why should I be poor

The whole pub stamps and cheers. And then he plays the piano like Errol Garner and sniffs up the 'Honeysuckle Rose' and the world feels good.

Jacky Appleton could never play the piano like Joey Burns – but he entertains like Sinatra.

'Welcome to the famous Sunday session at the Lord Wolsley ladies and gentlemen. Remember, you're here to hear, so fucking listen.' And then he launches into 'You're Nobody 'Til Somebody Loves You', 'Ain't Misbehavin', 'Bye Bye Blackbird', 'You Made Me Love You'. He breaks up the standards with a few 'newer numbers', like 'Be My Baby', which always gets one of the cocky barmaids dancing, and 'For Once In My Life'. Then there's 'Up A Lazy Widow' (not 'River') in the style of Bobby Darin.

The same woman sings 'Be My Baby' every week. She's the wife of a costermonger and they have a villa in Spain. She looks like Alma Cogan and sings like Barbra Streisand and everyone joins in when she shifts into first.

It was Phil Spector's masterpiece and it's never let me go.
I keep falling in and out of love with the same woman and it's driving me to distraction. I can't get Dina out of my head.

JOHNNY THUNDERS HEARTBREAKERS
(A.K.A. THE JUNKIES)

St Albans and Birmingham

Whaddya say to four cool-bar guys to whom the stars and stripes mean only what they've seen and suffered in steaming New York back-streets?

Hey, Johnny, what's the main thing you miss about your hometown?

'Hahahahahahaha!' He huddles in the front seat of the band's van before erupting in a paroxysm of piss-taking.

Ever felt stupid?

'That's neat,' he says. 'Everything man, everything.'

And then you get to thinking: they've just played to a half-empty hall in St Albans, it's dirty-raining, it's 2.30 in the morning and the band's still sober, it's cold, they're on their way back to London downers – and I ask that question.

'I wanna relate to you' but that's an English song and England is a million miles from New York.

The Heartbreakers are a bit special. An insular band in a heavy London climate music-wise, yet holding their own despite being intensely alone. And they're magic.

Tonight they're doing a gig at the St Albans Civic Hall. Hardly Manhattan.

The guys are congregated round a heavily stained table in a clapped-out pub. The show is an hour away. They begin to form in-band alliances to protect egos. Tonight it's Johnny Thunders and drummer Jerry Nolan versus Walter Lure and bassist Billy Rath.

Johnny: 'And I think we should change our name to the Junkies.'
Jerry: 'Yep, he's right'.
Me: 'But you won't get any airplay at all with a name like that.'
Johnny: 'Who needs it? The name will provoke a reaction. 'The Heartbreakers' has too many other connotations.'

Walter and Billy remain quiet. Antagonism in the air. Johnny and Jerry decide to split for a meal on their own. The Junkies interlude is over for another day.

'Chinese Rocks' should have been massive. Blame sound quality. It's one of the muddiest records you'll ever hear. A mess-up in the tape-vinyl transition. The song possesses all the hallmarks of a classic rock'n'roll record and it's a sad loss.

The band aren't what you could describe as happy. A lot of in-fighting and breakneck friction has led to a certain amount of dismay. They're homesick, and who can blame them? It's not often a band gets held up by a gunman in a Leeds hotel room and threatened by a maniacal bomb merchant.

As we arrive at the Civic a young guy is being beaten mercilessly by some heavies because he's a little drunk, y'know, and falling into a few people. Scenes like this are common up and down the country at punk gigs because the bouncers have shaken free of the menacing, tooled-up-spivs-in-mohair-suits era and punks are easy pickings.

A weak turnout. The band know it and there's not as much inspiration as there ought to be.

An audience split. The curious and the gingernuts. The latter are kids with bright red hair who beat the shit out of each other because the right kind of music's being played on-stage and what else is there to do in St Albans?

It's a throwaway night. The band aren't happy with their performance and Jerry refuses to talk to anyone. He's flaked out on a piano in the corner probably dreaming of his 24-hour city.

A pensive journey back to London. Disarmed and unattached and ungrateful. It's flaming June and it's raining.

Cut. A little thing entitled 'A Night To Remember'. It's not often in this game you get to see a band on a certain night who come on so strong they make your heart melt. A show you want to freeze and take home with you to defrost every time you're feeling hung up about soul raids and insecurity.

Well, boy, this one has everything.

First off, a meal in New Street where the toilets close early and the trains run on time. Disillusionment reigns. Nobody says much over their food but, let's face it, the food's not much to talk about. Sloppy omelettes and production-line sauces.

And, no, you've gotta be kidding – it's *still* raining? Birmingham hot just about makes it. Birmingham wet is nowhere at all.

Barbarellas can be an indeterminate gig. Limbo Land haunted

by transfixed stares and recalcitrant moods. But tonight that's all gonna be squashed by rock'n'roll, Heartbreaker-style.

The show very nearly doesn't materialise. The band sweat it out in the spacious dressing room declaring their intention to call it a day, pack their bags and head west. Seems it's a combination of two things – finances and disappointment at the turn-out in what is, after all, the second biggest city in the country.

Agonising moments. A handful of brides waiting at the disco altar while the grooms pace the backstage floor wondering whether to take the plunge.

They dive. In the best possible way. With a triple somersault and a double twist.

'Hi,' says Johnny. 'We're The Heartbreakers from NooYawk Ciddy and this is 'Chinese Rocks'.'

Jerry Nolan once said: 'Ain't nobody gonna hear the 'Chinese Rocks' single until we got it perfect.'

What went wrong? Hearing it live for the first time since I played the single only confirms the tragedy. The snake-pit degradation of the lyrics is rooted out by the cannibalistic double guitar of Lure and Thunders.

Thunders caricatures the demon drugged-up rockie between the numbers, lounging on each word until it dries up, ruffling the hair on the back of his head with both hands like he's all mixed up, y'know. Rock rookie personified.

Every song is a potential hit. Every song denotes a simple feeling.

'Get Off The Phone', 'All By Myself' – clear favourite for the next single – 'Can't Keep My Eyes On You', 'I Love You', 'Born Too Loose', not 'To Lose', the erroneous title on the record.

Hocus-pocus time. A made-in-New-York net designed to capture time has been thrown over the crowd. They struggle like fish in the throes of death and clamour for more.

First encore. 'You asked for it,' warns Johnny. 'If ya wanna pass the hat around all donations will be accepted.' And crack into 'Do You Love Me?'.

Everything is a blur. Rath cruises with his eyes creating a reliable foundation for the rest to gut-craze. Lure performs like there's no next second, let alone tomorrow.

Hey, Baal, you just can't let this end!

Second encore. 'Take A Chance With Me' and a stroke of genius, a 'Chinese Rocks' reprisal.

It's so good it hurts.

Mr Deejay they've gone, whatcha gonna do about it? Clash and 'Police And Thieves'. That just pacifies the murderous crowd.

Right. I gotta go now because it's time to unfreeze that memory. You can have one of them too. It's simple. All you've got to do is bowl along and see The Heartbreakers when they're in town. You won't regret it.

JULY 1977

Top ten singles
beginning of July

1. So You Win Again – Hot Chocolate
2. Show You The Way To Go – The Jacksons
3. Fanfare For The Common Man – Emerson Lake & Palmer
4. Lucille – Kenny Rogers
5. Baby Don't Change Your Mind – Gladys Knight & The Pips
6. You're Moving Out Today – Carol Bayer-Sager
7. A Star Is Born (Evergreen) – Barbra Streisand
8. Telephone Line – ELO
9. Sam – Olivia Newton-John
10. Peaches/Go Buddy Go – the Stranglers

Top ten albums
beginning of July

1. A Star Is Born – Soundtrack
2. The Muppet Show
3. The Beatles At The Hollywood Bowl
4. The Johnny Mathis Collection
5. Arrival – Abba
6. Hotel California – the Eagles
7. A New World Record – ELO
8. Exodus – Bob Marley & The Wailers
9. Deceptive Bends – 10cc
10. Sheer Magic – Acker Bilk

MARK P
Oxford Street

Half-way through the most crucial year in music and the likes of
Acker Bilk and The Muppets still permeate the charts. So we're in
this boozer off Oxford Street, Mark P and me. The jukebox is playing
'A Star Is Born'.

It's 11.30 a.m. and definitely not the right time for Cointreau. Mark's
talking about his band Alternative TV, and it's when he starts mentioning
Frank Zappa and Can influences that my mind begins to wander.

I get to thinking about blind alleys, dust-covered promises, the
blank fruition of Desolation Row, right-infested minds stunned into
submission by mediocrity. In other words, this guy's depressing me.

Now, it's not his fault – he seems sincere enough. It's just that he
makes me realise time is running out for a number of things – ju-ju-
juvenesence, clarity, improvisation. He obviously doesn't mean to,
but when he starts getting sentimental about events that happened
only a few months back, something's wrong somewhere.

Get a load of this, 'I used to really believe that the kids would
change something but they never will. They're naïve, they can't see
the truth. Outside London especially they're limited to reading the
gutter press and I don't think you can ever break that media system.
'International Times' tried to and failed. 'Time Out' tried to, and now
it's a conservative magazine. It's just no use having alternatives.'

See what I mean? But wait, there's more. 'Sniffin' Glue' will never
take over anything. The Clash can't go on for ever. I mean, what a
contradiction – CBS demanding a release of 'Remote Control' as a
single when that record is all about such manipulation. There's just
no unity any more. How can I possibly relate to kids in Bradford who
put safety-pins through their ears? And how can they possibly relate
to me with the Zappa and Can influences? And if that's the case
there's just no scene left. But I'm happy with that.

'I've lost the high I used to get back in September and October.

We meant something then. We knew who our audience was, people trusted us. But now I can't get enthusiastic about the scene.

'I like The Clash now in the same way I've liked any band over the last ten years. This is not the be-all and end-all. There will be other scenes. If my band don't relate to the punks – I'm sorry, I apologise, but I'm never gonna change. If you're expecting Mark P to destroy, to clamour for anarchy and trip up all the MPs then you're gonna be disappointed. I'm not into that at all.'

'Sniffin' Glue' fans might baulk at such sentiments from their 20-year-old guru. Maybe a newly formed association with Step Forward records, run by Miles Copeland and Nick Jones, the demon duo of Oxford Street, has had a calming influence on the Deptford gunslinger.

'It was a natural progression to being involved in actually making records.' Mark was directly responsible for signing the first and, as yet, only bands to Step Forward – the Cortinas, Chelsea and the Models. The Bristol-based Cortinas aren't bad but the other two are awful.

'I simply wanted to put out records I liked. I didn't want to keep on writing about bands. That got to be a bit of a high horse. People didn't think I had the right to say a band was good or bad. In fact, I've just written my last piece for 'Sniffin' Glue'. The 'Sniffin' Glue' office is next door to the Step Forward office. It has no electricity so a cable was fed out of the window along the ledge into our office.'

And now he's taken that 'natural progression' one more step forward by forming a band. 'I've had an idea for a band since last September. In fact, I actually had one – the New Beatles – a kind of anti-legend, but that never got past the rehearsal stage. So now I'm in Alternative TV. I can't play guitar so I play by a series of dots. I don't particularly want to learn how to play either. The concentration it would take to learn would spoil the on-stage experience, although I like things to be hard.

'I'm into Zappa and Can and jazz. I don't want to write songs for the people, I ain't a writer for the kids. But that doesn't mean I don't want people to be interested in us. I just want to get on stage and say something.

'The only way I can do anything now is through music. If ten kids say they really liked what the band played and it helped them change their attitudes, then I'll be happy.'

To date ATV have played four gigs – and they're already headlining. 'We did this really long slow number down the Marquee last week, 'Alternatives To NATO', which has me reading a speech from an anarchist magazine. It got a great reaction and I'm convinced if you wanna change anything you've got to do it through music and music alone. I ain't a good enough writer to do it through writing.'

His ideas of getting to the people are ambitious to say the least. 'I'm not interested in singles. I want to put out an album right away.

'It's no use coming out with all the anarchy bit and throwing it in their faces, they'll take no notice. Win them with music. I want to go straight into the big venues and not piss around with the pub and small club circuit. That's a complete waste of time. I wanna play the Empire Pool.

'I've never cared about getting a tight band. Alternative TV ain't tight and that's why it works. If I want to do an instrumental break when I feel like it, I will and it's up to the others to follow me.'

He but he knows what he wants. Can't make me mind up if he'll get it though.

Mark was a how-do-you-want-it-sir? merchant in a barber's for two years before cutting out to start 'Sniffin' Glue'.

'Problems with the job started mounting and I started hiding them. Two months after I left, they found drawers full of problems that I had stashed away.

'I haven't got old friends. I'm not one for a gathering of the clans. I was never involved in the gang thing. You play safe when you start relying on others. When most people leave school their brains ain't developed. They'll go to work in a factory and the most frightening thing is, a geezer will go there because his mate did. He's basing his whole career on something his mate did.

'So, then you get to thinking that the audience you're reaching is full of kids completely satisfied with their lot and that's why you can't preach anarchy to them. But I can give them music.

'We need a spokesman for the whole scene. Johnny Rotten was, but he's slagged everyone off so much he ain't any more. And there's no way I'm a spokesman. But we do need someone.'

Mark will help keep Alternative TV alive for the next 30 years. He has a website after his name.

RADIATORS FROM SPACE
Dublin

'Yeah, the Radiators From Space think your stuff is great and they'd like to invite you over to Dublin for Ireland's first punk festival where they're headlining.'

I'm flattered and agree immediately – I've never been to Dublin – but after I put the phone down to the band's manager a colleague puts me down by pointing out he probably asked everyone on 'NME', 'Melody Maker' and 'Sounds' in person before ringing me when they'd all declined.

'Don't forget, this is only 'Record Mirror'.' She's right. It is only 'Record Mirror', the clunk-click-every-trip music paper.

So I fly to Dublin, as fourth sub, to the saddest gig in the world.

'This is Irish history.'

The guy screams in the academic elegance of University College, Dublin, as the country's first new-wave festival begins...

Ten minutes into the first band, the Vipers, there's a scuffle in front of the stage. Nothing spectacular, just a couple of geezers with the taste of Saturday night in their mouths.

It's over in an instant. The band continue to play, the fans continue to sway. Then the news crawls out on all fours: somebody's been stabbed. People are told to cool it but no one's being over the top anyway. The next band, the Gamblers, trip on and that seems to be the end of the incident.

Shortly before the headline band Radiators From Space are due to appear, guitarist Pete Holidai is surrounded by four bouncers and bundled into the dressing room. Seems the stabbed guy is in a pretty bad way and somebody gets the wrong impression that Pete was involved in the fight.

Rough questioning ensues. They ain't letting anyone in to see what's happening. One girl tries to make a statement to a couple of journalists but another guy puts his hand over her mouth and hauls her back into the dressing room. The police arrive.

Pete's allowed to go on stage with the band, but the police are taking no chances and officers stand guard at all the exits. Nobody's getting out of this one.

The Radiators finish their set, the crowd clamours for an encore and the band oblige. The crowd wants another. The police don't, and an officer keeps beckoning them to come off-stage from the side. When they finish Pete is taken back downstairs into the dressing room. No one in the audience is allowed to go until they can provide some proof of identification and have undergone a search. The stabbed guy is now on the critical list.

It's three a.m. and all five bands who appeared are vegetating in the same dressing room, waiting to give written statements. Upstairs, kids are telling detectives what they saw or what they thought they saw. In the corner there's a bloodstained handkerchief on the table where the guy was carried after the incident

Four a.m. The guy is dead. He was an 18-year-old local schoolboy called Patrick Coultry from Cabra.

Fact is, people can be stabbed anywhere, anyhow, anytime.

Dublin is new to the current music set-up. The handful of bands in the city have experienced some hostility as a repercussion of this terrible event – an across-the-board ban looks on the cards and that's a tragedy.

A few points worth noting. The bands had nothing to do with the fight. That one-minute flashpoint was the only violence in an

otherwise peaceful evening. The show attracted well over 600 fans –
an unprecedented figure for an out-of-term college concert.

None of the audience looked in any way, shape or form like the kind
of punk most people envisage. They were a typically straight bunch
of Saturday-night Dublin kids out for a good time. The Stranglers
played two concerts to more than 6,000 people the following night
at the Roundhouse and there were no fights.

In the main, the press have reacted to this in a predictably
irresponsible fashion. The media alone has sown the seeds of hate
now firmly embedded in the minds of the ignorant. The following
morning one Dublin paper reported that the stabbing occurred while
the Radiators were playing – see what I mean?

And if you're still not convinced, read the 'Sunday People' for
distortion of the highest order: 'The Radiators From Space are the
ultimate in bad taste with insanity, sex, violence and blasphemy as
their stock in trade. They're in the sex business of shocking, which
may even have their usually raving audiences booing and hissing.
'We're the most hated group of all and the audiences cringe from us,'
they boast.'

The band's side. 'We'd been talking to this reporter and he realised
we were just ordinary blokes into our music and he said, 'Look, lads,
liven it up. We're read by 15 million people. We want something more
shocking than this.'

It seems hardly fair to review a show clouded by such a tragedy.
The Radiators are arguably Ireland's premier new-wave band but
they were clearly affected by the events that preceded their set.
'Blitzing at the Ritz' and 'Television Screen' are songs that deserve
more success.

The Undertones from Derry are a five-piece with potential. It's
surprising Northern Ireland hasn't thrown up more in-vogue bands –
they've got a lot to say. They sang 'Anarchy In The UK' adding *Resist
the UK* in the you-know-where-I mean slot.

The police didn't allow any of the bands to leave the college until
around 6.30 am. Sunrise. A friend of the dead youth sobs in the

corner after giving yet another description of what he saw to yet another detective.

I go back to lead singer Phil Chevron's Dublin home, where he lives with his family, and his mum cooks me a traditional Irish breakfast while I fall quietly in love with his sister.

I could sit here for ever…

But duty calls. I have a date in Camden Town with four scrumptious blokes with pain in their hearts and murder on their minds.

THE CLASH

Camden Town

Con Fucious, the celebrated Irish playwright, once said of The Clash, 'There is so much atmo within their 'sphere it's ridiculous.' And ol' Con knew a winner when he saw one.

But the question is – do you?

In case you don't – contained herein are several maxims. If you find one cut it out, fold carefully along the dotted edge, place in an envelope and post to the following people – The Royal Angus Hotel, Birmingham; the Matador Public House, Birmingham; St Martin's Church, Birmingham; several constabularies; 'The People'; the Dolce Vita, Birmingham; Tony Blackburn; Mr Bernard Brook-Partridge, GLC member; assorted dummies all over the country.

With any luck their principles might just explode in their faces, causing permanent brain damage.

In case you do – know a winner that is – then there's no need for me to tell you that Clash turbulence has smashed many a milk bottle on a bossman's doorstep (imagery), induced trash-can convulsions in high places (axiom), and played some of the best damn rock'n'roll the world's ever seen (and that's a fact).

Their sabre-tooth album chewed virtually every British rock record previously released into squelching redundancy. And you can see for yourself, round about sunset most days, gutless bands limping into the distance, towards an accursed horizon.

Constructive mayhem outside the mausoleum. How long before the doors open and the bodies burn?

Over the top? Nah. I just love 'em. That's all.

Well, I've had my say. I guess it's time for your weekly 'Set the Scene' show.

A rub-a-dub pub halfway down Camden High Street 100 yards from where The Clash hang out and rehearse. The remnants of a lost sun effectively blocked out except for the occasional flat cap-shadow flung across the carpet every time the door opens.

Like it so far? Well, don't stop reading even because The Clash will start talking any minute now.

But the 'SS Show' still needs touching up.

A table covered with lager, screwdrivers and French fags. Red vinyl seats. A piano soothes nearby, a pool ball collides with another pool ball. Mildew words lie strangled on the floor. There's blood on the hands of The Clash.

'So we gotta bring this carpet all the way back from Birmingham. ' Paul Simonon. 'What the hell are we gonna do with a grand's worth of carpet?'

'The Royal Angus Hotel says we damaged the carpet and want £935 in compensation,' Joe Strummer. 'It happened when we played Wolverhampton about six weeks back and stayed there."

'Could always knock out a few suits from the material.' Mick Jones.

'Yeah.' Nicky Headon.

The next bit concerns something that is going to happen in the future but will be in the past when you read it. Geddit? OK.

Joe: 'The Church and the police and the pubs have got together in Birmingham to prevent us from playing the Rag Market this Saturday. The Church says it won't be able to hear itself pray. The pubs say they'll all be destroyed and the police refuse to grant a dancing licence.'

Mick: 'They're calling us degenerates.'

Joe: 'We went into the Matador, the pub near the Market, and Paul put a record on the jukebox. Then him and me started dancing. When the record finished the publican said he thought it was disgusting to see two men dancing together.

'I told him I was dancing with myself. He said, 'That's even worse!' When punk rockers dance everyone gets frightened. So we're still gonna turn up outside the Market at eight pm on Sunday and check it out. We won't be playing – but we don't know what's gonna happen.'

Paul: 'They ought to have a huge aircraft hangar right slap-bang in the middle of Birmingham behind the church for us to play in.'

Joe: 'Older people in Birmingham are scared of the younger people in Birmingham.'

'Complete Control', 'Clash City Rockers', 'White Man In Hammersmith Palais', 'The Prisoner'. Four new Clash titles. Four new Clash instincts.

Mick: 'They're all based on the same theme. They have references to the mundane in-front-of-the-television way of life. They're a celebration of the power of music. The Clash have been pigeon-holed – everybody's favourite political band on the scene at the moment. We're sick to death of hearing all this kinda crap shoved at us.'

Joe: 'We take no notice of what people think we should or shouldn't be. They all need their heads seen to. They're looking for an easy escape route to a university degree.'

Mick: 'We're not 'Top of the Political Pops'. We're not the new leaders that everyone seems to be searching for.'

Joe: 'What the hell do we know about the international money market?'

Mick: 'We always wanted to be a rock'n'roll band. It gets a bit too heavy for us when you have all these people depending on you and expecting so much from you. I only want people coming up to me and saying, 'I really like your group,' not 'Why did you sell out?' They're pushing us around. We just want to do and say exactly what we want.'

Paul: 'Most of those people don't even know what 'sold out' means. So we played the Rainbow. A lot of people wanted to see us. That's why we played. So we signed with CBS. A lot of people wanted to buy our records. What's the point of signing for a tiny label with poor distribution so people have to come down from Scotland to buy your record in Rough Trade? They wanted us to lead the revolution – but we're only part of it.'

Joe: 'We haven't got any control over the situation at all. We haven't got any control over our lives. We just get tossed about like everyone else. Look – political power grows from the barrel of a gun. I haven't got a gun.'

Hold everything.

The Nicky Headon corner. Hullo, Nicky. What do you think of it so far?

'I joined the band three months ago. It's a lot better than I thought it would be and it's getting better all the time.'

Mick: 'He's now officially the fourth member of The Clash.

It's been a rough ride for the wafer-thin drummer. He and Joe spent three days in jail after failing to answer bail for a charge of stealing a key and a towel from a Birmingham hotel.

Joe: 'We jumped bail. They treated us bad. They gave us nothing. One cup of tea, chips, beans. No paper. No pencils, no cigarettes. No books.' I'm almost tempted to add *no phone, no pool, no pets*. The guy in the next cell was beaten up. We were hearing him getting knocked about.'

Nicky: 'They did it shrewdly, though, because when he appeared in the dock you couldn't see a thing in the front. But we sat behind him and his ears looked really bad.'

Joe: 'I guess we got treated the same as anybody else would be, and it's really rough.'

Nicky: 'The only time we got to see anyone in those three days was a face that appeared, poking some food through a little hole in the door.'

Joe: 'But we just kept very quiet throughout. If you give them an excuse they don't muck about.'

Nicky: 'The joke is they really do you for nicking a hotel key. But they told us straight, 'If you don't co-operate with us we'll oppose bail and you'll remain locked up.' That's what they said. They were against punks – definite personal things came out.'

Joe: 'The comment of the magistrate was a killer. 'If you check into respectable hotels you have got to behave like respectable people.'

A £100 fine between them on the theft charges, plus another conviction for Joe after he was caught spraying 'Clash' on a wall outside Dingwalls.

Joe: 'That was Nicky's first time acting as lookout. He failed.'

Joe comes on like a fluorescent lamp.

In the wake of the band's success what do they think of the minions – the don't-ask-for-the-moon-when-you-have-the-stars brigade? There's a preposterous number of bands attempting to emulate their idols.

Paul: 'When we first started we had nobody to look up to. Now all the second-wave second-rate bands have us.'

Mick: 'And a lot of them are getting fucked up by the entrepreneurs.'

Joe: 'I tell you, all the new singles that have been released are rubbish.'

Mick: 'They're recorded by people who are into totally different things – and that makes for one big mess. They're simply kidding themselves.'

Joe: 'They think it must be good because it's new-wave. That's nowhere.'

Mick: 'Fact is, there's too many surrogate bands without an idea between them.'

Joe: 'You've gotta sort through the crap before you find the wedding ring.'

In recent interviews, The Clash were demolished by the Pistols, a kind of incandescent indifference displayed by Rotten.

Joe: 'They sounded like ten-year-old kids. They said we wanted conscription brought back. They just don't listen. That quote's from 'Career Opportunities' and the words go 'I hate the army and I hate the RAF, they are going to have to introduce conscription'.'

Mick: 'It's just thick. All the bands are bitching and that just shows how weak the whole thing is. I respect the Pistols. They have a certain degree of accessibility to quite a few things and they could make it stronger. So many people seem intent on undermining the new situation.'

Joe: 'Everything changes. It's bad to take anything too seriously and we don't. Sometimes we come to blows among ourselves – but we always laugh about it after.'

Mick: 'It's a serious time, though. People are now more concerned about themselves than ever before. Nobody would fight line by line across the trenches. There's much more awareness. They'd rather go to a psychiatrist or a chiropodist or maybe have a tooth pulled.'

Joe: 'I don't believe in countries or states or tribes. I believe in a few people. Maybe I can count them on one hand, people I can trust.'

Mick: 'Right. It's our outfit. That's all that matters. Let people indulge themselves.'

Roadent the Roadie (who doesn't like being mentioned): 'But every time I indulge myself you shout at me.'

Welcome to the saloon bar two-step.

Mick: 'I never shout at you.'

Roadent: 'You do.'

Mick: 'I don't.'

Paul: 'You screech. You fucking S-C-R-E-E-C-H!'

Mick: 'I think everywhere now people are satisfied with the small group set-up. Y'know, not looking for more than two or three friends. That stems from a distrust of anything you're told.'

Joe: 'Because it's lies. Everything they tell you in school is a bunch of crap. Just do what you're told as they mould you to fit the machine. They don't want you to think. That's too dangerous. Things today are definitely more restricting. If something worries the authorities, they make a law to prevent it.'

And the Rainbow gig must have worried plenty of clinging-vine bigots.

Mick: 'Yeah. That night they tried to make Joe say something like, 'We want you to enjoy yourself, but we want you to enjoy yourself in your seats.' Nobody's gonna tell our band to calm down.'

Joe: 'And I never went to the party after. I just looked at all those people standing outside and the bouncers punching people in the face and I couldn't take it. Besides, I don't even think I was invited.'

There weren't many teds around that night.

Joe: 'A lot of teds are beating up punks. It gives them more credibility.'

Mick: 'The teds are very scared. They're living in the past. They were once the bad boys on the block but now punk is the bad boy. Punk rock is taking the piss out of rock'n'roll simply by playing contemporary rock'n'roll.'

Joe: 'The teds and Mary Whitehouse are on the same side.'

And now the one you've all been waiting for. The one that has alienated some of the band's followers with all the deerslayer vengeance of two Grunwick workers separated by a coach window. I'm talking about 'Remote Control' and CBS.

Paul: 'We were on tour when CBS decided to release the album track as a single. We came up to London to sort it out because if it had to be an album track we wanted 'Janie Jones'.'

Nicky: 'It was like a battle with everyone trying to establish that they knew best. So we finally turned round and said they can have it their way but we know how it'll turn out.'

Joe: 'We decided to lose that battle to prove a point. We couldn't win that one. There was nothing else we could have done. They had their way – they fucked it up. It won't happen again.'

Mick: 'There are a lot of people at CBS that don't want us there. They tolerate us. They've now got their safe punk band – The Vibrators – and they probably only signed them to frighten us. That band will do anything they're told to do. I don't lose a night's sleep wondering whether CBS like us or not.'

Joe: 'They're nice to your face, but wait till you turn your back. And another thing – we spent all our money on the other groups on the tour and CBS are refusing to refund any of it.'

Paul: 'They've got their own ideas and they include thinking that we can't do the tour by ourselves. We've been a social service.'

Joe: 'We're completely skint at the moment. We're treated like dogs. Nobody gives you something for nothing.'

Not exactly happy families.

Then there was the little matter of the Jam, who supported them for a while.

Paul: 'Their record company didn't want to support the tour. And they had their own tour looming up.'

Joe: 'Then they started coming up with that conservative shit, which was the total opposite to the feel of the tour.'

Paul: 'And to think we once saw hope for the Jam.'

Clash press?

Joe: 'There are a lot of masturbatory press articles about the band that make me puke.'

Mick: 'People who write about rock'n'roll can indulge in their own fantasies and I like to read it.'

Joe: 'I don't, like I don't believe in a leader. People are hanging on to our every move. I'm just someone doing something. I ain't gonna get taken in. I learned early on you should never believe your own press, because the minute you do you're doomed. People expect us to do their thinking for them.'

Paul: 'We don't preach. We just hope we're making things a little clearer.'

Malicious gossip about heavy university backgrounds surrounds these guys. None of them went to university; three went to art school. *Paul*: 'It was better than going into a factory.' His only hero, incidentally, is Jimmy Greaves.

Joe: 'Like I always say, trust the story not the storyteller.'

The confused blasts of disparity that this band seem to fire with alarming regularity are merely a camouflage. Mick Jones, the harbinger of the band's destiny, explains: 'We know we're the greatest band in the world, the universe. We don't care about the competition, because we're better than the rest.'

I'm planning a holiday with Dina. We're going to drive to Rome, via Paris, Lyons, Geneva, Aosta and Venice, in my 1973 Ford Cortina two-litre de-luxe. From Rome we'll head south to the coast and find a hotel for five days or so.

It'll be like retracing my steps.

Four years earlier I bought a Ford Consul for £30 and drove to

Cyprus with my mate Tony, using the same route to Rome, then cutting east to Brindisi for the ferry to Greece. I like an adventure. I'm also an incurable romantic.

I fell in love with Dina's hips when I first saw them sashaying round Russell Square from the top deck of a bus. I was 19 and had just got my first job in journalism as a court reporter at Marlborough Street Magistrates' Court, which backed on to the London Palladium and was directly opposite Carnaby Street.

I worked in a Dickensian office sandwiched between the jailer's room and Court One, and sat on the press bench every day writing down details of cases and sending abject shame in the post to local papers. If I thought the story warranted it, I'd come out of court and telephone the newsdesks of every national paper and try to flog it to them. If they liked the story I'd file it on the phone to their copy desk in their house style.

Everything – evidence, mitigation, judgement, the lot – I wrote down in longhand and copied out on a 1928 typewriter with no Tippex and no particular place to go.

My parents funded me a crash course for the ravers, two nights of shorthand a week at Pitman's in Russell Square, one of a series of squares that edge their way south from Euston Road.

On my first day I saw Dina. I looked out of the window as I was about to get off the bus and saw her from behind. She walked like Sophia Loren and had a body like Bardot. As she glided towards the entrance to Pitman's I prayed to God she'd walk in.

'You getting off or what?' said the conductor. I leaped out of the bus and ran to the college, but by the time I got there she'd vanished.

I was the only boy in the class. More than 90 per cent of the girls were foreign and training to be secretaries so they could return home in splendour. The teachers spoke slowly in the hope that a few students might understand. They didn't focus on any face; for them it was like sailing across every stretch of water from the Mediterranean to the Indian Ocean – dark-haired, dark-eyed girls, very much in the dark but amazingly good at learning shorthand.

Turkish, Persian, Greek, Nigerian, they tore through the books at an alarming rate and never got less than 80 per cent in all the tests, hitting 140 words a minute with consummate ease. Those girls actually thought in shorthand.

In that first lesson I noticed that the back of the head of the girl directly in front of my desk looked familiar. When she spoke to the girl next to her, there was something about her voice I liked. And when she got up and walked down the aisle to speak to the teacher I realised. It was her! The pretty flamingo from Russell Square.

I could hardly contain myself. I wanted to see what she looked like. Nothing else mattered. I imagined she'd have the face of a movie star kissed by an angel. She turned. She did.

The closer she got as she walked back down the aisle, the more agitated I became. With each step her beauty grew. With each heartbeat so did my love.

I must have had a smile on my face because she smiled at me as she went to sit down.

I stared so hard I forgot I was alive.

I'm looking forward to that holiday.

THE JAM
Battersea, Bond Street and York

A tale of love and adventure on the cracked road to success. In three parts.
Part One: In which our heroes Battersea

Town halls, bastions of English civility. Where local dramatic societies splutter, and demonstrative councillors stutter. Wasted spaces. Tonight Battersea Town Hall, an egotistical edifice in south-west London, is experimenting – and the test-tube babies are the Jam, tab-collar exponents of blitzkrieg bop.

The Jam are a very special band.

Paul Weller has managed to fuse, on occasion, the attitude of punk with the melody of Motown, betraying the skill of a magnanimous devil with thunder in his lungs. The Who? Bollocks. The Jam have more in common with Smokey Robinson than Pete Townsend. They ruffle the motor city smoothness and leap up and down and wave their knickers in the air. Nobody has ever done that before.

It's the third and final Jam jubilee acknowledgement. First was the abortive Stamford Bridge appearance, second Tower Hamlets.

But the council is clearly worried by the prospect of streetloads of punkoids swarming over their polished traditions. So precautionary measures – like no bar. Oh, sure, you can buy lemonade and crisps. One kid asks for a pint.

'Sorry, no alcohol.'

'Got any glue?'

The tickets have been limited to barely 800 and they're snapped up pronto.

And there's a Dock Green opposite.

So, now you've got the scene. Determination to keep the whole thing as low-key as possible. No maniacal debauchery down these cigar-stained corridors.

When the Jam walk on stage the hall is half empty. No way 800 people can make this mayor's ball hall look full. (That reminds me of a provincial newspaper placard I once saw rejoicing in the fact that its centre pages were taken up by photos of two recent dances held in honour of the town's mayor. It screamed, 'Mayor's Balls – Two Page Spread'.)

Naturally the sound isn't up to much. As echoey as the sobbing of a toilet attendant who hasn't had a customer all day.

But somehow that doesn't seem to matter. Paul Weller and Bruce Foxton stand apart like two speakers shuddering under the impact of burning watts, with drummer Rick Buckler providing the channel split. They're no stereohype.

Oh, and guess who's in the audience? Bill Curbishley, manager of the Who, and Keith Altham, publicist of the Who, and they love 'em. Julie Ege is spotted taking photographs. And Peter Gabriel?

They run through the usual set – most tracks off the album and a bunch of new numbers, like 'All Around The World', the next single, and 'Carnaby Street'. The crowd respond like they've known the Jam all their life and, in a way, they have because Weller has smuggled a Sixties sweetness into his songs, and a Sixties sweetness is a sweet, sweet sweetness.

One encore, an 'In The City' reprisal and 'Batman' – a mistake as a final song. Too abrupt an ending. The crowd may love it but only as an appetiser.

Rick kicks over his drum-kit and a cymbal slices the back of the neck. 'I thought it was this geezer at the side of the stage at first,' he says later. 'I nearly clobbered him.'

A sour epilogue – the morning papers tell of running battles between 300 teds and punks outside the town hall after the show.

That's bollocks. Minor bother and that's all. The Old Bill have things under control. One of The Boys, who support that night, is hit over the head and has stitches but he's the only one hurt. The 300 figure is a gross misrepresentation.

Part Two: in which our heroes go 'All Around The World' in Bond Street

A break in the band's massive 38-date tour culminating in a Hammersmith Odeon blaster.

The reason? They should have played Lincoln tonight but The Damned had some trouble at the same gig a few days back and the decision is made to pull out.

So, whaddya do on a day off? Make a single, of course.

But, first, an aspiring rock star's survival kit.

Ever wanted to know what highly personal belongings a guitarist in a successful band carries around with him while touring?

Come with me now into Bruce Foxton's bag, hidden beneath a control panel in the recording studio – Air Studios off Oxford Circus. Sssh.

What have we here? Large tube of Colgate, spray-on relief for legs, orange vitamin-C tablets, Kiwi Guard liquid polish (for children's shoes), Clearasil (for spots), Capriton nasal congestion tablets, Dequadin throat lozenges, Silverkrin pine herb shampoo (normal hair), Arid roll-on (extra effective, phew) Vicks Wild Cherry lozenges, Triomink catarrh tablets, Otrivine nasal spray and a toothbrush.

No self-respecting pop star would be seen dead without his Otrivine.

At the moment the boys are laying down the music and vocals to 'All Around The World'. The song is two-minutes 20-seconds long. 'Great,' says Bruce. 'That means we'll have eight more seconds on 'Top of the Pops.' 'In The City' was two minutes 12-seconds.

Recording studios are no more than hospital waiting rooms with rows of knobs, upturned dog ends on the control desk, lager cans in the corner, lacklustre sandwiches, dissection and disappointment.

Then, through the sterile gloom, Paul's bare, untipped, navy-cut vocals, stripped of all music, honeydrip from the speakers and spill across the floor like quicksand. You try to step out of the way but you can't because it's already covering your shoes and you're sinking into the painful sweetness.

A Surrey boy of barely 19 has no right to sing like a man hung out to dry, like a man disenchanted, like a man with the smell of death in his nostrils. But he does, and whatchya gonna *dooo* about it?

'Carnaby Street' is the B side to 'All Around The World'. They cut both songs in ten hours.

Just like Pink Floyd.

Part three – In which our heroes become the cat's whiskers

So, what have we got? York – a snap-happy town with monuments and tree-lined approach roads. Strategic lights on ancient walls in the subtle city centre. Tasteful.

We also get a hotel room where your feet touch the fucking wall if you decide to stretch out in bed. And the shower along the corridor leaks throughout the night.

A Cat's Whiskers, a name often used when Mecca want to change their ageing dogs-home image at the local Palais. Heavy smell of skin, deep fried scampi and chips as you walk through the entrance.

A great crowd.

A great band with a future as long as the Victoria Line and a talent to match. Nothing underground about the Jam, though. Accessible right down to the white tongue of Paul Weller's winkle-pickers.

They're one of the first new bands to hit York, but from the reaction you'd never guess. The place is packed out and, looking at the kids, you get to thinking, Boy, have they got problems.

Nobody dances like the girl in front of me, drugs or no drugs, without some deeply ingrained reason. She throws her head from side to side, her hair flashing across the faces of two guys. A girl in conflict. She collapses and is helped out by her friend.

Down the front the kids are leaping, their sweat-stained faces reflected in the silver-ring backdrop on stage. And the band haven't even started.

'Art School' and 'Changed My Address' kick off the show and already Bruce leads the pogoing. A guy shouts out, 'Substitute!' and they go into 'All Around The World'. Somehow, metaphors of the guitars-like-sten-gun ilk seem superfluous.

You just have to see them. That's all.

'In The City' is followed by 'Carnaby Street', Bruce's first song for the band, which he also sings.

'Midnight Hour' with a body-blow *nenenana* bassline.

Encore. 'This is the reason we're here,' says Paul. 'In The City'!' scream the fans. They oblige. 'Batman' next. Off.

They won't let them go. 'Jamjamjamjam!' Encore. 'This song's about this school of thought,' and 'Art School'. Gone.

Best concert that's ever stroked the Cat's Whiskers.

As guest singles reviewer on 'Record Mirror', Paul Weller says of the Jam's 'All Around The World', 'I was hoping for 'Modern World' as the new single from the Jam. I love them. Seen them play about 15 times and this is no disappointment. In fact, they make records that sound like anthems. Weller's guitar explosion in the middle is like a quick journey to the centre of the earth. Single of the week and number one. 'Carnaby Street' is on the B-side.'

In the same column Paul says of Cocksparra's 'Runnin' Riot', 'This is a record company's idea of new wave. Clichéd heavy-metal riffs and someone shouting in a Cockney voice. This is a con and I hate it.'

PENETRATION
Newcastle

Avoiding condescention.

Conditioning processes abound when Newcastle is mentioned to any non-Geordie, especially Londoners. Cranes and caps and dirty waves, steel and smoke and pitchfork houses, dislocated pubs and punk bands, corporate identities and

Wait a minute. Punk bands?

Well, punk *band*, actually. Penetration (don't go to my head), primo pushers of the big noise down in the boom dock. They're 16 to 19 and on the way up. They've played the Roxy – if that means anything – supported The Vibrators three times, seen the Pistols seven times, laid down a few demos, been banned from Newcastle University, written some pretty good songs. And been interviewed by 'Record Mirror', of course.

Tonight they're supporting The Vibrators for the third time at Sunderland's Seaburn Hall. It's easy to see why they've got an acre of a following.

Okay, introductions. This is Pauline, a real crackertoa with waylaid black hair and venomous eyes. She sings. 'Hi.'

And the Empire State on bass here is called simply 'K'. 'All right.'

The Bill Nelson lookalike on guitar is Gary Chaplin. 'Hullo'.

And on drums, 16-year-old Gary Smallman. 'How yer going?'

'Some of the people in our own town don't treat us the same as they would a London band,' says Smallman. 'That really gets up my nose.'

Their songs are complex, heavily influenced by the Pistols' wayfaring spirit. 'I like words, interesting words. I look at things way, way out in the distance,' says Pauline, who has titles to her credit like

'Duty Free Technology', 'Don't Dictate', 'Destroy', 'Silent Community', 'I'm Nobody' and 'Firing Squad'.

They smack of Teesside bleakness – oops, falling into that trap again.

'The Pistols made you feel as though you could go and try to do it yourself. They made me start singing. That's their secret,' she adds.

Penetration are creating enough interest for at least two record companies to be sniffing around. They laid down a couple of numbers in the studios of one and they seemed impressed. Early days. 'There's been a lot of crap put out recently,' says Chaplin, 'but we set our standards a lot higher. There's no way we would ever release something we weren't absolutely sure of. Okay, so we haven't got a deal yet, but when we do, we want control over anything that is released.'

They're not boastful, just realistic – and perhaps a little fanciful. So what's the scene like in Newcastle?

'There's not one place to go where they regularly play our kind of music,' says Chaplin. 'It's picking up fast now but it's getting frustrating. I think it's mainly to do with adverse publicity. Like, we'd never been threatened until this bunch of crap started appearing in the nationals. Now we're getting intimidated and we can't even walk around the streets of our hometown on our own. It's ridiculous 'cos who'd ever heard of teds in such numbers before the papers picked on it?'

'And the worrying thing is that people actually believe what they read.' Smallman. 'We wanna make music for people to enjoy, not for yobbos to go mad on.'

'We work out our frustrations on stage. I could no more smash someone's head in than walk a tightrope.' Gary Chaplin said that.

I wanna destroy passers by. Johnny Rotten said that.

Penetration sign a deal with Virgin two months after the interview. Their debut single 'Don't Dictate', is followed by 'Firing Squad' and 'Life's a Gamble', and two albums – Moving Targets and Coming Up for Air. They disband after a gig at Newcastle City Hall on 14 October 1979, but reunite for a UK tour in 2002 and have been gigging solidly ever since.

THE CORTINAS
Bristol

Well, you're a schoolboy in Bristol – a pretty well-off schoolboy at that. But that's boring y'know, so to alleviate the damage you form a band playing Dr Feelgood rip-offs. That gets boring too. Then you see the Sex Pistols.

So now you got direction, but you don't wanna be another voidoid and legless facsimile. That's no fun. How can you write songs about dole delights when you're sunbathing in your own spacious garden?

The Cortinas' dilemma? Not really. They don't inflict fake identities on themselves, just cigarette burns on the arm. The elevator-high-class structure has set them firmly on the second floor and they have no particular desire to walk down.

An all-embracing I'm-so-poor stance is out. The false-idol purveyors of the new now music can go hang themselves. But I disappear up my own garrulous black hole.

The Cortinas are – Jeremy 'Fatty Potato' Valentine, vocals, Dexter 'The-doctor-said-I'm-the-most-unhealthy-teenager-he's-ever-examined' Dalwood, bass, Nick Sheppard, guitar, Mike Fewins, lead guitar and Danny Swan drums.

We're in the living room of Danny's dad's house. The band have just played an open-air festival in a Bristol park. Abysmal set, thanks to almost non-existent PA. Okay, I'll say cheerio now and leave you with the boys.

Danny: 'A lot of people in London get the impression that we're a bunch of square kids just because we happen to be middle class. Okay, we know punk is essentially a working-class thing but that doesn't mean we can't have a place in it as well.'

Jeremy: 'Lower-class kids are bored kids. All they seem to want is football on Saturday afternoons and afterwards go out and get drunk. They don't want to think about things. It's always been down to the middle-class kids to say whatever they want.'

Nick: 'The hard-up kids haven't had a chance. They've been indoctrinated since the day they were born. They don't need anything, their life is planned.'

Danny: 'Working-class kids often resent middle-class kids and who can blame them when they get some university grad into Communism trying to flog them a copy of 'Soviet Weekly'? They'll just beat him up because they don't know what he's talking about.'

Dexter: 'Certain things are expected of us. Like going to university. Like getting a good job. Like thinking for yourself, although decisions have always been made for us.'

Nick: 'And when middle-class teenagers dropped out what did they become? Hippies, living in squats. Nothing positive. Now we're saying something.'

Like their song 'Further Education'.

Why should I sit for a board of metrication,
Just to go on to further education?
What's the point of qualifications
If it don't include the complications?

Nick: 'People say we should be working class but we fucking ain't.'
Dexter: 'And we don't profess to be.'
Nick: 'It's pointless us writing songs about class things 'cos we don't know anything about it. There will always be a class structure. If we did write like that and somebody came here and saw this house we would be maligned.'

Jeremy: 'There's always been London. We were terrified at the prospect of playing there but when we did we soon realised that a lot of what you read about it in the music press is a fabrication. I mean, we thought it was the centre of the world.'

They all roll up.

Dexter: 'The punk thing has already changed. It started off totally new but bands soon realised they had to use the establishment to get through.'

Nick: 'I mean, there's no real way The Clash are gonna change anything physically. They had to go to CBS and get money to get their message across.'

Dexter: 'Most bands in this area despise us because we've done in one year what they haven't in ten. We loved playing R&B, but after seeing the Pistols you get to thinking, er. See, you've got to support what you write.'

Nick: 'It's like the bands saying they've been on the dole and they haven't. Yet they're trying to create a movement against lying.'

Mike: 'Rebellion is getting stronger all the time. There'll be another one if this one doesn't do it. I may be getting a very privileged education – but I'm also getting a higher level of backlash.'

And to set the record straight about the single 'Fascist Dictator':

Jeremy: 'It's about a guy who doesn't want to be tied down in a serious romantic situation.'

I don't want love as it's a bore.
I don't want love just some street whore.
I don't want love cos it's a waste of time.
But don't forget that you are mine.

The Cortinas eventually sign to CBS and release the album True Romances that falls on largely deaf ears. They split up in 1978 and guitarist Nick goes on to replace Mick Jones in The Clash. Dexter will become a celebrated painter.

THE DAMNED
Hastings Pier

Wipe that pier from your eye.

It was only The Damned's last show in their massive nationwide tour – and what a finale. The Pier Pavilion, Hastings, home of fading

TV personalities serenading balding, demented souls in beige jackets and sunglasses. And you should see their husbands. The Damned, clearly pleased at the prospect of a long holiday, look relaxed and out for a good time.

The usual songs plus two new ones – 'Take My Money' and 'Politics', the latter a definite kick in the bollocks of the Pistols and the teeth of The Clash. And what's this? A drum solo? After covering his kit (drum) in talcum powder, then getting lost in the white smog, Rat lurches into a solo and it's only possible to make out his hands and head through the white wall of talc.

Countless encores culminate in Scabies throwing a cymbal – his favourite – 20 feet into the air and poking a hole through the polystyrene ceiling.

The sea crashed in and washed them away.

While reviewing the week's new single releases, Captain Sensible says of Rod Stewart's re-release of 'Mandolin Wind', that if he met him he'd gob in his face. 'I bet he smells worse than any other musician I can imagine. This record has a load of old hippies on it. Man, it's so peaceful. I could even play this to the neighbours at full volume and get away with it. He's worse than fucking Tony Blackburn.'

Among Johnny Rotten's top-ten singles for a Capital Radio show was 'The Pink', Captain Beefheart; 'Sweet Surrender', Tim Buckley; 'Lady Day and the Bed', Lou Reed; 'Revolution Blues', Neil Young; 'Rebel Rebel', Bowie and 'Doing All Right With The Boys', Gary Glitter.

THE SEX PISTOLS
Virgin offices, London

Trooping the Colour, with 'God Save The Queen' *à la* Sex Pistols providing the soundtrack, opens up the docupunk Virgin decide to screen this hot summer morning

There's the Queen, riding side-saddle wearing that nifty little beret. She turns her head slowly towards the camera and, wait for it, she's boss-eyed! And just as she double-dares into the lens, Rotten steams in the background, *She ain't no human being.* That's real style.

A collage: Derek Nimmo's dress sense being grossly insulted by Rotten, the toffee-apple-voiced Nimmo wanders out of the Kings' Road shop looking even more stupid than he did when he walked in; punked-up to the eyebrows, Bill Grundy egging them on in the most delightful TV interview in history. There's a discussion on punk by the 'Young Nationwide' TV team with the Pistols sitting in, the link woman over pronouncing the *k* in 'punk' and 'rock'.

On board the ill-fated 'Elizabeth,' where the band held their own jubilee celebrations, the fun begins when the police swarm over the boat after the captain sends out a flare warning. Things border on farce as they clearly have no idea what they're supposed to do so they appear to start laying into one or two crimson-haired punks.

'They've got Malcolm!' And there's McLaren being dragged into a police van. Perfick. The songs are all here – 'Anarchy' and 'God Save The Queen' recorded at the Marquee a couple of months back. They're miming but clearly loving it. There's 'Pretty Vacant', which you all saw on 'Top of the Pops'. And know why they appear to be living the song? Mike Mansfield was producing, enough to make anyone look vacant.

Last word to Mr Jones.

They're playing somewhere in Wales and the local carol-singing has-beens are out in force, converging on the theatre to make their protest, and a reporter asks Steve Jones what he thinks of them. 'Well,' he says, 'they're all outside freezing their bollocks off while I'm here, in the warm.'

It's the first holiday I've had since I started on 'Record Mirror'. Driving a Cortina to Venice and Rome with the love of my life beside me sounds more and more like one leisurely gondola ride to heaven. After all, I'd known her for five years, off and on.

I'd finally plucked up the courage to ask Dina out for the first time as a twentieth birthday treat to myself. I'd known her for weeks. I carried her books to the bus stop round the corner from the college, tried to hold her eyes with mine, listened to her glorious accent and thought about her in all my waking hours before she tiptoed through my dreams.

My birthday fell on a Saturday and I used that as an excuse to ask her out. She agreed. I was shocked, but I smiled and said, 'Thanks.' It made me sound an eyelid short of desperate and I imploded.

We arranged to meet outside Russell Square tube station. I was about to kiss my teens goodnight with the girl of my dreams, and my waking hours, on my arm. Dina arrived 30 minutes late accompanied by her older cousin, Nethi, to act as a chaperon. She was cool.

'She's got to be home by eleven,' Nethi said in no uncertain terms.

'Is that a.m. or p.m.?' I enquired.

She laughed. I took my dream date down the tube and on to a slow train to Whitechapel for a drink at the Blind Beggar, which had recently been refurbished. The Kray-induced bloodstains had been banished for ever. I knew it wasn't the most romantic of places but the music was good and the booze was cheap. Style or what?

Dina was on a year-long secretarial course and had already been in London for six months staying with her aunt. Our time was short but I loved her like I'd never loved anyone. I took her out maybe five times in four months, yet we kissed for the first time on our last date; stolen, brief, unforgettable, in the shadows of the block of flats in Camden Town where she lived.

When she went back to Cyprus I learned how to drive and took a Ford Consul across Europe to see her again, two days after my 21st birthday. It was the first time I'd been abroad. I thought I'd surprise her.

As we pull away from her flat in Hampstead Road, I turn to Dina and say, 'Next stop Rome,' and plug in my home-made cassette, the one I'd been working for days to perfect. First up, Tom Petty and The Heartbreakers 'American Girl'.

'Could you turn it down? I've got a headache.' We've only just reached the *raised on promises* line in the song and Mornington Crescent in the car.

What follows is two weeks of hell, interspersed with rare moments of sublimity. We argue about everything, everywhere – beneath the Eiffel Tower, by the lake in Geneva, at the centre of St Mark's Square, the Colosseum, the fucking Vatican.

She's exhausted after we've driven 300 miles, but I'm the only one driving. And navigating.

'God, it's so tiring sitting in the car. Could you go out and get me some matches?' Dina's lying on a bed in a room on the tenth floor of a cheap Milan hotel and she looks like she's just orbited the fucking earth. Just exactly how many 'l's are there in 'bollocks', Dina? I get the matches.

We stay in a little whitewashed wonder of an hotel on the beach just outside Sabaudia and around 80 miles from Rome, and have four heavenly days, but on the drive back she's unbearable. It's not me. It can't be. After all, I'm a man of the world. I know how to handle things. It's her. It's always her. Isn't it?

When we get back to London I've already decided to dump her. We go to see 'Rocky' at the Dominion in Tottenham Court Road, appropriate when you're about to deliver a KO. We go back to her flat. I don't go in. I say goodbye. Then I smile and say, 'Thanks.' And she closes the door on me. For ever. It's at that moment I realise I've left a shitload of difficult-to-get-hold-of albums in her flat.

I can't knock. That would be so uncool.

Fuck.

I shave off my beard, cut off my shoulder-length hair and head for the strangest punk gig of them all.

AUGUST 1977

Top Ten singles
beginning of August

1. I Feel Love – Donna Summer
2. Angelo – Brotherhood of Man
3. Ma Baker – Boney M
4. So You Win Again – Hot Chocolate
5. Fanfare For The Common Man – Emerson Lake & Palmer
6. We're All Alone – Rita Coolidge
7. It's Your Life – Smokie
8. Pretty Vacant – Sex Pistols
9. You've Got What It Takes – Showaddywaddy
10. Oh Lori – Alessi

Top Ten albums
beginning of August

1. The Johnny Mathis Collection
2. Going For The One – Yes
3. Live At The Greek – Neil Diamond
4. 20 All Time Greats – Connie Francis
5. A Star Is Born – Soundtrack
6. I Remember Yesterday – Donna Summer
7. On Stage – Rainbow
8. Rattus Norvegicus IV – the Stranglers
9. Rumours – Fleetwood Mac
10. Live In The Air Age – Be Bop Deluxe

Alan Jones works for 'Melody Maker' – fabulous writer but I've never seen him sober. Mind you, he's probably never seen me straight. That's simply because we only ever meet at receptions or on coaches bound for France. Sure enough, he's sitting in front of me as we head out of London on the way to Paris and he's pissed.

It's 9.30 a.m.

I can't drink in the morning but a line of speed I can handle. And I do, twice, before we hit Croydon. The coach is stuffed with bands – including new kids on the block the Police and the Maniacs – journos, photographers and PRs and we're nearly all either pissed or stoned or both before we get to the ferry.

The coach driver, a straight-down-the-line guy, is visibly shocked. He's taking us all the way down to the Mont de Marsan punk festival in a bullring on the toasted French-Spanish border and he is clearly appalled at the prospect.

I don't sleep for the next five days. In Paris 12 of us share a room for the night and by the time I get to bed, and finally manage to claw through the snoring, it's dawn and a builder starts drilling holes through the outside wall from a scaffold.

More speed down the highway. More stares from the driver, who turns into a complete sulphate freak by the time we get to Mont de Marsan. On the first night of the festival he loses his shoes, goes off in search of them and is never seen again.

THE CLASH, THE DAMNED, THE JAM, DR FEELGOOD, EDDIE & THE HOTRODS, THE BOYS

Mont de Marsan

Innocents abroad for speed-suction booze-junction on coach *en route* de Paris.

Police and Maniacs in a night grazed by a knife fight. Twelve in a room a fresh bread tomb. And on to Mont de Marsan.

Dancing driver breathless on the outskirts of the grasshopper town.
A bar full of stars. Welcome.

'You want to buy bed? *Oui*, zis is divine divan. Only 1,000 francs.'
And only those with influence sleep under crisp, ripe sheets.

So you wanna festival – you got it.

But before that, *j'accuse* the French of creating total bed chaos. The
organisers have failed. Result? Roadies living in the backs of their vans
and press on the streets, endlessly powdering their noses. Dreamless.
Oh, how I yearn for that Damned sofa and the Manhattan skyline.

And Skydog, the organisers, sleep like Heinz-stuffed babies.

Woodstock crazies had acid. They provided a backdrop for scruffy,
collar-up fantasies. These French kids are not into fantasy. They're
into long, tall Sally, all white and sharp and dizzy. Big-time.

Day one

Thrown out of my hotel room to make way for a blank-faced band,
name of Bijou. In the process of looking for another eight by eight
(fail) I miss the first three hours, which included Police, Maniacs and
all-girl band the Loose.

So the first band to come under the quickly fraying edges of my
critical scrutiny are The Damned, complete with Lu, their new fifth
member. He's there to lift some of the guitar donkey-work from Brian
James but on this showing he's not adding anything extra, or special.
Now, you can put that down to the wiped-out sound system, of
course, which leaves Vanian's mouth stranded like a dying goldfish.

The first three quarters of their set is ruined and the new numbers
– 'Politics', 'You Take My Money' and 'Problem Child' – are sounds
of silence.

Incidentally, Brian introduces 'Politics' with, 'This one's for The Clash.'
Don't need no politics to make me dumb

That is the first of many Damned/Clash aggro stances over the next
few days, culminating in Captain Sensible being forcibly carried off-
stage after planting stinkbombs during The Clash's set.

The final segment of The Damned's show is fine. They should have released a single months ago and if they're intent on keeping Lu they ought to use that as a basis for a rethink.

They're too good to lose out now.

The Boys

Yeah – here's the leaders of the second wave with a confirmation live of their soon-to-be-released wow of an album. OK, so their set is frantically short – but, sure enough, it's blissful brevity.

'This one's for Mick Jagger,' says Kid Reid before launching into 'Rock Belle'

A Riviera soul submerged in dollar bills has gone for ever…

The Boys, all meat and no decoration.

The Clash

Ten-second psych-out.

Six eyes.

Three sneers. LONDON'S BURNING!

The beginning of the longest Clash set in history – one and a half hours. And you know something? It's a disappointment.

Ever heard of the New York blade-in-the-back-alley dice game craps? Roll the dice. Here we go now.

…9…

Four new numbers, 'Clash City Rockers', 'White Man In Hammersmith Palais', 'The Prisoner', 'Complete Control', each sounding as good as, if not better than, anything they've ever done before. Weeks of devout rehearsing have made the songs Clash-sharp and that's sharp.

…3…

It seems nowhere near one and a half hours.

…9…

You win. That's it. Great. Another roll.

…6…

Paul Simonon has a huge needle shoved into his arse at the local hospital because of a blotch disease. He is very ill.

...9...

No monitors, so the back-up vocals, an integral part of the band's swipe songs, are lost.

...5...

Joe Strummer losing track signals on the lines, which throw the band into momentary confusion on several numbers.

...7...

Craps.

Know what I mean?

Strummer says later that he fails to click with the fans and when that happens he's dead.

It's just one of those nights, that's all, because even when they're bad The Clash are better than most. They're no garage band any more – they're a multi-storey car park.

Oh, well, there's always the Jam tomorrow.

It's just coming up to midnight in the all-night bar, packed to the rafters with bands and roadies and French speedheads. The three members of the Jam are seated in different parts of the bar, drinking, talking, being young, when their manager, Paul's dad John, walks in and tells them it's time they turned in because they've got a show to do tomorrow.

Paul, Bruce and Rick obey and dutifully troop out of the bar.

Scabies sniggers.

Day two

The Jam don't play. Bruce Foxton explains, 'We were contracted to appear before the Rods and the Feelgoods but then the promoters decided to put us on after the Feelgoods, which would have meant appearing at three a.m.'

Simple as that. But there's one hell of a lot of choked people around. A sleep overhaul prevents me seeing Little Bob Story or the Tyla Gang. Apparently, the Gang are given a bottle-blazing encore demand from their cult French following and receive the best reception of the weekend. It's now all to the Rods and the Feelgoods who have flown in on a special Southend charter.

They're both predictable. Maybe that's a little unfair. Curling guts and two-ton eyelids don't help. But that doesn't stop me thinking that Barry Masters's cartwheel isn't as spontaneous as it used to be. The Rods are backfiring into a blind alley and last year's raves are rapidly becoming this year's graves. The same with the Feelgoods. No special tingle. No transient solution to a blue night, no good-time blackout.

And in the running-sore all-night bar at six a.m. Feelgood rubs shoulders with Damned who bitches with Clash, who ignores Hotrod, while bottle-brandishing Frenchmen are laid out by Mick, The Damned's roadie.

This festival should have encapsulated everything good about the British scene over the last year. Instead, the only thing stabbed into submission by the two-day bullring show are 3,000 noses.

Quote Corner

'Either he goes or I go and you can quote me on that' – Captain Sensible referring to Lu, The Damned's new member.

'This festival makes me sick. The people here have a go at the Woodstock attitude but this is worse' – Paul Weller, referring to the use of drugs.

'She may look beautiful in this café at five a.m. but at nine o'clock on a Tooting Monday morning you wouldn't look twice' – Lee Brilleaux of a local smiling tart.

'I'm a vegetarian because when you eat meat you eat fear, fear of that first death call' – Mick Jones while tucking into a buttered roll for lunch.

'We were the best band at the festival' – Rat Scabies.

The French speed has staved off sleep for five nights solid and I'm starting to hallucinate. It's time to cut out. I've decided to grab five days in St Tropez and drive there with Tony – I seem to have driven round most of Western Europe with him – who followed the coach from London in his new Granada. We arrive in St Tropez in the early hours and spend the first night in the car but find a hotel the next day. Four days to think.

I'm totally unrecognisable from the person who drove to Rome with Dina. I've lost 10 pounds, the beard and the barnet. I look like a punk. A bit. But I'm also lost in tortuous ecstasy. As the speed is gradually flushed from my system in a river of cheap red wine, I'm tormented by a malignant misgiving: was I a fool to leave Dina? As I try to leap into drunken sleep it hurts so much to see her face, hear her voice, feel her hands on me. My life is wrapped in such delusions and I can't breathe properly.

In a café overlooking the harbour I write her a letter, explaining my feelings and saying I was a fool to let her go. I pour out my love as Tony pours out the wine. I'm not good company.

When I get back to London there's a letter from Dina waiting for me. She says for the first time that she loves me. I'm born again.

I arrange a meal for two at the ultra-luxury Belvedere in Holland Park on her birthday, 16 August, and surreptitiously slip the waiter a sapphire ring I've bought, instructing him to bring it out with the coffees.

When we arrived in Cyprus after that epic journey in 1973, Tony and I rented an apartment on Kennedy Avenue in the centre of Famagusta town. Dina worked for Kaisis, a big engineering company on the outskirts of Nicosia and I drove to her office within two days of arriving. She'd told me she worked there in one of her few letters.

I had written to her every week for a while, expressing my love in mysterious, metaphorical, epic ways, waiting helplessly for replies that took months to come and consisted of 150 words in that over-polite style of English taught to foreigners and imbeciles. But I couldn't forget her face. This time, the music wasn't gonna get me home.

I strolled into the huge reception and asked the girl at the desk if she could inform Dina Constantinou that Barry from London was downstairs and would like to see her. The receptionist looked more than a little surprised but dialled Dina's extension.

'Dina? There's someone called...' she looked at me quizzically.

'Barry,' I said.

'Barry – from…' She looked at me quizzically again.

'London,' I said.

'…London here to see you.'

There was a pause. 'Okay.' She hung up. 'Dina will be with you in a few minutes, if you'd like to take a seat.'

Take a seat. How could I, knowing all my dreams were about to walk down that staircase? I'd driven 2,000 miles for this moment. 'It's okay, I'll stand.'

And then she appeared – short skirt, long legs, face flushed fiery red. As she approached the redness grew brighter. I thought she was going to explode.

'Hullo, Dina.'

'What are you doing here?'

'I thought I'd come and see you.'

'Look, there's a café at the end of the road. I'll meet you in there when I finish.' She was actually squirming. This wasn't what I'd envisaged. I was looking for the slow-motion coming-together across a crowded room, not a Greek brush-off. Suddenly I felt very embarrassed and headed back out to my 12-year old Consul.

In the café I waited patiently for 40 minutes until finally she arrived.

As she walked in she checked the place out like a cop. 'What are you doing here?'

'You've already asked me that. I came to see you. Would you like something?'

'No. Why didn't you tell me you were coming?'

'I thought I'd surprise you.'

'You did.'

She glanced out of the window and saw a car she recognised. She slid down in the chair like she'd just been shot in the head at point-blank range. 'Has that big red car gone past?'

'What big red car?'

'The big one.'

'Well, I can't see one outside.'

She sidled back up from beneath the table. 'Sorry. It's just that people wouldn't understand. It's very difficult for me to be seen alone with a man, especially someone who's English.'

'But I came to see you, Dina. I drove a long way because I miss you and I wanted to see you again before I die.'

She laughed and not in a Tom Jones' 'Delilah' way, more like Ginger Rogers when she's dancing cheek to cheek with Fred Astaire. 'I can't stay. I have to go.'

'When can I see you?'

'I don't know. It's not easy. You should have told me.'

'I have to see you.'

'Where are you staying?'

'Famagusta. Kennedy Avenue. I drove here with Tony.' They had never met but Dina was familiar with his name.

'That's nice.'

'Nice'. She used it in all her letters. London was 'nice', the shops were 'nice', I was 'nice.' It was frustrating but, fuck, I couldn't write a word of Greek and never would.

'Look, some of us often go to Famagusta beach at the weekend. I'll meet you there this Sunday. Near the café. Now I really must go.'

I was overjoyed. 'What time?'

'We get there early, around ten, and spend the day there.'

'Let me drive you home.'

'No. It's okay.'

'I insist.'

She followed me sheepishly out of the café and dived into the car like she was in 'The Sweeney'. As we drove she kept ducking her head, then asked me to pull up at the end of her road, which probably wasn't. I put her through hell that hot afternoon after work.

The following Sunday I slipped into my white trousers and white vest – I was sporting the first tan I'd had in my life – told Tony to expect a few female guests and headed out of the door at 9.30 a.m. in the direction of the beach.

I waited the whole day. I think I gave up around four o'clock. I trudged back to the hotel empty-handed only to find Tony had laid on a buffet with food for six.

I phoned her at work the next day. She apologised and told me not to ring her again. 'It's too difficult.'

So, I sold the Consul for 150 quid, fell out of love, flew back to London and forgot about her, although her face appeared sometimes, like the remnant of a year-old acid trip.

I didn't count on a war.

Dina woke up one hot July morning in '74 to a sky full of parachutes. Hundreds of Turks falling through the hot, still, pine-drenched air with revenge in their hearts. Dina and her parents fled from their home in Nicosia, leaving everything behind. Her family put her on the first boat out of Cyprus and she made her way to London.

I was serving my indentures on a local daily newspaper in Gloucester and was holed up in the tiny Stroud-district office with two world-weary reporters and a heart full of soul when the phone rang.

Her lisp was a hypnotist's codeword and I was mesmerised. We met a week later in Kings Cross. She had changed her hair – it was much shorter. She wasn't as attractive as I'd remembered. I decided against seeing her again. I was young. I was fickle. I couldn't forget the pain she'd put me through. I wanted her out of my life for ever.

Then, two years later, a letter.

She was leaving London now that her parents were no longer refugees. She wanted to cook me a meal, a kind of charcoal-grilled last supper. I went. She looked great. I fell in love again. She accepted my love.

That's how it was with Dina.

We wrangled through the nights.

After the meal at the Belvedere, we head to the Élysée, a Greek nightclub off Tottenham Court Road that's hosting a reception for Gonzo rock god Ted Nugent, who has just played the Hammersmith Odeon.

When we get there the place is rocking. Everyone is encouraged to smash plates while a three-piece bouzouki band knock out everything from 'Never On Sunday' to 'Zorba'.

Suddenly the music stops. The Greek guy on the bouzouki, whose command of the English language makes Manuel of 'Fawlty Towers' sound like Rex Harrison, says, 'Oh, no, I just 'ear. Elvees Presley, 'e dead.'

There's a stunned silence.

Then Mr Bouzouki starts to sing,

I gave a letter to the postman
'e put eet in ees bag

The whole place erupts with laughter, then grown men start to weep.

Later that night I propose and Dina accepts.

It's now or never.

SEX PISTOLS
Wolverhampton

I've seen the Pistols play live only once – at the Notre Dame church hall in Leicester Square. I will see them three more times before they self-destruct. If they ever play any better than they do at the Lafayette club in Wolverhampton this hot August night then Jesus really was a sailor when he walked upon the water.

The field of vision is obscured by ten morose meatheads. The clarity of sound is debased – like a gurglng wino. Kids with fire in their eyes lash out in the darkness. This is the night that the silk-lined lid of Presley's copper coffin slams shut for ever. Who needs him when you've got the Sex Pistols.

Yeah. You heard right. The Sex Pistols, because at the little Lafayette club just around the corner from Wolverhampton station, the Pistols prove beyond a sliver-shadow of doubt that nearly everything you may have tuned into before was a sham.

A 40-minute blowtorch, leaving scars that will never heal. May the disfigurement burn its way through to your souls.

OK, so you've got a lot of questions to ask. Why the Lafayette? Why wasn't it publicised? Why was it being allowed? Why did they do it?

It appears the band decided they wanted to play in this country again, seeing as the last time was around four months ago and that had been a one-off gig. 'They came here late last year and really liked the place, so they contacted us and said they wanted to do it again,' reveals George Maddocks, manager of the Lafayette.

But the name couldn't be bandied about for obvious reasons. The born-again-Christian petition mongers would have had a field day if they'd known. So, they chose the Spots – 'Sex Pistols On This Stage' is one local's deciphered version. Make up your own mind, but secrets aren't kept, these days.

The nationals were ringing up a week beforehand for confirmation that their arch-enemies were booked to play. A radio station offered one of the club owners a free American holiday for a knowing nod.

The whole town knew about it on the night – but only on the night, although one guy I spoke to said he'd been told they were playing three weeks back.

'Hey. Just think, I'm actually sitting this close to him. I can't believe it.' Take away three bodies from the plastic lounger and she'd be next to him. No question.

We're in JB's, an aircraft hangar of a club in Dudley, five miles outside Wolverhampton. The band are due to play the Lafayette in an hour. Rotten's hunched up on the floor. Vicious is asleep on another chair. He looks quite cute with his eyes closed. A 15-year old dreaming of hell.

Steve's chatting up a local Richard, and Paul's smiling. Paul seems as much in the dark as anyone else. 'I really dunno what's happening. I dunno if we're supposed to be doing this surprise tour or not.'

He's referring to the top-secret gigs at selected venues round the country, heavily reported in last week's press.

Rotten looks tired. 'I am tired. Heavy night, as usual.'

The same sluggish monotones – Johnny Rotten drools. OK. What about the new album?

'Don't you read your 'Record Mirror'? It's brilliant.'

Did he mean the record or the magazine?

'That's cos it's the Sex Pistols.'

Oh.

'Anything Sex Pistols is brilliant.'

Scandinavia?

'It was boring.'

Nervous?

'Nervous? We ain't rehearsed for this. Straight out of recording studio to gig. Ain't got time to be fucking nervous, mate. It'll be all right.'

To Paul. Is it right Elton John will play Malcolm McLaren in the forthcoming Sex Pistols film?

'I dunno. I dunno anything about the film.'

You get the impression Paul dunno.

Meanwhile their beefy Spartan of a bodyguard is busy vilifying a greasy hip in a trench-coat. 'Can I have your coat? Remember how they all used to wear 'em? They needed 'em, queuing for hours in snow, knee deep, waiting to see Black Sabbath. I betcha did that, eh? I betcha did. Fucking mug.'

The hip ain't bothered none. But Steve loves it.

Right, time to go. I feel like I'm just about to team up with Richard Burton and Clint Eastwood and go where only eagles dare. Outside, a fleet of four motors is waiting to transport the timeless tearaways to the Lafayette.

The queue outside is endless and none of the punters are wearing trench-coats. The rain's falling heavily, dirty Wolverhampton rain that rusts your ears and sends you bald. The band try to push through to the front entrance. No dice. Nobody recognises them. A guy shouts, 'We want Rotten!' and doesn't realise he's standing next to him.

Inside now through a side-entrance. Already serried formation is the order of the night. A lot of people will be turned away. But they expected that anyway. Pessimism abounds when the Pistols play. It's natural.

Layout: tiny stage, rectangle disco floor stained by Donna Summer whinings, carpeted smooch skirting that area, a balcony going all the way round. Easier to sort out a girl that way.

Manchester United are playing Birmingham tomorrow at St Andrews. What better way for a lonely United fan to spend a night in the Black Country than at a Pistols gig? Sure, they steam into a few local punters but it's nothing bad. Just a few too many pints, y'know. Not enough fodder for the nationals. And there's quite a few of them around too, lurking in the shadows. Spot 'em by their grey macs and the press card in their trilbies. Hat-trick Macari might nick some kudos from the weekend but it's nothing to what Rotten will do to them.

Well, you'd better sit back now and listen to this gig. The Pistols have never played better.

Unannounced walk-on.

The crowd surge to the front.

'At least you're having fun for a change,' says Rotten. '*Right, naw! Iyamanantichrist, Iyamananarchiiist…*'

And that's the end of everything. Those opening lines to 'Anarchy In The UK' gunned down an era. From now on there's no looking back. The silky gestures that have enveloped the band are transmuted into diamond-hard endeavour the minute Rotten opens his mouth.

The kids press against the stage. The speakers are rocking. The PA's getting fouled up. The sound is chopping.

'How can I be a star when you all behave like that?' asks Rotten, before launching into 'I Wanna Be Me'.

Ten of them. Ten brooding, Bullworker bouncers materialise between the kids and the band like ugly maids all in a row.

OK, granted they have to protect the sound system, but there's always one, y'know, the King Kong, the tosser who thinks he's the business. He breaks the line and ploughs into the pogo merchants up front with blazing fists. It's totally unnecessary. When the Pistols play you don't protect kids from themselves, you don't protect the band and you definitely don't need the Saturday-night-at-the-movie Rorke's Drifters to look after the PA.

The crowd, spurred on by a pair of balding, barebacked 30-year-olds, pushes forward in retaliation and the guy falls back into the line. It's pandemonium.

Rotten climbs on top of a monitor behind the ten and belches out 'I'm A Lazy Sod'. The crowd starts to leap again but this time the bouncers hold back.

'Looking For Kicks' heralds the beginning of Rotten's stage schizophrenia. 'This one's called 'EMI'.' Lower, 'It's not worth it.'

During the number a guy faints.

'We're the first band in the whole world that's ever had geezers fainting,' proclaims Rotten.

'Holidays In The Sun', a new song from the album.

'Any Wolves supporters out there? ' asks the funny-looking lead singer, who's much taller than he seems. Hand over eyes Indian-scout stance. Lukewarm reaction.

'What about the lads from Manchester?'

'YEAH!'

'I ain't started off a riot, have I?'

Hold on.

Is that…no, it can't be – yes, he is.

He's actually SMILING!

Johnny Rotten smiles – sensation. Maybe he's ill. Or maybe all that spiel he gave a few months back about being there only for the fun was true. Perhaps he *does* enjoy himself. Well, would you credit it? And I thought it was all about pain and depression. Wrong again.

'No Feelings'. There's no better rock guitarist around than Steve Jones at the moment. Those months of intense rehearsing have certainly paid off. Maybe he'll apply for that job in Steve Harley's new band, after all.

'Problems'. Nah, surely not? Everyone loves the Pistols. It's got to the point now where you can't slag them off because they're, like, an institution. And do we need institutions!

'Pretty Vacant'. There's never been such a crowd. 'It's the best show I've ever seen,' observes Rotten, and that's after the second number. It's like watching the dance of death, round and round into the bottomless pool of trance. He can hypnotise them – do you know that? He can stab their minds with his eyes.

And they'll never be the same again.

'God Save The Queen'. Of course there's a future: they're creating one whether they like it or not. After you've disembowelled an entire industry the only direction left to go is up. As long as they never let the sacrificial sword fall from their grasp.

'No Fun'. The obvious encore and a contradiction. It *is* funny, in the best possible way. Rotten smiles because he's happy at the reaction the band get. Christ, the Pope would've been happy with it. When a band plays with such intensity you just know it won't be around for ever and you also know you're a lucky fucker to have warmed your hands at their fire.

That's it. The DJ slides 'Jumping Jack Flash' onto the turntable. A leather-clad kid yawns.

I wish I was a Sex Pistol.

SEPTEMBER 1977

Top Ten singles
beginning of September

1. Float On – The Floaters
2. Angelo – Brotherhood of Man
3. You've Got What It Takes – Showaddywaddy
4. Way Down – Elvis Presley
5. I Feel Love – Donna Summer
6. The Crunch – Rah Band
7. We're All Alone – Rita Coolidge
8. That's What Friends Are For – Deneice Williams
9. Nights On Broadway – Candi Staton
10. Nobody Does It Better – Carly Simon

Top Ten albums
beginning of September

1. All Time Greats – Connie Francis
2. Oxygene – Jean-Michel-Jarre
3. Rumours – Fleetwood Mac
4. A Star Is Born – Soundtrack
5. Elvis Presley's 40 Greatest Hits
6. Moody Blue – Elvis Presley
7. Going For The One – Yes
8. The Johnny Mathis Collection
9. I Remember Yesterday – Donna Summer
10. Rattus Norvegicus IV – the Stranglers

The leaves of brown come tumbling down when Elton John reviews the singles in 'Record Mirror' and says of Generation X's 'Your Generation/Day By Day', 'They've certainly got a lot of energy, but then again, so did Arkle. What a way to start the day. This is really dreadful garbage. It doesn't do anything for me and the Ramones do this sort of thing so much better. I'm all for rock'n'roll but not this. A hit? I can't see Radio 1 playing it. I suppose there's a market for this sort of music – Shepherds Bush market, perhaps. Hear it first thing in the morning and you'd want to go straight back to bed. It's hideously recorded.'

And Marc Bolan tells 'Record Mirror', 'If I was Pete Townsend and saw the Jam I would be staggered.'

And in the same issue the following letter reveals a nation divided.

'We are two musical appreciators of refined taste and broad mindedness. We believe everyone is entitled to their point of view and there's a place in society today for all kinds of music, ranging from classical to punk. Being so open-minded ourselves, we tend to get upset when some jumped-up little toad called Barry Cain has the clot-headedness to mention the late Elvis Presley and some paralytic idiot called Johnny Rotten in the same sentence. We thought it only fair to point out that should Barry by some chance find it fit to leave the mental establishment where he is at present staying and venture down to our neck of the woods he will probably find himself suspended on a rope by the bollocks with his safety-pins and razor blades rammed right up his arse.'
Jack and Jill, Cambridge

XTC, NEW HEARTS, THE MODELS
London

Disillusionment reigns. The season of the queue-wave is upon us. Suckling, talentless bands lining up to be knocked off by record companies scared of missing out, of being regarded as unhip.

So, whaddya get for your money?

You get crap.

One or two exceptions, maybe, but for the most part originality is smothered by a suicidal desire to assimilate everything that has gone before without thinking in terms of *now* and the *future*.

Like fireworks in damp grass.

The 'movement' will splinter and the '77 resurgence will die, if constructive thought is trampled in the rush to sign on the dotted line. Bands are nurturing identities in much the same way as their predecessors – and that isn't what the whole thing was originally about.

Take the other night. Well, perhaps the other night isn't quite a typical example – thanks to XTC. Here, at least, is a band who seem to be thinking, approaching music in an intelligent way without losing the honest thrust that has hitherto pervaded. Now, some may argue that XTC are an art-school band. The Clash went to art school too. XTC have that sharp-featured look so typical in ace young students intent on making the scene. Remember Roxy?

But if anyone can sing 'Fireball XL5' and get away with it they're all right in my book. Their secret? Andy Partridge in a rare tree. Straight out of a Shakespearian tragedy. Short fair hair, breadknife eyes, a Swindon Hamlet with Johnny Staccato style.

I keep thinking I shouldn't like this band, but when they hit numbers like 'Let's Have Fun', 'I'm Bored', 'Spinning Top', 'New Town Animal In A Bird Cage' and 'All Along The Watchtower', you can't help but smile.

Another secret? Barry Andrews on keyboards adds dimension

to the sweatshop skaters. XTC have just signed to Virgin, who have another punk band – their name escapes me. They'll deserve the success coming to them, and from the looks on faces at the Hope & Anchor, that won't be long.

On to the Speakeasy the night after a young kid was stabbed at the bar. Two bands – New Hearts, rumoured to have signed to CBS for some astronomical fee and the Models, who are just coming off Step Forward after a single 'Freeze'.

I'm sorry, I really am. Neither band cuts it. No doubt they mean well. Maybe the Speakeasy's atmosphere – colder than Elvis' Memphis tomb – doesn't help. But both come across as everybody's idea of a punk band and that's a contradiction. Nobody should have an idea, just a feeling.

The New Hearts insult, kick over mike stands, sneer, sing about the usual bland bollocks and get a typical reaction from punters who don't know any better. Result? Zilch. Nothing to offer.

Every movement is a preconceived act of homage to punk. They probably number plastic footmarks among their on-stage equipment.

Models. Static. Blazing blinks. Each member wears a clumsy black-leather jacket that lends nothing to the presentation. Actually, lead guitarist Marco isn't bad, but he's a dead ringer for a production-line American TV comic and incredibly difficult to take seriously. But, then, maybe that's the whole point.

The songs are weak, nothing you haven't heard before. Somebody tells me afterwards that these boys don't sham. 'They are PUNKS and they've been playing this stuff for ages.'

I remain totally unconvinced. Like New Hearts, the Models have a long way to go in the credibility stakes.

I guess there's always Gary Glitter.

In the face of these sub-standard, brainless bands with nothing to offer, I come to the conclusion that punk was only ever about five bands; anything after them is forever doomed to be a shadow-basker. The Pistols, the Stranglers, The Clash, the Jam and The Damned are all that really matter. The rest are away from the numbers.

Aren't they?

But what about the Buzzcocks? The new Messiahs or Freddie and the Dreamers?

I journey north with publicist Alan Edwards where he will famously piss on the Rovers Return in a glorious act of anarchic symbolism – but mainly because he was dying to go and there are no toilets at the 'Corrie' local.

The Buzzcocks live in glorious Victorian squalor.

First, the gig…

THE BUZZCOCKS
The Rafters, Manchester

A Manchester miasma causing GBH to the nostrils, or one of the best damned bands the rainy city has produced since the Hollies?

Of course it's unthinkable that two such theories could couple and produce the ultimate in miscegenation. Then again…

Adrift on a sweaty sea in Rafters. Beams criss-crossing amiably above your head, glee photos of Vince Hill dotted round the bar, chivs up the back, nerve ends down the front and a ping-pogo frenzy firmly embedded in the minds of every Buzzcocks troubleshooter.

Thursday night and it's raining. It's always fucking raining. Rafters, now well into its Thursday-night-is-punk-night season, presents the city's current saviours headed by one Pete Shelley, no relation, an unobtrusive little chappie with a nursery-book voice.

The band also boasts Steve Diggle, guitar, John Maher, drums and Garth, who bears a quaint resemblance to the comic-strip hero of the same name on bass.

The Buzzcocks are no baby-face newcomers – their songs have five o'clock shadows. Strange Shelley vocals sliding through a latticework of riffs like a blob of quicksilver negotiating a maze. 'Boredom', 'Love

Battery', 'Breakdown'. It's not a London sound anymore.

Stop Press: the Buzzcocks have just signed a record deal with United Artists. Poor sods.

And then the interview...

THE BUZZCOCKS
Manchester

I sang of the dancing stars,
I sang of the daedal Earth,
And of Heaven – and the giant-wars,
And Love, and Death, and Birth, –
And then I changed my pipings
Shelley (not Pete)

So what do you sing about when the objects of your frustrations are clinically removed and replaced with a foam-rubber life-style with a built-in guarantee to cushion any future fall?

The new substance bands adopted an iron stance that was bound to rust when the death card, Success, came a-knocking like Interflora. No more dole queues, no more squats, no more hunger. No more turmoil. Just fun, fortune, fame and a well-manicured screw-you scowl.

Sure, it's a dilemma. Their credibility is at stake. And if it's not causing them sleepless nights now they deserve a butcher's shop fate.

'There are still a lot of bands turning out Clash mentality,' says Pete Shelley. 'Third-fourth-fifth-sixth-seventh generation bands who are not changing from the originals because they thought that was what the whole thing was about.

'When groups sang of life on the road they were singing from experience. But now it's different.'

Pete pours another coffee from a silver pot in the lounge of one of those jacket-and-tie-only-at-dinner hotels at the heart of every

British city. It's a far cry from the dismal squat the band inhabit on the outskirts of Manchester, home of Shelley and the Buzzcocks. Pete still looks out of place, but maybe it won't be too long before it all comes natural.

'I mean, how can you sing about things like that, sitting in a hotel like this after a night in a four-poster?' That's Garth, guitarist and newest member of the band.

Pete continues: 'Song-writing is an outlet. A way of getting an opinion or feeling into a form which you can present to people. It's the same with all struggling artists. If I could draw I'd be a painter. If I could act I'd be on the stage. There's no more to music. It's very serious when people are expressing themselves. And with this whole new set-up I feel people have simply read the wrong things into it. If I write a song about my dole-queue experiences…'

'It would fill a double album,' Garth interjects

'It's because I want people to know about it,' continues Pete, ignoring the jibe. 'If I write about falling in love it's just how it seems to me. If you look at a painting by Van Gogh you can say either it looks pretty or it means something. He didn't want us to say 'pretty picture', he wanted to get an idea across. If you can see the feelings and sentiments behind it you'll feel more in touch with the picture and appreciate it more.'

The only time Pete was on the dole was by choice. He dropped out of college while studying electronics and started playing guitar, eventually forming a band with Howard Devoto. It folded after one rehearsal.

A while later Pete and Howard went to London for the day and picked up a copy of 'Time Out', which advertised one of the early Pistols' gigs. 'If you want a good buzz, cock, go along,' said the magazine.

'So we went along. It was a knockout and I thought, If they can do it why can't we? It was just so great to see somebody doing exactly what they wanted without a care in the world.'

So another band was born, this time with John Maher on drums and Steve Diggle on bass. Later, Howard left and Garth joined.

Now the picture is complete and Manchester will have its first punk combo with any modicum of success. The Buzzcocks have just signed a deal with United Artists after shrewdly shopping around and privately releasing the EP *Spiral Scratch*, which sold 10,000 copies. Red, blood-red rosy-nail-varnish future.

Pete talks like he's reading you a bedtime story and is frightened of waking the neighbours. And he sings like that too. Very much the negative narrator. In fact, the Buzzcocks are a negative band. They seem to go out of their way to present this image on stage, like they're being manipulated by an off-stage ventriloquist. Indifference reigns, and it works perfectly. Shy, fiddly, scratchy, clumsy, unsure, pent-up potency, nose-picking charm, cocksure originality.

Maybe that's what Mancunians are like. 'There's certainly more of a close community up here,' says Garth. 'Everybody's doing their part in the music scene. Anyone who can't play writes. That's very important.'

'But we still get more than our fair share of poseurs,' adds Pete. 'And the frightening thing is you can't tell them from the real people. They're the ones who get the punk plan from the 'Daily Mirror''.

'They throw the beer and spit while you're playing,' says Garth.

'They think they've got to adopt a totally different stance by jumping up and down and wearing leather jackets – especially when cameras are around.'

Could be it's just the boredom the 'Cocks so dutifully sing about. I can remember when bands vilified an audience that didn't jump up and down. Now they complain about the beer and spit. Dry nights are no fun. But that doesn't make them the devil's own children, as the vicar said on a Manchester TV programme. Pete happened to be on the panel of a tea-time chat show when this pew-pusher laid into punks saying they needed to let Jesus into their hearts.

'He hadn't done a gig for a long time,' quips Garth.

The vicar said punks were on the road to eternal damnation if they died with safety-pins stuck through their ears. 'This annoyed me,' says Pete. 'I thought it was very wrong of the guy to say you can't be religious just because you like a certain type of music. So I said, 'I'm a Christian' and the programme finished. And now I'm branded a Christian everywhere I go and, honest, I ain't that religious.'

I guess not. But then again, neither is Jimmy Pursey.

This is a guy determined to crack it. I'd never heard of him when he started ringing me at 'Record Mirror' and saying his band were more exciting than a dozen Clashes. I thought he was a crank, but sweet.

SHAM 69
Roxy, London

Shazam '77!

The antediluvian ideals of the pig-gutted swirl are in the process of a distortion that any blank-eyed chameleon would be proud of. Like we ain't getting what our readies craved in those blanched-out days before RCD (that's record-company deal, honey).

Then a geezer like Jimmy Pursey comes along. Worldly näive, full of wide-eyed assurance, a shelter in a bombed-out town. And the funny thing is, Jimmy is totally sincere, having a devout faith in his existentialist stance. But he's in no more control of his future than a puppy in a pet shop window.

Sham 69 will be big. Take my word for it. Deservedly so? Natch. Sincerity should always be rewarded. Sham pump glucose into London's Roxy club, the one that's been in a coma since February – I counted 25 people in the audience – with all the finesse of a bucking cannon. New bands have had nine months of tuition in the art of seduction followed by a course of contrived breadline bondage.

But the rot is already setting in. A deal with Polydor will lift the band out of the pram-pushing stakes and straight into gilt-edged Mothercare security. Songs like 'Ulster Boy', 'Borstal Breaker',

'Rich Kid', and 'Fuck All' will be chanted in council-block terraces by stone-stare kids swamped by graffiti. And Jimmy and Co will be worlds apart.

So it all smacks of pessimism on a tired old writer's part. So what? Sham mean well, but it's leading everyone up the garden path, including themselves.

Good luck, Jim. You don't need it.

I'm a big fan of The Boys but they should stick a beach in there somewhere and sing 'I Get Around'. I take a slow ferry to Holland at their invitation.

THE BOYS
Amsterdam and Groningen

OI! All you riff raffers looking for a £1 note by scraping at the dirt in the cracks between the pavements with your carefully manicured fingernails! All you mugs actually believing your own wasteland dreams, smothered by your own doctrines, creating your own little sweetshop world! Johnny Rotten or what?

You belong in that Sargasso Sea of petrified makeshift bands since you've got nothing we want. When the floods came the polystyrene ark could only take five bands – Pistols, Clash, Stranglers, Jam and Damned. The rest drowned. Now the rain's getting heavy again and the boat, like the bitch, is back. Four more to tackle the (new) waves. Climb aboard Sham 69, XTC, the Buzzcocks and The Boys. The rest can go take a shower.

The 'Boy's Own' world is nothing like the comic with its chunks of words and paucity of pictures. If anything, the band are more like the Victor, complete with Alf Tupper and Co.

At the moment, they are holed up in a Transit in the middle of Amsterdam looking for a circus tent. So far, they've been stripped by the Customs men of Sheerness who found many nasty things but nothing they could nick them for. They were also responsible for inciting a riot on the Flying Dutchman ferry coming over.

'We played in Holland only last week,' says pianist Casino Steel, a Norwegian who fled his homeland. 'We'd never have come back but we needed the money.'

Three of the band also lost their dough on the ferry's gaming table. When you're only on 20 quid a week that's bad news. 'If you don't arrive skint in Holland you're a poof,' says Honest John Plain. 'If you don't play the card table you're a poof. There are at least two poofs in The Boys, so what the hell?' Difficult to see if Honest John's eyes are laughing behind his ever-present shades.

Jack Black, drummer straight out of the Scabies stumbling-sycophant school, makes a rare speech: 'The Boys challenge any band to a game of five-a-side football, cards, pool, pinball, you name it. But in the rare event that we lose, can we pay you back on Friday?' Breathless, he's quiet for the rest of the journey.

The van pulls up outside a huge marquee erected in the middle of a park. Inside, girls dressed in extremes – jeans they've been shoehorned into or evening dresses. The guys look like lunching bank employees on a hot day. They ooze money. Where else would you find someone dropping grass all over the floor while rolling a joint and not bothering to retrieve it? The circus tent sure doesn't need a sideshow with a bunch like this. And then The Boys saunter onstage.

Now, in case you haven't sussed, The Boys are one of those rare bands with any real talent doing the springboard-gig rounds. Their songs have the kind of terse instability a psychoanalyst would have orgasms over and they're delivered in an effervescent, face-flannelling way.

Their first single 'I Don't Care', did a midnight stroll last April and was little more than an exercise in sign-there-and-release-this crass ignorance. But the follow-up, 'First Time', is a classic.

Kid Reid, a chemistry degree down the chute, stands up front swamped by his bass. Looks like he's taking the night off from his O level studies and at first he seems as out of place as the hairless knee poking through his black leather trousers. Until he opens his mouth. The Kid kids no more. He's flanked by the chewing stagnation of Honest John on rhythm and sole-flasher Matt Dangerfield on lead. Casino is slightly lost side-stage and Jack's doing what Jack does best at the back.

'Sick On You' leads off. It's also the opener on the new album. In fact, openers don't come any better. That segues into 'I Call Your Name' and you realise that Lennon, intolerably indolent at the time, never pumped the song with enough self-indulgent teen-pain like these do.

The Boys don't hesitate to admit their influences but they don't rely on them. Thus, an undeniable stamp on each number. Dangerfield and Steel have a penchant for writing tongue-in-cheek pubescent pop songs. Hence 'Living In The City', 'Cop Cars', 'Tenement Kid', and 'Kiss Like A Nun'.

The Dutch kids snort every number and that makes them dance. Not your maladjusted kind but in orderly hokey-cokey (plenty of that) circles. No way do they know what it's all about but the sweatfret kids get to their soles.

'First Time' is played twice. Magic. Dee Dee Ramone rang the band from the States and said the record was never off his turntable. It epitomises just about every torment a soaking-wet puppy-love mind has ever flip-flopped over.

Another Beatles run-out in the encore, 'Boys', and back to the Transit.

Noctivagant enlightenment in the red-light district. It comes in handy for Casino earlier in the day and he thinks he's in love.

John wrote 'First Time' and it seems inconceivable it was his virgin stab. His second is another gem, 'USI'. 'I hate everybody in this band,' he says. 'I'm just waiting to make my mark, for people to recognise just how talented I am. In fact, if any band's looking for a rhythm guitarist, I can be contacted at Castelain Road, Maida Vale, London, W9.'

The next day finds the band back in the van on the way to Groningen for their third Dutch gig.

So why isn't 'First Time' the biggest punkeen hit of the year? I mean, wouldn't it be great if everything went like (rock around the) clockwork. Did you see the movie on TV last week? A band playing 'new' music spotted by a receding straight with a 'You drive the strawberries wild' line in chat-ups. 'You kids will go far,' he tells Bill Haley, who actually looks like his dad. Barring one or two laconic love complications, the Comets' rise to stardom takes about as long as Haley does to lacquer his kiss curl.

Yeah, great if it was like that. But it's not.

Manager Ken Mewis, who's just been told by a stoned Dutchman he looks wrecked enough to be a manager, explains what happened: 'We signed with NEMS after they saw us play at Dingwalls. It was a cheap contract – a grand in fact – and the band used all the money on new equipment. NEMS have a distribution deal with RCA which has run into one or two problems. Result – 'First Time' has suffered.

'The song is far and away the biggest thing NEMS have had for a long time and they should have put everything behind it,' interrupts Reid. 'Now RCA ain't pressing many copies because they're too busy making Elvis records.'

'NEMS never got us many gigs. We got taken in by them because they bought us drinks at Dingwalls,' says a bitter Mewis. 'When we go to them for money there's always somebody who's on holiday. And all we've got to show for it is a single that went in at 84 with a bullet.'

'The publicity campaign for the record lasted just one week,' protests Black.

Dangerfield brings the subject to a close: "The more you get to know the record business the more you realise it stinks.'

Meanwhile, roadie Alan Anger watches the flat Dutch landscape cruise by. Water-fingers poking the coast. An all-embracing wetness pervades, and even the Dutch sun is damp. Alan decides he fancies a dip. 'The best place will be where the most fish are. Fish know about water.'

The band crease up.

Honest John talks about Alf Tupper. You must remember him. He was the guy in the Victor who never let a goal in, regularly bowled out an entire cricket side in ten balls and never lost a mile race – even though he used to arrive after it had started and ran in his hobnailed boots.

'He was always frowned on by his colleagues, all called Cecil. But he won out in the end.'

John's convinced that every comic-book hero since Tupper is really him in disguise. 'He was just too good to fade away. Anyone who trains on fish and chips is OK by me.' The Tupper psychology really gets to the Leeds-born guitarist that night. He ploughs into cod and chips twice.

Here's your chance to explain to all those 'Record Mirror' readers out there why The Boys ricky-tick-tick. Don't blow your credibility.
Jack: 'We write really good pop songs. Any band could use our songs and get away with it. I don't wanna be a flash drummer; the best ones are the simple ones.'
Kid: 'We just write about what happens to us. Nobody has seen the half of us yet because we're only just feeling our muscles. We've already got enough material for another album and musically it'll be totally different from this one. We don't care about what's punk – we care about what's us.'
Casino: 'Our main aim is to have fun. We don't intend to be political and we ain't stuck in one musical vein. We don't struggle to progress. It all happens naturally, and we certainly don't consciously strive for an identity.'
Matt: 'Sooner or later we're gonna be big. We're more adventurous than most other bands mainly because we're not limited to just one writer. Our only problem now is we've completely lost confidence in our record company and that's so frustrating. We're a sporting band.'
John: 'We're just five unprofessional kids who are getting more professional all the time.'

Nearly all the new bands keep recycling the same spew-spiel. A definite nick for causing malicious wounding to the brain.

But The Boys don't punish ears mercilessly with all the world-in-the-palm-of-our-hands shit. The band are as straight as the bottoms of their strides, as this Honest John quote typifies: 'I'm sick and tired of waking up in the mornings with birds who've got safety-pins in their noses.'

In Groningen they slaughter the audience with a gilt-edged set that sends two pigskin minds crazy, splintering chairs across the stage.

One criticism: Kid's inane intro to each number. Certainly unnecessary, very embarrassing and totally out of keeping with the band's personality. Kid is an intense little guy, obviously concerned about his character-building exercises. 'I'm homesick,' he intimates to Mewis after the gig. No matter. Energy and talent are two attributes already under his belt.

During the long wait for the encore, Jack nosedives into the ultra-heavy Dutchmen who are on the edge of berserkerama. Super-hero Jack Black retreats to the dressing room for a swift beer.

So, that's The Boys' world. A world of chips, ice-cream cornets, chocolate bars, meat pies and devastating gigs. Just buy their album, it's a killer.

If Alf Tupper had ever recorded an album it would have sounded like The Boys.

Alas, the band never manage to crack the big time and will go the way of the 'Victor'. They will re-form in the late Nineties and re-release some of their early albums, managing to sell 30,000 records in Japan. It's a strange world. Their big-living manager, Ken Mewis, will die of lung cancer in 2002.

The new new wave are pumping iron mercilessly. Some weeks I see a different band every night and none of them shakes my tree like The Clash in Paris or the Pistols in Wolverhampton.

Some of them are not that new – The Boys are the only British punk band to have a record deal in January '77. A handful are good but most are as predictable as the third shag in a night of shags. The first-shag excitement gene belongs to the Famous Five and

The Heartbreakers, but they're the Stones and The Who, the Small Faces and Hendrix, the Doors and the Beatles, Elvis and Motown. Punk has piss-all to do with it any more. The Famous Five – not The Heartbreakers – have climbed off that particular gravy train and headed for their own personal 'Ah! Bisto' utopias.

Oh, bondage, up yours.

It's what pop music is about after all – but you've still got to be good. And if you can't be good, be careful. And if you can't be careful, then put away that axe, Eugene, and piss off.

That's what I feel like saying every time a PR rings up and asks me to go and see a new band. But the PRs are all so nice and I'm a sucker for a sweet voice and a pretty face.

OCTOBER 1977

Top Ten singles
beginning of October

1.   Way Down – Elvis Presley
2.   Silver Lady – David Soul
3.   Magic Fly – Space
4.   Oxygene – Jean Michele-Jarre
5.   Down Deep Inside – Donna Summer
6.   Telephone Man – Meri Wilson
7.   Best Of My Love – Emotions
8.   Black Is Black – La Belle Epoque
9.   From New York to LA – Patsy Gallant
10. Sunshine After The Rain – Elkie Brooks

Top Ten albums
beginning of October

1.   20 Golden Greats – Diana Ross & The Supremes
2.   Oxygene – Jean Michele-Jarre
3.   Moody Blue – Elvis Presley
4.   A Star Is Born – Soundtrack
5.   Rumours – Fleetwood Mac
6.   Show Some Emotion – Joan Armatrading
7.   Best Of Frankie Laine
8.   Going For The One – Yes
9.   20 All Time Greats – Connie Francis
10. Exodus – Bob Marley & The Wailers

I ask for opinions from the permanent waves for a feature I'm writing on David Bowie.

Joe Strummer: 'David Bowie? I haven't got a very good memory. The first thing that comes to mind is he's got a great snare drum-sound on *Low*. What he makes is decadent disco music – he sure ain't rock'n'roll. The best thing he ever did was 'Get Off The Phone Henry' – or was it called 'Suffragette City'? I suppose he's contributed something. I dunno, I never raved about him.'

Johnny Rotten: 'He was good for a while but you couldn't really get into it because you didn't believe he was doing what he believed in.'

Hugh Cornwell: 'His head is where his new album's at. *Low* is quite a progression. Let's see what his *Heroes* tribute's gonna be all about.'

Paul Weller: 'He's the most inventive artist of the Seventies.'

As a result of action taken by the Belgian travel services, 60,000 copies of the picture bag of the Sex Pistols single 'Holidays In The Sun' are taken by court order from the Virgin offices. It's alleged that the artwork constituted a breach of copyright of the Belgian Travel Services summer holiday brochure.

SHAM 69
West End

Rooftop rumblings in West One.

George Davis Is Innocent.

And with that Jimmy Pursey leaps off the dross heap into the Wurlitzer world of stardom via a twisted arm, courtesy of the fuzz, and a slam-bam prison cell.

Sham 69 are celebrating a record deal with Polydor by holding an impromptu gig on the roof of the Vortex 24-hour coffee bar just off Oxford Street.

Coincidentally (yeah) that very same future domain of true-blue rock insomniacs and speedo merchants also opens on the same day – two bites of the proverbial cherry pie.

About 30 people join Sham on the slates while a large crowd gather below, comprising lunch-box secretaries, pewko punks and automaton tourists.

'There's gonna be a Borstal breakout,' sings Jimmy as the meat-wagon threnody spirals ever nearer from three streets away.

'What 'ave we got? Fuck-all!' chant the band, as the first blue-helmeted warrior appears 50 feet up. 'What's going on here then?'

'What 'ave we got? Fuck-all!' replies young Jim, and the copper pulls the plugs out.

Jimmy puts them back in.

The copper looks stunned. 'Right, er, you wait.'

Jimmy peers over the top of the building. 'What have we got?'

A few 'Fuck-all's.'

'D'ya want me to stop singing?'

A resounding 'No!' Pantomime was never like this. A thousand little Jimmy Purseys in the sanguine eyes of an amused mob and not one of them the right one.

Enter a sergeant with a little more experience in these 'Let It Be' moments. 'All right son. Pack it in. Everybody off the roof.'

'George Davis is innocent,' shouts Jimmy.

The police are clearly not very appreciative of that sentiment. He refuses to get down so they grab him. Maybe he's manhandled a little too strongly. 'Get some fucking pictures of this,' he screams, as a Fleet Street flasher closes in for the kill.

'Right, you're nicked,' and off they all drive into a wild blue yonder. Meanwhile two guys just behind where the band had played repeat 'Sham 69, Sham 69,' in typical three-card-trick fashion.

You must know the three-card-trick technique. An East End spiv pitches a table in the West End in close proximity to a bunch of babbling tourists. He produces three playing cards, one of which is the queen of spades, displays them to the thickening crowd and places them face down in a line on the table. He then asks someone to find the lady.

A guy – a plant of course – comes up, says very loudly, 'Oh, yes, I'll have some of that," lays 20 quid on one of the face-down cards. Surprise, surprise, he comes up trumps and walks away with a fistful of notes. He persuades a few mugs nearby – 'Nothing to it. You have a go." They do and invariably lose. Candy from a baby.

Those two guys on that roof remind me of that particular grift, only their queen of spades is Sham 69. The whole thing smacks of contrivance, a cheap escapade in the halls of shallow publicity, a desperate attempt to grab a fast buck.

Jimmy hasn't got that much to do with it – he's too pie-in-the-sky sure of his convictions. The ex greyhound-bollock squeezer and his boys don't need to resort to such tactics to get their name bandied about.

I suppose you could say the whole thing is a bit of a giggle. But getting nicked is no fun – Jimmy is eventually charged with criminal damage.

I don't see those two Sham 69 slogan-pushers getting nicked. They're soon off when the law arrives.

OK, let's go back a few weeks. Sham have just played a set at the Vortex. The skinheads are out in force from Islington, Lewisham and Hammersmith. They follow the band around like they're Arsenal.

Only difference is, Sham 69 never play away. Whenever Sham

gig, the skinheads take over, their cheap-shirted shoulders ousting the chic, man-about-town, debonair punks off the dancefloor.

'It's really great to be fighting to get somewhere,' says Jimmy. 'But now things are starting to happen, I dunno. When we were struggling I used to think they were real hard times. But I'll tell you something – they were better than they are now.'

Jimmy's not far from being hailed as a star in the scorpion Strummer/Rotten sense. It's been a long time coming. For over a year he's pummelled his head to get Sham's name known, to no avail. Then a couple of good reviews and everyone wants to know.

As he eats, his mini-Denis-Healey eyebrows bounce up and down. A filter-tip of a head on a long, lean body. He definitely looks the part.

'See, there's pressures on me now. Pressures for me to be something. And that's just like going back to work again. But a lot of kids are getting enjoyment out of us. They're the same kids that go and watch a match on a Saturday afternoon. People think we encourage them to fight. No way.

'Listen, if you have a knuckle and you win you enjoy it. But if you get your head kicked in you ain't too keen on doing it again.

'I think everyone should have a good kicking 'cos from then on they're gonna think twice before they have another go. But when they do they'll put everything into it. And the same applies to the band. Once you've had a good kicking at the start you don't care afterwards what you say. I just speak the truth.'

Watching Sham 69 is a total experience. A lot of people bottle out and retreat to the bar when the band gets on-stage because of Jimmy's rag-wringing stance and the antics of the crop-crappers up front. Grown men have been known to break down and cry.

'I enjoy getting on stage and slagging everything off. I don't worry about anybody any more.'

He's choked with the way the music scene's going. 'The whole punk thing was great at first because it shocked people. Not any more. The only thing that shocks me now is going down the Kings Road and seeing strides for 30 quid. The shock's in your pocket. Rich kids wanna look poor, poor kids wanna look rich. Poor kids earn their forties and fifties a week and they want to look real smart. But the rich ones get their dough from their mums and dads. Why should they care? It's not that I've got anything against the material side of it, it's just that the rich look down on the poor.

'As for all that heavy ethnic reggae stuff you keep hearing so much about – it's crap. I could do that reggae in my back garden. It's hip to like it but it's certainly nothing to do with what I'm about. Just 'cos Rotten or Strummer say they like it everybody has to follow. All I'm saying is, think for yourself.' He bangs a pointed finger at the side of his head as he splashes the last sentence.

There's a fan-belt urgency in everything he says. The day he needs an oil change is the day he'll die.

'It's going wrong because where we set out initially to create a movement the bands now are creating themselves. And the new bands are simply cashing in on what's gone before. Sham 69 want to take the glory away from bands who play simply for the sake of it. If it don't come from the heart don't do it. The songs I write are things I've personally experienced. People say to me I don't provide any answers. I tell them I simply show what's going wrong. I'm in no position to give answers. I'm no leader. I'm a human being.'

Probably a lot more human than most. When he speaks you feel that any minute the tears will come flooding out. He firmly believes in the entire Pursey philosophy to a nutcrusher extent.

'Take Victorian times. When somebody said they loved you they really meant it. How many people say that now, and if they do how many mean it? These days, you can't be sure that your wife ain' t nipping into bed with every Tom, Dick and Harry while you're at work.

'What does Lou Reed know about life?'

And then you start thinking his sentences aren't actually that uncoordinated. He can't control his gushing.

'I get worse and worse by trying to get something out of my system. My brain's getting eaten away. Like with the government, it doesn't matter who's in, I just want to get a shotgun and shoot the lot.

'We need leaders to be the same as us. They ain't got one idea between them. Maybe we should have leaders on a monthly basis. They're issued with a certain job and when that's done another geezer takes over. You can't call the government a load of crap in Russia – they'll shoot you. And people say Communism works.

'I always wanted to be somebody. After coming off the dog track, where I used to handle the greyhounds, I'd sit in the boozer and voice my opinion like anyone else, and now I'm voicing my opinion on stage within the framework of rock'n'roll.

'I just wanna make enough dough to look after myself and take my bird out for a good time. That's all. If it starts getting too much, and I realise I'm losing track of myself, I'll get out and find a place where nobody's gonna tell me what to do. Just me and my close friends.'

And the odd greyhound bollock.

Jimmy blows it a few years later when, on the brink of considerable stardom, he makes an ill-advised appearance on a kids' TV show and comes across as a complete dick – which he isn't. He never really recovers and Sham 69 break up after their fourth album. Jimmy works with Steve and Paul from the Pistols. He even collaborates with Peter Gabriel on the single 'Animals Have More Fun'. After a couple of resurrections Sham 69 get their first hit single since 1980 with a revamp of 'Hurry Up Harry' for the 2006 World Cup.

RADIATORS FROM SPACE
TV Tube Heart album review

A few months back this band released a single called 'Television Screen' that has since been hailed by 'Rolling Stone' as the best song, along with 'Pretty Vacant', to come out of the whole punk fing. Don't know about that, but it was a definite runny-nosed gem, whip lashing all the prerequisite snot nodules into lunar orbit.

I'm gonna smash my Telecaster through the television screen, 'cos I don't like what's going down

But it met with spectacular indifference and faded into alive alive-oh ambiguity. *TV Tube Heart*, however, more than lives up to the promise of that single and in many cases transcends it.

The Radiators are a Dublin band with treblin' talent. Since their inception they've had to rely on the junk-level second-handness of the English birth-right bands – odd records, odd reviews – while at the same time nurturing a distinctive Irish identity. Their condemnations can't include the northern catastrophe, and Dublin is a placid, verdant little town. Dilemma? Nope, because the one thing that deserves vilifying is the media.

This whole album is a concerted attack on Irish institutions like the 'Sunday World' – 'Are you getting it every Sunday?' – RNE, MTV. But don't worry kids, it's far from being oyster-isolated: the band's individual approach to each number makes *TV Tube Heart* universal. We can all identify with their grievances even if one or two fall into gaping näivety.

Erstwhile lead singer Steve Rapid took a back seat for personal reasons, but after I'd seen the band live in Ireland I thought that he'd never really connected. No matter. He's in the shadows, and that leaves Phil Chevron and Pete Holidai, guitars and vocals, Mark Megaray and the predictably named James Crash, drums.

Together they stumble, tumble and rumble into wickerworks like 'Enemies', 'Press Gang', 'Prison Bars', 'Blitzing At The Ritz' – *'Don't believe in the military, shoot them down with our terrorist guitars'*. Once they purge themselves of such hippiedom hopscotch they'll be a better band.

THE DEPRESSIONS

Speakeasy

'Listen, these boys have had it really tough. They've all been brought up on council estates in Brighton.'

Wow, my heart really bleeds, must've been hard, paddling in the winter. That was the Depressions manager, incidentally, after he'd heard there was a none-too-favourable review of his boys in last week's 'Record Mirror'. The review stated that the band used to be called Tongue and played heavy rock before signing on to the punk idiom with dyed-blond aggression and a banal line in socio-syncopation.

The Depressions are like cod-liver oil, hard to swallow. But if they sincerely (friends) believe in what they're singing, that sincerity is swamped by moronic sneers and carefully choreographed energy. Shame, because the band are no mugs when it comes to playing – a tightness rarely found on spit stage '77.

But eye-patches and black roots are no substitute for genuine, honest-to-goodness spontaneity. 'Honestly, everything I sing about actually happened to me. I ain't gonna try and change your views about us but we ain't shamming,' says guitarist Dave Barnard.

He's a nice feller. I'm still unconvinced.

They are all nice fellers, these splashes on the second wave, but the ill-fitting trousers and disingenuous lyrics smack of too little, too late. It's a road to nowhere, and I'm on it with them.

But sometimes you find a side turning...

L.A.M.F. ALBUM REVIEW
The Heartbreakers

You've got to get some gum first. Size of a table-tennis ball, stomach pink and icky-sticky. Pulverise it between those white pulp machines of yours good and soft. Then you gotta blow. A big, fat, Billy Bunter blow, and watch the bubble grow with cross-eyed delight. Then SPLAT!

You're in a heartbreak world full of gimmee-gimmee-gimmee,

primeval Johnny geetar breaks and the pockmark pangs of teen dreams. Every copy of 'L.A.M.F.' – and if you don't know what that means by now, brother, I really don't know where you been hanging out this past year – should include a stick of gum because juicy fruit it certainly is.

The Heartbreakers rip the atom-heart mother outta rock'n'roll' like they got a contract on its futile life. Comparisons? Naw, the Thunders' goggle gang got a league of their own full of baseball caps and numbered shirts. Live, they have an irrational transience, the breaking up of a cloud leaving a blue smirky grin. They knock out the songs with bacon-slice regularity – a definite beginning, explicit exposition and threadbare end.

On vinyl you have to imagine them live. That's no criticism. That's magic.

Thunders and Walter Lure have the kind of tacit understanding you find only in 'Batman' comics, hauling each other out of fiery traps with undeniable skill.

Billy Rath, bass, and Jerry Nolan, drums, bask in their shadows, providing the Fort Knox safe foundations. They're like heavies looking after their boys. Transfusion City.

An innocent derision pervades 'L.A.M.F.' – Johnny in the role of Wrigley kid taking off his rose-coloured glasses.

So 'Pirate Love' – *I never EVER needed it so bad* – 'Get Off The Phone', 'One Track Mind' – '*I got tracks on my arms and tracks on my face.*'

The miss of the year, 'Chinese Rocks', is regurgitated in all its squalid splendour – '*The plaster's falling off the wall, And my girlfriend's crying in the shower stall.*'

There's the succulently slow 'It's Not Enough', which sees Johnny sliding along his stem like a stoned gondolier on a Venetian beano. There's a duffer, 'Goin' Steady', not that there's any fault in the song, no, siree. It falls down on the mix, swamped by a gargantuan bass. The overall production is distinctly dodgy but buy it and you, too, can set the Reichstag alight.

It's like the guy says at the end: – 'Is that awlright?'

It sure is, Johnny. It sure is.

THE HEARTBREAKERS
Middlesbrough, Edinburgh

A mist. A moor mist, a molten mist, a Scotch mist obscures the three pissing figures to the point at which they bear a brief similarity to victims on an over-enthusiastic dissector's chopping block...

The treble-fountain sound of liquid colliding with damp grass becomes the only confirmation of their presence.

In the background a sheep moos. In the coach Siouxsie giggles. In the sepulchral distance a car stirs. In the sky a bird laughs. In the engine there's a phantom knock. In Gayle's head there's an image of an empty Edinburgh record shop. In the earth a worm smirks. In Alan's stomach a demon-hugging burp is conceived and born.

In the morning...

In the meantime the three figures, shakity-shake-shake, return, coughing windbreakers out of every orifice.

Surfbreakers on the shore, Heartbreakers on the moor.

It's an unlikely setting for an alfresco slash.

Even more unlikely when you consider the slashers are celebrated Noo Yawk mavericks Billy Rath, Walter Lure and little Johnny Thunders. But strange things happen when a band like The Heartbreakers take to the highways and byways of Britain.

It's difficult to write about the disparate airy elements that make up The Heartbreakers. 'Insular' and 'closed shop' immediately spring to mind. They don't go out of their way to be inaccessible – it's just that the sprawling urban conurbations of London and New York spawn opposites and it's difficult to find any common ground on which to take off.

Friction, whether it's of the supercilious kind or firmly embedded in some crazy past, is always apparent within the band. This has led to the departure of drummer Jerry Nolan, although, bizarrely, for this tour anyway, he's been retained as a hired musician.

Difficult to know if they're ever serious about their anger. Maybe it's just because they're Yanks. Maybe it's just because they're a rock band. Maybe it's just to relieve the black cloud of boredom that hangs over them as they travel from gig to gig.

A few months back they were all gushingly homesick. But when they were told to get out of the country by the Home Office they returned to New York and found they missed GB. Visa problems solved, they couldn't wait to come back.

Well, music is what it's all about. You don't get no politico palpitations from The Heartbreakers.

So, we're on this coach along with Siouxsie and the Banshees and the Models somewhere in the Scottish Highlands. The coach has a car engine and it's spluttering. On schedule it ain't. The trip is three-time tiresome and it's pause for dozing. Half-sleep produces the grandest illusions. First the immediate surroundings are intensified, the whiz-past scenery no longer holds any interest and dim mind scenes unravel a tangibility...

At Middlesbrough Town Hall a drunk weaves in and out the crowd, laughing to himself and spilling beer from the glass in his intermittently shaking hand. He stops to gurgle at various individuals who attract him, creases up and runs back into the audience.

What's that copy of 'Teenage Romance' doing ripped up on the floor?

'Got a cigarette, Johnny? Say, those curtains are gold.'

Marco from the Models reads a book. He looks bored.

There's spit in the air, spit in the hair, spit in the lair of The Heartbreakers. Then there's this sound of sirens growing louder. Police-car sirens first, then air-raid sirens, then the sound of marching feet, then a heavy-metal German voice. *Der Füehrer*! His hard, shifting tones incite the windswept German youth.

Then straight into 'Chatterbox'...

'*Hey!*'

'What?'

'Wake up and look at the cows.'

Sure enough, the coach has been detained yet again by a bunch of cosy cows. They've been milked and are obviously happy at the prospect of a dry day in the fields.

Middlesbrough. Oh, yeah. Yeah.

Back. 'Pirate Love'. The kids are standing on chairs, tables, one another to catch a glimpse of Thunders's snake mouth, of Lure's acid eyes. Johnny tells the kids it ain't cool to spit and heads for the hills on 'Let's Go'. A white splat of gob lands on his jacket as he sings...

In some Heartbreaker Hotel outside Middlesbrough, Johnny pouts that mouth in a look of incredulity. 'Naw, I ain't all that happy at the moment. Christ, I'm looking for a drummer.

'See,' he pours another brandy from the miniature, 'Rat Scabies didn't really fit in when he came to audition. Sure, he's a good drummer, a good rock drummer, but he can't play rock 'n' roll. He broke into 'Toad' half-way through one of our numbers.'

The hotel porter is getting an ever-increasing needle. It's late, he wants to go to bed. What with this load of jerks and the whore in the foyer having an easy time with a drunken salesman, 'Why didn't I become a night watchman?'...

Walter steps up to the mike for 'All By Myself' and carries on with the new single 'One Track Mind'. The bouncers straighten their bow-ties and dive into the crowds, slapping and warning. Middlesbrough kids got no fun

Walter and Billy join Johnny at the table. They define the difference between psychedelic bands and rock bands. 'Acid, man, acid.' There's the tale of the straight sound mixer with the Grateful Dead who never tampered with drugs despite the perpetual eighth heaven of the rest of the crew. So the band coated all the knobs and switches on the mixing desk with a layer of fine acid. Every time he touched something the acid seeped into his skin, up his nose, in his ears. He never got out alive...

'I reckon the Depressions are one of the best British rock'n'roll bands I've seen,' drools Johnny over yet another brandy. He could easily have played the part of Jimmy Doyle, the Robert De Niro character in 'New York New York'. A method rocker, the peachy Italiano kid with a suitable line in facial nuances...

The gig finishes and the crowd demand more. They don't get it.

Johnny talks about boring (musically, that is) New York, makes wide-eyed enquiries about the scene while he's been away, has many misgivings about the new album *L.A.M.F* and holds back the morning...

'Hey you guys, wake up. We're in Edinburgh.'

Edinburgh Schmedinburgh. After seven hours in a coach on a simple 150-mile trip, San Francisco wouldn't hold any interest. Walter stands up impatiently. He's looking freakier than ever, like a character out of a satanic silent movie, all pyramid eyebrows, ruffled hair and leather on an ever-diminishing dance of death. But he's cute with it.

On the other hand, Billy looks like a hit man with all the confidence of a cat. Tonight they're playing Clouds, where no alcohol is served, where plastic planes adorn the ceilings with the face of Prince Charles instead of a propeller, and where punches are hard.

In the dressing room before the gig a guy's telling Jerry (you remember him?) that his friend's main aim in life is to assist The Heartbreakers in any idiosyncratic indulgences they may want to pursue. In short, whatever they want he'll supply.

Jerry – 'Oh, really?'

And then we're into another Heartbreakers show. And 'show' is the operative word. The band plays rock'n'roll like guns fire bullets, like steamrollers flatten Tarmac, like thunder rolls, like trees fall, like – hell, like you've never heard before.

It's unfortunate in a way that their name has been linked with the London bands that have sprung up in the past year because The Heartbreakers brand of music is as timeless as it is iridescent. They've managed to forge a unique combination of indifference and burnt-ass fortitude, which, when rubbed together, sure makes big sparks.

It's the same show as Middlesbrough, only mighty meatier. They always manage to play like there's no tomorrow. It's probably to compensate for their off-stage opaqueness. The show merely confirms that you should get hold of their début album at the earliest opportunity, even though there's one member of the band who doesn't like it.

Throughout the past two days Jerry Nolan has been keeping a distinctly low profile. He refuses to pose for pictures and wanders around in a light blue coat with an air of dexterous frigidity. We're in the hotel after the gig and Jerry licks his lips. 'I quit the band mainly because of the album. I should have expected how it would turn out. I only wish we'd produced it ourselves. It was the same with the New York Dolls. Outsiders just don't know how to handle us on record.

'But there's another reason. There's one guy in this band I don't like. I've discovered he's a coward and I can't work with cowards. He's done things behind my back. He gave in to allow the album to be released. He's only interested in reading about himself in the papers. I can't live with that. There's also another guy in The Heartbreakers' set-up who acts more like a middle man in a drug deal rather than concentrating on what he should be doing. The whole thing is a joke and I want out.

'One thing might tempt me back into this band. It's a long shot and I don't know whether it's gonna work. We'll just have to see.'

He smokes a cigarette and I go to bed. There ain't a past around that's as crazy as a crazy Heartbreakers' past.

Johnny Thunders Heartbreakers will fall apart within months of the Edinburgh gig. Johnny will go solo for a while, gigging with an array of rock celebs from Sid Vicious to Phil Lynott. But smack continues to haunt him and finally guns him down in a New Orleans hotel room in April 1991. Silly fucker.

NOVEMBER 1977

Top ten singles
beginning of November

1. Name Of The Game – Abba
2. Yes Sir I Can Boogie – Baccara
3. You're In My Heart – Rod Stewart
4. Black Is Black – La Belle Epoque
5. Rockin' All Over The World – Status Quo
6. We Are The Champions – Queen
7. Silver Lady – David Soul
8. 2, 4, 6, 8, Motorway – Tom Robinson Band
9. Holidays In The Sun – Sex Pistols
10. Calling Occupants – Carpenters

Top ten albums
beginning of November

1. 40 Golden Greats – Cliff Richard
2. 20 Golden Greats – Diana Ross & The Supremes
3. Heroes – David Bowie
4. Seconds Out – Genesis
5. No More Heroes – the Stranglers
6. Home On The Range – Slim Whitman
7. Rumours – Fleetwood Mac
8. Thunder In My Heart – Leo Sayer
9. Live At The London Palladium – Bing Crosby
10. Oxygene – Jean Michele-Jarre

I've been to some strange places in my time but…

THE JAM
Dachau Concentration Camp, Germany

'The Totenkammer (morgue) was permanently crammed with corpses. According to the files of the International Tracing Service, 31,951 prisoners died in the Dachau concentration camp. An additional number of a few thousand prisoners who had not been registered at all were killed by shooting...'

'The experimental station of Dr Rascher was set up in Block Five where high pressure and exposure experiments were practised on defenceless prisoners. Professor Schilling had prisoners infected with malaria agents. Bio chemical experiments were also carried out in Dachau. Many of these experiments resulted in death...'

'At times there were 400 prisoners to each room. If a bed had been badly made the culprit would be hanged by his wrists for an hour...

'The Wirtschaftsge-baude contained the notorious shower baths where the SS tortured prisoners by flogging and hanging them at the stake...'
(Excerpts from literature available at the Dachau camp)

Out on the Dachau plain Paul Weller flicks flies away from his face. He's obviously uncomfortable in the shadows of the Wachturme where guards once mowed down prisoners in the rain, in the red-stained snow.

He wanders back to the Jam van with his girlfriend, Jill. In the crematorium, Bruce Foxton stoops and peers right down inside an iron-lung oven where the 32-year-old smell of burnt flesh still caresses the hairs in his nostrils.

Rick Buckler stands underneath a 'shower' next door. Anyone ordered to wash here was killed by the gas that poured down instead of water.

In the camp museum, manager John Weller looks at a picture of Nazis burning books before the war. The caption runs: 'where books are burnt humans will be burnt in the end.' Henrich Heine.

He remembers a newspaper report at the end of the war detailing the surreal sex life of a woman SS commandant. Every time a new batch of prisoners arrived she would choose the most virile-looking and lay him that night. The following morning she'd whip him to death, cut off his penis and pickle it in a jar. When her home was raided by American soldiers they found a room full of jars. She was known as the 'preying mantis'.

The Jews keep the camp alive because, as Santayana said, 'Those who cannot remember the past are bound to repeat it.'

Germany 1977.

Death in Dachau.

This is the modern world.

Sten guns in Stuttgart. As the band's van pulls out of the city the roads are lined with armed police. A team of international doctors is flying in to investigate the suicides of the Baader-Meinhoff gang.

'We won the war!' screams Dick, the tour manager, as they pass a policeman with a Luger.

The Jam are bored. Last night's gig was blown out, thanks to a crazy line of communications that meant the show wasn't publicised and the audience consisted of one man and his dog. Killing two nights in Stuttgart ain't a lot of fun when you're young and in love and clip girls in blue movie joints make their marks on a not-so-worldly-wise member of the band who's convinced that Monica with the long legs, coochie-coo laugh and expensive taste in alcohol is in love with him.

In the van 'Anarchy In The UK' blasts out of Rick's state-of-the-art cassette, which he bought recently in New York.

The band have just returned from a 12-day Stateside sojourn or promo as the music business short-cut merchants say, and they're continuing on a European tour.

They came to look for America.

Rick: 'It was just as I expected.'

They played New York (CBGB's), Los Angeles (Whisky-A-Go-Go), San Francisco (Old Waldorf) and Boston (Rat's Skeller).

Rick: 'LA was the epitome of America.'

Bruce: 'What did he say?'

Me: 'Epitome.'

Bruce: 'Oh.'

Rick: 'Big and clean and nice. A place to visit, that's all. '

Bruce: 'I hated New York. But maybe that's because we only had three hours a day to look around the place. Some people thought we were a real heavy rock band. There was one guy, a brickhead DJ, who interviewed us on his show.'

Rick: 'He never had a clue about what was going on. All he kept saying was 'punk'. 'Well the weather's really punk here in this punk city on this punk day in Punkland.'

Bruce: 'The radio's a waste of time out there, anyway. We hardly get any airplay and neither do bands like the Ramones. It's all Fleetwood Mac and Yes.'

Rick: 'Americans are more into the music than the punk thing. We've never been part of the hard-core punk idiom anyway so if they just want the music that's great. But they liked the way we dressed, especially in New York where new wave is stronger anyway.'

Bruce: 'Patti Smith came into our dressing room in CBGB's and walked out again. Dee Dee and Joey Ramone also came to see us. In LA, Blondie paid a visit. They all seemed well out of their heads.'

Rick: 'Bing Crosby couldn't make it.'

Bruce: 'Bruce Springsteen and John Lennon were rumoured to have come but I never saw them.'

Rick: 'Out there kids tend to copy British fashion although there's no strong fashion thing simply because of the country's vastness.'

Paul (yep, he's in the van): 'They're still really into the Kinks, Who, Beatles. Everyone I spoke to loves them. Despite all that Frampton crap they still crave the basics. Seventeen-year-old kids have got all the early Kinks stuff. But there's still a lot of crap over there. I found the place really boring. England's the best country in the world.'

Rick: 'To create any impact in America you've got to spend a long time out there. The Damned didn't seem to go down too well when they were there – well, nobody talks about them. British bands have got to keep plugging away, there's too long between visits.'

Rick slips on another tape, *This Is The Modern World* (an album by the Jam). Cover: underneath the arches, Westway.

Side One

'Modern World': 'It's a micky-take really,' says Paul. 'Is *this* what we've worked for?' He twists his head around to talk, occasionally dropping his eyes when you stare, a subtle lack of confidence that's academy-award-winning appealing. 'I guess it's a concept album reflecting different shades of life. It's more in depth, more personal than *In The City*.

'There's so many people, so many groups who think they're so hip to the modern world. They're full of crap. So you think I know nothing of the modern world?'

'London Traffic': Bruce wrote this one. 'I want to get into writing, contribute more to albums. I guess when I write I imagine how it would sound performed by the Jam. But I still get very embarrassed, I still lack confidence. This song just came into my head while I was getting bored in a traffic jam. Nothing heavy about it.'

'Standards': '*Standards rule OK*', chorus-bash. 'Whatever you do to fight against standards you always find yourself making your own,' says Paul. 'It's like a system within a system within a system within a system.' He pauses, turns away, continues. 'When I write a song I get this big relief. I get annoyed by something, I write a song about it and I seldom return to that subject.'

Paul: 'If people could only try to stand outside of themselves and try to look. Use your eyes as a window.'

'The Combine': 'Ken Kesey, author of 'One Flew Over the Cuckoo's Nest' used the word 'combine' for 'system,' explains Paul.

The song goes on to list a series of names ranging from Ena

Sharples to 'News At Ten' to page-three-girls. 'Whichever way you turn you can't get away from the Combine. We're all slaving for a system in which nobody cares about the obvious coming destruction. You just can't get any truth from anyone.' I never read the book but I saw the film.

'Don't Tell Them You Are Sane' is another Bruce song.'
Bruce: 'It's just about someone being put in a nuthouse. Like prison, I reckon there must be a few people who don't deserve to be in one.'
Paul: 'It's great how that follows 'Combine'. You can lead your lives, you can read the Sunday papers and all the while a subversive 1984 situation – Winston Smith behind the closets – is being created.'

Side Two

'In The Street Today' has lyrics by Dave Waller, a mate of Paul's.
Paul: 'It's just about the way we all take so much crap.'
Paul: 'London Girl': 'There are still so many people around who have the Whittington theory of London – that all its streets are paved with gold. They just get off the train and fall asleep at Waterloo.'

'I Need You' is the first of the album's two love songs. Simple words, simple song.
Paul: 'I wrote it in a tea break while we were recording the album.'
'Here Comes The Weekend'.
Paul: 'We originally intended to record 'Friday On My Mind' but decided to write one of our own. The weekend starts here.'

'Tonight At Noon': Acoustic guitar intro to medium-paced ballad.
Paul: 'It's adapted from a poem by Adrian Henri. I admire his sort of poetry and I think it's time the band really started getting into ballads and acoustic stuff. A critic once wrote that the Jam are going to find it difficult to slow down. That was true once but not any more.'

'Midnight Hour': Wilson Pickett. Jam took it.

The Jam van arrives in Munich traffic. A car cuts it up. 'We won the war!' screams Dick.

Jam after jam. Check in at hotel. Shower. Leave for gig which is above a Schweinaxen restaurant. They play before just 100 people.

Now, the Jam have long been regarded as uncool by the knife-sharp-crease-in-their-plastic-bin-liners brigade. In other words, they ain't liked. Reasons? They don't indulge in that studied on-stage Librium look so favoured by their contemporaries. Funny how people can be afraid of black suits and ties. They also don't allow their stage pose (which is kept at a minimal level anyway) to interfere with their personal lifestyles. Too many bands have nurtured an image that dictates their out-of-show activities.

So, they have a slick act. Isn't that infinitely superior to the contrived madness inherent in many of the second-division leaders? Standards rule, OK.

I confidently predict that Jammania is but 12 inches away and will approach at a speed of approximately 33 r.p.m. Colour it silver, gold or platinum – colour it diamond, if you insist – but don't colour it by numbers. Do that with the others.

They're three blokes who like a drink, a giggle, a wardrobe full of smart gear, a bird on each arm and a few bob in their pocket. Sounds familiar? Yeah, because the Jam are you and me and your best mates.

All right, they made a few clumsy moves early on. Union Jack jackets aren't likely to be next year's big thing. And the Queen statements didn't help win friends and influence people. But when you're 18 and surrounded by smartarse journalists and executives, loose-tongueitis is as easy to catch as NSU.

John Lennon had the same trouble once – 'We're more popular than Jesus' – and he was much older and wiser than Weller. Everyone's entitled to err in front of a Kodak and a notebook.

The night they played Munich wasn't the happiest. The sound was distorted, leaving Paul's vocals high and dry and Bruce's bass sounding at times as if it had been mugged in the corridor leading to the dressing room.

But disparate they ain't. The nexus is strengthened with every performance. No more the boys-off-the-street show, they set out to entertain in the only way they know how, with two guitars, a set of drums and a string bag full of rock.

Maybe that sounds clichéd, but what the hell?

After all, we won the war.

Didn't we?

SEX PISTOLS
Never Mind The Bollocks Here's the Sex Pistols, album review

'The first thing that has happened after applying the vinyl rule is that it has become the first point of attack for resistance. Rotten attempts to escape from it by every possible means.

First he says nothing comes into his head, then that so much comes into his head that he can't grasp any of it.

Then we observe with displeasure and astonishment that he's giving in to his critical objections, first to this, then to that; he betrays it by long pauses which occur in his singing. Instead of simply remembering certain of his feelings and states of mind of his past he reproduces them, lives through again such of them as, by means of what is called the 'transference', may be made effective in opposition.'
Sigmund Freud

'Joe Public bore aloft a drawn dagger, and he approached, in rapid impetuosity, to within three or four feet of Rotten who turned suddenly and confronted his pursuer.

There was a sharp cry — and the dagger dropped gleaming upon the sable carpet upon which, instantly afterwards, fell prostrate in death Joe Public.

Then summoning the wild courage of despair, a throng of revellers at once threw themselves into the black apartment and, seizing Rotten, whose tall figure stood erect and motionless within the shadow of

the ebony clock, gasped in unutterable horror at finding the grave
cerements and corpse-like mask.

And now was acknowledged the presence of the Red Death. He had
come like a thief in the night. And one by one dropped the revellers in
the blood-bedewed halls of their revel and died each in the despairing
posture of his fall.

And the life of the ebony clock went out with that of the last of the day.
And the flames and the tripods expired. And Darkness and Decay and
the Red Death held illimitable dominion over all.'
Edgar Allen Poe

'I played an album, which was not all an album.
The bright sun was extinguish'd, and the stars
Did wander darkling in the eternal space,
Rayless and pathless, and the icy earth
Swung blind and blackening in the moonless air;
Morn came and went – and came, and brought no day,
And men forgot their passions in the dread
Of this, their desolation.'
Lord Byron

'If they'd have included all their B-sides it could have been released
on K-Tel.'
A disgruntled critic

This descent into the maelstrom is merely a reaffirmation of the Pistols'
secular position in the shape of things. The presence of the band's four
singles to date – 'Anarchy In The UK', 'God Save The Queen', 'Pretty
Vacant' and 'Holidays In The Sun' – indicates a desire to strengthen
and gather together the incidents of the past 18 months. More than
anyone McLaren realises that disparity leads to maladjustment.

Then again, they might have been included because the band didn't
have any more songs.

Anyway, they're there and you can't do much about them, except maybe listen again. After all, they are four of the best ten singles released this year. If only the band themselves hadn't said a few months back that they were only going to include 'Anarchy' because they felt including previously released singles on albums was a rip-off.

It hasn't hampered sales. The album's gone gold on advance orders alone.

Never Mind The Bollocks is a predictable Pistols album, i.e. an exciting mess, a torture chamber full of perverse caricatures and verbal defecation. Most of the songs have been performed live since the band's inception and ten of the 12 tracks include Glen Matlock credits. Only 'Holidays In The Sun' and 'Bodies' mentionVicious alongside Rotten, Jones and Cook.

A lot of 'knowledgeable' people reliably inform me that Matlock was the real talent in the band, the instigator of the music. I profess total ignorance to the backstage Pistol squabbles but I do have ears and 'Bodies' is one of the standout tracks on this album. It traces the heart-warming story of a young Birmingham girl who has a baby, wraps it up in a package and leaves it in a public toilet.

She was a case of insanity...

She was an animal

She was a bloody disgrace

Body screaming, fucking bloody mess

Rotten spews: *She don't want a baby that looks like that, I don't wanna baby that looks like that.* And amid the squirms and gurglings in the dying moments of the song Rotten becomes the baby in the toilet: '*Bodies – I'm not an animal. Mummy?*'

Then there's 'No Feelings', a tribute to narcissism, reminiscent (in sentiment only, you understand) of 10cc's 'I'm Not In Love'.

I 've seen you in the mirror when the story began...

I 've got no emotions for anybody else

You better understand

I'm in love with myself

My beautiful self.

The tinsel teenie with the jackboot streak…

You never realise
I take the piss out of you,
You come up and see me
And I'll beat you black and blue,

Again, the affected brainwave guitar of Steve Jones churns the whole thing up and spurs it on to more appealingly repulsive heights.

Rotten's nobody's fool in 'Liar'. '*You're in suspennnnsion*' he screeches over Cook's beautifully deranged drumming.

In 'Problems', those who've seen the Pistols as the saviours of '77 youth are pilloried:

Too many problems oh why am I here?..
And I can see
there's something wrong with you,
But what do you expect me to do?
At least I gotta know what I wanna be.

So you've got to
Eat your heart out on a plastic tray.
You don't do what you want
Then you'll fade away...
Bet you thought you'd solved all your problems.
But the problem is YOU.

'Seventeen' and celluloid Pistols with cinematic reality:

You're only 29, got a lot to learn
But when your mummy dies she will not return,
We like noise, it's our choice,
It's what we want to do...
I don't work I just speed,
That's all I need I'm a lazy sod

The love song of the album, 'Submission', is also the slowest (that means it's faster than 'Virginia Plain'). The Doors' 'Moonlight Drive' immediately springs to mind.

'NewYork' is a little ambiguous. The lyrics are difficult to decipher, with references to gays, pills, cheap thrills and bullshit.

'EMI' is a fitting finale, a golden lesson in vehement retribution and a cackling bit of fun:

There's unlimited supply,
And there is no reason why
I tell you it was all a frame,
They only did it for the fame.
Who? EMI

Rotten's unique r-r-roll and vindictive vowel succulence have never been so effective. The public-toilet backing chorus has never been so public-toilety.

You thought we were faking,
that we were all just money making,
You don't believe we're for real.

Oh, yeah, but readers, it appears they were erroneous thoughts because

We are ruled by no-one

So there.

The end is glorious.

Hullo EMI, goodbye A&M (a raspberry is then blown)

A Pistols album could only end on a raspberry when you *really* think about it.

And doesn't Johnny Rotten bear a remarkable resemblance to Stan Laurel?

The album has the desired effect...

In Nottingham under instructions from the chief constable, police visit Virgin Records, Fox's Records, Bradleys Records and Select A Disc and seize window displays and copies of the album sleeve of *Never Mind The Bollocks*.

At the Virgin shop the manager replaces the display and has so far received two summonses.

At Small Wonder Records in East London the police advise the shop to take down the *Bollocks* display or they would be prosecuted under the 1899 Indecent Advertisements Act. Ads on TV and radio have now been banned. Although provisionally cleared by the IBA, the Independent Television Companies' Association and the Association of Independent Radio Companies have banned the ad even though it did not contain the album title.

To Virgin and many in the music business the ways of the independent broadcasting companies appear to be passing strange.

As punk dies screaming, working for 'Record Mirror' seems a little pointless. Years like this don't come round very often – the next 20 might be shit.

United Artists offer me a job as head of press which I politely turn down. PR doesn't appeal – I'm a journalist; I want more from that. But I also want more money – I've proposed. I've bought a ring. I've started to hack my way into the mindset. Marriage.

Though, come to think of it, Dina and I haven't discussed marriage for months, not since the first flush of speculation cooled down. We did enquire at the Cypriot High Commission in London about the possibility of me working in Cyprus as a stringer for one of the nationals, but that lead has gone cold. Dina wants desperately to live in Cyprus but I want more here.

It's a dilemma we never confront, too busy drifting in the loveboat to care.

POLY STYRENE
'Record Mirror' offIces, Covent Garden

X Ray Spex's Poly Styrene looks surprisingly radiant and shows no sign of the traumas she's suffered over recent months. At the outset her manager informs the dazzling array of journalists assembled in the plush ballroom at 'Record Mirror' headquarters, that Poly will not be answering any questions about her rumoured relationship with a mystery Hollywood movie star.

Poly smiles a lot during the conference but occasionally the tension she's tried so long and hard to hide appears on her face as she toys

222 '77 Sulphate Strip

with the plastic flower in her hand.

Bearded teetotaller Robin Smith opens the proceedings with one of his customary searching questions: 'Have you got any boyfriends?'

'I've got some friends that are boys. What do you mean by boyfriends?' she snaps. 'I don't know. I don't care. I'm not interested.'

Undaunted, Robin fires back, 'Well, why aren't you interested?' Unfortunately Poly's reply is lost amid the fits of uncontrollable laughter from the back four rows.

'How old are you?' asks young, blond Tim Lott, a reporter with an innate sense of style.

'I'm 19.'

'When did you leave home?'

'When I was 15.'

At this point there's a long pause. Then old reliable Robin breaks the silence. 'What does your mum think of all this?'

'She thinks it's good. She doesn't come to my concerts, though, because she's convinced she'll get her head kicked in. She's going to wait until I get really famous and play the Palladium so she can sit down in comfort.'

'Perhaps she'll come when she gets bigger,' quips John Shearlaw

'So what's 'Oh Bondage Up Yours' all about then?' enquires Robin who looks decidedly uninterested in the whole affair as he rips the wrapping off of his Milky Bar.

'It's about everything,' says Poly. 'It's about life. Everybody's in bondage, but on the other hand people say, 'Up yours,' to everything. It's about the duality of it all.'

'What do you write first, the music or the words?' asks Tim.

'I write them both at the same time.'

'Do you believe in women's lib?' asks Sheila Prophet.

'I don't believe in following any movements. Why should I resort to women's lib when I'm already liberated? It's just an attitude. I don't want to be pushy but I also don't want to be stupid.'

'Do you have any pets?' interrupts Robin.

'I've got a lot of little gay friends. They're my pets.'

The day draws on.

'What books do you read?' asks Tim.

'Yellow Pages,' says Poly, clearly frustrated at the line of questioning.

'Are you a fun band?' wonders John.

'We're a satirical band. We're having fun and we want other people to have fun as well. Some people thought when Laura Logic left the band we wouldn't do so well and said we should replace her with another girl. That's really silly.'

'Will money change you in any way? If not, do you believe in God?' asks, yes, Robin.

'I haven't got money. That takes time. I don't believe in just one thing because everything's changing all the time. I once read this book called the 'Magic Mushroom' which…'

'Does that mean you take drugs?' asks Phillip Hall.

'Not particularly. I have taken drugs but I wouldn't get into the habit of doing it.'

'Why do you dress the way you do, with plastic jewellery and plastic flowers and things like that?' asks Jim Evans who just has just popped in to pick up a few free albums before returning to the local boozer.

'Clothes express a certain type of attitude. They take you away from reality because reality is pretty boring. I left home because I wanted to escape from reality but I'm still a survivor. I used to play truant from school in Stockwell and wander round Biba. I never had any friends. People were wary of me because they didn't want to think for themselves. I presented a threat and they felt uncomfortable in my company. When I left home I had lots of jobs – salesgirl, barmaid, DJ in a disco, you name it.'

'Name what?' shouts Shearlaw.

'Do you believe in sex before marriage?' asks Sheila.

'I don't really think it matters. Marriage or sex, it's just something you do. Marriage is all right if you want to get married. There's no way I'm ever gonna become a typical housewife. Maybe I'll have kids but I won't be married or living with anyone.'

'Yes, that's all very well, but what about the children?' says Robin.

'I mean, just think of them instead of yourself for a change. I'm fed up with people in this permissive society when…' at this point Robin Smith is quietly strangled by an unknown assailant.

'Do you regard yourself as a sex symbol?' asks Tim.

'I don't want to be regarded as one in the classic mould. You should be able to be more than something nice to look at. Robin Nash, the producer of 'Top of the Pops', intimated that he liked X Ray Spex's single 'Oh Bondage Up Yours' but had to bear in mind the sensitivity of his viewers.'

'I went up to see him and he said he sympathised but thought Shakespeare ought to be shown. I told him Shakespeare was dead. 'Well Betjeman then,' was his reply.'

'Who's this mysterious Hollywood star then, eh?' asks 'Record Mirror' editor Alf Martin, who arrives late.

The manager advises Poly not to say anything and they leave.

'What did I do wrong?' pleads Alf. 'And who strangled Robin?'

Deputy editor Ros Russell is on holiday.

KENNY ROGERS AND CRYSTAL GAYLE

Dublin National Stadium

Country singers make me puke. I'm talking about the real hard-assed variety. Women – lacquered hairstyles as complex as a Concorde engine, lips that red-glow in the night so they can see their keyholes, mammoth H-bomb mammaries, a great line in cumbersome candyfloss banter and a spittoon full of fake love songs. They are sexless in their Goliath efforts to be sexy.

Men – cocksure confidence bordering on stupefaction, redwood smiles that crack like plaster, ties with tiny knots, cook-in-the-can suits and inert songs.

These predominantly American animals were once confined to their Nashville zoo but thanks to abominations like George Hamilton

100 CLUB

Rat Scabies roadie for Sex Pistols first appearance at 100 Club

ABOVE: The Pistols' first appearance at the 100 Club. The image is from a Sex Pistols publicity handout and the writing is on the original. Rat did indeed help out with "guitars and things". John Lydon says of Rat, "We had good rows, me and him. He never ran from a row". *Pic: Barry Cain collection*

LEFT: Hello Goodbye at EMI starring the Sex Pistols. The label released 'Anarchy in The UK' but pulled it when the single reached Number 36 and the band became too hot to handle. *Pic: Barry Cain collection*

ABOVE: Wilko Johnson – a one off with a Chuck Berry walk and Bette Davis eyes. Interviewed In January '77 Wilko said "In the Feelgoods there's a lot of heaviness." Within three months he'd quit the band and the 'harbingers of British punk' never again had quite the same charisma that had seen them catapult to the Number One spot in 1976 with *Stupidity*.

LEFT: Stiv Bators of US act The Dead Boys at CBGBs supporting the Damned's disappointing American debut. Only the Damned's last gig at the venue showed what they were capable of. The Dead Boys split in 1979 and Bators went on to form Lords of the New Church with the Damned's Brian James and Dave Tregunna from Sham 69. Bators died in a car crash in France in 1990.

TOP: The Damned were the real deal. They were hit and miss live but when they got it right they blew you away. They were the most American of the punk bands musically - but on stage they had a very British 'Carry On' feel. Despite the humour there was a darkness about the band. They were the forerunners of goth, particularly Dave Vanian.

RIGHT: Marc Bolan and The Damned's Brian James join forces on T. Rex's 1977 tour. Within six months of the end of that tour Marc was dead.

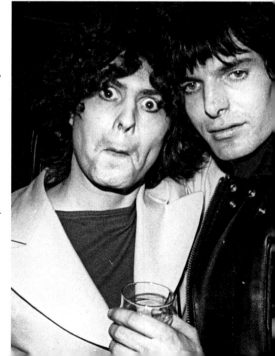

LEFT: Knox and John Ellis vibrate – together. The Vibrators were a decent band with song writing talent but lacked real bollocks live.

RIGHT: Sex Pistols play at Notre Dame Church Hall in Leicester Square in 1976. The following March it was the scene of Sid Vicious' first live appearance, after the local priest took pity on the band who couldn't find a venue to film a free concert for US television channel NBC.

BELOW: Mick Jones looking remarkably like Pete Townsend, and Joe Strummer looking remarkably unlike Roger Daltrey. The Clash had the look. Of all the people I'd have liked to met up with again, Joe was at the top of the list. He once told me I was, "the most original writer in the music press". A man of impeccable taste.

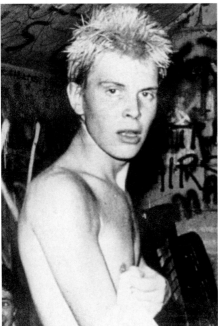

ABOVE: The Jam down in the Hope & Anchor at midnight. The only trio on the scene, they made more room on the dance floor. A sound to cherish. The Jam were a drug free zone but liked a drink. I remember Rick Buckler coming off stage once and downing two bottles of Bulls Blood wine in quick succession.

LEFT: Generation X frontman Billy Idol. As a showman he was the Freddie Mercury of punk, as a singer he was more Roger Deacon. His voice did get better and, coupled with that look, he couldn't fail. And he didn't, living it up in Hollywood and becoming the star he always knew he would.

ABOVE: A rare shot of Johnny Thunders and the Heartbreakers shooting up some good ol' smack and roll. Johnny was the Georgie Best of punk – dazzling one minute, pissed the next. The ex-New York Doll was lost in space when he came to the UK but became an integral part of the scene. Although mad, bad and dangerous to know, Johnny could also be a charming man.

RIGHT: Venus in blue jeans. Debbie Harry, who put the pop into punk. Blondie bloomed in '77 but blossomed big time in '78 on both sides of the Atlantic, making them far and away the most commercially successful of all the bands to emerge at that time.

ABOVE: That's me second from left – with the tasty trainers – with the Buzzcocks in a Manchester squat in '77. Steve Diggle (left) looks on bemused as I ask another penetrating question of Pete Shelley (far right) and John Maher. *Pic: Barry Cain collection*

TOP RIGHT: Radiators Pete Holidai and Phil Chevron. They're from space y'know.

LEFT: Mr. Pursey. Mr. James Pursey. Sham 69 gigs were the most violent. Punk as football hooliganism. I never saw another frontman like Jimmy. A real star.

RIGHT: Fanzine editor Mark P definitely not sniffing glue but watching the tide roll away. His band, Alternative TV, celebrated their 30th anniversary in 2007.

ABOVE: The Boys, with the unmistakable face of Kid Reid (second from left). Should have been stars but never had a hit. Classic teen angst songs with a hint of cool.

RIGHT: Fee Waybill and the Tubes. Quite simply the most spectacular stage show I've ever seen and purveyors of possibly the first proto-punk single. They were managed by Rikki Farr who had been involved in organising the 1970 Isle of Wight pop festival.

LEFT: Poly Styrene, who was really too nice to say 'up yours' and mean it. And as for bondage... A delightful woman who kept her shit together.

LEFT: Ticket for Pistols' Atlanta show.

BELOW LEFT: Press conference with Polly Styrene (out of view) at Record Mirror in Covent Garden. The author (right) with Robin Smith and Tim Lott in the front and, left to right behind: Chris Westwood, John Shearlaw, and Philip Hall.

RIGHT: Hugh Cornwell and a strangler. A definite contender for the 'what happened next' spot. The Stranglers released two albums in 1977 – probably the most successful band of the year.

BELOW: Shades, pint of lager: Graham Parker deep in conversation at the Nashville with Southside Johnny.

HUGH CORNWELL, 2007   JOHN LYDON, 2007

RAT SCABIES, 2007   ALAN EDWARDS, 2007

Pic: Paul Weller

PAUL WELLER , 2016

Vibrators
(the becoming establishment beaters)

Mickie Most may be the Vibrators record producer, so you would expect them to agree on most things but it seems they don't agree on anything. Barry Cain keeps them apart.

Most
(the beaten establishment beater)

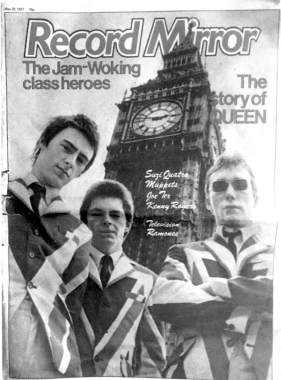

ABOVE: Mickie Most, the Seventies answer to Simon Cowell, sharing a sofa (somewhat uncomfortably) with The Vibrators (who he was producing) for an interview with the author.

LEFT: The bands loved the fact that in an issue of Record Mirror you could find Television and The Ramones rubbing shoulders with Kenny Rogers, Suzi Quattro, Joe Tex and The Muppets, and the Story of Queen could be competing for a share of the big type with the Woking class heroes – The Jam.

IV and BBC 2 they've emerged as a task force in this country – witness the recent number one album from Slim Whitman. How anyone can get their rocks off to someone singing about American idiosyncrasies is way beyond me. The audiences over here are usually the same – somewhere between distilled Eagles and heavy Max Bygraves. Dublin's National Stadium is no exception, audience-wise anyway – mainly young married couples in search of complacency. Maybe Kenny can alleviate the mortgage worries.

The stadium is very Irish. Now, that don't mean all the seats are facing in the opposite direction to the stage. It just means it ain't ornate, it's functional, just like their bars where the pints of Guinness, already poured and waiting on the counter, add the only touch of glamour to the grey.

First up, a little band called Peace and Quiet. Fey and funky. It turns out they're Crystal Gayle's band and she makes her entrance after they've warmed up.

Denim waistcoat, white blouse, blue skirt and knee-length brown boots. Now, don't she look cute for someone who's just beaten the female country heavies to take the top-girl-singer award back in the States? She's pretty tiny. No, what I meant is she's pretty *and* tiny. Brown hair that cascades right down to her bum. And not the merest trace of Harmony–a welcome relief.

She's a 'This is'merchant. 'This is mah group', 'This is mah blues song', 'This is a song which ah'm so proud of. It was mah first gold record back home and I'm so *proud* of it.' Well ain't that jest so doggone sweet? Don't it jest go with her voice? Don't it jest go with her charisma? Don't it jest get ya right here? Don't it, huh? Well, *don't it*?

She wraps her lily-of-the-valley larynx around things like 'Green Door', minus the Frankie Vaughan Tiller Girl kick, 'Somebody Loves You', 'I'll Get Over You' and her current hit single 'Don't It Make My Brown Eyes Blue'.

Sometimes it's just a little too much, a little too clinical. But she's got something. She looks slightly uncomfortable, especially when trying to provoke audience reaction. Maybe Miss Gayle is better suited to a smaller, more intimate venue – like the toilets at Piccadilly station. Jest mah little joke. No, in a large hall she's good, in a club she's probably great.

And she ain't got big boobs, thank goodness.

Kenny Rogers doesn't have big boobs either – but Dolly Parton does. 'Dolly Parton will never drown,' he informs the audience half-way through his set.

This guy is just so affable. He's certainly no Adonis, he's a little adipose, but he's sure as hell adroit in the art of winning an audience. Not that he has to try hard. The moment he strolls on, dressed in simple grey jacket, open-neck white shirt and blue jeans, the Dubliners are his for the taking.

His first song is all about his Omaha honey or something and then he introduces himself 'Well, hi there.Y'know, Harry Chapin told me you were the nicest people in the world and he was so right.' (Pause for frantic Irish cheers.) 'It's mah first time here and I jest love it.

'Now, before I start I wanna know what sort of music you wanna hear tonight. Who likes rock'n'roll?' (Cheers.) 'Who doesn't like rock'n'roll? (Cheers.) 'Who likes country music?' At this stage I hope and pray for silence. In vain. They don't just cheer, they go fucking hysterical.

'I'm not making my music for money, y'know. And if any of you believe that, I got some watches in my car outside which you might be interested in.'

Neat, huh? Then he sings 'Reuben James' from the Kenny-Rogers-and-the First-Edition file. That's followed by his version of 'Desperado' amid swoons from adoring colleens who've had to get babysitters in for the night.

But there's no denying the innate professionalism of the man. He's just so goddamn confident that if a bomb had gone off he'd probably bang his fist against his chest and say, 'Excuse me.'

Somebody shouts, 'Ruby!'

'If you wanna hear 'Ruby' and 'Lucille' you wade through the rest of the crap first.' His greying beard, his hairy chest, his suntanned face – all the right qualifications to make him Phyllosan playmate of the month.

His new single 'Sweet Music Man' is next. 'I feel really excited about this 'cause it ain't often I write a good song.'

That's followed by 'Lucille' which segues into 'Ruby Don't Take Your Love To Town', arguably one of the most effective anti-Vietnam war songs ever written.

The encore is Kenny's first major hit straight out of the dripping psychedelic era – 'Just Dropped In To See What Condition My Condition Was In'. Phew. It's full of phrases like, 'Found my mind in a brown-paper-bag.' But the crowd lap it up with slobbery lips.

It's an Irish kiss, full of cream and flowers, alcohol and blarney. Just like country music, in fact.

I stay round Dina's flat most nights. Every Friday we watch 'Rich Man, Poor Man', a TV mini-series. It stars Nick Nolte and is riveting and romantic and will end sadly.

'What The Papers Say' follows directly after the show and tonight there's a special edition on the music press. Anne Nightingale, who I had never met, is the guest host and, predictably, all the snippets read out in the first 12 minutes of the quarter-hour show are from articles in the 'heavy' three – 'NME', 'Melody Maker' and 'Sounds'.

And then, to add insult to injury, a piece that appeared in 'Sounds' that week accusing 'Record Mirror' writers of being shit, is read out in a dutifully – and brutally – sarcastic way.

I was pissed-off when I read it in the office and I'm even more pissed-off now.

When the offending sentences are removed from the screen the camera flashes back to Anne.

'Oh, really?' is all she says and then my words appear on the screen. They come from a concert review of The Tubes taken from this week's issue of 'Record Mirror'. The voice accompanying them becomes increasingly breathless...

'Time is running out...

The Tubes are: 20 years of piecemeal conditioning distilled into two piebald hours, an erogenous zone, the boulevard of broken dreams, Gary Glitter's deformed offspring, Ex-Lax easy to the constipated, gloriously patchy, a baroque daydream, Sunday Night At The London Palladium, a Ken Russell confusion, unsexy, technoflash tight, a grandiose overkill, a '77 sulphate strip.

The Tubes star: Fee Waybill, a ketchup-splattered synchronised chameleon.

The Tubes: help you heave more easily.

The Tubes are: some kind of wonderful.'

I'm smiling. I can't help it. I light a cigarette.

My cynicism grows bleaker by the day but the trips keep coming. Indifference appears to breed popularity. I'm spoofing and goofing when I should be slippin' and slidin'. Hence this completely untrue Radiators tabloid piss-take written after the band had been much maligned by the gutter press.

RADIATORS FROM SPACE
Kassel, Germany

An Irish punk rock group ran amok in a sleepy German town over the weekend.

While parents took their children around the picturesque grounds of the town's university – celebrating its 200th anniversary – the group:

drank themselves legless and vandalised gaming machines!

played their punk songs extra loud, causing deafness among the younger members of the audience!

wandered around the streets in the early hours of the morning, singing, shouting abuse and waking drowsy Germans!

watched disgusting blue movies!

The group, Radiators From Space, were booked to play four shows during the two-day festival and were billed as coming 'from the ruins of Belfast', although they actually come from Dublin.

'They have totally changed my way of thinking about life,' said the organiser after seeing the band play their final set when frenzied Germans 'pogoed' for the first time.

I can exclusively reveal that the band, who all dress in way-out leather and fake leopardskin, drank enormous amounts of German beer and retreated to the special blue-film room after each show. There in the darkness they watched filth – 'Bodies On The Beach, Sex In The Cow Shed' and 'Naughty Knickers' were shown continuously.

On one occasion lead singer Phil Chevron took off his trousers and *continued on page 5*

continued on page 5

A diminutive blonde model wept as she told me of her affair with Radiators' guitarist Pete Holidai. 'I first met him when he arrived in London from Dublin,' said Mandy X, well-known Roxy socialite with caved-in nostrils, warpaint eyes and a sulphate glow. I was immediately attracted to him and we made love in the backstage dressing room after his first show at the Music Machine. But I knew it wouldn't last. He wanted to be famous and didn't care who he stepped on, on his way to the top. But I still love him, despite all that's happened in Germany. '

Mandy is the 19 year-old daughter of Lord *continued back page, column 3.*

continued back page, column 3.

Controversy has dogged the Radiators From Space throughout their short career.

The German fiasco has not surprised people who know the group. 'I expected something like this to happen – they're that type of band,' said publicist Rick Rogers, from his hospital bed. Both his legs were broken and his head was nailed to the floor by drummer Jimmy Crash in an incident at a West End nightclub.

'But I don't hold any grudges. Deep down they're a nice bunch of lads really,' said Mr Rogers.

Drug taking at all-night parties was alluded to by ex-member of the band Steve Rapid, but he refused to confirm the rumours. 'They'll fucking kill me if I do,' said Mr Rapid, whose kneecaps were drilled after he threatened to quit and come clean.

Father Patrick O'Rourke, the band's resident priest, said, *Going My Way* was my favourite

continued on page 9

'I don't care who I step on, on my way to the top,' says Pete Holidai, guitarist and self-styled punk guru of the Radiators From Space.

'We're different from all the other bands – more developed,' Phil Chevron, a dedicated anarchist and ski-instructor, agreed as he opened his fifth bottle of Scotch after their last Kassel gig.

'If I'd come to England a few months earlier our album would have had ecstatic reviews instead of the good ones it did receive. We're naturally different from the London bands because we've developed in Ireland. We regard ourselves more as a pop band who try to say something.'

'Our music and image appeal to a wider audience,' says Pete.

'We don't want to be stuck in the Roxy all our lives,' interrupts Phil. 'We want to be a 1980s pop band. We put a lot more thought into the actual songs and arrangements than most bands dream of doing. The London scene was exactly what we expected – and it's disappointing. There are much better bands in Ireland – although we're now getting more than our fair share of 'Sunday People' punk bands.'

Their début album on Chiswick is heavily dominated by their opinions of the media. It's called *TV Tube Heart* and has songs like 'Television Screen', 'Press Gang', 'Sunday World' and 'Prison Bars'.

'The next album will be different, though, more personal,' says Pete. 'If you want to get a better life for yourself and your children, just realise who your enemies are.'

'If you get a compulsion inside you, you've got to do something about it,' says Phil. 'I write songs about what I'd like to see happen. I know we're not going to change anything radically but if you carry on repeating yourself, you become totally boring.'

'Nothing's going to prevent us succeeding,' says Pete. 'When we get a hit single – and that's not too far away – watch out. 'We've got to bring the pressure up slowly. Supporting Thin Lizzy on the next tour is obviously gonna help us a lot.'

That's true.

What can be done about these punk junk skunks?

In Kassel I witnessed scenes of gutter degradation. Chevron, the lead singer, frantically attacked his guitar as he and Holidai sang of anarchy, sex and violence. The unsuspecting German audience was egged on by the band as they smashed chairs, punched each other and danced hysterically.

In the last set the Radiators whipped through 45 minutes of music with a venom that horrified me. They played four encores and I for one was glad when the whole sordid evening came to an abrupt close. This shocking punk movement has got to be stamped out once and for all. Bring back conscription, bring back the cat, bring back my bonny to me.

I tell the 'Record Mirror' designer to make the copy look like snatches from newspapers. He forgets and it reads like an ordinary feature. Stupid. The obvious piss-take of the sanitised, satanic red-tops dripping with tits and shits is lost for ever. A bit like the band itself after four years of cracking reviews and indifferent sales.

The Radiators will disintegrate in 1981 and Phil Chevron ends up in the Pogues. After a couple of false starts, the Radiators re-form in 2004 and release the Trouble Pilgrim album in 2006.

And then the white punks on dope drop into town with the most spectacular stage show since the Cuban missile crisis.

THE TUBES

Manchester and London

It's raining in Manchester tonight. The night The Tubes put the SF back into 'San Francisco', the PPP into 'pre-pubic palpitations', the GR into 'gosh really', the VW into 'visual wipeout', the B into 'bananas', the E into 'epic', the RR into 'rock'n'roll'.

As I step out of the Free Trade Hall through a stunned crowd into the neon rain, calendar pages fall past my eyes. I think of the Fifties – clock rock, Elvis rock, Brighton rock; I think of the Sixties – Mersey rock, limbo rock, heavy rock; I think of the Seventies – singalong rock, glam rock, punk rock; and I realise I've just seen the whole job-lot through the eyes of a bunch of TV generation nomadic Spartans in two fun-filled, action-packed, don't-miss-next-week's instalment, here-is-the-news, good-night-and-don't-forget-to-switch-off hours.

The Tubes make you think like that. Weird. I love you get outta here.

But in their efforts to squeeze every pimple on the rock face, they end up parodying nothing.

Dilemma? Nah. Because their act is so immaculate, so eye-orgasm-popping that you begin to forget the parody and just enjoy The Tubes simply because they're The Tubes and not just some multi-million-dollar lascivious, supersonic Barron Knights.

Britain, with its neatly packaged spontaneity, could never produce such an animal. Only the Yankee-manufactured lust for glory is capable of creating The Tubes.

Describing a Tubes show is like describing a Frankenstein mish-mash monster – plagiarism personified. A bloody leg here, a severed arm there, a massive overdose of electricity and voilà! A two-hour Boris Karloff cataclysm in glorious crackling black and white.

There's TV sets, dancing girls, kendo, trampolines, Tom Jones, gigantic cigarettes, colossal cameras, chainsaws, bondage, motorbikes, fellatio, Quay Lewd, drum solos, the Osmonds (eat yer heart out), 'West Side Story', basketball, fire-eaters, smoke, cinema, two-foot platform heels, Apache dances, White Punks On Dope, 20-foot tall collapsible speakers, fights, the Sex Pistols – oh, and Fee Waybill.

Now, Fee Waybill just happens to be the centre of The Tubes' particular universe. He's a takeaway tall guy with a distinguished nose and a shock of red hair. He looks like one of those infuriating school chappies who always got to be prefect or attained the dizzy heights of head boy after seminal successes as captain of the cricket, football, hockey and chess elevens. In fact, you'd swear he was an old

Etonian until he opens his mouth. Accent circa mid-Sixties, Phoenix, Arizona. The Desert King.

Don't he look swish in his shaken-not-stirred white whistle? Don't he look positively dangerous but spiffing in his leather jock-strap and black hood, whipping that poor defenceless girl? Don't he look like hell itself on that motorbike? Don't he look flasher-dirty in that raincoat and trilby? Don't he look glim-glam in that glitter gear? Don't he look straight backstage at the Free Trade, chatting to Hugh Cornwell, long-time Tubes adulator.

'Hey, Fee, I loved your show.'

'Thanks, Hugh. I loved your Roundhouse show too.'

'Thanks, Fee.'

Enough of this intellectual banter. The two continue to talk late into the night over beef stew in the band's hotel and a sociable blitz in Fee's room.

If The Tubes committed commercial homicide in Manchester it's a haemorrhage holocaust in Hammersmith.

The hypercritical/cool London audience, forever on their guard against the hype, go overboard. Don't they just gasp at Mingo Lewis's bongos! Cry at Michael Gotten's bizarre synths! Guffaw at Bill's Spooner-isms! Shriek at Prairie Prince's snares!

And after the contrived lunacy?

What better way to relax and unwind than with your friendly neighbourhood 'Record Mirror' hack just two minutes from this theatre?

'Hullo, Fee. Loved your show.'

'Gee, thanks. I like your paper too. '

'Thanks, Fee.'

Throughout our little tête-à-tête, Dickie Davies's Goldilocks smile curls quietly in monochrome at one end of Fee's hotel room.

'I just love your [I hope he ain't gonna say 'wonderful country'. That's a definite zero rating on the old credibility scoreboard] adverts [phew!].'

So how come a band that's sold such a pitiful number of records can still cause a rollercoasting commotion over here?

'Don't ask me. I never expected anything like this. People told me this would happen but I never believed them. I thought it would be just the same reaction as the States. I mean, they go nuts too but nothing like this. People used to describe our audience as made up of those who came to see The Tubes to be seen seeing The Tubes. They'd wear all their silly clothes and pose.

'We've probably been better than we've ever been. The only place where people used really to go nuts over us was Cleveland. They got the real weirdoes in Cleveland – Alex Harvey broke first in Cleveland. America is just getting so computerised and the people are reflecting that. Radio stations even choose their playlists by computer surveys. And we never get on the radio.'

So why ain't your brand of pernicious paranoia sold vinyl-wise?

'I just don't think we've succeeded in putting what we can do on record. It's just the nature of the band – everyone sees us as a visual act and nothing more. It's a curse. I sometimes wish I could be an Eagle and just stand there on stage, play and not move. Just sell millions of records. Naturally I don't wish that for long. I mean, who really wants to be an Eagle?'

The albums – Fee Waybill's personal view.

The Tubes: 'Al Kooper produced it. He was a nice guy but he kept kicking us out of the studio. We were all just babies and didn't know what was going on. He combined instruments on the same tracks so it was impossible to remix. I guess the record was way ahead of its time. All we knew was that we had a pile of money and an album. That was all that seemed to matter then.

'The album was just one headache after another. We had to put a sticker on the front saying, 'This album has been cleansed of dirty words for people who don't like the word 'fuck'. But that was censored to 'nasty words'.'

Young And Rich: 'When this came out we were hailed as an art-rock band. People called it just too weird. But strangely enough one track, 'Proud To Be An American', won us the best country and western band award for 1976. Amazing. Another song, 'Don't Touch Me There', was a big single hit but, thanks to some bad timing, we were sent out on tour before the album was released so it never took off.'

Now: 'At the same time as we recorded this we were playing two two-and-a-half-hour gigs a night in the Whisky. It just wasn't on. Nobody would buy our albums because we were too visual, right? So we decided we wanted people to think of us purely as a musical band. We got more serious, fired all the dancers and managers. And what happened? The DJs wouldn't play it because they thought there wasn't enough rock'n'roll on it and it flopped completely.'

At this time it looked like curtains for our heroes. The recording company were thinking of giving up the ghost and a split was imminent.

'It was the fifth of June this year. Everyone was burned out. We were due to play the biggest gig of our lives – a 56,000-seater baseball stadium with Alice Cooper, the Kinks and Flo and Eddie. There was also a guy who jumped 80 feet into 11 inches of water and an escapologist. It was that kind of show.

'Alice was terrible, pathetic. He was just so drunk. He had to be continually surrounded by people so it wasn't possible to see him falling about. Anyway, we knew this might be our last gig so everyone went over the top. There were 50,000 people singing along with 'White Punks On Dope', man. It was incredible. After that the company renewed its interest and we got Rikki Farr [son of Welsh heavyweight boxer Tommy] in to manage us.'

So how would you describe the act?

'A unique fusion of rock'n'roll and theatre and dance and – hey, is that rugby?' He points to the TV. 'Wow. Look at those guys, will ya? Wow. What was I saying? Oh, yeah. See, everyone in the band was raised in Phoenix and when you're raised there you can never be normal. It's a city with one million people slap-bang in the middle of a desert. The temperature remains at 100 degrees 24 hours-a-day and everyone's blood gets so thin that you just can't take cold weather at all. All people do is watch TV and I was typical.

'Phoenix was also a testing place for new commercial products. The companies figured that because it was so far away from any other major city the inhabitants were not affected by any external stimuli. The very first McDonald's in the world was in Phoenix. They put it right on the main road where all the guys would cruise looking for chicks so you always stopped and bought one. The very first Kentucky Fried Chicken was cooked in Phoenix. They also developed these colossal slides for people to slide down for ten cents a throw. But after your fifth slide you got to thinking, Jeez, this is fucking boring.

'The town also had a trampoline 'city'. A huge area was covered in trampolines but they could be fixed only into cement. I used to know so many people who broke their legs on those trampolines. The company that started it got sued for millions and went bankrupt.'

The band members bounced into each other in high school.

'It all just developed from there. We fed off each other's cynicism. That's why we could never be a straight band. We make fun of everything and everybody. Put it down to a media overload.'

How did 'White Punks On Dope' evolve?

'It doesn't have anything to do with us. When we moved to San Francisco it took us two years to become a happening. We began to attract a certain type of kid, a real heavy clique. They were mostly from Pacific Heights and were stinking rich. We let them hang around with us because they kept turning us on. They could buy all the coke they wanted, all the Quaaludes. They used to get so fried they'd make total spectacles of themselves – dancing on tables, fighting. They could always buy their way out of their fifth drunk-driving charge. One guy totally smashed his brand new Mini Cooper one night and just went out the next day and bought another. They're still there. Some are burned-out, some have straightened out.'

Fee's definitely straightened out his act. He's up there with the greats like Sophie Tucker, Lon Chaney, Eddie Cantor, Errol Flynn and Barnum and Bailey.

He's a natural and I love you get outta here.

The Jam's second stab at supremacy receives patchy reviews. But I love it, mainly because it's got my name on the back. 'Special thanks to Mr B. Cain'.

Apparently I inspired Paul's song 'Life From A Window' because of a phrase
I used in a live review of the band earlier in the year: 'teenage blue'.

THE JAM
This Is The Modern World
album review

Forget the Sixties. Forget comparisons. Forget Jam = The Who,
the Beatles, the fucking Kinks. Forget the naïve neurosis of the
plagiarists. The Jam are here, and now. They have carved out a
formidable future in three pronged monomania.

Here comes the weekend.

This Is The Modern World reflects a definite progression (remember
that?), a definite identity.

In The City was probably a little too eclectic. Sure it was raw, but
there was an undoubted, underlying sense of vacillation that left too
many rough edges. But here Weller is making an obvious attempt at
creating a Jam 'sound'. He succeeds. Brilliantly.

It is, in fact, a ceremonial pulling back of the post-pubescent
metropolitan veil. It's also fun to listen to.

'I Need You (For Someone)' is one of the prettiest love songs
to come out of a new mind in ten years. The name of the game is
simplicity. The guitar is straight off *Rubber Soul* – oops, don't mention
the Sixties. The system, and the perpetual adolescent battle against
it, is a recurrent theme.

On 'The Combine' the vocal's not as harsh as before. It's not that
Weller is softening, just that he's learning. Like young love, he's
picking up the turn-on techniques hit-and-miss fashion. Thankfully,
there are more hits than misses.

His cracked-pavement voice has often been a cause for concern
in certain circles, which I could never understand. It's perfect for his
songs and, anyway, whoever heard of streetsongs (excuse the cliché)
sung so sweet? That would be implausible. He sings like he looks.

Freddie Garrity could never say that. Strangely enough, two of the album's highlights don't have the Jam true-grit ring of confidence – 'Tonight At Noon' is the band's first lullaby.

And 'Life From A Window', a cleverly constructed smoky skyline of a song:

Staring at a blue sky tried to paint it blue, teenage blue

Weller has never written a better line!

A week after the album is released the band's record label, Polydor, decide to fly a bunch of journalists, PRs and record-company execs to Newcastle in a 20-seater private jet to see the band play.

I don't know, there's something about me and planes. In the absence of Rat Scabies I enlist the aid of a journo, who shall remain nameless, in another sting. The sweep I organise this time is guessing the nearest town the plane passes over at precisely four p.m., the answer to be dutifully provided by our pilot, a touch that gives the whole operation the stamp of authenticity.

The cheating answer to be dutifully provided by my partner in crime.

I dutifully collect two quid from everyone on board – 40 quid altogether. I love a captive audience, especially when it contains lots of journalists. The only correct answer comes – would you believe it – from the man sitting next to me.

We dutifully split the winnings when we alight from the plane. Twenty quid will go a long way in Newcastle tonight.

THE JAM
Newcastle Mayfair

Oh, man, look at those cavemen go.

The dancehall Dan Dares of the far-flung Mecca outposts are out in force on the opening night of the Jam's world tour. 'House Full' notices promote shockabilly tactics and the Geordie hellraisers rise to the occasion in typical kamikaze, iconoclastic fashion.

Only trouble is, the journalists find themselves on the receiving end for a change. As a bunch of us attempt to get through a mob at the front entrance, some fans start to lash out. In the subsequent bundle our usual cool, calm exteriors are demolished – one writer gets his nose broken and another suffers a fractured jaw.

But, never fear, your Thor-like 'Record Mirror' man, visibly shaken and stirred, manages to lay out five of them before hacking his way inside.

That's what I'd like to say. Fact is, I immediately adopt a passable Geordie accent and strike up a conversation with one of the brawlers about the plight of Newcastle United this season and narrowly escape a couple of right-handers.

Cowardly? Sure, but the football interlude works like a charm. Why should I take a punch for Polydor? When the boat comes in I'm the first one on, believe you me.

So, what about the Jam? Irrespective of the death-watch Bela Lugosis outside, the audience are the white-collar gobbers of the regime. They throw plastic pint pots, spew methodically and dance sporadically. They're a chain-store crowd, as opposed to the boutique bootie boys in London. The Jam have nothing to overcome, as simple as that. A reflection of their acceptability is the almost morbid frequency of black-suited, white-spatted punters oozing out of the centre of the booze-splattered crowd like blood from a Stanley knife stripe.

The band have already achieved two-bell greatness in the pinball seat of power and it won't be long before bell three and the jackpot. They play tracks from their delectable new album *This Is The Modern World*, except for the slow-paced cuts like 'I Need You' and 'Life From A Window'. They haven't the confidence to play them because of the contemporary stigma of breaking up a fast set with a ballad. Silly, because it's about time Weller woke up to the fact that this is the Jam and nothing but the Jam.

They're out on their own and should present a Jam show, with all that's inherent in the phrase, and if they don't know that now they never will.

But they will.

What's this? The Damned? I'd completely forgotten about them.

THE DAMNED
Music For Pleasure, album review

So everyone keeps telling me this is crap. I'm brainwashed into hating the record even before I hear it. And, sure enough, it is crap. Then I play it again...

The Damned have always been first of the fun-filled crop to get off their arses and do things. Like releasing the first punk single. Like releasing the first punk album. Like going to the States before anyone else. They've always prided themselves on this so it was all the more surprising when The Damned method-show ground to a systematic halt. Nothing seemed to be flowing from the Brian James pen. We waited months for a single and when it did come, coinciding with the announcement of Rat Scabies' resignation/sacking, it was disappointing to say the least. Like they weren't spontaneous any more, they weren't shocking us any more. And with the addition of Lu on guitar they weren't The Damned any more.

But, hell, I like this album, and I'll tell you why. It doesn't smack of a desperate attempt to push out product because of external criticism. It's well thought-out and, although not exactly meticulous in its production, it manages to reproduce the vampirical, volatile nature of the band. And it's not a rerun of the first album either.

First up there's the flop single 'Problem Child', which has been rejuvenated, thanks to a much needed remix. Now you can actually hear a guitar at work. That's followed by the next single 'Don't Cry Wolf':

You don't have to listen to what your parents say
They don't understand us because we don't obey
You can wear what you want now there ain't no uniform
Go where you want to go don't say life is hard

True, the sentiments may be passé but they are effective on this little roadster. 'One Way Love' presents us with a unique animal – The Damned plus slide guitar! And it's a frantic gem.

The band have been performing 'Politics' live for some time – '*I don't need politics to make me dance*'. It was written initially as a chip against The Clash but it's not as powerful as the title suggests. 'Stretcher Case (Babeee)' you all know and love by now, and side one concludes with 'Idiot Box', which starts like a Stones number, complete with honky-tonk guitar, and finishes with a very untypical, almost-Spanish-in-its-wizardry, guitar solo. Mmm.

Side Two is not so strong but does contain one of their finest songs, 'Alone', which has all the metallic intensity of a skidding Pullman about to derail:

Lying in a wiped-out park with silver screams from the dark
There's no direction a steel erection to feel.

Oh, yeah, there's a love song, 'Your Eyes' – though I know it's difficult for you to imagine Dave Vanian being tender – and Lol Coxhill playing sax on 'You Know', a five-minute marathon with a riff even Black Sabbath would be proud of.

And you can't say more than that.

The Drones are a band I wouldn't usually give the time of day to, although I love their rendition of 'Be My Baby'. However, their record company decides to pull out all the stops to promote the band's début album by organising a reception at a massage parlour in Soho where two women are on hand to bring express relief to any number of boozy journos.

THE DRONES
Massage parlour, Soho

So, I put talcum powder over my jockstrap, slip into a clean pair of pants, adjust the stains on my raincoat and venture out into the night.

Naturally I'd heard all about massage parlours. The Sunday splurge had provided me with the lowdown on the cheap, essential scenery, the bosomy, creamy thrills and the dehydrated delicacies of these depraved establishments. But I wanted to make up my own mind.

In the protean blue of Soho I pick the most likely-looking place, tucked away in an alleyway with 'massage' emblazoned on it in vertical neon splendour and by Andrea's Pleasure Parlour. Glossy colour photographs of voluptuous girls adorn the window. Inside, a blonde files her nails behind a table. Behind her a price list, ranging from a fiver for a simple shower and massage to £15 for assisted shower with two girls plus massage with special powder and mysterious oils.

I flash my press card and say I'm from 'The Essential Guide to Houses of Disrepute in the UK'.

'Oh, in that case, you can have today's special – assisted shave and footbath at £1.50.'

I walk nervously downstairs into the gloom. Okay, I make no bones about it, I'm looking for the kind of fast, active relief that Rennies just can't give me. A girl taps me out of my reverie.

'Take this towel, go in there and strip off.' I obey. I guess it's the knuckleduster she was wearing and the scar across her cheek that somehow got me thinking she wasn't the type of girl you take home to meet Mum. I'm just removing my trousers in this dark cubicle when I realise I'm not alone. 'Who's there?'

'It's only me, MJ Drone.'

'Who?'

'MJ Drone. You must have heard of The Drones. A pop band from Manchester.'

'What are you doing in a place like this?'

'We're launching our first album, *Further Temptation*. It's on Valour.'

Now, in case none of you have sussed, I'm guilty of perpetrating a cheap plug for a neat little band under the guise of a grossly exaggerated Soho sex story. But wait a minute. The Drones did launch their album in a Soho massage parlour, and we've got the pictures to prove it. It's all true. Honest. Read on.

The steaming water splashes on our lithe bodies as we stand in the shower.

'Where are the others, MJ?'

'Well, our drummer, P. Lambert Howells is at this very moment having a blow-job.'

The management would like to make it clear that their massage parlour does not, I repeat not indulge in mouth to mouth resuscitation, and fellatio will get you nowhere. The occasional hand shandy maybe, but...

'Our lead guitarist Gangrene (Gus) is recovering in the local casualty unit after his massage. Our bassist S (Whispa) Cundall is dead. No, he's not. He just goes that colour after a hectic session.'

The water has a strange effect on me. As it hits my back I feel a weird, tingling sensation in my groin and my mouth dries.

'Our press officer John Thomas thought this might be a good idea so he contacted the owner of this gaff – and then the whole thing just steamrolled.'

When we finish our shower, two well-built girls help us into bathrobes. They lead us into a small room with two couches, a sink and a table covered with bottles of oil and cologne. They slowly undo the belts on our robes and we climb on to the couches. During the ensuing squelches of firm hands kneading muscle, or, in my case, flab, MJ outlines the band's career: 'We just used to play R&B with a street image – you've got to start somewhere. The band used to be called Rockslide and we played for 18 months in and around Manchester before Gus joined, and we changed the name in October last year. Since that time Manchester has got together a really good scene, especially when the Circus was still open.

'Unfortunately, with every new scene you get a clique and Manchester is no exception. It's like when we first started to play the Roxy in London. Then it was great, but every time we went there subsequently it got more unbearable. It was the same in Manchester but it still ain't as bad as London where people don't go to watch the music any more. I wouldn't play the Vortex if someone offered me 500 quid.'

A fever is rising in me as my masseuse takes off her boilersuit to reveal a heart-shaped tattoo carved with pride on her chest – 'I Love HMS Reliant'. It's when MJ starts to talk about the time he first saw the Pistols and how the band anticipated the change that was happening in music at the time and how they never really changed direction, that a happiness-is-a-warm-gun glow devours my very being.

Love comes in spurts.

And talking of spurts...

DEMIS ROUSSOS
Birmingham

Okay, I admit I'm expecting a fat, uncouth, big-mouth. A balding rent-a-tent with a circus-ring ego and a mania for greenbacks. A quivering, absurd, incoherent babbler

How wrong can you be..

But the moment he rises with a resurrection shuffle out of the ground, arms raised in all the joyous ceremonial pomp and splendour of his glorious waistline, it's love at first sight. I'm hooked.

Demis à la carte Roussos, I love you. I love your galvanised grossness and your insatiable capacity for greatness.

Anyone who can wear an unflattering frock at the Palladium and surround himself with simulated stained-glass windows, false fog, over-the-top stage sets and finish up holding a single red rose can't be all bad.

You can say what you like but at least Demis puts on a show, in every outrageous sense of the word. His week-long Palladium extravaganza – he paid £100,000 for the staging alone – was a golden-calf indulgence in entertainment.

There's nothing wrong for a guy like Roussos to strike up the bands in such an extravagant way; it's merely a further extension of his despicable/lovable persona. And I enjoyed every baroque moment of it.

Ever seen the sunrise at nine p.m.? Ever seen a 60-foot dove? Ever seen the hills of Athens? Ever seen his friend the wind? Ever seen a 20-stone Greek sing falsetto and receive a tumultuous reaction?

No?

You ain't seen a Demis Roussos show then, because that's what you get – and more. You ain't seen him eat either, have you? Well, welcome to dinner with Demis where the proof really is in the pudding.

Midway through his show at the Birmingham Odeon, Demis takes a breather while his band Black Crow do the interval stomp. I bump into him sidestage. 'Hullo, you are writing about me for the 'Record Mirror'?'

"S'right, Demis.

'Thank you.'

So very 'umble, these Greeks.

'I have booked a nice restaurant after the show. Indian food. Very good.' He makes the kind of exit Bette Davis would be proud of, his frock sweeping the floor, his hair flowing in the door draught. He's nothing if not regal. The customary flowers embellish the gushing finale as over-excited pre-Phyllosan lovelies in flowery dresses surge towards the stage.

'Goodbye, I geeve you my music, I geeve you my love – I geeve you myself.' Gee.

At the stage door a shimmering quadriga awaits to transport Zeus at Ten. As he hauls his massive frame out into the night the Birmingham Aphrodites surround him. 'Let me just touch him, *please.*'

'Sorry, darlin',' says his bodyguard, hired after a harmonica incident up north somewhere. 'Not tonight, awright?'

I climb in the back of the 80-foot long limo with Demis and his mate Van Gelis and for the first time in my meagre life I feel like a star.

'Wave to them.' I wave. Demis laughs. A 60-odd-year-old woman actually swoons.

'You are engaged to a Greek girl, yes?' asks Demis. He remembers meeting Dina when I took her along to interview him for the *Three Sides of the Coin* money feature a few months back. 'Good memory, Demis.'

He turns to Vangelis and says something in Greek. They both roll up. What do they know about Greek girls that I don't?

Cash and curry for the next two hours. VIP treatment at the restaurant.

Demis is shown to his table and it takes him a while to sit down but when he does he orders in a chicken-supreme voice. 'Bring me the menu.' See, when Demis sits down to dinner he doesn't just select, he engulfs. 'I cannot be bothered to choose so I tell them to bring me everything. It's much easier, hehehehehehe.' He laughs like he sings. And it seems to go on forever and ever, his brown eyes sparkling under the soft, tasteful Indian lights.

He's getting hungry and impatient – it's ten minutes since he ordered. So he plays drums with his knife and assaults a salt cellar.

'These people who write about me, they don't know what they are talking about. They only interested in one music, rock. If they don't like me why do they come? Eh? Why do they come?' His fermenting anger is quashed by the arrival of plates – big plates, small plates, oval plates, square plates, contem-plates Demis. Sausages, chicken, Indian kebabs, aloo chat, hot sauces, mild sauces, mango chutney, peshwari nan, keema nan, puris, bhajis, chapatis, samosas and a million poppadums.

Demis performs the ancient Greek ceremony – eating. He grabs three large pieces of tandoori chicken and two huge stuffed, spiced and speckly sausages. 'You like?'

'Not bad.'

'Splodgelishlickgood.'

In five minutes his plate is empty. He washes it down with a large bottle of mineral water, orders a whisky, which he downs in one swig, orders a pint of lager and then says, 'Those starters were good, what's for the main course?'

He hasn't smiled once since the food arrived. Serious business.

Next up, curries. Lamb dhansak, vegetable biriyani, sag dahl, tandoori chicken massala, sizzling murgh tikka, raja chingri bhuna, mushroom pilao, mattor pilao. They disappear in moments.

'It's good, yes? Ah, here comes the sweet trolley.' And there's brick-heavy cakes oozing jam and enormous meringues full of eeechh, kulfi, soft fruit and profiteroles.

And the hot chocolate sauces and custard and mangos engage in a demon dance with the bhunas and dahls and tikkas inside the black hole that was once my stomach.

After a few days with my cute little portable stomach pump, I've recovered sufficiently to pop along and see Demis in his London hotel suite for…

The interview

'Would you like some cream with your coffee?'

'Er, nothing for me, please, Demis.'

He sits, legs apart, on the sumptuous settee, scratching his scantily clad scalp and wearing a flowery blue thing that reaches to his knees. Demis turns out to be an ultra-friendly guy with boyish charm, reflected in his lovable habit of scanning newspapers for a mention of his name.

At the moment he's engrossed in a magazine that talks about his sojourn at a Swiss health farm.

'It's not that I worry about my weight, it's just that sometimes I like to relax. It's funny. I am from the seaside, but I find I relax more in the mountains.'

So why do all the critics hate you, Demis?

'It has happened for all the artists all the time. I read very bad critic in the paper recently about a new album from Leo Sayer. The album is a big hit, even before this article appeared. I also see a very bad article concerning a concert by George Harrison in Canada. The concert was a sell-out. People loved it. It was fantastic. I also see a bad review of Neil Diamond in, er, Woobum? He is a great artist and the people they love him. They also criticise him at the Palladium.

'For me, the Palladium was a sell-out. To fill the Palladium for one week, it does not happen. But I could have filled it for two weeks. I have a lot of fans and I sell a lot of records in this country. But bad critics, they always there.

'The most important thing is to have critic – bad or good, I do not care.'

And he doesn't, and who can blame him? I admire big, fat blazing egos, I guess I admire Demis Roussos.

Now he's getting annoyed. 'I don't give a damn. I am there, I have sold out these concerts. The critics, they not insult me, they insult my public. They call them stupid. If I was one of those critics, I would be very afraid to meet them. I am not afraid of these critics, but I am afraid of my public. I live for them. The man in the street will harm me more than these critics who don't buy records but are given them.'

He says some American critics from magazines like 'Time' and 'People' came to see the Palladium shows and loved them. This heralds Demis's assault on the US with what he calls his 'Mediterranean Country Rock'. 'The most important thing in show business is the relationship between the artist and his public. Everything depends on this one thing. I believe that the public does not know what it wants but they always want what they know. And they want something they are used to.

'In America they are used to country rock like the Eagles. But I am not American, I am Greek, and I have a way of feeling the music and performing the music. It is the Mediterranean feeling of music.

'Put it this way – if I was talking in terms of food...' I clutch my stomach at this point with bitter memories... 'I will give the Americans my meat with their sauce. My sound that I brought from the Mediterranean with the sound that they know.'

It may sound ridiculous but there's no way ol' Demis is gonna fail to cut it in America. A guy like him could never fail at anything.

'My music is massive. It has never happened before that a European artist has sold over 30-million albums. I am someone who works and works hard. All the money I have got I have worked for. But I am not mean. Shortly I am going to Paris to dress up as Father Christmas and give £10,000 worth of clothes and toys which I have bought to the children. I have helped a lot of people.'

Demis is moving from his Parisian mansion to a little place in Monte Carlo. He's off to the States shortly where he will spend six months a year in Los Angeles.

'I wanted to take England first as a door to America. Now I take America.'

Tomorrow the world.

DECEMBER 1977

Top ten singles
beginning of December

1. Mull Of Kintyre/Girls School – Wings
2. We Are The Champions – Queen
3. Rocking All Over The World – Status Quo
4. Name Of The Game – Abba
5. How Deep Is Your Love – Bee Gees
6. Dancing Party – Showaddywaddy
7. Daddy Cool – Darts
8. I Will – Ruby Winters
9. Floral Dance – Brighouse and Rastrick Band
10. Live In Trouble – Barron Knights

Top ten albums
beginning of December

1. The Sound Of Bread – Bread
2. Disco Fever – Various Artists
3. Never Mind The Bollocks Here's The Sex Pistols
4. Footloose And Fancy Free – Rod Stewart
5. Rocking All Over The World – Status Quo
6. 'News of the World' – Queen
7. Feelings – Various
8. Out Of The Blue – Electric Light Orchestra
9. 30 Greatest Hits – Gladys Knight And The Pips
10. Moonflower – Santana

Plus the annual 'Record Mirror' gongs...

Top ten singles of 1977

1. Don't Give Up On Us – David Soul
2. Don't Cry For Me Argentina – Julie Covington
3. When I Need You – Leo Sayer
4. Silver Lady – David Soul
5. Knowing Me Knowing You – Abba
6. I Feel Love – Donna Summer
7. Way Down – Elvis Presley
8. So You Win Again – Hot Chocolate
9. Angelo – Brotherhood Of Man
10. Chanson D'Amour – Manhattan Transfer

Top ten albums 1977

1. Arrival – Abba
2. 20 Golden Greats – the Shadows
3. 20 Golden Greats – Diana Ross & The Supremes
4. A Star Is Born – Soundtrack
5. Rumours – Fleetwood Mac
6. Hotel California – the Eagles
7. The Sound Of Bread – Bread
8. Endless Flight – Leo Sayer
9. Greatest Hits – Abba
10. The Johnny Mathis Collection

The Pistols *Never Mind The Bollocks* album is number 12, the Stranglers' *Rattus Norvegicus* is 21, and their follow-up *No More Heroes* is 32.

Suddenly I don't see a future and when that happens I have to change. I feel like flying and I feel like making bucks and, more importantly, I feel pretty and witty and bright. There's talk of me co-running a record label with Alan Edwards, which really appeals.

I hand in my notice at the end of the month to the editor Alf Martin, who expects it. A fine man, Alf, for whom I will always have the deepest respect. Best music editor I ever worked for – only music editor I ever worked for.

It seems the right thing to do.

But, once more, unto the breach…

GRAHAM PARKER
London and Birmingham

Talking to Graham Parker is talking to two mini-images of yourself immobile on black glass. Ever tried making conversation with a pair of shades? Catching the occasional glimpse of the eyes underneath is like spotting an eel swimming near the surface of a murky river. Those few feet might as well be a million miles.

Parker hides behind them. He admits that. 'It's funny, some people think I'm aloof and don't want to talk to them when I walk into a room. But the truth is I can't see them.'

So why wear them?

'I wore shades a lot during the long hot summer last year and when my then future manager Dave Robinson saw me he said they looked cool and advised me to wear them all the time. He's good at sussing out what's best in the business.'

It seems pretty incongruous to think that this little guy, who probably can't even reach up to see those 'Please mind your head' notices let alone heed them, is one of the most exciting rock'n'roll stars to emerge from this country since Billy Fury took everyone 'Halfway To Paradise'.

And he ain't even got a quiff, more an ain't-it-about-time-you-got your-'aircut-Private-Parker regu-cut perched uncomfortably above his anaemic brow.

'I'm a lazy sod,' he says as he takes a roll-up from a ten pack as if it were a Benson's. That's a good opportunity to leave him, pondering on the primeval Pistols' problem, in the tiny room above Stiff's London headquarters where they plan all those bizarre assaults on the unsuspecting British public, and head north.

To Birmingham, in fact, where men are men who aren't even allowed to stand up in the local Odeon to support their favourite band until 15 minutes from the end of the show. Stopwatches are provided.

Among the audience: the Adverts who are appearing down the road at Barbarellas later, the Pistols' personal bodyguard and Bernie Rhodes, celebrated manager of The Clash. Later, when asked what he thought of Parker's performance, Rhodes, who doesn't look unlike the singer himself, will be overheard to say, 'Three million nice people can't be wrong.'

Old Rhodes might not be a Colossus but he's adroit at the art of delivering below-the-belt-one-liners.

True, it sure ain't a Clash audience out there. I guess a typical Parker fan would also like the Stranglers, Abba, the Eagles, the Feelgoods, Bruce Springsteen and Otis Redding – though not necessarily in that order. In other words, the music he and the Rumour make is pretty much universal, hence the 'nice' reference. He's dynamic without being pretentious, professional without being methodical – two attributes as rare in the current impoverished music whiz-biz as malaria down the Old Kent Road.

The made-in-Hollywood light-show drowns any remaining functional quality the Odeon stage clings to and the band don't waste any time with formalities: they launch straight into 'Heat Treatment'.

After the next song, 'White Soul', the brasses exit, leaving Parker, Brinsley Schwarz, Martin Belmont and Co. to eradicate any Chicago hangover with a three-number set of good time, pleasure-cruising kosher bop – 'Soul On Ice', 'School Days' and 'Hotel Chambermaid'.

Re-enter brass for the most intriguing, ambitious, complex song Parker has ever attempted – 'Heat In Harlem' from the new album. Street-corner blabber pace initially, sliding into action-replay street-pimp stroll.

Yeah, it's got sequined girlie chorus and customary police sirens. And it's also aggravated the derisive 'Cockney-kid-trying-to-be-a-Yank' syndrome.

'I don't want to be an American, no way,' says Parker back at Stiff. 'It's simply that I've been there a lot in the last few years and it's bound to have some effect on your writing.' A sardonic smile follows, and that's all you can see on his face in that tiny room.

'Look, if I was trying to be American my music would be much more laid-back. It's British and nothing in America sounds like it. 'Heat In Harlem', just happens to be about Harlem. It came to me while I was looking out of the car window as we passed through. You live for the moment and you write about the moment. The structure of the song is the way it is because I'm into the big musical buttons-and-bows Busby Berkeley stuff. 'Heat' is a white man's view of a white man's view of America. It's just a feeling off the streets. Anyway, 'Watch The Moon Come Down' is about Finsbury Park.'

It's true. American towns have much more impact than British ones in song titles. I mean, could you imagine 'Heat In Hounslow' or 'Clapham Junction Here I Come' or even 'Lullaby Of Broadstairs'?

As the Finsbury Park moon brightens up a lonely Birmingham night, 'Thunder And Rain', another powerful cut from *Stick To Me*, soaks him through and he shakes off the prosaic pleadings like a wet dog. His clothes are limbo-coloured, his I-wanna-hold-you-but-I-feel-you'd-break body makes Leo Sayer look as if he's pumping iron, and his face is perpetually masked – but the Thin Man creates a unique atmosphere on-stage.

'The US tour helped us a lot. Before, there always seemed to be something lacking live. But now I feel confident. Confident enough to look someone in the audience right in the eye. We're theatrical, living out the songs on-stage, something we've never quite done. I also have a great confidence in my songs. They're a sight better than most people's. Then again, I've always known that and now this confidence is manifesting itself. The audience want someone strong up there to lead them.

'But sometimes I wake up in the morning and think everything I've done is useless, but I guess that kinda thought keeps you going because you end up saying to yourself, 'Hey, I can be better than this.' True, that whole thing might drive you to an early grave but you'll sure have some fun getting there.'

Let's Go On With the Show…The lights are really cooking by the time the band reach the last number 'New York Shuffle'. A blinding iridescent double-decker row of lights heralds the intro and, with only 15 minutes to go, the crowd rush to the stage and do what comes naturally when you ain't got a bureaucratic strait-jacket blow-torched on to your body.

The encores include 'Soul Shoes', 'Hold Back The Night' and the perennial 'Kansas City', or should I say 'Kirkby City'?

The show is infinitely superior to the last time I saw the band at the Rainbow on that absurd double billing with Southside Johnny. The Yank brasso was classier on the night, but on current form Parker is streets ahead in the white soul stakes. And when you really think about it, he doesn't sound *that* much like Springsteen, except maybe when he goes 'Ba-a-a-b-ee, ba-a-b-ee, ba-b-ee, baby,' and then it's only the merest intonation. You ask him.

And while you're about it ask him about his stream-of-consciousness days.

'My streams-of-consciousness days? Oh, you must mean when I got so frustrated with writing songs and singing and getting nowhere that I took up writing books. I didn't have a deal then, and all these people were telling me to get a band together and go out on the road. I'd been through so many kinds of music that I didn't know who the hell I was any more. So the stories I wrote got all this confusion out of my head. None of them got published. Maybe I'd like to do it again but there are so many people who do it better.'

The next night finds Parker in the sterile surroundings of Fairfield Halls, Croydon. It's a stereotype sarcophagus venue, more suited to HMS Pinafore than G.B.H. Parker.

Still, it's the kids that make a gig and there was a little crew up front who did more rooting than a potato farmer. And there were, er, punks too.

'If we'd been called a punk band from the beginning we'd have sold more records. Not everyone's a punk band. I just want it to be hard for people to categorise, that's all.

'I've always believed that a single personality is best for a group. It's a very attractive thing and I've always been into solo artists. But at the same time you know the band is great, so there are two things working together and when we sit down and talk about the music, we talk about the band. Like, if I ain't on form one night the band will drag me back up and vice versa. But that doesn't happen much any more. Brinsley told me the other day that the UK tour we've just completed was the best he'd ever been on – and he's been on some.

'I'm a lazy sod. I don't have sleepless nights about my chart position. What I do have is a lot of fun because, when you really think about it, the whole thing is a joke. It's just so funny. I mean, there are punters in the audience walking around in shades, black jacket, the whole Parker bit. Now that's funny. But what I do take seriously is when some half-wit writes a bad review of one of the shows simply for the sake of being snidey. Still, I ain't gonna kill myself over it. No, when I die it's gonna be onstage – if only for the moment. I guess I just live at different shades,' and we're not talking sunglasses here, 'whatever I happen to be at any given time. Sure it's neurotic and that's maybe why I never look into myself. But if you went through life continually analysing yourself, you'd never be confused. So how the hell are you gonna write rock'n'roll songs if you ain't confused?'

'Don't Ask Me Questions'. 'The readers will get so bored with this.

I know that people close to me will read this sort of thing and tell me I'm saying the same old things. It's just a variation on a theme.'

After the show Graham loses his voice. It sometimes happens to rock stars. Some *Heat Treatment* should cure it.

And I'll tell you something else. If you've got a bad dose of the blues and your symptoms persist, consult your GP.

You know it makes sense.

Graham and the Rumour will disband in 1980. In June 2000 he starts to swim in those streams of consciousness and a collection of short fiction – Carp Fishing On Valium – is published. In 2003 Graham produces his first novel, The Other Life Of Brian, and in 2006 he releases a single, '2000 Funerals', on the Internet.

A few days after that bonny but ultimately bony Parker interview, I find myself staring into the wrong end of a gun in Bedlam, one mile outside Amsterdam, on the most frightening night of my life.

THE STRANGLERS
Paradiso, Amsterdam

Pass me the aphrodisiac honey, we're in Amsterdam. And all the cutie canal streets and all the clapperboard clubs and all the demonic deckhands of this cold Indonesian restaurant night lead to the Paradiso.

The Paradiso is Amsterdam's premier hole. Imagine the Roundhouse only dirtier – a huge filter tip after the cigarette has gone, the death-brown fusing of nicotine, tar and spit all the way through. Then you look up, way above the stage, at the stained-glass windows that provide the only clue that this was once a church. Yeah, that's right, a church. Now there's a dope bar where the font used to be, kids snort in the shadow of the altar and the Stranglers have replaced Christ. Hey, is that a tear on the multi-coloured cheek of Mary up there?

Christ he told his mother, Christ he told her not to bother

There's a thousand punters inside, another thousand outside and a Dutch TV film unit celluloiding the lot.

The Stranglers – high-rise exponents of the kind of devout decadence inherent in pre-war Berlin. They always remind me of a scene in the old Alexander Korda movie 'The Thief Of Baghdad', when a wealthy Indian merchant falls in love with, what looked to me as a sweet seven-year-old in front of the TV, a life-size mechanical doll with eight arms. He pays a fortune for it, then indulges in some Eastern delight. The doll has huge fingernails and it proceeds to dig them into his back as he caresses it. Slowly at first, then harder, until the blood gushes and he collapses dead to the floor.

There's something very unclean about the Stranglers. I always feel like taking a shower after seeing them.

Their phenomenal success among the pre-pubes baffles me – what 13-year-old has ever heard of Trotsky? They're not glamorous. Their clothes are straight out of a Black Sabbath queue of fans. They don't exactly come on like teenies. 'What did you do in the war, Daddy?' But the far-out, bombed-out, bleached-out fall-out that is the Stranglers somehow gets across to them.

Like dirty old men offering sweets to little girls…

Same applies to this spaced-out Dutch-capped Paradiso audience. They don't have the faintest idea what the band are going on about but they cheer every familiar chord.

The show is their usual sex act without taking their boots off. One new song, 'Five Minutes', indicates a variation but the tried-and-trusted format is retained. Why change success? If that's what the proles want, give it to 'em and give it to 'em good.

I enjoy their shows, their records, their pose. It may be real cool to slag them for writing anti-feminist songs (though I thought most songs professing to be 'love' songs were anti-feminist anyway – writers from Porter to Lennon have regarded women as merely love objects, gossamer fantasies) or for making dough, but their desirability rating is high in my estimation. I'm down to ten a day now.

They bring out the prurience in people – and that can't be all bad.

Now we get to the meat of the story. Half-way through 'Ugly', just before Jean-Jacques Burnel screams, '*It's only the children of the fucking wealthy that tend to be good-looking,*' a kid jumps on stage and dances.

A security guard strolls on and hurls the kid off stage. Nothing out of the ordinary you might say. But the guard is a Hell's Angel, built like a brick shithouse, and the stage happens to be eight feet off the ground. Burnel stops playing and tells the Angel to cool it. But that's all he can do. The Angel grudgingly nods. The first taste of what's going to happen on this mordant Amsterdam evening.

The band finish the number and the rest of the show runs relatively smoothly, with only the slightest hint of Angel cakewalking sidestage. But the kids take the hint and limit their enthusiasm to soccer sways while sitting on the stage in front of the band.

The Dutch Angels have muscled their way into the Stranglers' camp. Whenever they play Holland the Angels are there, offering friendly advice and five-star service. The band like them, there's no doubting that.

But it wouldn't much matter if they didn't.

The Hell's Angels of Amsterdam are different from their counterparts in Britain, America or Timbuktu. They're government approved! No kidding. The Dutch Government allocated a £150,000 grant to enable the Amsterdam Hell's Angels Society, as it's officially known, to set up shop. With that money the society built an Angel complex on the city outskirts. It includes a large clubhouse complete with disco and bar, sleeping quarters, a garage to house their 1000cc steeds and a makeshift shooting range. And, wait for it, each of the society's 25 members receives an annual grant of £2,000!

Altogether now – *why*? Fear appears to be the prime motivation for such an insane policy. It seems the government are afraid of this happy band of men, and the money is merely a ruse to keep them quiet. A DIY Nazi-jacketed protection racket. But it's not on any little speakeasy owner. It's on the government, maaaan!

Backstage after the show, the Stranglers enjoy a spot of quiet relaxation with their new-found buddies. I get a long, ludicrous, electric-drill-in-the-kneecaps stare from one of the Angels as I walk into the dressing room. 'He's all right,' says Hugh. His timing's perfect. The Indonesian meal I had earlier is ready to make an unscheduled appearance.

'They took us back to their clubhouse after we played last night,' Hugh continues. 'I stayed till six this morning. They gave us anything we wanted. They treated us like kings.' Hugh is clearly loving every Evel Knievel moment of it. Dave sits nearby cuddling his missus. Jet surveys the scene and Jean-Jacques is AWOL. 'He's gone to pick up his motorbike.'

By this time the dressing room is pretty crowded and one of the roadies locks the door.

'Let me in. It's Pedro.' He's one of the Angel clan.

'Sorry, we're too full.' says one of the roadies

'Let me fucking in. It's fucking Pedro,' says Pedro who starts punching the door.

'Piss off.'

Pedro kicks hard at the door in utter frustration and pisses off.

A few minutes later after two hefty blows on the wall by the door, Pedro emerges through a pile of masonry carrying a sledgehammer. 'Which one of you said 'Piss off?' Nobody was gonna own up to that one.

'We're all going back to their club tonight,' says Hugh.

Oh, great.

It's somewhere between the *b* in 'club' and the first *t* in 'tonight' when the loudest banger you've heard explodes at my feet. A group of three bearded (ain't they all?) Angels with dirty faces chuckle in the corner. 'You come with us, ya?' said, yeah, you guessed it, Pedro.

'Er, well, if it's all the same to you I'll go in the van with the band.'

The last time the Stranglers played here the boize took them along to a pleasant little bar slap-bang in the middle of the red-light district. Their birds are whores who pop up between grovelling clients for a sociable drink.

But this time it's da bizness... the Angel Club.

The building is well away from residents' areas, one of the government's stipulations. But a prison, a rather luxurious block (well, you know what these permissive countries are like) is under construction nearby.

'They'll never finish building that jail,' a visiting Angel from Brighton informs me. 'The Communists don't want it so they keep bombing the place every now and then.'

There's another reason why the building won't be completed for some time. In the back garden of the club a large machine gun is mounted on a tripod. When an Angel fancies some fun he strolls out, loads up the gun and sends hails of bullets through the prison windows. Cute, huh?

The clubhouse is tastefully lit, probably because most of the light bulbs have been smashed. Hugh plays pool with a guy affectionately referred to as 'Loser'. His face has been eaten away by the acid shower he got in a bundle.

Half-way through the game the barman starts showing home movies. Well, they can't be that bad if they make cosy family films. Why, look, isn't that this very same club? And isn't that the pool table Hugh's playing on? How sweet.

Oh, look, there's a... er... gulp... naked lady. Giggles at the bar. 'Look, that's me, haha-hahahaha,' says an Angel. And sure enough it is. He's holding a milk bottle, which he inserts into the woman as she reclines on the pool table.

'She was a German girl who wanted to be shown round,' whispers Loser in my ear. They certainly showed her everything.

That's followed by a film of two German Angels who got stroppy. They're dragged back to the club, searched at gunpoint and their weapons confiscated. Big Al, the president of the society, tells them to get out of Amsterdam and they plod mournfully offscreen.

Then there's the guy with the ginger beard in the cowboy hat acting the fool in a film. Loser says he's in a lunatic asylum after mercilessly beating up three men and putting them in hospital. When the lights come on after the show there he is drinking beer at the bar.

Get the picture?

A few fancy revs and in comes Jean-Jacques on his Triumph bike along with an Angel on his Harley Davidson. Jean-Jacques' mascara is smudged but he still retains his cucumber cool.

Why the stunt? Bob Hart from the Sun is doing a feature on the Stranglers/motorbikes/Hell's Angels/and his photographer has set up a contrived but effective happy snap.

The Angels indulge in a spot of frantic posing. Stranglers' posing comes natural anyway, and the shot has more than a passing similarity to one of those Barry Sheene victory scenes after a world-championship race.

After the session Hart drags Jean-Jacques into a room for an interview, Hugh continues playing pool, Jet continues drinking and Dave continues to cuddle his missus.

A guy in a balaclava wanders over to where publicist Alan Edwards and I sit. 'Look at this yah.' He pulls out a small revolver and places it against Alan's head. He pulls the trigger. There's a click. 'Good, yah. It is .22 calibre. Powerful for such a little gun, yah'.

'Oh, yah yah!' says Alan, who looks totally stunned.

Balaclava Billy wanders off. 'Bet it wasn't loaded,' says Alan.

The photographer walks in. 'Here – they're all shooting bottles off walls with revolvers out the back.'

I ask Big Al if they have problems with the police. 'The police? Hahahahaha! They never come here. They're too scared.'

What about licences for their shooters? 'Hahahahaha!' He gives me his card: 'Amsterdam Society of Hell's Angels. President Big Al. Vice-President Stanley.'

As we leave, the Angels shake our hands and tell us we're welcome back any time. With every shake I keep thinking a knife will be plunged into my back. That ice-cream soft entry, comblike parting of the flesh, the rose-red spill, the thump-thump of the heart, the dirty steel caressing the bone, the cool call of death.

I get to thinking about newspaper headlines 'Pop Group and Friends Slaughtered by Hell's Angels'. Of only the good-die-young. Of bright future epitaphs, of me mum and dad, Dina.

SLAP!

A hand hits me on the back. 'Goodnight. Safe journey.'

Phew.

So I'm left to think about the night. And you know what I think? I think the Angels are nice guys in their way, but their way ain't my way. The government pay them to keep schtum and out of the limelight. The Stranglers, unintentionally, have brought them out of abeyance.

A few people have since mentioned unpleasant scenes they witnessed on the band's last British tour involving some of the Angels.

Remember Altamont? Maybe that sounds a little drastic but it's not just the Angels you have to worry about. It's the ordinary punters reaction as well.

While the Stranglers keep insisting on playing smaller venues there will always be the danger of violence. Playing a place the size of the Paradiso is not fair on the fans or the band. Christ, they could pack out the Empire Pool two nights in a row, maybe even three.

Slapdash security just won't work any more. Nice gesture, sure, but something better change quick.

Whatever happened to the Finchley Boys?

A week later Jean Jacques sends me a letter about the Amsterdam article on and I realise for the first time that the artists actually read what I write. It feels like some kind of honour. Our conversations lengthen considerably in 1978 and I develop a tremendous respect for him. He has a lot of bad press, some of which is unwarranted, but I have a sneaky regard for his fists of fury attitude. This is punk rock after all, it has to have an edge, and JJ is on hand to push you over it if necessary. Fiercely intelligent, he doesn't suffer fools gladly. Oh, and he plays bass like an angel.

DEREK AND CLIVE
Richard Branson's houseboat, London

There's wanking and there's wanking. Just ask Peter Cook and Dudley Moore aka Derek and Clive, the Armitage and Shanks of the rock world.

I mean, a Bermudan Wank isn't half so much fun as a Wank of England or a Centurion Wank. And nothing beats a Top Wank.

So it seems strange that the naughty duo should decide to jettison their new album *Derek and Clive Come Again* from that very same sceptred isle.

The scene: former London home of khazi-paper entrepreneur Peter Cook currently awaiting trial on a charge of assaulting a Delsey football fan. 'I just wanted to get it out of my fucking cistern,' he's reported to have told his mother.

Gathered around a special amplified telephone are a number of well-known journalists ranging from the bespectacled chappie representing the 'Guardian' ('Derek and who?') to the meticulously rehearsed smirk-and-collar-up platitudes of Blast Furnace from an equally well-known music paper.

The phone purrs. 'Er, that must be them in Bermuda,' says an uncharacteristically edgy Al Clark, press officer and glib comment merchant of Virgin Records.

'Hello, you two. There are a lot of journalists here, all eager to ask you lots of questions about your new album. I hope you're ready for them. Right, over to you, chaps.'

Pause. Longer pause. Lifelong pause.

'Er, what's the weather like over there?' queries Al, laughing a mite nervously.

'The weather is fine and Katie Boyle is with me, Al,' says Clive. He's the tall one.

'Is it true,' asks Blast, 'that the...'

'What?'

'Is it true,' asks Blast again, 'that Derek and Clive are fathers?'

'I'm sorry, you'll have to speak up. [Aside] I always knew this was a fucking stupid idea, Derek."

'Are Derek and Clive fathers?'

'What?'

'ARE DEREK AND CLIVE FATHERS?'

'They are childless because they are ignorant,' says Clive. 'They've heard rumours about copulation but they haven't actually experienced it. They just wank. They're products of the Seventies.'

Pause.

'Why are you so preoccupied with cancer?'

'What?'

'Why are you so preoccupied with cancer?'

'Money causes cancer. I've got cancer of Dudley Moore.'

'What?'

'What?'

'What did you say?'

'Oh. Money causes cancer. I've got cancer of Dudley Moore.'

'Would anyone like a drink?' says a Virgin girl.

'Could I have a glass of white wine please?' says the man from 'Melody Maker'.

'What?'

'Oh,' says Al, 'that was just the man from 'Melody Maker' asking for *another* glass of white wine.'

'Oh.'

Pause.

'How would you describe your new record?'

'What?' asks Derek.

'He said, 'How would you describe your new record?'' says Clive.

'It's a rare thing in this world to find a pure work of art like this,' says Derek. 'Derek and Clive have gone deaf like Beethoven.'

'What did he say?' asks the man from the 'Mail'.

'What?'

'That was just the man from the 'Mail' asking what you had said,' says Al.

'Here's your white wine,' says the Virgin girl.

'What?'

'Tell my wife I love her very much,' says Clive.

The year is nearly dead on its feet – a bit like Ian Dury.

IAN DURY AND SOME BLOCKHEADS
Queensway Ice Rink

Key (in order of appearance)

tabby (cat): fat

comics (cuts): guts

taters (in mould): cold; taters is short for potatoes

golly (wog): fog

oilies (oily rag): fag

Richard (the third): bird

frog (and toad): road

Scotches (Scotch pegs): legs

raspberry (tart): heart; jam tart is also quite permissible

titfer (tat): hat

two and eight: state

barnet (fair): hair

Rory (o'Moore): door

half rug: mug

Cain (and Abel): table

whistle (and flute): suit

laugh and a joke: smoke

nanny (goat): throat

hackney (wick): there's one for your fertile imaginations to deduce.

If Bill Sikes had been six inches shorter with a little more *tabby* round his *comics* and had written song lyrics, he would have been Ian Dury. *'He had a brown hat on his head and a dirty belcher handkerchief round his neck: with the long frayed ends of which he smeared the beer from his face as he spoke. He disclosed, when he had done so, a broad heavy countenance with a beard of three days' growth and two scowling eyes; one of which displayed various parti-coloured symptoms of having been recently damaged by a blow. And man was he a performer.'*
Charles Dickens – rock critic

It's not difficult to imagine Dury skulking along a cobblestone street in the darkness looking for a likely person to roll. A moribund limping figure out of the grey, out of the midnight grey...

You could be forgiven in thinking that Dury is a novelty, just, I suppose, 'cos *he ain't never 'ad nuffin' worth 'avin never 'ad and never ever – ever*. One album *New Boots And Panties*, which only just scraped into the 50 ain't exactly the Ritz.

But remember the old saying, 'You can like it or limp it'?

Oh, yeah. You won't read anything about his association with Kilburn and the High Roads in this article or other misdemeanours. That's over. It's boring now.

:So that leaves us with December Dury – on ice. See, we were supposed to be going to the dogs (okay, I know he's probably already gone) this particular night. But it's *taters* and the *golly*'s thick so the meeting at Harringay's cancelled.

'Let's go ice-skating,' beams Kosmo, well-known Stiff and raconteur. 'Yer. And if we go down Queensway we can have a chinky afterwards,' says Ian.

He's got this voice, this cinematic butcher's voice. A voice you could light *oilies* with on a blustery day. Loud enough to be heard coating somebody six floors up. Gentle enough to fall asleep to if you happen to be six years up.

A voice that's tumbled over sex 'n' drugs 'n' rock'n'roll, and workhouse slime and sneaky Scotch and hooky hooch and tear-stained nights. A bootleg voice having a proper wriggle in the naughty naked nude.

In other words – I'm partial to his abracadabra…

So we, that's Ian's *Richard* Denise and three Blockheads – drummer Charley Charles, bassist Norman Watt and jack-of-all trades Chaz Jankel – saunter down the *frog* to participate in some frozen delights.

Unfortunately, Ian ain't what you could call Upminster's answer to John Curry. So he sits by the side of the rink, rather like a night-watchman round his brazier, taking illicit swigs from a bottle of brandy hidden in his inside coat pocket. *Takes eight to make him randy.*

See, ol' Ian's dodgy on his *Scotches*, thanks to an overdose of kiddywink complaints. But remember the old saying – 'A bird in the workhouse is worth four in the bank'?

So while he sits out the dances The Blockheads indulge in a spot of slippin' and a-slidin'.

You must have seen Blockheads in raucous teams
Dressed up after work
Who screw their poor old Eileens
Get sloshed and go berserk

Sometimes I can't help thinking all that's sitting on that tiny chair in this huge hall is his coat. Then he pops up, alert like a back-street mongrel, and you know he's been at the brandy again.

So, Ian, do you think this sudden rise from obscurity is going to last?

Casually he twists his head. 'Too soon to say. I think I'm worried but I don't actually. A multiple statement – I don't like to take for granted that I can't handle it.'

Why?

'Because I can't handle it.'

Maybe I shouldn't say anything. Maybe he's winding me up.

'See, I've got to keep looking forward to obscurities.'

Why?

'Because obscurity is all any of us must expect. And in the light of this current dairy…'

Current what?

'Dairy. Just stick 'limelight' in brackets, seeing as you're an Angel boy and don't understand these subtle Elephant expressions. Now, where was I? Yeah. In the light of this current dairy it would not be withstanding of me to cop hold of that as being in the nature of the result.

'Sometimes,' he continues, 'I think there's a little bit of clever Trevor in all of us.'

And it ain't not knowing that
There ain't nothing showing
And I answer to the name of Trevor

And it ain't not proving that his mind's not moving, either.

And if his *raspberry* ain't as sound as the next man's I'll eat my *titfer*. The romantic riddler from the East End isn't half clever. Never. Clever.

So we sever (never) all connections with the rink after the manager refuses permission for our demon photographer to take snaps of Ian lying face down on the empty ice. He's game for anything, this boy, and is prepared to jump over the rink barrier in the name of cheap publicity. But he doesn't count on the size of the surly, burly security guards.

But remember the old saying 'You can't be judge and Dury'?'

And no one can shimmy like my Sister Skate.

Also, it takes much longer to get to the Chinese the Dury way. Despite the curious nature of his gait, there is a certain nobility in the movement. A bit like Richard III on a cold day. You can imagine him, in a right *two and eight*, wandering around some moor screaming: 'A gee-gee, a gee-gee, my kingdom for a gee-gee!"

Thirty-five with the Hamlet *barnet*. Bill Sikes was 35 too. That, if you recall, was his last year, his last ring round the bark.

At first there's a Shanghai dismay as the motley crew walk through the *Rory* and Ian says, 'Table for eight, please. 'I thought he was going to add the durable 'me ol' china' but he doesn't go in for the predictable. He's probably the first true rock purveyor of rhyming slang which is now fast being covered with a bland varnish. Like backward slang (originated by 19th-century Smithfleld meat market porters who conversed in words pronounced backwards – hence yob), rhyming slang is, quite simply, beautiful. A flamboyant, baroque vocabulary that epitomised the extrovert barrow-boy, barrel-organ, bellowing Cockney.

Now? It's all been relegated to coffee-table discussion. Something to swallow mints to. 'I say, Nigel, what do you think boat race means? Face, heeheeheehee.' And these *half rugs* don't even realise you're supposed to chop off the last word anyway to make it totally incomprehensible to naught but the trained listener.

That's ear stupid.

Anyway, we all sit down at the *Cain*, and Charley, a connoisseur it appears of all things Chinese, orders. I continue with the thankless task of interviewing.

What about...

'See, the gigs we do are full of old age pensioners and children and workmen, who don't want to work, and idle rich, who wish they were doing something, and other deprived minority groups. Basically, what I'm saying is – everybody's deprived so we must be on a winner. I ain't got a clue what's going on, so all I want to do is work hard.'

We're in the khazi when he starts saying how he can't change people. 'You won't come out of a Clash gig left wing.' He says he doesn't really want to give interviews because 'I did them in the Kilburns and where did that get me?'

Then there's Liberace. 'He's surrounded by a crowd and an eight-year-old boy presses up to him. Liberace shows him this big ring on his finger and says, 'See, son, this is what you get if you persevere.' That's what it's all about.'

He then proceeds to stuff his mouth (you must know north and south by now) with boiled rice and Pacific prawns and all manner of Oriental delicacies, and turns round to have a little tête-à-tête with Denise.

And somehow that got me thinking about Dickie. You know, the one who had

A love affair with Nina in the back of my Cortina.
A seasoned-up hyena couldn't have been much more obscener.
She took me to the cleaners and other misdemeanours,
But I got up right between her rum and her Ribenas

And remember after that he
Bought a lot of brandy while I was courting Sandy.

Took eight to make her randy and all I had was shandy.
And another thing with Sandy, which often came in handy,
Was passing her a mandy, she didn't 'alf go bandy

Who needs interviews when you've got lyrics like that?

But remember the old saying, 'When you've wet yer *whistle* you'll have to have another one made.'?

By this time we've finished eating and Ian's having a *laugh and a joke.*

'It's got to be fun, y'know. It's all about fun. Like, your van's broken down and you've got to dropsy the AA geezer 12 quid for something that's gonna cost 40 quid and you get to the Blue Boar roadside café and see the same egg and chips you saw the day before and you get back to London at seven a.m. and suddenly you feel great 'cos you see everyone just going to work and you know you're going to bed and that makes you want to stay up and there's nothing better in the world than having breakfast and going to bed. Nothing.'

And if that ain't the most succinct summing-up of life on the road I'll slit me *nanny.* Like looking at the world through the bottom of a pint glass.

'People are waking up to the fact that being in a rock band is a lot better than going to work. In ten years' time there ain't 'alf gonna be a lot of bands around. In fact, there'll be more people playing rock'n'roll than actually working.

'And the only way they're gonna get those few to go to work is to have Sha Na Na playing at the factory all day.

'It's like when people ask you, 'Is it true what they say about...?' Yeah, course it's true 'cos if it wasn't they wouldn't be asking.'

These off-the-cuff, scratch-yer-head remarks ain't as baffling as you first think. They have a habit of falling together into a cogent conglomeration of Dury philosophies. They also protect him from cherishing the purity and depth of his disdain.

He's quieter now (his own words) if only because 'When I jump around now people only say that's Ian Dury acting flash whereas before people would only stare and ask who that little wanker was in the flat cap.'

But there's a few people around who'd still ask just that. Despite the hysterical reviews, Ian Dury remains a name a lot of you aren't familiar with simply because somehow he just appeared. The sword out of the lake with Stiff playing Lancelot. Talk about being handed something on a plate.

But once you've seen him, savour him like he used to savour his idols. 'Kids who were into Roxy Music went along with their dyed hair and right strides just to see the band and nothing else. The boys didn't want to pull a bird and the birds didn't want to pull a boy. They wanted to go home, get to bed and hold that concert in their arms. There ain't nothing in the world comparable to that feeling.

'Otis Redding's like the Windmill Theatre – he'll never close. Buddy Holly was only 22 when he died, 22! Eddie Cochran was 21. When Bob Dylan played his first electric concert at the Albert Hall someone in the audience shouted 'Judas!' He replied 'I don't believe you.' He was 22. These days you've got to get old quick and stay there for ever. Like they do in Barbados. But there they look old at any age.'

Kosmo, meanwhile, is flaunting his talent for after-dinner conversation. He's talking about this geezer who used to tie up his *Hackney* with nettles and whack it with a peg.

'Then there's the patron saint of Blockheads,' says Ian. 'Joan of Belfast. We came across her picture in a girlie magazine.' She was one of those readers' wives photos. A flesh in the pan. Wonder if he'll ever add her to his pearly hall of characters. Like Plaistow Patricia, for example, *the lawless brat from a council flat who liked it best when she went up west where she took some smack from a Chinese jack.* And after that, if you remember, *an affair began with Charlie Chan.*

I could say Dury is more down to earth than two dozen Max Bygraveses, a gross of Arthur Mullards, a brace of punko pantomimes and a score of spiv-scrawls on brick walls.

I could say he's charming, maybe a little too distrustful but ultimately real. No shop window mannikin like many sham stars in the January sales.

I could say he's a two-up, two-down toreador.

I could say his secret is what he describes as his 'nudges'. The lyrical nuance inherent in every line. The delicate shove into comprehension. There's more meaning behind, say, 'Candyfloss is sticky,' than in any of the songs streaking past the top of your head making the milk-rounds now.

I could even say Ian Dury is one of the most exciting and original artists to emerge in an exciting and original 366 days.

I could say all of that. But I won't 'cos it's much easier for you to take the initiative by doing the alternative.

Just ask Joyce and Vicki.

Ian will go on to become a working-class icon and shrivelled legend before dying of cancer in March 2000.

RAMONES, GENERATION X, REZILLOS
New Year's Eve, Rainbow, London

Resilient Rezillo Fay Fife, she of the misspent midriff, comes polka-dot splashing on to the Rainbow stage like a Prisoner balloon and kisses goodbye to '77.

She juggles round lead singer Eugene Reynolds, he of the sweaty shades, her great lipsmacking thighs slapping and folding through each number. Songs like 'Top Of The Pops' and '2000AD' indicate an interesting future for the first British band to appear on the Sire label, home of the Ramones and Talking Heads. Powerful yet always under control. Heavy, heavy. Rumour has it the Ramones wanted to rearrange the bill after they saw the Rezillos because they rate them highly. Watch out.

However, Generation X are a bit of a sham. They just don't feel right. Billy Idol's pseudo menacing curled lip is an inconsequential bore, but he's just so good-looking that the have-face-will-travel mode switches into automatic every time he sneers into a camera.

This is not punk, this is washing-powder and it certainly cleans a lot of teenage stains judging by the regularity of their appearances on 'Top of the Pops'. Idol puts the hunk into punk and he wears it well.

Operative word – okay. Never knocked me out. Probably never knocked themselves out. Yet. Billy Idol has a somewhat tuneless voice which sometimes grates. No denying he looks good – all piebald and mash – but that ain't everything. Still, Derwood is a cracker of a fringe-in-the-eyes guitarist and the crowd does stand up.

The Ramones. First time I've seen them. They're a giggle, as far as giggles go. I counted 193 songs and three encores. Like driving a tank at 150mph. Long hair and shades. Sweet-talking raids. Hey-ho, let's go into 1978. So long, Ramone. You were last year's thing. Most of you will die pretty young and pretty vacant. You have to.

I feel like last year's thing too: *I look pretty young but I'm just backdated.*

In the foyer of the Rainbow after the gig I have a quick chat with Magenta Devine who works for PR guru Tony Brainsby. As she walks away I realise I'm standing, bearded and alone, in the middle of a heaving pride of punks just like I did 12 months earlier. Just like I've done the whole fucking year.

For me nothing has changed – except, maybe, my life.

1977 is already a dream to me now.

And so it ends…

SEX PISTOLS: ATLANTA AND MEMPHIS
14–15 January 1978

Radio phone-in show, Atlanta.
Listener: 'Say, Ah've heard them Pistols even crack hamsters in half on stage.'
DJ: 'Yep, reckon Ah've heard that too.'
Listener: 'Ah jest want them suckers back in London.'
DJ : 'Ah was a little disappointed with them last night, y'know. The

worst thing thrown was a plastic football. Why, up there on that stage the worst thing them boys did was to blow their noses.'

Listener: 'Anyway Mike, Ah wanna bet ya that the All Stars are gonna win the big game tonight.'

Purge your minds of everything you've read about this tour. This is the real McCoy.

My observations are limited to two shows – Atlanta, Georgia and Memphis, Tennessee. They are the opening dates of this strange Pistols' tour centring on the southern states, which ain't exactly hip to what's going down anyway.

The big cities were out. Reasons? Mmm, difficult. McLaren digs the holes his boys fall into – some day, maybe, one will be six feet deep.

The Wringer of the Publicity Flannel doesn't do anything without guaranteed Fleet Street reverberations. Every move isn't just coldly calculated, it's way below freezing, man. Even the simple announcement of a single makes the editorial columns – especially if that single happens to bear the title 'Belsen Was A Gas'.

Don't fall into the trap of thinking that the papers will write about them, no matter what. No. Just think of McLaren sitting in a back room with a graph charting multifarious courses to magnificent stardom.

The band is a unique animal. Spawned out of sensationalism, they must continue to feed upon it until they reach a grotesque level of obesity. Sure, that's happened in the past, but the Pistols, and this is where the unique factor comes in, have actually lived up to the initial hype and even transcended it.

Not content to consolidate their position as this country's number-one group they, or rather McLaren, embark on preposterous missions that can only ultimately lead to commercial suicide – but maybe that's what they want.

Publicity begins to dwindle. Solution: an American tour. Select a bunch of ambiguous venues usually patronised by whistling cowboys and singing saws. Where hick cracks hick and never the Twain shall meet.

The papers are sure to go for that one. You can easily envisage the editor's office the day before the tour gets under way. 'Those cowboys sure aren't going to take too kindly to four slurping, burping tramps from England. There's bound to be trouble. Christ, there might even be a murder.'

Now, I'm not saying that's what happened. And I'm not pointing the finger at anyone. But Randy's Rodeo, San Antonio?

Anyway, the papers move in for the last round-up, following the band all over the south without a helping hand from the Pistols' American record label, Warners, who become increasingly intolerant of the British press as the tour wears on.

The band is aware of the press and in an oblique way, they pander to it. Let's face it, the Pistols have never been outrageous on-stage. Exciting sure, but shocking? Yet the old dream-machine whirlpool has prepared the Americans for the worst. They expect defecation, they expect urination, they expect blood, they expect genocide, they expect Hiroshima.

They get the Sex Pistols and the occasional flob.

The whole thing is an anticlimax to all but the discerning critic and the punk purist.

Sure, the band provide a little rock'n'roll fun, like dirtying up hotel rooms and burping in public. Real run-of-the-mill stuff and probably things they would never have done if they hadn't read about themselves doing it – before they did it that is.

After all, why knock the system, especially one you've helped to create? Play ball with us and we'll play ball with you. Simple as that. But is it? They've yet to win over an American public untouched by human hand, though maybe a little shop-soiled, given to plagiarism and the occasional infidelity – but, despite Woodstock, LSD and hash-browns, still God-fearing and respectable.

First blood (in the strict, figurative sense, you understand) is at a snazzy little hall situated in the middle of one of those indoor shopping precincts where blue-rinse housewives buy non-dairy milk while floating on a cushion of Muzak. Soap-opera city. A glance across the margarine shelf was all it took. She just couldn't tell the difference.

The Great South-East Music Hall. True, it's in the south-east but the rest is lies. It certainly isn't great, just a gleaming reminder that you can actually watch live music, if you shut your eyes, in what seems like the comfort of your own home. And music hall, never; just a flash little place with seats and a bar that sells pints of Coke and beer if you produce your ID card.

The strange collection of people gathered seem, on the whole, to appreciate the band simply because they can no more draw comparisons than a bunch of stoned chimps.

A crowd of 600 that comprises two city vice squads (the Memphis mob just checking them out), British press, American press (in force), transvestites (some of them real darlings) and drunken rednecks. Hardly typical.

Snatch of garbled conversation: 'Two stems turned me down tonight. And why did you bring your wife to see punk rock?'

'Hell, she don't know nuthin' about punk rock.'

His wife: 'I jest bought this book. It's called 'Hallucinogenic Plants'.' 'Pigshit'.

See what I mean?

Maybe the band is crap because of an over-reliance on facial expressions and bodily stances. In other words, posing. Rotten appears to be so engaged – no, entrenched in trying to look like what he thought the Americans thought he looked like that he pays no attention to sounding like what he thought the Americans thought he sounded like.

And that's a very complicated way of saying that he sings real bad.

TV interviewer to southern belle; 'Whaddya think of the Sex Pistols?'

Belle, trying to make herself audible over Steve Jones's cacophonous guitar: 'Ah think it's the worst thing Ah've ever heard – but Ah'm havin' fun."

And that's what it's about, after all. As long as the band remember that – they always used to. It's during 'Submission' that I start to draw parallels between the Sex Pistols and Muhammad Ali.

Remember how Ali, then Cassius Clay, used to outrage boxing pundits with his predictions and crazy ring repertoire? He picked the idea up from a wrestler – Gorgeous George, who used to laugh a lot around his home town Louisville. Clay was as good as his mouth and rejuvenated interest in what was then a flagging sport. Likewise Malc's boys deliberately set out to shock, to pulverise a coagulated music industry. Initially, they weren't as good as they boasted. But they got better. There's a lot of Gorgeous George in Johnny Rotten and it'll take the Yanks some time to realise that. Let's hope Rotten never forgets it.

'It's real good fun knowing we're all going to die, isn't it?' Rotten's introduction to 'EMI'.

Right then a guy standing behind me accidentally treads on another guy' s foot. 'Don't step on mah foot.'

'Hell, man, Ah'm jest havin' mahself a little fun.'

'But don't step on mah foot.'

'Ah'm havin' fun.'

'Ah think we better settle this outside.'

'Fine by me.'

Exit.

Somebody throws a dirty handkerchief on to the stage. In one instinctive action, Rotten picks it up, wipes his nose and throws it back.

This was the one gig where image ousted music – and thankfully, the band knew it.

In an Atlanta airport waiting lounge the next day Sid Vicious comes strolling in. He missed the band's bus. There's blood on his vest. 'We were fucking terrible last night. Do you like *Spiral Scratch*?' and then he breaks into 'Boredom, boredom, boredom'. Then he burps, then he spits, then he drinks some more Coke, then he burps again. 'Cutting yourself is all right at the time but the pain after is a bind,' he tells me.

See, young Sid went missing after the gig. He was eventually found wandering the streets with blood spouting from a self-inflicted rip to his neck caused by a broken bottle and a three-star body full of five-star smack. 'I can kill myself if I want,' he tells the weary Warner Brothers' press officer.

Sid is the only Pistol I manage to speak to – and you've just read the entire conversation. To say that the band is taciturn is an understatement.

Their mouths are full of concrete when the press is mentioned. McLaren is determined to imprison them in splendid isolation.

Ten-foot-tall guys with steel helmets and sten-guns guard the band's dressing-room doors. I thought they might like to see an old face, y'know, a bit of southern comfort in a strange land.

I venture up to one of the guards and ask him if he would mention to the boys that Barry Cain from 'Record Mirror' says hullo.

That way they'd realise I was there and maybe invite me in for a drink. The guy goes into the dressing room and reappears ten seconds later.

'Did you tell them?'

'Yep.'

'What did they say?'

'Hullo.'

Outside, TV units are firing the stock 'Whaddya think of them?' at people.

' Too loud.'

'The warm-up group was a helluva lot better.'

'I'm a journalist.'

'The warm-up group was more than that.'

' I'm a journalist.'

'Ah thought it was hot. It was real good. Ah enjoyed it.'

'I'm from another TV company.'

'It sure makes a change from disco music.'

'Ah'm a security guard.'

'I'm another journalist.'

'I'm a Sex Pistol.'

Well, what do you expect from a country that prints a photograph of the boys in a daily newspaper arriving at JFK airport with the caption, 'The Sex Pistols 1. to r.: Steve Jones, Johnny Rotten, Paul Cook, Glen Mattock.'

And so to Memphis. The band arrive on the day of a farmers' strike. The plainsmen invade the town in tractors causing a five-mile traffic tailback. Ironically it's also Elvis Presley's birthday weekend and there are queues of fans at his Memphis home, Gracelands, to celebrate his 43rd.

Five-thousand tearful fans are expected to pay homage at the wreath-laden fog-bound mansion over the two-day festival. Meanwhile, police director Buddy Chapman has given the go-ahead for the Pistols to play. 'Ah saw them in Atlanta and the worst thing they performed was their music,' he tells the TV cameras.

The newsreader on the local TV station gives a toothpick sticky grin. 'Hey, people, we gotta bit of a scoop for ya. A Sex Pistols interview. Yep, we were intimidated by them at first but thought, What the heck? I asked their guitarist Steve Jones what he thought of the American reaction to the band.'

Switch to scene outside hotel as Steve pokes his head out of the band's coach into one of those phallic mikes. 'Dunno what reaction we've 'ad an I don't care.' Sniff.

'Well, whaddya think of America, Steve?'

'Too many cowboys, ain't there?' Sniff.

'How do you think the band will go down over here, Steve?'

'Dunno.' Sniff. 'We're nuffin' big anyway.' Exeunt coach and co.

'Well, folks, they were kind to us.'

Change channels to NBC. Toilet-faced announcer says that when one of their reporters tried to interview the band they demanded ten dollars per word. 'And when they did talk it was a bleep bleep all the way through.'

Then their music specialist, a grey, fat 40-year-old, makes a few evaluations: 'The Sex Pistols are outrageous and also vile and profane. When their hotel room was examined in Atlanta, the maids found beer cans on the bed, spit on the carpets, food debris on tables and empty bottles of Clearasil. The band told reporters they were off to a local sex-devices store.

'Each member of the band looks like a reincarnation of Gary Gilmore. Their music is primal, driving, and as ugly as the young men make themselves.' All said in dulcet presidential-election tones.

Another station.

'No group since the Beatles has created such an interest through their hype – and that turns into money very easily. We asked people in the street what they thought of them.'

Little old lady: 'Disgusting. They ought to know better.'

Truck driver: 'If they keep themselves clean they'll be all right. As long as they stay within the law.'

Black guy: 'They oughta be horsewhipped.'

Little boy: 'It's jest sick.'

Then, without any kind of warning, adverts.

'Frankly, I could sure use some advice about *laxatives*,' says the beautiful blonde. Y'know, the kind of girl you think never goes to the toilet. She doesn't, anyway, by the sound of it.

The Taliesyn Ballroom stands on Union Avenue in downtown Memphis. There are a dozen armed policemen and 150 ticket-holding fans who are being refused admission. Seems the local fire department is complaining that 900 people inside the hall is against regulations. Lame excuse but effective, nonetheless. The kids try to storm the place – but it's the kind of riot you only hear about later. In other words, you get more violence at Millwall when there's nobody playing.

An organ-and-cloak school-assembly-hall atmosphere pervades the sarcophagus Ballroom. People (real people this time, not the quilted patchwork audience of last night) sit neatly in rows of wooden chairs.

Nashville is barely 150 miles away – close enough to hear the agonising Indian death-chant screams of cats choking on guitar strings. In Memphis you can always spot a country fan – his petrified hairstyle doesn't blow in the wind.

An irrational impatience rules. They've read, watched and heard so much but never *seen*. Like internees at Japanese PoW camps forced to drink pint after pint of water till their stomachs reached nine-month pregnant proportions before they were jumped on, these kids are determined to spew out all the bullshit.

Rotten leaps on stage. The kids leap up. Cries of 'Sit down!', reminiscent of open-air festivals, drown his voice on 'God Save The Queen'.

'You all celebrating Elvis's birthday?' asks Rotten. Then a ten second psych-out before 'I'm A Lazy Sod'. He's wearing a Max Miller special, blue suit with purple hoops and tails. 'I'm so fucking lazeee.'

'Didja hear that?!' one guy asks his bird. 'Didja hear what he jest said?'

'You fucking cunt!' says Sid, as the number closes, obviously doing a surf special on the shockwaves. He then slips out of his black-leather bomber and screams, 'Who wants a fight?'

Sid's a rock'n'roll casualty and he ain't even dead yet. The Sword of Damocles looms ominously above his malignant skull. Count the days.

'New York' sees Rotten doing an Egyptian jerk with his head. 'I'm not here for your amusement – you're here for mine.'

They're playing much better, having realised they'll be accepted as unacceptable simply by being themselves (as far as they possibly can, that is). The kids love it. But one wonders if that's the reaction of automatons afraid to dislike the band or a mob of rednecks who get off on it because they find the band exciting and original.

'EMI', 'Bodies' and an unrecognisable song ('Belsen Was A Gas' perhaps, if indeed it exists), 'Submission', 'Holidays In The Sun', 'No Feelings' and 'Pretty Vacant' follow without mishap. 'Anarchy' is the last number and Rotten adds, 'In the US of A,' much to the delight of the crowd who are by now standing on their seats.

Rotten holds his hand above his eyes and surveys the scene Nelson style as if to say, 'I see no hips.'

'No Fun' encore enhanced by the liberal distribution of *Never Mind The Bollocks* T-shirts, all ludicrously small. A simple 'Goodbye, y'all' from Mr Jones, and the band flee to their waiting bus, which heads straight away for San Antonio, south Texas.

The Pistols stand at 108 in the Billboard album charts – that's a fair way behind Elvis Costello. It's still too early to tell whether they'll storm the States. Six-hundred people a gig is not exactly Madison Square Garden.

Like I said, McLaren moves in mysterious ways – but it could be that this tour is a little too mysterious for the Americans to comprehend. After all, they're still a new race and they ain't that hip to rock prestidigitators outside Colonel Tom Parker. You can almost feel sorry for them.

The album will move up and they'll become quite popular. But without continuous press it may be a case of out of sight, out of mind. Like a country singer told me in a local club, 'I like their style – but they ain't no musicians.'

But neither were the Stones nor Beatles at the beginning.

The Americans are notoriously fey. They enjoy novelties, especially if those novelties happen to speak with English accents and look as if they've just shot up 50,000 volts of liquid electricity.

Maybe the Pistols will always be treated as essentially a novelty over there simply because they're so English.

So, they've done the big tour. What next?

Solo albums?

DESPERATE HOUSEWIVES, MEMPHIS

After the Memphis gig I'm itching for reaction and talk to a few punters outside. I'm the first English guy these people have ever seen in the flesh. I feel like a movie star. Everyone I speak to loved the show and two on-the-ball dudes – more Mott The Hoople than Bob Dylan – invite me to a bar that's heaving with country and Lynyrd Skynyrd, and introduce me to a succession of girls heaving with country and apple-pie breasts.

The guys won't let me put my hand in my pocket all night (a journalist's dream) then insist on buying me dinner (a journalist's wet dream).

We smoke some dope in the car as we drive to an all-night hamburger joint. One of the guys tells our waitress I write songs for the Pistols which I guess means he hasn't grasped what I do. I'm about to correct him when I notice the spark in her eyes.

'No! Really?'

'Er, well, yes,' I say. 'In a way.'

'Wow!'

By the end of the meal I've told her the name of my hotel and even the room number. Shit, I'm pissed and stoned and in Memphis. Elvis would have approved.

The guys drive me back to my hotel. I've made their night. And they've certainly made mine. It's six a.m. by the time I crash out.

Two hours later a furtive knock on my hotel-room door wakens me. I'm still a little pissed and a little stoned and a little in Memphis but I make it to the door and look through the keyhole.

It's the fucking waitress!

And she's with another fucking woman!

And I'm in my fucking underpants!

Thank you, God.

I open the door.

'Hi. Remember me? The waitress from last night? This is my friend, Mona. Can we come in?'

Two women. Two fucking women.

I'm usually a coy boy but I suddenly feel free in my underpants and ready to be taken advantage of. Repeatedly.

I sit seductively on the bed, one leg on, one leg off. Then I notice I'm still wearing socks and hastily remove them putting the off leg on in the process. The movement makes me feel distinctly uncool and at a loss for words.

'Mona, this is Barry. He writes for the Sex Pistols.'

'Hi, Barry. And you've come all the way from London?'

'Er, yes.' I cross my arms to cover my nipples. I feel totally naked. It's like a bad dream.

'I've never met anyone from England before,' says Mona. I grab my first real look at her. She's got dyed blonde hair, wears spectacles with pretty thick lenses and looks around 35. Turns out she's divorced with two kids, aged ten and eight.

The waitress, raven-haired Karen, is also divorced and 35 and has three kids. Last night she looked 17, 'well you know what I mean'. Karen, Mona and their five children live together in a house on the other side of town.

This isn't about sex. This is about prestige. They tell me to get dressed because they want to take me out for breakfast.

Twenty minutes later I'm eating ham and scrambled eggs in a restaurant where the waitress begs me to keep talking in that 'beautiful way' and hands me a joint as we leave. Mona and Karen drive me to their house – via the gates of Gracelands – and proceed to spend the afternoon ringing all their friends and inviting them over to meet the English guy. I feel like Christopher Columbus as they file in.

They cook me a slap-up meal and in the evening take me to a country-and-western bar where I dance with several women on the outskirts of middle age who thrust their legs between mine, causing my knob to have a hoe-down every time we move.

Karen gets a headache and goes home, and Mona drives me back to the hotel. We sit in the car and talk for a while as I bathe in this glorious southern hospitality. I'm tempted to invite her to my room but, shit, Dina's better looking. And I love her.

And Mona would probably tell me to piss-off anyway.

'Goodnight Mona. And thanks for everything.'

She actually says, 'Goodnight, sweet prince,' as I get out of the car. I don't know what shocks me most – the idea of me being sweet or Mona knowing 'Hamlet' – and as she pulls out of the hotel car park I'm *stuck inside of my mobile with the Memphis blues again.*

I try not to disturb anyone as I close the last volume of 'Record Mirror'. In the reading room of the British Library nobody can hear you scream.

For the first time I notice the silence.

As I turned the pages of those volumes the glorious pageant that was 1977, bursting with colour and condoms and clear consciences and sweet, sweet life, danced before my eyes. It was as if another person was recording my life for me, a pseudo-Boswell with a Mohican, 'turning me up and turning me down, making me smile and making me frown'. My youth has been sleeping in these huge books for 30 years and I awakened it with a kiss.

A Locarno kiss.

You're all I need

To get by…

2007

Ever feel the world's caving in?

I do. Often. Especially when bills drop like bricks on to the doormat and people close to you fall ill and die.

Trouble is, bills continue to fall like bricks on to the doormat, then *you* fall ill and die. And all for what? A few crumbs of praise? £1,000,000? £1,000,000,000?

The way of all flesh is the same.

Still, a few crumbs of praise...

The Stranglers sang about 'Dead Ringers' in the strictly spitting image colloquial sense – 'You're a dead ringer for Gwyneth Paltrow.' But rumour has it – bollocks, probably, but intriguing – that the phrase actually dates way back to the days when Post Mortems was the name of your mailman and the odd pronounced dead bod wasn't, in fact, so very stiff after all but, whoops, too late, we've just buried you. After some 'corpses' came back to life just before burial, a curious local dignitary ordered a few recent graves to be exhumed. Finger nail scratches were discovered on the inside of one of the coffins, with eyes on the point of explosion, an acre of snot and an ocean of blood-red vomit.

To prevent more such tragedies from occurring, a hole was bored in all coffins into which ran a string attached, via a wooden tube, to a bell on the surface that the unfortunate victim could ring with a flick of the wrist and alert the gravedigger (who was probably pissed and shagging his sister in a shed somewhere and, logically, thought that the bells he heard were round the necks of cows that cavorted outside). If the bell hadn't rung after three days the tube was removed.

It's probably an etymological urban myth but it suits my purpose because I feel like a dead ringer, not in the Johnny Depp sense, although some might disagree, but a dead ringer as in buried-alive-but-unable-to-reach-the-string-because-the-silly-fuckers-stuck-the-hole-in-the-other-end dead ringer. I feel I've been badly designed and, like a Sixties tower-block, an increasing eyesore with each passing year.

I'm getting older and I hate it to fuck. I never realised it would carry such baggage, such unmitigated sorrow. It feels like I've been yearning for my lost youth for an eternity.

Thanks to the British Library, I got the chance to spend a few hours with it, much like the boy android in the movie 'AI' who waited thousands of years to spend just one day with his human 'mum'.

As I turned the pages, I felt the flame of youth up my arse, and a ripple ran across my soul in much the same way as an itchy ear indicates someone is talking about you. I suddenly wanted someone to talk about me to someone about something that I'd done.

I think it's called desire.

I needed a bigger fix. I wanted more than words. I wanted bodies. Bodies that rang bells.

The more I wrote about 1977 the more I fantasised about seeing some of the main players again, the ones that were so good they sounded like two people playing when they performed. I wanted to see their faces, their eyes, their smiles. I wanted to hear their voices. It was important, somehow, like a premonition of death.

HUGH CORNWELL
Notting Hill

When I finished reading my January '77 interview with Hugh Cornwell, I found it painfully hard to believe that it had taken place 30 years ago. I'd got to know Hugh pretty well, the band had invited me along to some magical places – from Kyoto to Reykjavik via Paris, Rome and Amsterdam. I was even the Stranglers' PR for a while. We corresponded when he was unjustly jailed for heroin possession and I recorded his experiences behind bars, which the Stranglers published independently as 'Inside Information'.

But I forsook the writing to publish pop magazines and life suddenly got serious with offices, secretaries, filing cabinets, and being married to a woman who hated the music business with Mediterranean intensity.

In short, I've seen Hugh on three occasions over the past 25 years, all in 1990, and haven't laid eyes on him since.

I thought it might be a good idea to celebrate that first interview in 1977 and decided, during the course of writing this book, to try to track him down and ask him what he thought of those dusty quotes I'd unearthed in the British Library.

But would he be interested? Or would he be fed up with regurgitating the past?

I discovered the name of his music agent on the Net, and a girl with the surname 'Cain' actually represented him. This was the first in the long line of coincidences that haunted the new interviews. I emailed her immediately.

Hi Michelle

I wonder if you could confirm that you represent Hugh Cornwell? And if so I wonder if it would be possible to interview him for a forthcoming book I've been commissioned to write about the year 1977?

My name is Barry Cain and Hugh knows me well – although I haven't seen him in some years.

Apologies for troubling you but I felt sure you wouldn't mind as you're obviously my long-lost sister!

Look forward to hearing from you.

It hit the spot.

Hi Barry,

Always nice to meet another Cain! David Fagence, who is Hugh's manager, may be able to help you. I've CCd him above.

Thanks

Michelle

Lo and behold, an email from one David Fagence arrived within the hour.

Hi Barry

I am David – HC's manager. Can you tell me a little more about the book and who has commissioned; publisher etc? Hugh has informed me that you did the interviews for the 'Inside Information' booklet and as such I would be delighted to hear more about the project. As you can imagine we are approached on a daily basis for such things and I need to be certain of the validity and credibility of the project before entertaining. I would also appreciate an idea of who else you have contacted for interviews? Let me know by return.

Best regards

David

I was elated. I was a reporter again and I'd come up trumps! I hadn't lost my touch. My reply was swift.

Hi David

Thanks for getting back to me so promptly.

Basically, the book is about the year 1977 when bands like the Stranglers exploded onto the scene. At the time, I was a journalist with 'Record Mirror' and got to know the main players pretty well. The book will feature interviews and reviews I did during those crucial 12 months with my take on the events that unfolded as the year progressed.

I also want to talk to several of the most influential people at the time and get comments from them about the things they said and what the year meant to them. I am approaching John Lydon, Paul Weller, Mick

Jones and Rat Scabies.

I hope that covers your queries. Please don't hesitate to ask me for anything else you may require. Of course, Hugh will get to see his words before anything is published. I envisage the interview taking no more than one to two hours.

Besides, it would be great to see Hugh again.

Look forward to hearing from you.

Cheers

And then – nothing. Six days later I sent a soothing reminder.

Hi David

Just a quick line to check that you received my email OK and whether you've had a chance to speak to Hugh.

All the best

Still nothing. I re-read my earlier email – had anything I'd written turned him off? 'One or two hours'? Should I have said, 'one hour max'? Was I a fucking jerk or what? I haven't seen the guy in 16 years – maybe I should have been more deferential? What have I done wrong?

A week later I sent another email.

Hi David

Sorry to trouble you again but I wonder if you could possibly let me know whether Hugh is up for my suggestion? The publisher is on my back at the moment and I need to finalise my plan of action. As an alternative suggestion, I could email you some questions and maybe Hugh could email me back the answers, although, as I said, it would be nice to see Hugh again over lunch or dinner perhaps.

So, if you could let me get back to me David I'd really appreciate it.

Regards

As I pressed send, I saw the mistake. 'So, if you could let me get back to me David I'd really appreciate it.' *Let me get back to me?* David must have thought he was dealing with a schizophrenic. *Let me get back to me.*

Fuck.

Bingo!

Hi Barry [Which one did he mean?]

Hugh and myself have been in the Middle East for the last 10 days; hence you not hearing from me. Hugh is leaving immediately for Europe tomorrow and after 24 hours back in the UK leaves for a 1 month tour of Australia, returning at the start of July. We have no problem with helping you with the book, but timing is not ideal. I am surprised the publisher would be on your back so soon? You only made contact a couple of weeks ago.

Let me know your timings.

Best regards David

I replied swiftly.

Hi David

Thanks for coming back to me. Sorry to be a pain and many thanks for your co-operation.

The publisher is looking at the Christmas market, I guess, and is anxious to get his hands on my words asap. Nice to know someone wants me for something other than my body.

Anyway, it looks like Hugh can't make it until early July. If we could set a date, say, sometime in the first or second week when he's recovered from the tour that should be fine. Hugh will be the first interview that appears in the book so I'll leave a space for it!

Glad to hear he's doing well. Please send him my very best wishes, and thanks again David.

Look forward to hearing from you with suitable date.

Cheers

Another two weeks went by. I was about to give it up as a bad job and start pursuing other avenues when the phone rang.

'Barry Cain.'

I knew his voice immediately as it slid through my memory like the steel sphere in a pinball machine with the tilt light on.

'Hugh Cornwell.'

'Hi, how are you? I've been given your number concerning this interview you want to do.'

'Are you up for it?'

'Absolutely.'

We arranged to meet outside Notting Hill Gate tube station on a Wednesday afternoon around 2.30. I hadn't been to that station for years and had forgotten there were a zillion exits.

It was two o'clock. I was early. I dropped into the Old Swan in Kensington Church Street and ordered a pint of Spitfire. I'm a sucker for a quiz machine and spotted one in the corner. I won two quid and then sat down to check over my notes, which amounted to a couple of questions and a copy of that first interview.

The last time I met Hugh was in a Greek restaurant in Camden Town 17 years ago when I interviewed him for an extended biographical press release that CBS had asked me to write on the band. He was reticent and guarded, and didn't like my line of questioning. He wasn't the guy I remembered.

I remembered a cool, laid-back dude who seemed to like me. Sharp, erudite, supremely intelligent, but always a musician.

The Stranglers were musicians first and foremost. Only a fool would deny that their initial three albums – all recorded in barely a year, the time it had taken Yes to pick their noses – contained bewitching music of strange structures and lyrics dripping with mature delinquency. No shit.

Within weeks of our last meeting, Hugh had quit the Stranglers after a gig at Alexandra Palace. He dug some deep roots to grow a solo career and disappeared from major public view for a while, last seen carrying a giant spade and a fucking pneumatic drill.

But Hugh knew that the answer, as Kenneth Williams always maintained, lies in the soil, and his solo career has now started to blossom, 17 years down the rock island line. And that's a mighty fine road.

'Hugh, you told me to ring when I got here. I'm just round the corner from Notting Hill tube in the Old Swan in Kensington Church Street.'

'Pick you up outside the Bank of Scotland by the station in 15 minutes.'

Half an hour later we're sitting opposite each other in a nearby Italian café, empty, with a dizzy waitress apologising that there's only a thimbleful of Parmesan to shake over Hugh's meat lasagne and my gnocchi with tomatoes, onions and garlic.

He looked far, far younger than his years and was as lean as a Grand National jockey. It's in his genes to be tall and tanned and young and lovely: his 94-year-old mother swims every day in the open air.

I suppose Hugh was the first pop star I could actually call a friend and that meant a great deal to me. Although I'd interviewed musicians regularly, I was nervous in the presence of celebrity – still am. Most journalists are, because they're plagued by self-doubt and inferiority complexes. And the biggest joke of all? So are the pop stars. Talk about the blind leading the blind.

Jean-Jacques Burnel was a lot less accessible and I didn't get the chance to have any kind of insight into his complexities until after '77. In fact, I never interviewed anyone in the band except Hugh during that year.

From the moment I saw Hugh again outside Notting Hill tube I felt comfortable, as if it was only a few months ago that we were in that Greek restaurant sharing pitta bread and paranoia.

I guess I was always relaxed in his company because Hugh was a north London boy and went to William Ellis school in Parliament Hill, which was my first choice although I didn't get in.

I explained across the gnocchi, *sans* Parmesan, that I was hoping he'd comment on that other first interview, 30 years ago.

'Fire away.'

What I really want to do is melt down Led Zeppelin and reinforce all the church roofs in England.

'I wanted to what?'

Melt down Led Zeppelin and reinforce all the church roofs in England.

Laughter. 'That's a great quote. Nice turn of phrase. Very funny.

'You simply weren't allowed to like bands like Led Zep then, but when I first got into music I bought *Led Zeppelin I* and *II* and I was wigging out to it at university in Bristol. I was there when these bands first appeared. I was hitching back to university once when I got a lift from Led Zep's road manager. He was on his way to meet them at a houseboat and it must have been just before a tour. When I got back to uni I couldn't wait to tell everyone – 'You'll never guess what! I just got a lift from the road manager of Led Zeppelin in his big Range Rover.' I was so excited. So that quote didn't mean I didn't like Led Zeppelin, it was just the lead connection, I guess.'

Old ladies are being mugged on their way to churches and it's a shame.

More laughter.

Things won't change by violence. There will be a silent revolution.

'Uhhhh!'

There are a lot of very intelligent people around today who are fed up with our constitution. They're slowly increasing in number and something's going to happen soon. I see my role as someone trying to make the country understand that all these 60 and 70-year-old politicians have absolutely no contact with the public. They start off with good intentions but after years of crawling they become meaningless. Like Denis Squealy, they don't want to lose what they've got.

'As you get older you realise that it's always the case that the government, whoever it is, is despised. Everyone loves them during the honeymoon period when a party first gets in and then, once they start messing up, everyone's disgruntled and wants to get rid of them. You suddenly realise that's the ebb and flow of government. That's what happens.

'I don't know many young people now so I don't really know what they think, but I would say that they're just as disgruntled as we were then. I'm sure there are lots of things they can complain about now; it's just that the things to complain about used to be more obvious.

'Now there are more subtle changes. Like the fracturing of society, constant but undetectable.

'Like the way in which education in this country is slowly

crumbling. Teaching is the most important job in society yet one of the most poorly paid. Teachers should get a hundred grand a year and then the profession will attract all those far-thinking people who currently eschew it. It's the only way of attaining the very highest standard of education that is so required. This is what we're basing the future on.

'Like the litter. I get very sad when I see people, and I guess it's mainly young people, throwing wrappers on to the floor. Nobody's ever told them to pick it up – where's that come from? At the risk of repeating a terribly old cliché – I'm sure it wasn't as bad as that before. I know I never threw things on the street when I was that age. So there must be something intrinsically wrong somewhere.'

I'd like to make enough money to buy a huge mansion and put all the politicians in separate rooms so they can play with themselves. A majority of people have come to the conclusion that the government has no credibility.

'Ooh! I was obviously on a sort of, kind of... It was obviously all the drugs I was taking. Young people now are dissatisfied but they don't really know why. They can't put their finger on it. It's subtle.

'Everything is legislated now, enforced by law. In 1977 there was an it's-the-way-of-the-world acceptance of things. You know, shit happens.

'There was nothing special about that era in terms of disaffected youth. Youth has always been disaffected. You don't see that either until you get older. When you're young you don't have the opportunity to see things repeating themselves in cycles. When you get older you begin to recognise repetition.'

This is the Hugh I remember with such affection, the one who could talk the talk while Jean-Jacques walked the walk. His innate cool hasn't been tarnished by the rust of decades.

What we need desperately is a Robin Hood character. I used to know this bank robber who shot someone once. I asked him about it and he said, 'Look, if someone is stupid enough to get in the way then I'm gonna stop them.' And he's right because the only one who's gonna lose out if he gets away with it is the bank. All it would mean is that someone, somewhere, will have one ounce of caviar less a week.

'I still think like that. I remember a sketch on *Not the Nine o'Clock News* when a guy goes into the bank to make a withdrawal and is informed by the teller that the bank has been robbed and all they stole was *his* money. 'What do you mean?' asks the guy. 'Well you see, we keep everyone's money in boxes out the back and they took your box and no one else's.'

'That's so ludicrous but it illustrates the fact that nobody loses out when a bank is robbed because they're covered by insurance, and insurance companies are the biggest money-making scams in the history of capitalism. I don't lose much sleep over the plight of insurance companies losing money.'

People have got this weird idea that if they see a thief they've got to stop him. What they should do is try and help him escape. The thief will spend the money and spread it around. This country isn't poor. If people can spend 50 grand on a flat then we can't be broke.

'Absolutely right. I'm not talking about a mugger in the street, I'm talking about a professional thief. Why would I need to stop him? Good luck to you, mate. If I was looking out of my window one night because I couldn't sleep and saw someone robbing a bank, I'd watch. It would be fascinating.

'It's funny how we're brainwashed to do certain things in order to uphold society when, in fact, some of the things we're told to do are simply a way to maintain a certain hierarchy and class structure, something that has always held this country back.

'Some people would argue that that's what's best about Great Britain, but it's also one of the worst things about it. It's all about keeping the status quo, keeping the rich rich and the poor poor. This country is experiencing a boom based partly on all the cheap labour that's available after expanding the EU. They all want to live in London because it's the best town in the world. London has everything you could possibly want. I met a French painter in the local pub recently who's moved to London. When artists start moving to London from France that's when you know you're living in the best place in the world! The tide has turned. London is the centre of modern art, of music, of so many things, and the more people come here the more they're reinforcing it. There's also the best money-laundering business here – the City of London.

'Yet I read recently that people across the globe had voted Melbourne the best city in the world to live in. Who's voting? If I lived in London and voted, I'd go for London. So who's voting in this competition? There must be more people from Melbourne voting than anyone else, spread out around the world. Why aren't they living there if they think that? I just can't get to grips with how they've calculated this and if they have – it just doesn't make any sense.

'I've been to Melbourne and I didn't like it much. It's as big as London but there's nowhere near as many people. It's the one place in Australia I can't get to grips with. I understand Sydney, Brisbane, even Canberra, because they're essentially an Australian experience – lovely semi-tropical weather, perfect location usually in a bay, wonderful place to live, extremely friendly people. And then you go to Melbourne and there's this vast expanse of flatness. I just didn't get it.'

The Sex Pistols opened the floodgates and must be credited with that. The Damned are a bit lightweight but they've got a couple of really good numbers.

'True.'

And Eddie and the Hotrods are even more lightweight than The Damned. The Feelgoods are very good at what they do but they've got to come up with some new material quick.

'I should have been running a record label with chat like that. That's pretty accurate. I never slagged off the other bands. Johnny Rotten said the Stranglers were old-age pensioners but I don't think The Clash ever slagged us off. The punk thing could only have happened here, really. I can't imagine it happening anywhere else.

'There was a great rivalry between everybody. I was in San

Francisco at the time – I used to go there a lot to get my head together. I strolled into a bar with my friend Robert Williams, who was recording with Beefheart, and ordered a drink. Out of the blue, The Clash came running over from a corner of the bar. 'Hugh, how you doing?' They were so pleased to see me and suddenly all that rivalry thing disappeared. To experience that over there was so refreshing.

I take all the music papers with a large pinch of salt. I find them far too heavily opinionated and the style has become more important than the content. They're dealing with music which is an escape clause from the con tricks of life. The papers exist in their own ivory towers. They don't have to search for stories because they are always there.

'Absolutely right.'

'Melody Maker's got no humour and takes itself far too seriously. 'NME' is the direct opposite but just as bad – I've had a few shit experiences with them and I think you can distil the whole thing down to one reporter. The rest are probably old hippies.

'Who was that? I got on quite well with Tony Parsons so it can't be him. Wouldn't it have been someone else like Phil McNeil, or maybe Phil Spencer? That remains a mystery.'

'Sounds' treats new bands and established bands in the same way which is pretty good. I find 'Record Mirror' quite refreshing because it contains articles on totally different things and that's healthy. The papers don't always cite the truth and I reckon stories are far too heavily tampered with between writing and printing

'I still believe that, but I just accept it these days. Now I always make sure that when I do an interview I'm perfectly aware beforehand of the angle the interviewer wants and do my best to supply it.

'You get used to tailoring what they want into what you need, so I give them their angle. That way I don't get so disappointed when I read it because I know I've got something out of it and they've got something they can use. It's give-and-take, it's a business. You start realising you've got to treat the whole interview process in a more business like fashion.'

If music leads to violence then it's not music anymore.

'A lot of this at the time was a reaction on my part to John's [Jean-Jacques] attitude to it all which was it's not music unless maybe someone gets beaten up. I just kept going back trying to create an antidote. I felt he was pushing the band in that way and I wanted to defuse it. He could be very intimidating but I must admit that such an attitude really did help to raise our profile. We were the bovver boys. We were the band that people feared.

'We used the whole punk thing, but it wasn't just us. The Jam, the Police, Blondie, they all did. People called us punk and our attitude was, 'Who cares? It's getting our records played on the radio, people are coming to our gigs, we're making records and selling records. Why should we complain about being dragged into the whole punk scene?

'A guy once wrote a bad review of the band so John went out, found him and smacked him. The free press? I told him not to get so wound up about it.'

The function of the artist is to reflect the environment.

'Most definitely. I've been up in Sheffield working with a new group and you wouldn't believe how similar it is to the old punk scene. The Arctic Monkeys have opened the floodgates up there in the same way as the Sex Pistols did down here.

'Sheffield isn't that big a town, but while I was in the studio, whenever I went to the toilet or to make a cup of tea I'd pass these rehearsal rooms and every day throughout the week there were three different bands in each one, all rehearsing at the same time. And they're playing pretty decent stuff. They've got a revolution going on up there. I rehearse in studios in central London and you don't get anywhere near that number of bands coming through.

'The Arctic Monkeys are okay but I'm not sure how they're going to survive in much the same way as I was never sure how the Pistols would survive. But at the same time I can see them being just as influential as the Pistols because of the way they've done it

– through the Internet. It's great – you don't need to be with a big record label any more, you don't need a big advance. This incredible demonstration of the capability of the Internet has made kids start to think, Oh, I didn't realise you could write a song about what happens to me on a Friday night, and they're doing it. Punk was writing about your life and that's exactly what's going on up there.

'After '77 music went out of the control of the people who were making it and into the hands of faceless corporations. But now it seems to be moving back into the right hands. The influence of the big record company is nowhere near what it used to be. The only reason I've got any kind of profile now is because I do a lot of live work. Record royalties, these days, are so bad because, with all the downloading going on, there's nowhere near the sort of income that there used to be. Today, the only way you can survive, finance-wise and PR-wise, is by having a live profile. The days when record-company press offices backed their artists with seemingly bottomless pockets have long gone. The only way to survive is to go out there and do it for yourself. You need that presence simply for people to know you're active. It's a substitute for that big record-company involvement and it's very exciting, being in charge of your own destiny.

'It's only ever been about playing music, it was never about making records – that was something else, a bonus. I enjoy playing music now more than I've ever done because every time I do a new tour I'm not sure who my bass player and drummer are going to be – I may have a different band every time, and that's wonderful.

'I'm gathering a team of good people around the world, not just the UK. It's true that more effective team work has meant I'm selling more albums, but it's also because 16 years after I left the band most people in this country have finally cottoned on to the fact that I'm not in the Stranglers anymore, that I'm a separate entity now.

'It's taken this long because the Stranglers were such a strong brand – as strong a brand as Pink Floyd at the time. I use them as an example because when they were making records in the Seventies no one really knew who the individuals of Pink Floyd were. Most people didn't know who the individual members of the Stranglers were but they knew the name.

'For a long time after my departure the band's management didn't publicise the fact that I'd gone. For years after people would come up to me and say, 'I saw your band the other night but you weren't there,' and I'd tell them I left in 1990!

'It's taken me that long to re-brand myself, but my autobiography, 'A Multitude of Sins', has helped.'

A band should demonstrate to people that they're well within their rights to hold a certain view. There's no point in making things up, the artist has got to be true to his experiences. Music's function is not to create. It isn't a spark in a fuse: it's a separate entity.

Laughter. 'It's not creative? Sounding a bit confused there. If it's not creating it should be a spark to create an explosion and it's not that either? So what is it? Didn't I qualify that statement or did I just fall over at that point?'

And the great thing about punk is that the guy singing on-stage has the same problems as those watching.

'That's right. Most people who write songs are writing about themselves or something that's happened to them. It's a cathartic experience rather than a creative one. I get much more of a therapeutic benefit from writing a song than I do thinking I've created something. I'm doing it for myself absolutely: I want to get something out.

'It's ironic that something so personal becomes so public. Maybe it's so personal that you want everyone to know about it.

'People now know what the Stranglers' songs mean because I wrote a book about it, called 'Song By Song'. I felt I could do that because it was so long since they'd been written. I couldn't do that with my solo stuff. The Stranglers was a shared experience so I could be a little more objective.

I'm fed up with those little schmucks [that's glitzy rock stars] who live, breathe and have the same bodily functions as everyone else yet strive to be inaccessible. Even Rod Stewart gets diarrhoea. Punk could be the first step towards Utopia.

'That's being optimistic, isn't it? I'm still quite optimistic. You have to be optimistic to succeed. If you're pessimistic you think, This will never take off, and you give up on it. I've always thought there must be a way through all this and there's a chance something will happen..

'I had a down period before I left the Stranglers. I was despondent because we didn't seem to be getting anywhere. It was as if the band's career had plateaued out. I'm ambitious and I always like to be achieving. I don't want to have time to be pessimistic.

'I feel good. I don't think I've changed that much. You see some people you haven't seen for a while and you get a shock.' Shit, I hope he's not referring to me. 'And then you get to thinking they must have been through some pretty bad times to end up looking like that.'

Shit, he *was* referring to me.

'That's when you realise you haven't had such a bad time of it. Maybe optimism keeps you young.

'In the last seven months I've hardly had a moment to myself, and even though I don't like being at home too long, it's a perfect place to revitalise the soul, like being plugged into a battery charger.

I studied biochemistry at university which comes in very useful, especially when applied to narcotics. I know everything there is to know about drugs.

More laughter. 'That's classic. What an entertaining interview. I haven't smoked a joint in 16 years. I was in Los Angeles at the time and borrowed one of the band's cars on a day off and went to see Robert Williams. As I walked into his cottage he was finishing a joint and he offered it to me. I had a quick hit, like you do. I came over really weird. I felt absolutely terrible.

' 'What was in that joint?' I asked. He said it was just some grass. "What sort of grass?'

'He told me it was this new skunk stuff I'd never had before. It felt 50 times stronger than ordinary weed and I sat in this chair for four-and-a-half hours unable to move a muscle. Robert asked if I was okay and said I looked terrible, really ashen-faced. I don't think I've ever felt so bad in my entire life. I literally thought I was going to die.

'I kept saying to myself, 'What an absolute waste of time,' and vowed never to touch drugs again. If skunk was the shape of things to come I didn't want any part of it. That's what kids are smoking now. No wonder they get cannabis psychosis. I don't miss drugs at all.'

I'm into decadence – you've got to enjoy it because it comes only from warped, privileged minds. My definition of decadence is having a huge table covered with grapes and instead of taking one at a time you leap onto the table and indulge yourself in the juice of the squashed fruit. Indulge yourself, get completely wiped out. Forget your problems. You can OD on acid, start smoking dope, get a rush in your head and take off like a rocket.

'Sounds like I was definitely having a grand old time. That is very optimistic, isn't it? I used to make a point of enjoying myself. It was very important to take pleasure in that position.

'I wouldn't change my life. I feel very fortunate. I'm still doing what I enjoy doing. Old rock stars fade away less and less these days. Everybody's still out there doing it. The Stones look really good. Let's face it, people half their ages look worse than that. I'm very lucky, very privileged.

'My scheduling is terrible – I forget that I've been told to do something, and if I write it in my diary I forget to take my diary with me. But one thing I've learned is that, in the end, things always get done. It really doesn't matter. That's the way to look at things and that's why I feel quite relaxed at the moment.

'I'm laid-back now but I don't think I used to be. In a review of my book someone said that after reading it they'd found out nothing about me. He said I was very guarded and didn't reveal anything about myself. I couldn't believe it. I tried to be so honest about everything. Events shape your life, anyway. My attitudes to the events that happened around me has shaped me. Maybe he didn't like the fact that I wasn't providing an insight into the Stranglers any more.

'I can't remember if something happened in '76, '77, '78 or '79. I couldn't even remember what year I was put in jail. I thought it was '84 and it turned out it was '79. Now I know because I had to look it all up while writing my autobiography. I used David Buckley's book 'Stranglers No Mercy' as my bible of dates because he's very hot on the chronology.

'I was shocked to see how many things happened in such a short time. The first few years, especially '77, proved to be such a huge explosion. After that it got much quieter. *Rattus* and *Heroes* came out in '77 and *Black and White* in '78.

'I guess '78 didn't shape me as much as people thought it did because I was shaped before that. I was a late starter, so I took a lot of it with a pinch of salt because I wasn't fresh out of short trousers, I wasn't as impressionable. So even though I was toeing the line in the sense of the revolutionary talk, a lot of it you can interpret as just interesting ideas with not a lot of consequence – like reinforcing church roofs with Led Zeppelin.

'All the outrageous things I said, all those so called lies I spouted – yet it turns out most of it was true. I used to get a lot of stick for speaking the truth.'

He smiled and that's the end. Apart from...

Better and worse now than in 1977?

'One thing that's worse is litter. Sorry to keep harping on about it but I really, really hate it. Even the countryside is covered with litter and I find that very upsetting.

'What's better now is it's easier to get proper food in England than it was in '77. It used to be such crap. Now you can eat well wherever you are and it's not expensive. There's more variety and more choice of where you buy it as well.'

Favourite '77 single and album?

'It's gotta be 'In The City'. I remember seeing the Jam perform it live on 'Top of the Pops' and thought, This is amazing. A truly great song that reflected an era. I loved the first Ramones album.'

I reminded Hugh that that was released in 1976.

'In that case Blondie's *Plastic Letters*,' he said, quick as a flash.

Hugh insisted on driving me back to Notting Hill Gate station.

'Who else have you spoken with?' he asked.

'I've contacted six key people I got to know back then. Four, including you, have said yes. The only two I'm not getting any response from are Paul Weller and Mick Jones.'

'Mick. He and I were going to maybe do something a little while back. I've been meaning to call him so now I will. I'll tell him the interview isn't really about the past at all.'

These bands must be sick of dishing out the same old shit about those days of whine and poses. It must be bad enough listening to yourself in a state of constant repetition, but it must be even worse to know that the person doing the interview is invariably someone who has a 30-year-old image of you frozen inside their skull that they expect you to live up to. So, when a voice comes out of that '77 quagmire, i.e. mine, they assume the worst. My efforts to persuade Mick Jones, through various representatives, to do an interview had fallen on stony ground. The offer from Hugh provided a lifeline.

I thanked him as we pulled up at the station. 'Yeah, I'll give Mick a ring. See you, Barry.'

It was five o'clock and I didn't fancy the prospect of a sweaty rush-hour tube home. Hugh and I drank mineral water over lunch so I decided to return to the Old Swan for a more relaxed pint and quiz-machine session.

Cue 'Twilight Zone' theme.

As I walked through the door of the pub the first person I spotted was Mick Jones. He was sitting alone at a table, nurturing a lager. I hadn't seen him for 25 years. 'Mick.'

He looked up and smiled.

I offered my hand. He took it.

'Barry Cain, remember, from 'Record Mirror'.'

'Sure.'

I wasn't, but pressed on. 'Can I get you a beer?'

'No, thanks. When I finish this I've got to shoot off.'

I told him about Hugh and this amazing coincidence, I told him about the book, the interview, the days. He loosened up. Yep, it was Mick Jones all right, The Clash city rocker.

He told me about his Carbon-Silicon project with Tony James – ex-Generation X and Sigue Sigue Sputnik. He told me about Paul Simonon teaming up with Damon Albarn. He told me John Lydon lived in Mae West's old house. He gave me a direct email address and said he'd do the interview in September when he came back from holiday in France.

He left. I pinched myself and ordered that pint.

Several weeks after that interview I saw Hugh play live at the Scala in rejuvenated King's Cross. The last time I'd seen him perform was on that fateful night in Alexandra Palace when he did the Captain Oates number and walked out into the blizzard. He nearly got frozen solid, but Hugh has a blinding pair of thermals that deflect the cold and retain constant heat. His voice was still hanging around and polished up good. The inclusion of old Stranglers' favourites worked like a charm and sharpened the impact of the newer material, of which 'Picked Up By The Wind' was a standout.

Any show that features 'Always The Sun' and a shit-hot bassist in the wet-dream shape of Caroline 'Caz' Campbell – the sexiest woman to pick up a bass this side of Robert Palmer's 'Addicted to Love' video – is a number one in my book and I couldn't wipe the smile off my face until the dawn tapped on my window and interrupted a particularly lascivious dream.

Backstage, Hugh was this charming man and we chatted for ever.

And then it happened.

Hugh introduced me to a guy, who, on hearing my name, looked shocked and said, 'Barry Cain! You're a legend.'

Fuck me sideways.

I won't reveal his name in case he was getting me mixed up with someone else. If he wasn't, he's way up there with Joe Strummer and Tony Parsons.

And if he was, fuck it. There's always the sun.

RAT SCABIES
Soho

I found Rat on myspace.com, a kind of Yellow Pages for pop legends. It took a lot of searching – 4,000 sites featured Rat Scabies and his myspace was on the sixth page. By then I'd found out about the fascinating 'Rat Scabies and the Holy Grail' – surely a contender for any best-book-title award – by Christopher Dawes. I found out all about his post-Damned life in a beautifully written piece penned by the man himself. I found out all about the punk hero who had punched his way through 1977 like a man on fire.

But I wanted more.

I fired off the same email I'd sent to Hugh and crossed my fingers, then crossed my fingers again in the hope I hadn't sent the 'Hi Hugh' email by mistake.

And sure enough…

Hi Barry

Of course I remember you. Call me and we'll hook up.

Rat

It was touch and go, with the emphasis on go, but we finally met up at Rat's old haunt, the Ship in Wardour Street. I hadn't seen him in 24 years and had convinced myself, in the wake of Hugh's immaculate appearance, that if anyone was bound to have a faceful of wrinkles and a scalpful of grey eels, it was Rat. After all, he'd looked years older than the rest of the band when he was 19.

What the fuck will he look like at 51?

And what the fuck do I look like at 54?

'Hullo Barry.'

He looked the same – I swear. Same sad eyes, same air of resignation, same fuck-you attitude. The rock'n'roll lifestyle is obviously the elixir of eternal youth.

We embraced. It felt right, like two war comrades meeting for the first time since the end of hostilities nearly a quarter of a century ago. I'd been there and he knew it, and I knew he knew it. I guess we just fucking knew it.

'I knew it, Rat. I knew you wouldn't have changed.' Duplicitous or what?

The barnet was still there, with more than a hint of its original carrot. The glasses made him look confident. The jacket was leather, the words were cool, the beer was Guinness, the tobacco was rolled in king-size Rizlas. The Ship seemed to cut loose from its moorings and the memories came gift-wrapped.

'People always thought I dyed my hair back then.'

I never did.

'Other people seem to be more affected by my age than I am. I used to get fucking breathless running for a bus when I was 18. To me, life hasn't changed. My teeth are a bit looser and my eyesight ain't as good but I'm the same, although other people do tend to talk to you in loud voices –'You all right, Rat!"

Almost immediately I felt obliged, to ask – in a normal voice – if he had any objection to me mentioning the scam at 35,000 feet.

'Be my guest. I've always wanted to say, 'Bless you', for that. Came in well handy. I was thankful of that extra money within the first fucking hour of arriving in New York. Jake Riviera, our manager, said, as we checked into the hotel, 'Right, someone's given me some weed but no Rizlas. Captain, Rat, go and get some.'

'What?' we said, in a kind of shocked unison. 'In New York?' Don't forget, none of us had ever been on a plane before, let alone to New York. We were as ignorant as shit.

'Just fucking go,' he said.

'You couldn't argue with Jake, so we went down into the street and walked a couple of blocks in a complete daze to a newspaper stand.

'Rizlas, please,' I said, a bit sheepishly.

'What?' said the guy, in the gruffest, heaviest Brooklyn accent you ever heard.

'Er, fag papers.'

'What?'

'Cigarette papers?'

'What ones?'

'Some of those.' I pointed to one – I didn't recognise any of the packets. He pulled out these really heavy ones. 'Got any lighter ones?'

'What?'

'Anything lighter?'

'Yeah,' he said. 'These,' and he gave me a different packet. 'That'll cost you an extra dollar.'

'Er, they're still quite heavy. Anything else?'

'These, an extra dollar.'

'I ended up paying five dollars for a packet of fag papers. Every time I asked to see another packet the cunt put the price up.'

Twenty-five years ago, New York was a sleazy, whore-ridden giant that chilled and thrilled me to the bone. When I returned last year, I saw spotless streets stinking of zero tolerance. It was still spectacular, but ultimately sterile. I preferred its chic Seventies decay; the New York of Ratzo, Popeye Doyle, steam gushing streets and Johnny Thunders. It made Americans seem so much more human.

'The most disappointing thing about that whole trip to the States was walking into Max's Kansas City and discovering it was fucking horrible,' said Rat. 'I couldn't believe it. We were told it was this happening, jumping place where all the punks congregated, but it was empty – we were the only ones in there. It had about as much glamour as a public toilet.

'And when we went to CBGB's that was even worse. I mean, it

had tables and chairs.

'We had death threats warning us not to go, and to watch our limey arses if we did. Over the first two nights we overplayed our hand on-stage and the whole thing was a circus. We then decided not to play the game and just play the music and we pulled it off. The Stones, who were in town at the time, even sent along a bevy of topless girls to the club to celebrate our arrival.

'The rest of the US tour was disastrous. We went on to Boston and played to ten people eating pizza. Then we went to LA to do three nights at the Whisky-A-Go-Go with Television, but Tom Verlaine didn't want a punk band supporting him so we were stranded in LA without any money. Jake took us down to the Whisky where Television were playing and we just hurled abuse at them all night –'Get yer tits out, Verlaine.'

'We went over to America to show them how it's done and fucked up completely. Still, it had its compensations. I remember talking to American girls over there and trying to persuade them to give me blow-jobs on the strength of how big we were back in England. But when they saw the size of —'

I put my hands over my ears.

'—the audiences we attracted there, they never believed me. I guess I was pretty insatiable then – but you're only young once. Wasn't that the point? Life was for living.

'To be honest, I was one of those kids who couldn't get a girlfriend, straight out of Gawky Park. Women weren't really interested in an unemployed drummer from Croydon. But when you're in a successful band, other people's perceptions of whether you're good-looking or not change, thank God. I'd never been anywhere, we'd just made our first record, fucking hell. Just doing gigs for me was such a big deal, it was all impossible to imagine.

'I always used to think that whole New York thing was very constructive but Warholism ran right through it. It was all 'Let's go down to the Bowery and be poor.' But I guess it was somehow brilliant in its dumbness.

'What people don't realise is when the whole punk thing first started all we had in London was 'Punk' magazine. I used to go down to Skydog in Praed Street and look at photos of the Ramones and Blondie and The Heartbreakers and try to imagine what they sounded like because none of them had put out a record. I liked their haircuts and ripped T-shirts but I didn't have a clue what they sounded like. It was all guesswork. Then we finally heard Television's 'Little Johnny Jewel' and that gave punk complete validity in the musical sense.

'When me and Brian James first heard it we thought it was brilliant. It matched our vision. At the same time we knew we'd be regarded as worthless because all the bands we were into, like the Dolls and the Stooges, were regarded as worthless.

'Iggy Pop's big thing at that time was that he was perceived as being shit because he wasn't Robert Plant. He sang about nasty, unmentionable stuff. The rest of the world was going with the Eagles and King Crimson and he totally didn't fit. Lou Reed was looked upon as an American bloke who didn't really have a voice. People forget the time shift when they look back. They forget how these people, now classed as great artists, were regarded then.'

It was time for another pint. The years drifted, I'm 24 again, buying a drink for Rat Scabies in the Ship. There were lights on the horizon, far across the sea. They were getting dimmer.

'On the sixth of July Brian hired the 100 Club to celebrate our very first gig supporting the Pistols. I was very scared. It's like being a boxer who reaches a peak and realises he'll never be as good after that. You build a reputation when you're 18 and now I'm 51. That's frightening.

'It's about being in shape and having attitude and doing it for a reason. Me and Brian are lucky because we're too blinkered and stupid to change, and when we played together again at the 100 Club it was great. You get more precise as you get older, but there's something raw about anger, frustration and stupidity – it just gives you brute force and nobody can touch that.

'I've been totally stupid from day one, but you just keep on and hope that eventually it all comes right.

'Funnily enough, I sat at this very table six months ago with Captain, Brian and Dave for the first time in a long time and talked about going back to CBGB's next year to play, if it's still there.

'But now there seems to be even more animosity than there was before we met up. Jake and Paul Conroy said they wanted to manage the band in 2006, Alan Edwards would do the PR, Neil Warnock would be the agent and Peter Barnes was going to be the publisher. What a fucking team! The idea was to play as many barns as we could across the world. We were guaranteed to make a small fortune each, but we had to be with Jake for a year. It all went pear-shaped because the Captain and Dave had the current line-up and refused to stop gigging.

'Jake and Paul had 150 shows arranged. They'd get the same as each of us. It was a great deal but I didn't think the Captain and Dave wanted to go for it. I guess they were being loyal to the other guys in the new band and I suppose they didn't want to lose control of what's become something of a cottage industry. But I think we couldn't have gone wrong with that deal. It was all first-class hotels, the works, laid out nice, whatever you want you can have. All we had to do was say our arses were theirs in 2006.

'When we met up I looked at the Captain and Dave and I finally realised it was dead. I guess I just didn't respect them any more. The magic had gone. The thing with Dave was, it didn't matter how much he pissed you off, when he walked into the room you'd forget everything and think, He's a cool guy. It doesn't matter about the past, let's deal with it and move on. But that feeling had gone when we met up again. Everything used to melt away and you dished out instant forgiveness – but I couldn't do it this time. We'd all changed. His attitude was different. I thought we'd do the reunion tour, build bridges and it would come back like before. I was wrong.

'They probably say the same thing about me. When the magic goes, it's over.

'Dave wasn't a singer when we got him, he really was a gravedigger. But that's what made him great because he went out there not knowing what he should or shouldn't do and just gave it everything. He'd trash the stage and turn into a raving, psychotic, vampire-biting bull but off-stage he was as quiet as a lamb. Dave always looked great whether it was five p.m. or five a.m.

'But then, as the years passed, he began to build up his own concept of what he wanted to be and that wasn't what The Damned were all about to me. Although having said that we did 'Eloise' and at that period I guess that's exactly what The Damned were all about.

'Dave hardly ever turned up for rehearsals. When we asked him where he'd been he'd say, 'Doing the garden,' and that meant he was taking everything alive out of it and just leaving an area of grey mud and dead plants. Brilliant, a totally awesome commitment to his lifestyle.

'The Captain was a total one-off and that's the hardest thing about disliking him now. You have to own up at some point along the way – I liked that man. We were mates.

'A couple of incidents spring to mind that sums him up completely. At the Paradiso in Amsterdam he strutted up to the front for 'Neat Neat Neat' – the first song in the set – and stepped off the front. He actually fell off the stage and as he went down his guitar neck bashed him on the head. He was knocked unconscious. We carried on playing, and ten minutes later he came back as if nothing had happened. Another night me and him had a couple of tarts in tow and we went to Dingwalls because it was the only place open until two a.m. As we sat at a table the whole place was staring at us. We ordered a beer and I said to the Captain, 'I don't feel good.'

'Why's that?'

'Everyone's staring at us. We're a fucking freak show. We're too conspicuous.'

'Yeah,' said the Captain. 'I know what you mean.'

'So he picks up a bottle of ketchup, takes off the top and downs it, the whole fucking bottle. He stared at everyone in the club and they averted their eyes.'

'When I left the band it wasn't through personal differences or animosity, it was the band not the individuals. Only later on it became the individuals.'

I rolled one of Rat's Rizlas (now, that's a great name for a band) and wondered whether he agreed with me in thinking The Damned were interfered with when they were one step from true stardom. I never understood why they became a five-piece with the inclusion of Lu.

'I must admit, I didn't want Lu in the band,' said Rat. 'And the Captain certainly didn't want him. It was Brian who insisted. He thought Lu would make us more like the MC5. But I tell you something, Lu could really play. Hold on.' He suddenly ran out of the pub...

Cue 'Twilight Zone' theme.

...and returned with...Lu. He'd spotted him strolling past the door. He had a suitcase and guitar in hand and looked very young. Lu and Rat hadn't seen each other in ten years. I hadn't seen Lu since 1977.

'Mont de Marsan was my first Damned gig,' said Lu. 'Deep' and 'end' sprang into my mind. 'And they gave me a lead so short that when I got excited and jumped – which was pretty fucking often, I seem to recall – it catapulted out.'

Lu, who has played in the Mekons since the year dot, looked a little stunned throughout his swift sojourn aboard the Ship, but still managed to conjure a 600-page Russian grammar book from his case. He speaks the language fluently, along with a dozen others.

I'm impressed. He left us to it.

'Amazing,' said Rat.

I tell him about the serendipity that was Mick Jones.

'Amazing.

'When I went to gigs before The Damned I used to look at the door that led backstage and thought it led to Wonderland. I used to watch the people coming and going and think, That's where it's all happening. And when you do eventually go back there you realise it's fucking worse than where you were, but you try to counteract that disillusionment by thinking that when you get bigger and play bigger venues it'll be exactly as you thought it would be – but it ain't.

'In Mont de Marsan I'd already decided I'd had enough. It was intolerable. Brian had dried up and I was earning 30 quid a week schlepping around with tour managers I hated. I never had any money. I never ate properly. I loved the first album but I didn't think anyone would get it, apart from us. I was wrong. So Stiff, naturally, wanted a second album. Trouble was, Brian didn't have any songs – it was the classic scenario, a lifetime to write the first album and three months to write the second.

'Up to that point we called Brian the Füehrer because he wouldn't let anyone else write the music. Don't forget, we didn't know what publishing was. We just thought it was an extra credit and didn't realise you got paid more money for being the writer. So me and the Captain would ask if we could write some songs – never having written any in our lives before – but Brian was adamant that nobody would do the writing except him. It was his band and we respected that.

'But we weren't ready for another album because Brian didn't have any songs. I knew we were in trouble when he said to us one day that maybe we should write some songs for the new album. Then he started trying to palm off previous stuff he'd written which we'd originally rejected. To me it was all starting to lose its shape. My main man Brian looked out of ideas and all the while I'm getting gobbed on and bashed up.

'Mont de Marsan was the final straw. We'd made our point. It was time for me to do something different, be different. There's nothing worse than being a failure once you've been successful. I was terrified of The Damned crashing and burning. I didn't want to be associated with that. I loved being in the group, it meant so much to me. It was heartbreaking to watch it implode.

'It didn't help that Brian insisted on taking his girlfriend, Erica, on the road. In the van we used to throw paper planes at each other and spray shaving-foam and stick chewing-gum in hair. But Erica would turn round and tell us to cut it out. And Brian sided with her.

'We were still travelling in piece-of-shit vans. Everyone seemed to be making money out of us but us. The music business seemed to be full of pirates who wouldn't show you the map. Jake Riviera told me that.

'*Music For Pleasure* wasn't the record we should have made then. Jake was getting disillusioned with Stiff. We were on the road non-stop, still sharing rooms in B-and-Bs that wouldn't even let us in half the time. They'd look at us and say, 'We've made a mistake with the booking now fuck off,' and you'd end up dossing on someone's floor again. I just couldn't take it any more. We used to play to upwards of 1-2,000 people and I'd think, If this is the top of the pile, then it's shit.

'I hadn't fallen out with the band. We were still mates. It was everything around it that made me want out. So I just said to them, 'You know what? I'm going home.' We were in France and someone gave me a big handful of pills. Me being me, I necked them without knowing what they were. The Captain had passed out on stage yet again. It was all getting too much. Then, to top it all, some guy threw a bottle at me from the audience. You don't throw a fucking glass bottle. It's just not on.

'I stopped playing and jumped into the crowd. I was gonna fucking have him, but the nearer I got, the bigger he got, and the spotlight's on me and I thought, Oh fuck! but I grabbed him by the hair and dragged him out. Luckily he didn't beat the shit out of me.

'Fuck knows what those pills were but I was on one. When we got back to our hotel the porter didn't know we were staying there and thought we were trying to gatecrash a wedding party that was going on in the basement. He couldn't speak English, which I found incredibly frustrating so I started trashing the lobby.

'The porter called a couple of passers-by and it went off outside and I ended up getting the shit kicked out of me by three or four French guys while the rest of the band just stood there and watched.

'Ironically it was the tour manager I hated who came and got me out. That really did it for me. Everything was falling to pieces and now these guys, my mates, stood by and did nothing. I thought they'd let me down.

'I'm sure they've got their own version of what happened. Maybe, because of the way I was carrying on, they thought I deserved a good kicking. I probably did, and perhaps I'd have done the same in their shoes. These were strange times. But in my own mind at that moment it was the last straw. I left and got lost in Paris for two days. Stiff said I was having a breakdown and tried to commit suicide, which was a pack of lies.'

We finished Rat's Rizlas and headed off to a nearby Italian where, as we perused the menu, he confessed that he occasionally reverts back to his pop star days. 'I always like people to order for me. That way you don't know what you're going to get. If I order I always have exactly the same. For example, whenever I go to an Indian I always have a lamb biryani. Always. I can't change it. Having someone else ordering makes it a much bigger adventure at mealtimes.'

We both order the same – marinated fresh sardines with cod. Very punk.

'Do you know what sums up 1977 for me? Doc Martens and gobbing little shits.'

It seemed an appropriate moment to introduce his quotes from that first 'Record Mirror' Damned interview, way back in February 1977.

I always knew we were gonna be big. We're about to tour with Marc Bolan. How good the fuck is that? And we'll have room to move on stage, to breathe. It'll be like moving out of a council house into a mansion.

'I'm amazed I was that astute.

'I always said The Damned could be the best group or the worst group in the world, depending on what night it was. We worked on our emotions. The Pistols and The Clash rehearsed and were in control of their songs. We'd go up and say, 'Fuck you.' I suppose that's probably why we didn't really retain the essence of punk. It all sounds a bit shabby now.

'Maybe we weren't as tight or neat, but so fucking what? It was 30 years ago – what are you gonna do now? The uncoolest thing was to be like another band.

'We had a real problem with all the gobbing from the very first date of the Bolan tour. Marc's equipment got covered with phlegm. He still had an audience, but there were always a couple of hundred Damned fans pogoing down the front. We hung out with him non-stop. He was great. I mean, there were the Pistols trying to shaft us on the Anarchy In The UK tour and here's Marc Bolan, a proper star, inviting us to sit with him on the tour bus, buying us dinners and guitar strings. He really did look after us. He was so cool. He did all his own sound at the gigs as well which really surprised me.

'Initially, Bolan was 'I'm the godfather of punk and can I jump on this bandwagon.' But then he gradually started to understand the concept – three-minute moments of brilliance with very few chords and great melodies. And then it dawned on him that that was what he was all about too. Marc was re-evaluating what he was doing and his death was a tragedy because he was probably the only old-wave star who could have successfully crossed over.

'The reason why punk became so big was 60 per cent down to the media and the rest down to the musicians. The time was ready for that change and it was going to happen regardless. It was dreams coming true and none of us expected what we got.'

But what about the buzz, the memories, the adventure? Your kids must think it's very cool having Rat Scabies for a dad.

'I've got three kids, two boys aged 21 and 19 and a girl aged 16. They're completely uninterested in my past. They hate every record

I've ever made but I don't really expect them to think otherwise. Every generation is entitled to its own art and culture. What we've got now is a sanitised music industry. My kids listen to very diverse garage and drum and bass, obscure hooligans from west London who sing about mugging and wanking.

'The really hard part is, I can't go and say, 'Turn it down, kids,' can I? Instead I say, 'Can you just roll a bit of the bass end off there, son?'

'Mind you, they used to like it if there had been film of me on the telly smashing things up because the next day at school the other kids would say, 'Was that your dad? Fucking brilliant!''

Look, no matter what a lot of people may think, The Damned ain't out to change the world. The other bands like The Clash and the Pistols might have such ambitions but that doesn't mean we come from different backgrounds than them. We're all working-class and have been on the dole.

'We were council-estate fodder. None of The Damned had a proper secondary education. None of us went to art college. My dad is a very knowledgeable, learned man, but I wouldn't have stayed in the same room with him for more than two minutes in 1975 for those very reasons. What he expected from his child wasn't what I was. I always thought that in his eyes I was a total loser – I'd had over 30 different dead-end jobs – who could blame him?

'But I could play the drums. I started drumming when I was eight. I was attracted by the sound while watching Eric Delaney, Jack Parnell and the Dave Clark Five. That sound hit me deep inside and tore me apart. Millie's 'My Boy Lollipop' was the very first single I ever owned – it came free with my Dansette record-player.

'I used to listen to Steve Race's jazz show on the radio every Sunday morning and there'd be quizzes about jazz and I'd learned how to spot the different bands – if it was a clarinet it was Benny Goodman, if it was a drummer it was Gene Krupa. The main thing I loved about jazz, though, was that every track had a drum solo. I had a Glenn Miller album featuring 'Sing Sing Sing' that had a great drum sound.

'To me, there's two ways you play drums – orchestral or you keep time. Most drummers are timekeepers, like Charlie Watts. I've got a lot of drums and I like hitting them. All the punk bands were drum and guitar – the bass player didn't really matter, and me and Brian were a great combination. I suspect we were the last of a generation of players with that empathy between the drums and guitars. That chemistry has long since gone. If you can play a bit, 60 per cent of the time it will sound okay and the other 40 per cent is shit. You don't need a great success percentage to be a successful band. If two of you click that takes it up to 75 per cent, and that's what happened with our first album.

'The songs were great but they were already in place. They became greater because of the chemistry between Brian and me. Any idiot could have sung them, any idiot could have played bass. The fact that those 'idiots' happened to be two of the best stage performers in the business made us a winning combination.

'The music industry is such a readable, structured game. There are rules and parameters, and if you play by those rules and within those parameters you can become Simon Cowell. For me, that was never what is was about. It was purely about the power of music.

'Kids now have a certain favourite tune and that tune goes on the CD player and stays on the CD player. Today when someone compiles an album they'll put the best tracks at the beginning because nobody ever listens to an entire CD now. So you'll get the singles first, followed by the B sides, followed by the shit that's just a filler. When we used to make an album we'd say, 'Side one's gonna be like that, and that will take you emotionally to this point.' The spaces between the tracks were often as important as the songs themselves. Timing and rhythm is 80 per cent of everything.

'Drums are the oldest instruments along with the human voice. They are primeval, central and a weapon because you'd scare people with volume. It sounded like thunder and thunder only comes from the gods. People talk about ethnic music but what you're really talking about is 150 people sitting round a fire banging coconut shells together.

'Public Image Limited proved that if you gather the same people together with the same intent it will sound like shit until one magical point when it will become coherent and transform into such a massive force. When it hits it's undeniable.

'That's what music is – a tribal gathering, people being communal.'

Why did you all dislike The Clash so much?

'I had a lot of time for Paul Simonon, but Mick I was never sure about because he and Tony James had blown me out of the pre-Clash band London SS. Mick really enjoyed the whole star trip and that put me off him a little bit. He was a rock star, in fact, he is a rock star and he should be treated as such.

'I replied to an ad in 'Melody Maker' for a drummer in London SS. I didn't want to do an audition along with a hundred other drummers. This ad, which ran for two months, said the applicant must be into MC5 and the Stooges and the current New York scene. I rang the number and Bernie Rhodes answered.

"So you like The Stooges?' he asked.

"Sure.'

"The MC5?'

"My favourite band.'

"What do you know about the New York scene?'

"I live in Caterham, mate. How the fuck would I know what's going on in New York?'

"The ad says you must know about the New York scene. Why bother to ring up if you don't know the New York scene?'

"Look, mate, you either want the best drummer in the world or you don't.'

'That was good enough. He invited me down to meet Mick and Tony but they were so uninterested. They both had hair down to their arses, flared leather trousers and ruffled shirts. Brian James was there as well but he was cool. They were so bored with watching people audition that they had an old black-and-white telly, and while I played they were watching that rather than me.

There was a war film on and we were playing The Stones' 'You Can't Always Get What You Want'. That's where Mick and Tony were coming from – it had nothing to do with 'White Riot'.

'When it came to the guitar solo in the song there was a dogfight going on in the movie and Brian started playing in time with the dogfight. The four of us are all pretending to be bored with each other in this sweaty little room, and as the planes were zooming in the background Brian's doing this awesome guitar solo. I thought, Right, I'm gonna show them what I can do, and I kicked in and played along and me and Brian just looked at each other and knew.

'After, Brian told them, 'We're either gonna have him or I'm leaving,' and they said, 'We don't want you to leave. It's just that we're not sure about his trousers'!

'We only fell out with The Clash when Bernie and Malcolm and Jake locked horns. In fact, we originally asked Paul Simonon to be in the band. Paul was cool. He'd never front it. He knew. We'd all meet up at Hennekeys in Portobello Road and, come closing time, we'd go shoplifting in the market. Paul had just got himself a bedsit and he painted the whole room luminous pink, the bed, light switches everything. I remember being hammered and playing the Ramones' album for the first time in that room, smoking a joint. At the end of side one we just looked at each other and thought, Yeah, magic.

'With Joe, you wouldn't know which way he'd flip. He was unpredictable. If he had a knife he might stab you or talk about politics. With Mick, if he had a knife he'd clean his nails with it or take up the hem on his jacket.

'After I left The Damned I went to Hollywood for a while. One day, while I was hanging out at A&M studios, I bumped into Joe. Ministry were playing the Palladium that night and we both went along. At the gig we noticed Timothy Leary in the crowd and we decided to try to blag our way backstage to see him because we knew he'd be dead soon. Joe was very bad at hustling but I managed to get us in. We chatted to Leary for a while and I ended up carrying him to a car that took him home because he couldn't walk any more. He died a week later.

'There had been so much bad blood between The Clash and The Damned but Joe was so forgiving and Christian and was prepared to forget everything.'

What got me really annoyed about the Pistols was that when they released 'Anarchy In The UK' they were staying in fucking flash Holiday Inn hotels while we checked into two-quid-a-night rooms. Then they wanted to charge us a grand to stick all our gear on their special coach and there was loads of fucking room on it.

'Very true. I'm telling you, that's really how it was.

'The difference pre- and post-Grundy was that people actually turned up at the gigs. Before that nobody was there. On the Anarchy tour at the end of '76 the only people in the audience were journalists, half a dozen football hooligans and a few blokes with spiky hair who knew what it was. You got no more than a dozen punters down the front who were really into it and they'd get a good kicking, so you ended up dragging them into the dressing room to keep them out of trouble because they were the only allies you had.

'And that was where that whole freedom of going backstage with the punk bands originated. It was a case of safety in numbers. There was less chance of getting beaten up if there were 20 of us rather than ten. You'd let them come in while the local rugby team fucked off.

'My take on that whole Anarchy tour was that I finally realised Jake Riviera understood how to put a band on the road. He knew all about life in a van and the dividends that paid off in terms of building up a hard-core audience, and that's what we'd been doing. They tried to put that tour together for a long time with the Ramones, Patti Smith, Talking Heads and the Pistols heading it up. The Pistols were getting all the publicity but they weren't getting any shows. They needed to be seen.

'On the other hand, The Damned had a person in the shape of

Jake who could get us as many shows as we wanted – more than we wanted. We'd done our homework and before the Grundy show I'd have put The Damned up against the Pistols anytime, and we'd have always caned them in terms of punters. We were getting just as much press and people were seeing us.

'Then when it came to the Anarchy tour we were only on it because we had to be. The Clash hadn't done a gig at that time and didn't even have a name until a couple of weeks before the tour started. And nobody knew who Johnny Thunders was. They had to have us on it because we put bums on seats, and they knew that, but they did everything they could to make our lives shit on that tour.

'We were on Stiff, an independent that Jake and Robbo [Dave Robinson] started with two grand they borrowed from the Feelgoods and they didn't have the money for air-conditioned buses and rooms at the Holiday Inn. But Malcolm wanted us to pay half the costs. We were the only two bands that had record deals at the time.

'Stiff was so hot then. Just being on Stiff was great – it couldn't get any better than that. Then, after Grundy, it was all about 'News of the World' journalists. I just got fed up with the tossers who interviewed us most of the time because you knew, no matter what you said, they were gonna tear you to pieces. So you might as well be the biggest arsehole on the planet to them and give them something to write about. So when we made these outrageous statements to the 'News of the World' or the 'Sun', loads of people genuinely believed it was true. I thought it was all transparent horseshit – how could anyone take such statements seriously? But they did and we ended up being branded the comedy rock band. We were aware of it at the time but it was difficult when the Captain was involved and, of course, everyone likes a laugh and a mess.

'It really used to piss me off that we were regarded as a cabaret punk act with me as 'the mad drummer'. I didn't realise there would be so many different factions in the media – there was a lot of jealousy and resentment about the band and I could never understand why.

'With the benefit of hindsight, I wish I'd have kept my mouth shut about the other groups. That was the big mistake that punk made – slagging off each other. Caroline Coon was right: we should have been more unified.

'Mind you, we still took a few kickings that were meant for the Pistols. We were cannon fodder because everyone hated them.

'But I thought it was hypocritical at the time to claim they were street and that everyone should be unified and then they're trying to take the fucking money out of our back pocket, though the band themselves probably had nothing to do with it. It was the whole set-up. It was a hippie trait. It was hippies did all that artificial-social revolution shit. Punk was all about not having anything and when you got it you pooled it.

'I remember Vivienne Westwood going up to this hippie in the Nashville, accusing him of sitting in her seat. He told her to piss off so she had a real go at him and a fight started, then Sid waded in and the rest of the Pistols were trying to break it up because they didn't want to be associated with any aggro. But someone took a photo and it looked like they were right in the thick of it and it made the front cover of 'Melody Maker'.

'The first time I saw Sid Vicious he was wearing a gold lamé drape jacket and black spiky hair and he looked so cool. I thought immediately we should get him into the band. People who looked good in those days were worth having because they were a rarity. It was all about the leather jackets. Chrissie Hynde would turn up in winkle-pickers, Dee Dee Ramone haircut, leather jacket, parallel trousers; no other women looked like that because you'd be regarded as a Hell's Angel and be thrown out. In those days it was a real statement. We went scouring gigs looking for people who looked great.

'I remember people who never made it but were part of the scene and were brilliant. People like Chaotic Bass. They were the truly innovative ones and would wear the most outrageous clothes and had the best ideas, but nobody knew who they were. I used to go to places like the 100 Club and look around and think that the world was full of brilliant minds. But after 1977 that all disappeared. You stopped seeing people with that flair, with that virtuosity, making everything out of nothing. Why did they vanish? I always felt there were a lot of people who should have broken through and didn't, and to me they were the coolest, the ones with the most integrity. They backed off because they thought it wasn't cool to be bigger than other people with great ideas.'

What were The Damned?

'I think McLaren felt seriously threatened by The Damned. We were better looking than the rest. Caroline Coon once said that The Damned were way out there in terms of sex appeal. Brian was an androgynous rock god. And Dave was all muscle. The Pistols, on the other hand, had a slightly flabby singer with a lot of personality that everyone wanted to mother, not fuck. With Vanian they wanted to fuck him.

'The Pistols weren't very good, but they tried very hard to be. They were a regular rock band with Johnny Rotten singing – which is not to take anything away from the songs or what they did. The Damned just were. There was no kind of ethic that went with it. We formed because I could never find people playing what I wanted to play.

'I got kicked out of a lot of bands as I searched around, and suddenly there was Brian with short hair – nobody had short hair then – and straight trousers when everyone wore flares. He had pointy shoes and a black leather jacket and he was loud. But he could play from the heart, and if you gave him an ounce of inspiration he could run with the ball

'The Captain? I was never sure why he joined the band. He was a guitarist who hated playing bass. He thought he was a better guitarist than Brian. Captain had his fortune read on Brighton pier and he was told he'd join a group and get on the telly and be famous. That was all the push he needed. He would probably have just sat there and listened to Soft Machine records and tried to be Alan Holdsworth, and that's why he went completely over the top because that wasn't really where he wanted to be. This was punk and anything goes, so if anything goes he was gonna fucking go there. We were totally us. There were no rules, just honesty.

'It was get the hair off, get me out of these fucking high waisted baggy jeans, get me out of this Harry Fenton tank top and put me into clothes that say this is me. I really did find me then. Sounds shitty, I know, but I found a place where I thought I really belonged.

'I originally just wanted to be a drummer. I never expected to be in a big group. I thought I'd play weddings or cruises. Just a normal, regular player in a nine-to-five life. This was a dream come true but not a dream I expected.

'We had the kickings, y'know. We were chased out of gigs by big fucking bikers. We did the groundwork.

'The gigs were always jam-packed. Always big queues. Always gobbing, flying glasses, fights, if not with security then with each other.

'I remember a gang of bikers turning up at Eric's in Liverpool. Now these were men, big men, all dressed like punks for the night and taking the piss. The real punks, aged about 15 and 16, were down the front. The bikers liked us and ten of them jumped on stage as we played and started pogoing about. Security told them to get off and a huge fight started. One guy took the microphone off the drum kit and was beating people around the head with it. This medieval battle raged around me while I continued to play.

'Miraculously, the whole band went through the gig totally unscathed, not a hair out of place. But as I walked off-stage, I tripped over and landed on broken glass and fucking stabbed myself in the arm. I had to go to casualty later that night, and there were all the bikers and bouncers with broken limbs and huge gashes down their faces and ruptured spleens, comparing notes about the punch-up.

'What a fucking show we used to put on.'

Now the money's coming in we're just about breaking even.

'In those early days, breaking even was about the best it got. I never really felt successful at the time. I didn't have any money, had nowhere proper to live. That's one of the reasons I liked going on the road – at least I had a room for the night with a bed. When we came back off the road it was shit because I'd have to go and doss on people's floors. To the outside world we were rock stars, but in reality we were schmucks.

'I used to question all this but never got a proper answer. It was my job, it was what I'd always wanted. I wasn't going to turn my back on that.

'The longer you're in the music business the less work you get because you're wise to all the deals so nobody wants to get involved with you – they can't take advantage of you anymore. But I wish more people had made more money out of me then because that would have meant I earned a lot more as well.

'We only started to make a few bob in the Eighties when my kids were born and life suddenly got much easier. We had the whole 'Eloise' thing going and had sorted out the business end so we went on expensive holidays and lorded it up in flashy restaurants.

'Sadly, 'Eloise' was the biggest thing The Damned ever did. People forget that. In the most disposable, forgettable period in the band's history – 1984 – we had our biggest hit. At the gigs then we had hard-core punks who wanted to hear 'New Rose' and 'Neat Neat Neat', a bunch of Goth dollies who dreamed of giving Vanian a blow-job and the rest were crusties who weren't sure. So when we did 'Eloise' all the little Goths would rush down the front and knock the punks out of the way. Then we'd do 'Neat Neat Neat' and all the punks would rush back. And all the while the silent majority would look at us and think, Is this a good band or not?

'It was just like the end of 1977 all over again, and when the music becomes meaningless there's no point. I'd really rather drive a truck. I went back to The Damned because we had great songs even though nothing else was working.

'The only song I ever wrote for the band was 'Stab Your Back' and I make about 50 quid a year from that. I also receive odd royalties from back catalogues, which pays me enough to stay poor. Obviously, it's not enough to live on so I make up the difference by hustling. I do odds and ends, like the Donovan tour recently. The strangest thing about that – and also the nicest thing – was Donovan insisting on introducing me as Chris Millar. I prefer Rat but he wouldn't use it. It was the first time in over 30 years I'd been introduced by my real name and people actually applauded and suddenly I thought, Ooh, that's me, that's really me. Not this bloke in The Damned. I suppose I was never really me. I thought the whole punk thing wouldn't last more than six months because the nature of it was so explosive you couldn't see beyond that.

'Shit, if I'd known I was gonna live this long I'd have taken better care of myself!'

Too many drugs?

'The drugs didn't help but I was never too far gone. I didn't ever have a serious habit or anything like. In fact, there weren't an awful lot of drugs around, but we didn't need a lot. We never used to buy drugs – they were provided by fans most of the time.

'It was lively and I got fucked up occasionally, but it was always redeemable. I could always come back to reality if I wanted to.

'Hugh Cornwell had such a responsible attitude to drugs – he said it's all about controlling the drug and not the drug controlling you.

'When we did the first festival at Mont de Marsan in 1976 we were on a fucking mission and just looted our way through. I'm convinced if there'd been more than four of us we'd have taken the whole of fucking France. We used to go steaming – before anyone had coined the term – in the shops nicking everything, and there was nothing anyone could do about it.

'I remember sitting next to Paul Weller on the coach from the airport to the '77 Mont de Marsan festival and I was absolutely hammered. He was a good bloke and I got on quite well with him. I said to him, 'Y'know the trouble with your band, Paul?'

"What?'

'You don't fucking drink enough.' Then I threw up.

'The Jam were from Woking and my parents were from Redhill so I knew that Surrey-belt mentality. The Jam were the classic example of a band formed by geography.

'I've come up with a theory over the years. A bloke who starts out in suburbia and wants to form a band is limited to the amount of musicians he can unearth. So, if he finds someone who's the same kind of age and who's got a bass or a drum kit, they'll be in the band automatically, even if they don't really cover the same musical ground.

'That's why a band like the Jam split up. But it's also what makes a band great because they don't have that personal empathy. If you all agree it sucks. Rick Buckler wasn't as interested as Weller was in being a mod but he went along with it because it was more interesting than being a mini-cab driver or something.

'The Damned were made up of blokes from Crawley or Reigate who couldn't get a job, but we could connect with people. We didn't know why they got what we were doing but they did. We'd go to Glasgow and they'd be, 'Come on then, you English fuckers,' but by the end of it they'd say, 'You're just the same as us.' And that was our secret.

'It was all about aggression and communication and really pissing off people who were content with the Eagles and that lame pub rock. We never had time to work it out, to define it. We just concentrated on getting out of the gig, into the van and back to the hotel without getting our heads kicked in or bottled or nicked. If you avoided any of that you were ahead.

'We were rock stars without limousines. The only time we had a limo I made the driver drive 40 miles out of his way so my mum and dad could see it.

Everything happens in a seven-year cycle. Music progresses but attitudes remain the same. There was Liszt then this geezer Wagner bowls up with something a lot heavier and he gets slagged off.

'It used to go in seven year circles. The next big revolution in music after punk was rave. The ska revival and New Romantic thing didn't count because I'm talking about genuine, life-changing music. There'd been the skinhead thing – the Dave and Ansil Collins, the Upsetters, Desmond Dekker. That was very much part of our culture and accepted as such but not in the mainstream. I remember the first time I went to America and someone asked me what music I liked and I said reggae and the response was, 'What's reggae?'

'Because of punk, reggae began to get known. I must say Rotten was the biggest champion of reggae and dub. He really knew a lot about it

'When Simon Cowell was on 'Desert Island Discs' he came up with something very profound. He said a lot of people come on to 'The X Factor' looking for a short cut. They haven't done five years on the road, harbouring dreams they've had since childhood. They want stardom without working for it, so fuck them, they don't deserve it. For that one comment I realised Simon Cowell is part of my generation and I respect him for that.

'But somewhere in High Wycombe or Luton or Milton Keynes there's a bored 15-year-old kid who's so sick of what we've got at the moment that he'll create the next big thing.

'I haven't heard much in music for years that actually has something to say. Maybe Mike Skinner of the Street and Eminem have opinions that are worth listening to but who else is there? Pete Doherty? He's the worst kind: he's trying to be a rebel, but he's not in the same league.

'Most bands back in 1977 played their album on stage and it sounded like their album, whereas we quickly worked out that gigs were about the sensationalism of the moment. We liked Hendrix when he set fire to the guitar. We liked it when Townsend smashed up his guitar. We liked it when the Small Faces were incorrigibly cheeky.

'We were given the licence to do anything we wanted. When you've got nothing to lose you can only win.'

I just hope we can do something constructive for the kids years from now. I'd like to open a club and put on the kind of music that won't be acceptable then like punk is now. That's something bands like the Stones and The Who have never done with all their millions. I like to think we give people their money's worth. The fans know they can come and see us and do what they like. It's a party. We don't want to influence, just make people feel a bit freer.

'That's pretty good if a bit hippie. If I'd have earned enough money I'd probably have done that. Remember the Roxy? The way Andy Czezowski ran that was great, even though we ultimately fell out with him. I remember going into the toilet one night and there was a guy trying to kick a urinal off the wall. Andy walked in and told him, 'You can smash it up as much as you like. It just means you won't have anywhere to piss.' It was do what you want, there's no father figure but, remember, if you punch the ceiling out there is no more ceiling.

'It was a generation in decline. What Andy realised was it didn't matter how shit the club was, it was ours and provided us with freedom. It was a good place to hang out and relax.

'It's very easy to put money back into the business once you've been successful. It doesn't take much to have a club and turn up once a month to jam. I felt really let down in '77 by the Who, Zeppelin, the Stones and Dylan.

'All they did was sell records, which I know is what they were supposed to do, but they sold those records on promises that they were a different kind of people. They weren't selling us the promise of a new album, they were selling us the promise of a new lifestyle, a new future, and when we were 15 and 16 we bought into that.

'But when I got older, it was painfully obvious this was never gonna happen and they didn't really want anything apart from the next royalty cheque. Without the public you're nobody, and if they do like you, you should reward them – all that adulation they give you and the lifestyle they give you, there should be something you can do along the way that says, 'Thank you.'

'No-one was aware of longevity. We were saying to Zeppelin and the Stones, 'You've had your turn, your ten to 15 years of success. Now fuck off.' It was time for us, the three-minute pop-song merchants. It was all about being trash and disposable. Nobody dreamt you could possibly carve a career out of this.

'Yet here we are, 30 years down the line, and you wouldn't believe the number of people that have asked me to form a punk supergroup. But you could never do it because you could never find a singer. I even had Dee Dee Ramone round my house talking about it.'

Regrets? He's had a few...

'I guess I regret nearly all of it. I regret the mistakes, like being coerced into the second album. I regret the lack of communication we had as a band. I regret the lack of understanding of what we were and what we should have done. I regret not coming off the road for six months in 1977. I regret Jake not being more involved.

'The worst decision I ever made was to have cream cake plastered all over my face on the first album. Maybe if we'd played our hand differently we'd have taken more of the comedy element out of The Damned. The band didn't know what was going to happen so I'm sure the audience didn't. Remember, in those days the Captain was more like the Joker – not the sanitised model responsible for 'Happy Talk'. He was a big, lumbering, threatening mass.

'In the band we all believed we were the best. You have to be like that to have any degree of success. In reality we were a bunch of fucking losers who had nothing else and because we had nothing to lose we managed to win, at least, I think we won.

'My two biggest ambitions when I started out was to play the Marquee and appear in the 'NME' crossword. I did. I was famous. It was great.

'I miss the adulation and the hour of being someone. During the course of a week, I think of those days a few times. It's not like I sit there yearning for the lost years but I do miss everything buzzing around me. When we went to somewhere like Nottingham to play a gig, we were that week's news. We were different and special – and I admit I do miss that.

'In a funny way I also miss people being scared of us. There were four of us, and we were all unpredictable so consequently more threatening.

'I've never really known what I should think of myself. I think I'm still schizophrenic. I like to think I'm a bit more astute these days, don't make such an arsehole of myself. I could have done with thinking like that 30 years ago. It's probably too late now.'

What isn't too late now?

'I go to America fairly regularly. My wife is an understanding woman because she realises it's either that or me sitting on the porch smoking dope, drinking tea and watching the sun set on my life. If I go there, there's always a chance that I'll bring something back.

'Over there they know their icons. Like, if Iggy Pop comes here and you see him in the supermarket it's a big deal. There it's not often you'll see one of The Damned sitting in a bar in Long Beach drinking a Bloody Mary and playing pool. I thrive on that minimal success – it's like being back in '77.

'Don't get me wrong, I wouldn't hesitate to play them my new album if I had one but I'm not a prolific enough writer or artist in terms of sales to have that sort of career – it's not like I became a Billy Idol. I do some things really well and I do other things really averagely.

'It's just that when you played a place you never got to know it. So when I went to hang out in Orange County for the first time I became part of the people who lived there and did the things they did and saw the things they saw – skaters, surfers, girl guides selling cookies and raffle tickets, the cops and the hassle they give you even today for having the wrong haircut.

'There's a different kind of respect: they like you but you have to be all right, and just making a few records ain't enough. It's up to other people to interpret what I mean to them. I don't mean much to me but to some people maybe I do.

'I'm very happy with the interest people still have in my life and what I do. myspace.com is great because it lets me hear the applause. I don't go out that much to gigs unless it's something really special. I don't do a lot in terms of getting public recognition or being any kind of media figure. I don't really count myself as having any worth or value.

'I think, That's what I did then and if that means something to someone then that's good. Let them have that, let them cling to it. What it meant to them isn't what it meant to me. I never really asked to be recognised as anything.

'I wanted to be a drummer and when I got the chance to be one I grabbed it and did it as loudly as I could. I knew that was my chance to be someone and I did everything I could to be someone. But at the same time I don't feel any responsibility to people for the way they feel about my career. I get people come up and say, 'Hey man, I was 15 when I heard your first album and it changed my life.'

'It's almost as though they expect me to give them some kind of blessing like the fucking pope.'

We polished off a bottle of red and two Irish coffees each over lunch, plus a few more Rizlas. A line of speed in the toilet would have made a perfect liqueur, followed by a swift ten Bensons. Alas, it was two cappuccinos and the bill.

We were going in opposite directions so we shook hands outside the restaurant. I watched him walk down Wardour Street towards Oxford Street and wondered if I'd ever see him again. In the sunshine I imagined a distant meeting celebrating 50 years of punk with a 71-year-old Rat, whose Scabies had long since crusted over, telling me that The Damned had re-formed after the magic returned.

Dame Caroline Coon said they were the sexiest geriatrics ever to do the gruelling UK retirement-home tour, especially since Captain

Sensible had managed to get back into the tutu after having all those varicose veins surgically removed.

I felt a little Sad. She told me she came from Eudipida, the capital of Sadia.

That seems like an appropriate end to an interview about The Damned circa 1977.

I cut her head off in a dark alleyway. Never did like Sads.

That seems even more appropriate.

The Damned's cabaret was the cabaret of the damned. People forget that.

2007: THE ONES
THAT GOT AWAY

When Joe Strummer finally found the hole in his bucket five years ago after he succumbed to a heart attack, my immortality died with him. For the first time in my life I felt vulnerable – like the last white man in Hammersmith Palais knowing it was gonna be off outside where a host of maniacal speedo skinheads were skipping through the shadows waiting to smash my brains in with milk crates.

It was time to start thinking about dying.

I never got to know Joe that well. I had no idea how he lived, if he liked tea better than coffee, if his shit was more thick than thin, if he cried over spilt milk or laughed at Morecambe and Wise. But his honesty shone through his voracious music, and when he spoke, that odd, glutinous voice resonated with integrity.

Or so I've always hoped.

Let me talk about a treasured moment, one of the *genuine* treasured moments when someone notices something about you and you alone.

Women and professional praise are the two commodities that conjure up such moments, both sadly lacking in my life. But one night, late '77, in the upstairs 'VIP' bar at Richard Branson's Venue club in Victoria, Joe Strummer cast a spell over me worthy of Merlin or even David Blaine.

I was talking to a few people at the bar when Joe wandered over to say hullo. Then he turned to me and said gently, 'I think you're the most original writer in the music press.' Pure and simple.

Now, I don't know about you but I fucking adore praise. I didn't care if Joe said that to all the boys, all I knew was he'd just hit the spot, the bullseye.

But now he's dead. And I can't prove a thing.

Unless I wanted to employ the aid of a spiritualist, a Joe Strummer interview was out.

But I was confident a Paul Weller interview was in.

Now, Paul I did get to know a little and watched the sharp-suited boy grow into a sharper-suited man in months rather than years. I adored every Jam single, especially the breathtaking 'Down In The Tube Station At Midnight', which grabbed my dick and pulled me up to rock heaven.

I even invited the band to my wedding party in 1980, above a pub off New North Road in Islington. I felt a little embarrassed to invite anyone famous so I never told a celebrity soul. But I casually mentioned the party to Bruce Foxton one night and, in a fit of desirous expectation, told him to invite the others.

Bruce came with future wife, Pat, but he had neglected to inform Paul and Rick. The next time I saw Paul he thought I hadn't invited him and looked a little peeved.

We were *that* close!

I hadn't seen Paul in nearly 23 years but I guessed he might spare an hour to talk about love, like a walk in the park, a kiss in the dark, a sailboat ride.

I guessed wrong.

I tried. I really did. But the days turned into weeks, the weeks into months and apparently the months will turn into another 23 years when he'll be 72 and I'll be 77 because a wall of PRs awarded me *nul point* and every move I made got the bum's rush. This was an example of that incredibly difficult martial art, Nokandu. Gee whiz, I thought I was in with a chance of interviewing someone who'd once walked into my dreams.

Shame.

I really wanted to see how time had changed Paul. I went to the last Jam concert in Brighton and noticed, at the after-show lig, that he looked happier – and cockier – than I'd seen him before. A weight had been lifted from his shimmering mohair shoulders and he exuded confidence.

I felt proud – I'd been in at the start of it all – but I also knew I wouldn't be seeing much more of him. I wasn't far wrong. I saw him once, at an afternoon record company-reception with Mick Talbot, just after Style Council released their début 'Speak Like A Child'. He was friendly but distant. I felt he regarded me as the 'that was then' part of the 'and this is now' statement. A familiar face in the snapshots of his youth he'd take a look at maybe once every 20 years around Christmas.

I belonged to his Jam life, and his Jam life was no more.

A few more years of success as a Councillor would be followed by several years of dejection. But when you can sincerely bang them out the way Paul Weller sincerely bangs them out it's inevitable that you'll crawl through that 500 yards of Shawshank Redemption shit to freedom.

If Hugh, Paul and Rat were my brothers, Mick Jones would be a cousin I only saw at weddings and funerals. All right, so my beard and long hair must have been off-putting. I don't know why I had a beard for so long; I started growing one at 21 and kept it – on and off – throughout my twenties. I think I just wanted to hide my face.

Here I was, on an island of facial hair with just Jet Black for company, in a sea of smooth.

I didn't look like someone out of The Clash, that's for sure. I guess I never insinuated myself into their land of 1,000 dances. I could never have rung up Mick Jones and asked him if he fancied a drink because (a), I'd feel like a wanker (which actually *made* me one) and (b), I didn't know his telephone number. Maybe I could have given him mine but I figured he could always reach me at the mag.

We had a guest-list relationship.

I was great at communicating in interviews but socially not so hot. That's why I needed the speed. It gave me a transfusion of confidence and a taste for Marlboro and Jack Daniel's, preferably all at the same time. But it only papered over the cracks. I could never shake the feeling that I was outside looking in.

Still can't – especially at home.

I liked Mick, though. He was the closest thing to an actual rock star that punk ever threw up. He looked great on stage, sang compelling songs in a cool rasta Sta-Prest voice and played a guitar that got inside your head via your arse.

That was all I needed from him.

But I hoped he might now spare me an hour, like Joe spared some coins for that Soho beggar we passed after my first Clash interview. At one bizarre moment – when I bumped into him after the Hugh Cornwell interview – it did indeed seem the fates had decreed I would get to interview him.

How wrong can you be?

Both Paul and Mick's representatives assured me, via email and phone, that their clients would rather not talk about punk. I tried to explain that the book was about a year rather than a style, about people rather than a scene

I was banging my head against brick walls.

I emailed Paul's PR.

Hi Barry ,

Thanks for the email. I'll run it past Paul but be warned he gets asked to do things like this all the time and ALWAYS turns them down. But you never know…

Polly

God knows how many weeks went by. I emailed again. I needn't have bothered.

Hi

*Thanks for the email – I will mention this to Paul again but I'm afraid I'm
sure he'll decline again – he's also having a bit of a break from stuff at the mo.*

Annoyingly he doesn't have email – so I can't forward this!

Polly x

Wasn't sure if the kiss was compensation for lack of Barry after
'Hi'. But I recognised a brush-off when I saw one. Eventually Polly
told me that Claire at V2 Records might be better able to handle my
enquiry as she saw Paul more frequently.

I spoke to Claire a dozen times on the phone, posted her –
recorded delivery – rough drafts of pertinent extracts from the
book for Paul to read and a personal letter. Zilch. She was charming
and I sensed she sympathised, but I guess her hands were tied.

'I'm seeing Paul tomorrow and I'll mention it then,' was the
standard answer.

Tomorrow, tomorrow. I felt like I was listening to 'Annie' only
without the bit that said the stars come out 'cos they didn't fucking
shine for me.

I discovered Paul was completing a swift nationwide tour with
two nights at the Forum in Kentish Town. I checked the availability
of tickets on-line and was greeted with a predictable 'sold out'
notice.

But I'd chance it.

I'd slip into the old blagging suit, which, like the King Kong-
shouldered, double-breasted navy blue jacket next to it at the back
of my threadbare wardrobe, I hadn't worn in countless years. I'd
glide down to the gig in Dina's black Yaris and turn the clock back.

I'd saunter up to the backstage door and say, 'Tell Paul that Barry
Cain's outside,' and they'd usher me in with a smile.

I got down to Kentish Town about 10.15, parked up and listened
to James Whale interview David Cameron on 'Talksport' before
strolling to the Bull & Gate pub next door to the venue. My plan
was to mingle with the fans as they left the gig, spot a familiar face
and get invited backstage.

As I wandered past the Forum on my way to the pub I spotted a sign on the front doors proclaiming 'Tickets available on the door: £35'. If I'd known I'd have come down earlier and bought one. I'm sure the publisher would have covered the cost – well, about as sure as Moses was when he raised that rod over the Red Sea with a shitload of Egyptians on chariots in hot pursuit.

Someone opened one of the doors and I caught a whiff of 'A Town Called Malice'. It was the first time I'd heard his voice live in almost 25 years and for a moment I felt like George Bailey in 'It's A Wonderful Life' when he realises he's been born after all. I bitterly regretted missing the show.

I looked out of the window in the Bull & Gate – a pint of Guinness cooling one hand and the sweet smell of a duty-free Benson's warming the other – and watched the punters as they streamed by. Seventy per cent looked just about ready for a Mediterranean cruise and the rest were thirty-something mod cons and twenty-something 'Bladerunner' mods.

I looked frantically for a familiar face until it dawned on me that those familiar faces – Paul's dad and ultimate shrewd nut John, tour manager Kenny, Polydor A&R man Dennis – probably didn't do gigs any more. The Jam split up a quarter-of-a-century ago, when Wayne Rooney was minus five and counting; any shit could have happened. I'd forgotten that.

Suddenly my blagging suit started to feel four sizes too small.

Around 30 people stood by the stage door – 'X Factor' junkies with the Jam in their hearts. There was a grille on the door, behind which lurked defiant eyes. There was no way past it.

So I waited.

I'd never in my life stood outside a stage door in the hope of grabbing a word with the star of the show. It felt mighty strange.

Apart from two girls in their late-twenties and a couple of similar age, who sat in a car with their baby asleep in the back, the small crowd comprised of blokes in their forties who talked mostly about football, Paul Weller and the Jam. These were fans; fans for whom the music was not enough, fans, prepared to wait nearly two hours in the freezing cold on the off-chance of glimpsing their hero.

I asked one guy who was wearing, predictably, a parka, why he waited.

'To see Paul. I love the guy.'

Two floors above laughter streamed out of brightly lit rooms. I had two Bensons for company.

Around 12.30 Paul emerged from the door with the grille, his distinctive barnet blowing in the bitter wind. He looked startled as the fans surrounded him. He exchanged a few words with some of them before jumping into the back of a waiting car. One guy in the crowd pleaded, 'Oh, come on, Paul, please sign this picture. I've been waiting for fucking ages.' He took the picture and signed it. I couldn't get anywhere near the car, let alone Paul.

Shit, did I feel cheated.

But as Paul's car sped off into that cold December night the smiling faces of the people around told a different story. For a moment they'd inhabited his space and they were happy.

The next day I rang Claire four or five times and got voicemail. I tried once more and was finally put through. I asked if she'd had any response from Paul. It was a stupid question. While Paul was on a UK tour my request for an interview was hardly going to receive top billing. But I'd been trying for more than four months making all my nowhere plans for nobody. I was frustrated.

'No, sorry, I haven't asked him yet,' she replied.

'You gave him the documents I sent?' I asked.

'Oh, yes. Look, I'm seeing him tomorrow and I'll ask him then.'

I told her I'd been down to the Forum.

'Did you? What did you think of the show?'

I remembered those two cold hours by the stage door. Lying came easy. 'Amazing.'

'Yes, I heard that. Shame, I couldn't go last night.'

'Oh, you missed a great show. It was the first time I'd seen him live in a very long time.' I started to feel a little uncomfortable. 'Thanks again for all your help, Claire. I'm sorry to keep troubling you about it.'

'No problem.'

But I couldn't resist one last hit. 'And when you see Paul please tell him I loved the show.'

I didn't care anymore.

Claire eventually gave me the number for Paul's tour manager who turned out to be Kenny, The Jam's original road manager, a Spurs fan and all-round decent bloke. He remembered me. In fact, as it turned out, he remembered me big-time. He told me on the phone that Paul was busy rehearsing for a US tour and wasn't doing any interviews. I mentioned I went to the Forum gig.

'I know,' he replied. 'I saw you there.'

'Why didn't you come over and say hullo?'

'I was driving the car that picked Paul up at the backstage door. I thought it was you standing there.'

Now, that's entertainment.

Oh well, there's always tomorrow.

A word here about punk provocateur Malcolm McLaren. In 1977 our paths rarely crossed and when they did I was suitably deferential. He was, after all, the puppet master and, to me, unapproachable. I interviewed him for the first time towards the end of '78 and obviously made an impression because he later asked me to ghost write his autobiography. I'd just got married and Malcolm came round to our flat nearly every night and told me the story of his life while swigging vodka and smoking pack after pack of Marlboro, which, I seem to recall, I supplied.

I felt like his psychiatrist. He'd recline on my sofa and talk sweet somethings late into the night. It was startling and I felt privileged. I knew more about Malcolm than anyone else on the planet.

However, when the tape transcriptions were completed, Malcolm, who'd been managing Bow Wow Wow at that point, decided to up sticks and move to the States and I've never set eyes on him again.

Was it something I said?

ALAN EDWARDS
Outside Organisation,
Tottenham Court Road

Alan Edwards was just about the most sincere and, unwittingly, shrewdest man I met in the music business. I first came across him when I was working on the 'South-East London Mercury' in Deptford and he was doing his PR apprenticeship with Keith Altham, who was top-dog pop PR along with Tony Brainsby. I'd been working as the entertainments' editor for the 'Mercury', getting squirted by Sooty and interviewing anyone from David Kossoff to Vince Hill via Susan Hampshire and Arthur Mullard. I blagged the job even though the ad asked for an entertainments editor who could sub and design. I could do neither.

Alan and I spoke on the phone about a press release he'd sent me and ended up talking for ages about music, football and the meaning of life, which I said was a combination of Alvin Lee and Rodney Marsh.

'I can't get you Rodney, yet, but we've recently signed Alvin,' said Alan. 'Would you like to interview him down at Pinewood Studios and watch him rehearse?'

The rattling of plastic against the side of my head from the chunky grey phone in my shaking hand brought me round. Meet Alvin Lee? I saw Ten Years After in the Bluesville above the Manor House pub in 1967 filling in for a no-show John Mayall and fell in love with Alvin's fingers. They could make a guitar cum faster than anyone I'd ever seen. I was an ejaculation-free 15-year-old and became an instant voyeur.

Over the next three years I travelled far and wide to see them – well, from the Isle of Wight to Bedford. I liked my blues at the speed of sound. Then, like Concorde, Ten Years After were taken off the market. It wasn't cool to move too fast anymore.

Alan might just as well have said, 'Here's a million quid.'

Incidentally, the Alvin Lee interview took up a lot of space. I must've written 2,000 words, far too much, in a tribute to one of my all-time heroes. The two pictures of him I used were the biggest in the whole paper. I'd stayed up until dawn designing it. I was expecting a favourable reaction.

Instead I saw 'This is utter crap,' daubed in thick, black, felt-tip across my spread by the editor, Roger Norman, when it was handed round to the editorial staff at the Friday meeting. He was clearly not a Ten Years After fan, but he knew bad journalism when he saw it.

Naturally, after Alan introduced me to Alvin, I loved him like the younger brother I never had, and he went on to introduce me to a galaxy of stars including, in order, Midge Ure (at number one then with Slik), Rick Parfitt, Marc Bolan, Robert Plant, Keith Moon and Bob Marley. And all before I joined 'Record Mirror'.

Both he and Keith Altham said nice words about me to Alf Martin, the newly appointed editor of 'Record Mirror', which helped me get the job. For the next five years Alan and I saw each other regularly, travelling the world and laughing like kings.

In 1978 we teamed up together to run an independent PR company called Modern Publicity from a Covent Garden squat. Alan had started the business in 1977 and asked me to join him and handle the publicity for Blondie, the Buzzcocks, Generation X, the Stranglers, 999, you name it.

I stayed for four months and left with the abiding feeling that most journalists were complete arseholes and I wanted to be one again. I also realised that PRs must possess arses of steel, manipulative minds and hearts of gold. My arse, like those of most journalists, was made of lard.

Along with everyone else I met in the business, Alan drifted out of my life when our paths ceased to cross professionally and the friendship was, in the immortal lines of Private Fraser, 'Doomed, *doooomed*!' It's the one damnation I truly regret. It's hard to find a saint in the city.

Not only that, he's moved out of the Old Kent Road and successfully circumnavigated the board to Go, avoiding jail, the waterworks and that fucking hotel on Mayfair. He now runs the Outside Organisation, employing 60 people swathed in showbiz splendour in cavernous West End offices and has, among other things, helped to launch Brand Beckham, managed the publicity for the Spice Girls and become David Bowie's right-hand man, not to mention looking after Paul McCartney, the Four Seasons Hotel, Robbie Williams, Jamie Oliver, The Who and Naomi Campbell.

Serious shit.

I'm doomed, I tell you. Fucking *doooomed*.

The offices of the Outside Organisation are situated half-way down Tottenham Court Road behind an inconspicuous doorway. I wasn't impressed. When I walked out nearly three hours later, I felt like Lucy returning from Narnia for the first time.

I had seen Alan once in 16 years, on the day of the total eclipse in 2000. After a fascinating but inconsequential meeting at his office about nothing much – my idea, not his – we went on to the roof to check out the eclipse, which turned out to be a damp squib. I guessed Alan may have been a bit of a hypochondriac when he thought there was a chance he'd lose his sight after momentarily catching the sun's reflection in a mirror while, I might add, wearing sunglasses.

Now I know why he reacted like that. He had big dreams and he wasn't going to lose sight of them. If anyone caught a falling star and put it in his pocket it was Alan Edwards.

I was highly impressed with his set-up back in 2000. What – 15, 20 staff? Big stuff for an independent entertainment PR.

This time round, I sat on a very comfortable sofa in reception for ten minutes chatting to a spot-on receptionist who really did *receive* me, until I was greeted by Cassie, one of Alan's personal assistants.

'Hi, Barry. Come this way.'

I followed her into a lift where she pressed the button for the top floor which happened to be the sixth. As we soared upwards I asked about the nature of the other companies in the building.

'It's all the Outside Organisation,' said Cassie.

All six floors?

'Yes.'

No shit! How many people work on each floor? I mean, these could be offices like the ones in 'Being John Malkovich'.

'Eight, ten.'

No *shiiit!* I was tempted to ask if they were full-size human beings but I soon came to my senses.

This was a guy who had worked single-handed out of a shithole squat in Covent Garden and hit the town night after night in pursuit of the unknown and usually finding it. Alan was a rare example of a nice guy making good in a rip-roaringly bad industry.

He was devilishly handsome, which always helps provided you have the nous to go with it. Six years ago he still looked great, but in your forties six years can be a broken rope-bridge suspended hundreds of feet above a crocodile-infested river – even if you make it across, chances are the effort and fear will have turned you grey, fat and miserable.

All those floors, all those people, all that pressure. I bet he looks like shit. My defence mechanism was kicking in again.

The lift stopped. It led straight into an impressive office with lots of light wood and smiles. I was shown to another comfortable sofa while Alan's assistant went into a room in the far corner. I flicked through that day's papers and the latest magazines spread out on the coffee-table in front of me, all stuffed, no doubt, with stories about his clients.

Yep, he's definitely going to be grey, fat and miserable. I'd stake my life on it.

'Hullo, Barry.'

Big baby blue eyes dominating a slick-feature face carrying not a cigarette paper's width of extra weight or a silk thread of a wrinkle. Alan used to look like David Essex. Now it was George Clooney. He was obviously cruising on Ocean's Eleven.

Rich too.

And single.

That says it all. I've said it once and I'll say it again: single keeps you sane, single keeps you focused, single keeps you a king. Needless to say, I'm still married after 27 years and I'm insane, unfocused and a fucking queen.

He invited me into his own office and we sat down on yet another comfortable sofa in the far corner. This building had lots of far corners. And comfortable sofas.

'This morning I was thinking punk has influenced everything I've ever done.'

Alan had just written the headline to his own tale of mystery and imagination. He's a natural.

'I wouldn't be sitting here now without punk rock and '77. When I got involved with the Spice Girls it seemed to me they were a natural follow-on to the Sex Pistols. Both cartoon, both incredibly British, all regular girl/boy-next-door people, irreverent, funny, tabloid, off the wall.

'They were chaotic, anarchic. Both released movies. They were *Carry On* bands – I always expected Sid James to pop up at any time.

'Of course, musically there was no connection. But culturally there was. The Pistols had a lot to say – 'Anarchy In The UK' and 'God Save The Queen' are two of the greatest pop singles ever written. Now, I don't know whether it was down to McLaren or John Lydon. I've read all the books, I've heard all the theories and I still don't know who wrote what or who influenced whom.

'But to get a record to number one that was so subversive it had to be blanked out of the charts? That didn't exist in the eyes of society? That wasn't played on the radio? That attacked the Royal Family but had people queuing in the streets to buy it? And all that within the context of three minutes of pop? Are you fucking kidding me?

'And it was me they were singing to. The way *I* felt. I was living that life at the time – renting a room I couldn't afford in Islington, even though it only cost four quid a week, walking to work to a dingy little office in Oxford Street because I couldn't afford the bus fare.

'Sometimes I remember walking home in the evenings through the West End and the world seemed to be in turmoil – no lights because of power cuts, people buying candles, muffled bomb explosions in the background, piles of rubbish, riots. I know all that didn't happen in one day but it sure felt like it. The world was falling apart. It was like the end of civilisation. But, fuck, it was exciting.

'And punk grew out of that decaying world in much the same way that Elvis grew out of the decay of the pallid Fifties and hit with rock'n'roll and people smashed up cinemas and dressed strangely. He changed the landscape of the world in the way punk did.

'People like Bill Grundy were terrified and intimidated and appalled by punk. Without realising it, the Pistols were the sledgehammer that knocked the door down. But they didn't know where that door led to any more than we did. It didn't matter. It was just about destroying the door.

'When I heard 'Anarchy In The UK' it made sense. I understood it.'

In 1975 Alan left the bright lights of his native Brighton for the darkness of London with a fucking big torch and the desire to write about music. He started freelancing for 'Sounds' and 'Record Mirror', writing about classic pub rockers the Feelgoods, Kilburn and the High Roads, the 101ers.

'These were the roots of punk and I loved it.'

One night, at a Who gig, Alan bumped into pop PR supremo Keith Altham and his life, as they say, changed for ever. The seeds of six floors in the West End and a worldwide reputation had been sown.

'Keith asked me to work with him for £25 a week and I thought, Great, I can pay the rent, I can eat. I thought I'd do that for a couple of months and go back to writing. Thirty years later I'm still waiting to go back to writing. I never wanted to be a PR. Fucking terrible job. I wanted to be a writer. But I guess I didn't have the technical skills to be a journalist.'

I wouldn't worry too much about it Alan.

'Keith and I worked in an upstairs office in Victoria and Tony Brainsby, another top music PR, was downstairs and Magenta Devine worked for him. Keith tutored me brilliantly, and I served what was tantamount to an old-fashioned apprenticeship. He took me down to Fleet Street and introduced me to the news editors and showed me how the picture desk worked and made me understand the cold, hard fact that if you don't get a story on the news editor's desk at the right time, you ain't gonna get it in the paper.

'But at that stage I didn't realise there was a powerful creative process inherent in PR. I didn't realise how mad you could go with it if you wanted to.

'Then the Pistols came along and showed me the way. Keith handed me the rule book, punk grabbed it and threw it out of the window.

'In Keith's day you'd rewrite the press release ten times with all the *t*'s crossed and all the *i*'s dotted. But what McLaren and Co. showed was that nobody really gave a fuck about what the press release said or if it was spelt incorrectly or if the picture was out of focus. It was all about the moment and the angle – was there a riot or wasn't there? Did the gig get cancelled after the police were called in?

'I learned it wasn't about if the record was good, or whether Jean-Jacques Burnel's bass playing was great. It was more like, had they smashed up something? Had Jean-Jacques been with some amazing girl? Had they been in a fight with a load of Hell's Angels in Amsterdam? *Those* were the stories.

'When I got involved with the Stranglers I understood how to connect those two key elements – the madness of the band and the tabloid desire for sensation. The Stranglers were much more than a pub band but they didn't know it. They were a squatter band along with the 101ers and I got very close to them and loved them dearly. In a way though, I was more punk than they were.

'I don't know if Hugh blames me or gives me any credit for helping to pull them towards punk, image wise. Maybe I was pulling them unnaturally into something that wasn't really them but because they were highly intelligent, it was something they soon comprehended and ultimately manipulated.'

'Manipulated' might be a euphemism for terrified when applied to certain members of the press.

'I recall Jean-Jacques pouring a load of whisky down the throat of a journalist in Iceland and we all thought it was really funny 'cos the guy was a bit of a boozer anyway.

'I recall JJ hit the journalist Jon Savage – who incidentally brought out a magnificent book on punk years later called 'England's Dreaming' – because he didn't like his review of the band. It was ignorant and malevolent behaviour on JJ's part.

'I recall JJ kidnapped the 'Sounds' writer Chas de Whalley, who got the police involved. I recall the band tying music writer Dianne Pearson to a tree in Portugal and leaving her there. It was fucking disgraceful.'

Alan started to smile – there was a ridiculous side to it. He couldn't help himself. Neither could I.

'Okay, I know it's easy to laugh about it now but, my God, it was heavy duty then. By the end of '77, a lot of people were scared of JJ. On a personal level we got on at the time though.

'I never knew just how much I liked JJ until the last days of '77 and I never knew how much I respected him until halfway through '78. He was a fantastic bass player who influenced a hell of a lot of other musicians. The Stranglers haven't had the respect they truly deserved. The writing was wonderful – Trotsky, Shakesperos? Jamelia's recent hit has a Stranglers' sample in the middle of it. Even after all these years they're still popping up.'

In '77 Alan felt confident enough to branch out on his own, taking the Stranglers and Generation X with him. It was risky, his face was maybe too fresh, like that of a jumped-up teenager. His experience was of barely a year's duration. What was he doing?

'I was young, although I didn't know it at the time. But this was 1977. I became the reluctant businessman. I didn't know how you formed a company because I'd never had any intention of starting my own business. It'd never crossed my mind. I had absolutely no training in business but I had all these great punk groups and I wanted to promote them in my own way. So I found an accountant and started my own company. I signed a form and never thought any more about it.

'At the time I didn't make any money out of it. The Stranglers paid me 25 quid a week. I can remember the first big cheque I ever had was from Arista for some punk band and it was for a month's work – £225. I couldn't believe it. I immediately went to the Gaylord Indian restaurant with Ian Grant, the Stranglers' manager, and spent the afternoon eating curry and drinking.

'I'd knock out press releases and mini fanzines and talk to journalists. Punk was a crash course for the ravers. It was seat-of-your-pants-stuff and I didn't have Keith behind me any more. I had to make decisions, do what I thought was right, follow my own instincts. I had no idea of the ramifications. I'd go to gigs every night of the week, hang out with bands, go drinking with journalists and it never occurred to me that the rest of my life was going to be like that. It wasn't a job, it was 'this is what I do', which is a different mindset altogether.

'I was influenced by people like McLaren and Lydon in terms of not just being a PR but also to be entrepreneurial, to take a risk, to confront and deal with the media.

'The classic PR thing before then was 'No comment. We'll keep out of it, thank you, and let's not do national-paper stuff'. The nationals didn't write about music on a day-to-day basis like they do now. Not until John Blake started *ad lib* in the 'Evening News' in the wake of the punk explosion. When I worked with Keith on The Who it was still really about the music press. It was much more important to get something on the cover of 'Melody Maker' or 'NME', and I was trained in the discipline of that.

'But the Pistols changed everything overnight. It wasn't just a music revolution, it was a media revolution, a fashion revolution. I probably couldn't have done any of this without punk. It was the strand that ran through my entire career and many other careers from the So Solid Crew to the Spice Girls. Both Keith and the Pistols were fantastically influential to me. They helped me to combine my apprenticeship with anarchy. It was a great advantage. The Pistols made me realise you could cross all the barriers. They were suddenly far bigger than showbiz. This was right across the board and a national newspaper editor's dream come true. This was the power and the strength and the value of what music could do. It was that great ethos – you can do it yourself. You don't have to go to university or be something you don't want to be. If you've got the energy and enthusiasm you can do it.

'Bizarrely, because it was very much get-on-your-bike-and-create-something – start a fanzine, start a club, start a band – it was a precursor to Thatcherism. Punk gave birth to more entrepreneurs than any other movement.

'I remember when we were in the old squat in Covent Garden, Lynne Franks worked round the corner doing bondage pants and all the punky fashion stuff. I often come across heads of corporations who started off being involved with punk in some way. It was the perfect young person's business opportunity. You teach yourself three chords on the guitar and see what happens. You pay 100 quid, buy a company off the shelf, start trading and see what happens. That was the legacy of punk. And you'll find loads of creative people, from design to filmmaking to TV, who set up businesses after they saw the Pistols because it changed their way of thinking. It was a watershed.

'Start 'Sniffin' Glue'…'

I never went that far.

'…the magazine, go form your own band, read a Strummer

interview, open a club. Before that it was all about the rock *star* and him alone. 'I've got a big car, a big house, I can buy a private plane.' It was never about 'How can I give you, the audience, anything back?' It was, 'How much more can I take off you?'

'Punk flipped it in its strange socialist-Thatcher way. That's why it didn't last. People like Strummer and McLaren and Rhodes were aware of what was going on. They were political animals but, as with most revolutions, the wheels came off very quickly as people's self-interest started to glisten.

'But 1977 was the most amazingly selfless year. A young, disenfranchised generation helping each other. A generation the government had forgotten. Nobody cared about youth, so youth cared about nobody.'

In '77 I hadn't felt disenfranchised – I guess I'd never felt disenfranchised. Other than when I'd spent a couple of years doing my indentures on a local daily newspaper in Gloucester, I'd always lived at home.

'You and I were close enough to the street to know the struggle of paying the rent and having to pay for a cab home after the after-show party.'

I never paid the rent – I gave my mum 20 quid a week to do everything for me, the egg-and-bacon sandwich in bed on the rare Sunday morning I was home included. But I wasn't about to refresh Alan's memory on that score. And I also refrained from mentioning that I always drove home from the after-show party in my own car, very often pissed and as high as a kite. One night I hit every parked car – and the odd van – in a whole street as I went on my jolly way and didn't bat an eyelid.

'But after spending all of your money on that cab home from the party and realising you now didn't have enough to pay the rent, the next day you'd find yourself on a plane to LA where you stayed in the best hotel you could possibly imagine and partied until dawn.

'We straddled both camps which very few people – 50, less? – did at the time. It was a privilege.

'There are still traces of that '77 feeling in minority groups to this day. I'm talking real minority groups, like young black kids in the US ghettoes reflected in rap and hip-hop, and here with bands like So Solid Crew. Punk was a completely white thing but dealing with So Solid reminded me of the old punk groups – bright kids straight off housing estates with no chance of a break. They were angry and wanted to get it out in music and art, but didn't know fully how to articulate it. They weren't musicians in the strict sense of the word – they'd never been in a studio. It was do-it-yourself music.

'It just confirmed to me that if you put a lot of young people together and give them no help whatsoever, they'll create something regardless of colour or creed.

'I looked after a Croatian teenager, Jasmin, for a couple of years. He'd been going out with one of my daughters after they met on holiday in Croatia and she invited him over. He was 16 and an absolute rebel. He was angry with the world, with politicians, with governments. I spent a lot of time with him and really got to like him. My daughter told him to come over to London to live. He didn't have a penny in his pocket when he arrived and we felt somehow responsible for him so we put him up. He reminded me a bit of myself at that age, full of anger, full of frustration.

'I sat him down one night to watch Julien Temple's 'Rock and Roll Swindle' movie. It blew his mind and he went out and bought every Pistols record. He started reading about The Clash and The Damned and it was great to see this kid 30 years later pick up the essence of all that energy and aggression. It was still completely relevant to him today. Hip-hop was Jasmin's main love but he could identify with punk. The music helped him to channel all that anger, just as it did with me.'

What happened to the boy?

'It was great because I managed to persuade some of my friends to sponsor him and he's gone to college and got his life together.'

That story is so typical Alan Edwards – heart of gold, head of marketing.

Would people have reacted to punk now as they did then? Would the Anarchy tour be banned?

'Probably not. In one sense you can do anything now, yet in a way we're much more strait-laced because we've gone down the American Republican road that pervades everything. We live in very conservative times and people are quite polarised.

'Although it felt very severe back in '77, there was probably a lot more freedom. You can't walk down the road today without being on CCTV. We're constantly monitored and we're not half as free as we like to think we are. I felt free in 1977.'

To Alan, the punk legacy doesn't stretch to music.

'My biggest regret about punk is that, musically, almost none of it has lasted. You'd be hard pressed to name about 25 great songs. I do a punk compilation every so often – I'm a bit like the guy in Nick Hornby's 'High Fidelity' – and that's about the number of songs still playable, which ain't great considering how much influence it wielded. It hasn't aged well at all.

'It's the opposite of Motown, which left a lasting musical legacy but fuck all culturally. I might be wary here, on reflection – Motown was probably all part of the new emerging black middle-class in America. Motown was completely working-class, from the performers to the fans, whereas punk purported to be working-class although many of the main protagonists were faking it. Strummer was middle-class. Some of The Damned were and so were the Stranglers. The Jam were suburban. The Pistols were the only 100 per cent working-class band. You can still listen to a lot of the stuff from the big five, but have you ever tried listening to the rest of it? Bands like the Adverts produced some truly awful albums.

'Punk left nothing much in the way of music but its influence *on* music ever since has been enormous. Think of the Police, Bob Geldof – that whole Band Aid affair was spawned by punk rock. Movie directors were influenced by punk – Russell Crowe even talks about its influence.

'It changed everything but it left nothing. It was a cultural bomb that exploded into a million pieces.'

Alan handled the PR for the Sex Pistols UK concerts that took place.

'I didn't really enjoy it. John Lydon has a fantastic wit but he sometimes goes over the edge a bit. But at least he's a big Arsenal fan.'

When the infamous Anarchy In The UK tour was cancelled in '76, Alan and I were in Zurich to see John Miles. The next morning our flight was delayed.

'There was snow on the runway – and we heard that the Anarchy tour had been cancelled after just one gig. It felt like the storming of the gates at St Petersburg. There we were with the ultimate boring-old-fart music while the revolution was happening. I remember the sheer excitement of it.

'I kept all the cuttings and funnily enough Virgin borrowed them for the Sex Pistols reunion concerts and they used them on all the packaging.'

Last year Alan, as Rat Scabies mentioned, also flirted with The Damned for a week or two.

'I wasn't sure how much depth there was to The Damned but I could understand their popularity. Paul Conroy, the ex-head of Stiff who originally turned me on to the Spice Girls, and Jake Riviera approached me not long ago and said they wanted to do a big Damned reunion tour. I was really interested – this was something I was made for. I really knew how to make it a big deal and concocted a fantastic media plan. We could have made it so big – Paul's got money muscle, Jake's got entrepreneurial skills and I'm the media man. Each one of the band would have made a substantial sum of money and they could have milked it for years. I was disappointed when the band decided against doing it. I think they made a mistake because now the moment has gone and it won't ever return. You've got to take the chance when it's offered. I always wondered who put the kibosh on it. I thought

Rat didn't want to do it.

'I knew Brian James really well and managed his band Tanz Der Youth in 1978 after The Damned split up. He was a real nice guy but he seemed to go off the rails a bit with booze after getting involved with Stiv Bators. Hopefully he's got it all back together again.

'I can look at 1977 from many different perspectives but one thing's for sure, I lived it. I lived it at the start, middle and end. And, in a way, I'm still living it. I'm close to drama, close to tabloid. I like to be at the centre of things. I love it. It's exciting.

'My life has changed less than that of most people who were around then. I'm still in the West End every day, I'm still in and out of gigs and clubs and having late nights. I'm at football. I'm still living that life, there's still a bit of an edge to it – unfortunately, in some ways!'

An edge dulled, no doubt, by a leisurely drive in your Ferrari to the office from your rambling Ascot home.

'Sadly, I don't live in a mansion in the country. I live in a one-bedroom flat not ten minutes from the office. My car's nine years old and at the moment I can't quite remember where it is. I've reinvested every penny I've ever earned back into this and hopefully it's working.'

At what price? Are you married?

'Pretty separated really. My private life is complicated. All right, I'm not a happy man in every respect. Of course I've got regrets but that's another interview.

'I suppose if I could do it all again I would invest more time in improving my personal life. The grass is always greener. But I'm rich beyond imagination in terms of excitement and adventures. I've been privileged to be in the middle of some extraordinary situations. I don't know many people who can say they've never had a boring day since they left school. Can you ask for more than that in life?'

What, like a wife, kids, Jack Russell?

'I've got two stepdaughters and two daughters, who are both at university now. I've known their mother for 30 years.'

Something clicked. Alan had introduced me to his girlfriend at a Stranglers concert. She was beautiful and I seemed to recall she had two daughters from a previous relationship.

'Relationships have made me realise I don't have a great consciousness about material things. I don't know why. It's a source of some regret. Making money was always a secondary thing. When you talk to people like Branson, they say they had a vision about something and were determined to see it through. Making a hundred million was the boring bit – well, not that boring but you know what I mean! If you'd said to David Beckham ten years ago that he'd only ever get ten quid a week playing football he wouldn't have cared. Money had nothing to do with him becoming a footballer. One night, just after he started going out with Victoria, I went to David's digs on the outskirts of Manchester. It was freezing cold because he didn't have the money for the electricity meter. He couldn't even open the tin of baked beans because there was no can-opener.

'I think people who are not true to themselves invariably have the most regrets. We've all met the bloke who says he should have quit his job in insurance and been a boxer or a writer or an actor. Why didn't he?

'Luck does play a part, though. The luck of being in the right place at the right time. The rest is down to you. Teddy Sheringham scored goals because he hung around the six-yard box picking up the scraps.

'You make your luck. You go out every night. You talk to everyone you meet. You'll come across something.

'I probably would have made a ton of money by making more clinical decisions but that would have been at the expense of the adventures. In the Eighties I'd probably have gone into marketing Diet Coke and made millions and gone to live in America. But it wasn't right for me. Punk was. I liked the shock of it. I liked the fact you could get away with lunacy.

'I remember concocting the story about Jet Black having a Victoria Cross. I think he bought one but I implied that he'd been awarded it in the Second World War.'

At which point we both rolled up laughing. My abiding memory of Alan, after I bury him when he drops dead at 95, will be his laugh, a schoolboy's infectious, eye-watering laugh.

Could you get away with that now?

'Er...yeah, just. The peak of PR would have been the mid- to late-Nineties when the Spice Girls and Oasis dominated the headlines. It was out of control and some papers seemed to write almost anything. It's calmed down quite a bit. There are a lot more lawyers in the mix now and people mumble about privacy laws so everyone's a bit more careful.

'Basically, there are only about ten possible crisis-management scenarios in PR and we deal with one on a weekly basis. People get into a fight, people get arrested, people shag the wrong person. Everybody gets into the same scrapes.'

A typical day in the life of Alan Edwards would be...

'I guess there isn't one. On a good day I'm in at seven.'

What, a.m.? I shivered.

'If I'm in at nine a.m. that's very late. I've usually read all the papers by 6:15 a.m. and deal with things relating to that. I'll hit the computer at seven and spend a large part of my day on it. I go out at least four nights a week to various events.

'Yesterday I spent the afternoon with Simon Cowell. I'm getting involved in 'The X Factor' brand. There's a tabloid line from 'X Factor' that stretches right back to the Pistols. I've known Simon for quite a while. He's very clever, very bright, very sharp-witted and still quite untouched by it all. He's a modern Mickie Most – good-looking, articulate. Do you know that when Mickie Most was a pop singer, he played the townships in South Africa and he told me that he got stabbed touring there something like 47 times?

'After Simon left I had a meeting with an agent and discussed all kinds of projects including, Tony Bennett, and now I'm handling the publicity for an exhibition of Tony's paintings in Camden Lock. How brilliant is that?

'I finally left the office at eight p.m. – I'd been in since seven that morning – and went and got a falafel before heading off to the first party for London Fashion Week in Bond Street with Naomi Campbell's agent where I was surrounded by skinny models and Pete Doherty hats. I stayed until ten, had only one drink, and was in bed by eleven. I was up at six this morning and in here by eight.

'Music is an essential part of my life. I listen to it three or four hours a day, every-day. Today so far I've listened to early Stones, bit of Dylan, Shakira, Rainbow, Sara Vaughan and Steppenwolf.

'I deal with hundreds of emails,' he said, as he walked over to his desk in search of his diary.

I remarked that the years had been kind to him.

'I think that's down to weight. I don't have time to get fat. I'm hyperactive. I can't sit still.'

I sat opposite Alan in that Convent Garden squat for four months and he was constantly on the phone, constantly smoking, constantly the man in search of something, a deal, his head, his heart, his soul. And constantly finding it.

You were the biggest fidget I ever met. Every time the phone rang you lit a Marlboro. And every time you lit a Marlboro the phone rang. Every day was a Marlboro-phone day in the squat, which was alive with pop stars, roaches and rats.

'I'm still the same, but instead of smoking I write emails when I'm on the phone. I must write 200 emails a day. I'm trying to cut down.'

Do you still like going to parties?

'What I find now is I can get away with less. I have a more responsible role. People work for me now and I'm seen as the *sensible* one, so there's no way I can slip off half an hour into the show if it was shit, like in the old days. I have to see the artist or the manager or the agent afterwards.'

He flicked through his diary as if it was the latest edition of 'FHM'.

'This is interesting. Usually I tend not to dwell on old diary dates.

It's not too good for the health. Let's see, I went to the 'GQ' awards because we had some acts there and the editor, Dylan Jones, is a friend of mine. Went to the MOBO's – we do the PR for it.

'Er, I went to a couple of gigs, went to a birthday party where I met a potential African presidential candidate. Oh, yes, I saw a Westlife concert, then flew to New York to see Usher. Er, I went to a leaving do at SonyBMG and the next night I met up with Andy Coulson for dinner – I got home at four a.m.. I also found time to pop along to a 'News of the World' party.

'I like the company of journalists. It's kind of instinctive.'

Alan reads from his amazing diary in a very matter-of-fact way. He hasn't got a boastful bone in his body.

You've got 60 people working for you for Chrissakes. Can't you delegate?

'I suppose, deep down, I'm a hands-on man. I go out four or five nights a week as I've done for the last 30 years.

'Two or three years ago I tried to market the company in order to sell it to take the pressure off me. I'm not joking when I say I really do live a modest life. But it would be nice if I lived a slightly less modest life. A couple of deals fell through, and my attitude now is, if it happens it happens. I'm not actively looking to sell it. Business is great. It's growing. There's hardly anyone here over 30 so I'm working with really buzzy kids half my age and they're the same as we were at that age. It's fantastic, it's completely invigorating, really energising.

'I'd like to broaden it out. We do a lot of fashion stuff now, sports, hotels, Virgin Radio, WWE wrestling – anything that's roughly in the area of entertainment. Sometimes I do think I should be more strategic but largely I've gone on instinct. There's always another adventure round the corner.

'I guess I'd like it to be global in some shape or form, inject a more international dynamic to it.'

You must be fit.

'Luckily, I'm blessed with a bit of stamina. I run and train every morning and I don't eat excessively. I've never been one for long boozy lunches.'

For some, 1977 was the year of boozy lunches. Attractive record-company PRs would invite you out to lunch in the West End, ply you with all kinds of alcohol, then invite you back to their office to browse through the record cabinet and take whatever you wanted. It was like a date, with something much better than sex at the end of it.

At RCA once I was invited to help myself from their impressively large mint-condition record collection. I was left alone and I went bananas. I loaded 40 albums into my arms – including the entire Bowie back catalogue – then sneaked out of the back door and hailed a cab with my leg.

And if you didn't go out to a boozy lunch with a PR you had three or four pints at the pub round the corner from the 'Record Mirror' office and rolled back at around 2.30.

It wasn't work: it was pure, unadulterated pleasure.

Working as a music journalist in 1977, while living at home with my mum and dad, not a care in the world, was some kind of wonderful. It was the closest thing to heaven I'd ever seen. And then God threw punk into the mix.

''77 memories are amazing memories. Remember that trip to Manchester to see the Buzzcocks? Remember that filthy squat where they lived? Remember going to the set of 'Coronation Street' where I had the pleasure of pissing on the wall outside the Rovers Return? How infantile is that?'

It's that schoolboy laugh again.

'Pissing on Corrie was symbolic, and I've got the picture to prove it.

'And did you know I came up with a Buzzcocks song title on that trip? We were standing outside a library and Pete Shelley said he was stuck for a song. I saw a sign inside the library and said, 'What about that for the song title?' 'Fiction Romance' was released as a single and I got a credit.

'And what about the Hell's Angels in Amsterdam with the Stranglers? God! Occasionally I tell that story and at the end people look at me with such disbelief that even I've started to question it. It did happen, right?'

It sure did.

'Remember the guy with no face? These guys were shooting people. Then one of the Angels drove a Harley through the club as we were talking. What did we think we were doing? We were lucky to get out of there. But it's funny, we weren't scared even though they were fucking gun-runners as well.'

Do you remember the Russian roulette moment?

'It all seemed so unreal, like I was watching a gangster movie and it was Al Pacino who had a gun poked into the side of his head, not me. I think it was the click of the trigger that brought me down to earth. Violence was part of punk. Sometimes it seemed as if every time you went to a gig there was a fight. There was a direct connection between punk and football. I grew up on football and I saw a fair bit of violence at matches. Punk spilled on to the terraces and it was real hard core and seriously working-class.

'Weirdly, when the rave thing happened football fans started dropping E and smoking weed and that calmed the violence. They were more worried about what trainers they were wearing.

'Then Rupert Murdoch came along and football became a corporate beast. It's still essentially working-class – I've worked with a number of footballers and the majority of people involved in football are working-class. Whatever that means now.'

Is music corrupt?

'The music industry of old had a long-standing connection with crime, certainly in the Sixties and well into the Seventies. But the music business has become increasingly anaesthetised.'

Alan is a devoted Arsenal fan and has been through the bad times, the good times and the breathtakingly beautiful times.

'Football and music were my passions and I ended up working for some fantastic footballers. How good is that?

'In 1977 I drifted down to Highbury occasionally to watch Arsenal but I'd lost interest by then. I didn't have the time, and football didn't seem relevant somehow. It wasn't really in my radar and the music was so incredibly exciting. I started to go to Arsenal regularly again in 1980. It was the crap Sanson-Woodcock-Mariner era, but I've hardly missed a home game since. There was a period in the early Nineties when my business wasn't going well and I was having a rough time. I managed Big Country and the Cult with Ian Grant and everything was fucked up. But football kept me sane. We had our own team and we played at Market Road. There was a couple of the Cult guys, Phil Daniels, some 'NME' writers and loads of King's Cross hooligans, one who played with a fag in his mouth.

'I used to go to many of the Arsenal away games, including European ties. It was my salvation.

'Football wasn't quite so commercial then, and there was a feeling of punk about it. It was exciting, it had an edge, a sense of everybody being in it together. They weren't all megastars living in mansions.

'I read Niall Quinn's autobiography and he said that after the matches the players would go down to the greyhound stadium in Harringay and blow all their money. They used to leave a fiver under a stone outside the stadium so they could afford a mini-cab home.

'He even worked on a building site part-time while he was playing for Arsenal because he was only on £280 a week as a player.

'Funnily enough, in 1977 Ian and I formed a football agency and it went spectacularly wrong. The first year was great. We were backed by an estate agent who Ian had met in a bar near Victoria station. The agent knew Steve Perryman and we met them both for dinner and signed him for the agency.

'Agents hardly existed then. If I'd stuck at that I can't tell you how much money I'd have made. We went on to sign Gerry Armstrong from Watford and Steve Foster from Brighton and England.

'Suddenly Ian and I were going to all the big games but not as fans – we'd walk straight into the boardrooms and wander round the dressing rooms like a couple of punk rockers, Ian in his leathers and me in my Damned T-shirt. It was amazing. We didn't realise what we were sitting on.

'Then we had a really bad week. Ralph Coates came in as a director of the company through the estate agent, Perryman contracted jaundice, Armstrong broke his leg and Foster suddenly remembered he'd signed a contract in Brighton with someone who wanted to reclaim his rights. I took that week as a sign that we weren't supposed to be in football and we went back to Big Country.'

Alan got involved with football again years later when he was working with the Spice Girls.

'I got to know David Beckham through Victoria. He'd only just got into the Manchester United team and it was after he scored the half-way line wonder goal and we'd chat about the beautiful game – me from a Highbury perspective, of course!

'As a result, I started looking at football again from a business point of view. When I saw Freddie Ljunberg's red hair I thought, This bloke could be a brand, he could be everywhere. I jumped on a plane to Stockholm, went to see his family lawyer and signed Freddie up during his first season at Arsenal. I was excited but it never really worked out.

'I also looked after Mario Melchiot. The problem with football is getting people to commit to paying for PR because a lot of them don't value it.'

David Bowie has played a significant role in Alan's life. Alan still pinches himself from time to time to make sure it's not all a dream.

'In 1977 after many nights out with Hugh Cornwell and a few lines of speed, we'd get back to my place at four in the morning and Low would be the album we'd play. It would take you to this moody, weird, futuristic place. I never imagined I would ever meet him. David was a mythical, godlike figure, and I remember seeing him at Aylesbury when he played with Iggy. Talk about the man who fell to earth – it was almost a religious experience. If you'd said to me, 'You'll be working with this man for 25 years,' you'd have knocked me down with a feather.'

How often do you see him?

'He lives in New York so I see him in waves. Some years I've spent an incredible amount of time with him, others very little. I saw him recently when he was in the UK appearing in 'Extras' with Ricky Gervais and where he got up and did a couple of songs with Dave Gilmour at the Albert Hall.

'I've been privileged enough to share some amazing moments with him.'

Now I've got an issue – a not inconsiderable one. Okay, so this has nothing to do with 1977 but I won't ever again have the chance to get this story off my chest so…

In January 1979 I went on a trip with Alan to Jamaica to interview Jason Miller's Inner Circle. On the way to the airport, the two of us pulled up in a cab outside Island Records' London offices and Alan jumped out, telling the cab driver to wait. Ten minutes later he returned and as we headed off to Heathrow he pulled out a thick wad of cash Island had just handed him for the trip.

That's what I call a good start.

'Where are we staying, Alan?' The sound of rain bouncing on the cab roof as we splashed down the M4 was particularly satisfying.

'The Kingston Hilton, the Pegasus. For eight days.'

It was getting better by the minute.

'Oh, and business class on the plane.'

Shit, fuck, piss.

Chris Salewicz of 'NME' and Hugh Fielder from 'Sounds' were to share these delights. Both English music journalists – don't forget that: it's crucial.

'I've got pictures of that Jamaican trip,' said Alan. 'God, it was a different world then. Unbelievable. I remember a surreal conversation with a couple of the guys from Inner Circle. We'd gone out there on the basis they were a rasta dreadlock band living close to the edge, and there we were, in this swanky house in the hills where they lived, and it was like Miami or something.

'I remember we had a quite intellectual discourse about racism in the UK. They were wary at first, but because we weren't trying to pretend to be anything other than honest, they appreciated it.'

But that's not the story Alan. You know what I mean.

'The highlight of the trip was going to Bob Marley's house and he showed us round and was Mr Polite.'

Yes. And then?

'He gave us some ganja – lamb's bread – and he said Bunny Wailer had given it to him.'

Yes. And then?

'Smoking the stuff and not being able to lift the cup out of a saucer for two hours. Then we went to a party of the Tribes, a deep rasta thing in the hills in the middle of the night. We drove into the back of a car at a crossroads at the bottom of a steep hill.'

Yes. Before that. A few years ago I bumped into Hugh Fielder in an East Finchley pub. He'd known what I meant.

'Playing football with Bob Marley and a bunch of other guys in his back garden.'

Bingo!

'If people ask me whether I ever met Bob Marley and I say, 'Yes, I played football with him in his back garden once', they look at me like I'm a bullshitter.'

Exactly.

But what really spooked me was a story I read a few years back that said Marley aggravated an infected toe that ultimately became cancerous while playing football with a bunch of English journalists in a government yard near Trenchtown.

Alan wasn't familiar with the story.

And you know what that means? One of us may have shot the sheriff.

'But he probably played football with lots of English journalists. They always went to see him at the studios and he was always playing football. The odds on that happening when he played with us are very high.'

Yeah?

'Yeah. Don't you think?'

Alan smiled. After living in cutthroat city for 30 years, little fazes him any more.

'To quote Harold Wilson, 'I'm an optimist but I always carry a raincoat.'

And an old raincoat won't ever let you down.

JOHN LYDON
Marina del Rey, Los Angeles

John Lydon lives a fuck of a long way from Finsbury Park. 5,422 miles to be precise.

But purely in the interests of research you understand, and that seeing him again after 26 years would be one of life's more interesting events, I hopped a plane to LA on the impressive Virgin four-movies-and-20-games-of-Who-Wants-To-Be-A-Millionaire-and-you're-there Atlantic, splashed out on a queen-size room in a motel on Santa Monica Boulevard, which reminded me of a million road movies, and waited patiently by my mobile phone for Johnny's sweet and sour tones.

And I still got change out of 500 quid.

The interview had been prearranged by Rambo, John's old Finsbury Park buddy, who lives in Arkansas and helps John with his affairs. If he was going to live that far away from the Arsenal, Rambo had at least to be in a place that began with the same two letters and Arizona was never in the frame.

He rang me out of the blue in response to a fax I'd sent after tracking the number through a press officer at Virgin, which had released John's last album, *The Best of British £1 Notes*, a compilation featuring prime Pistols and Public Image Ltd cuts. Rambo was a bit wary at first, but we ended up talking for more than half an hour and that's rarely happened to me before with someone I didn't know from Adam.

He sounded like my youth and I sounded like his, and it doesn't get much better than that.

He must have given me a favourable review because Johnny agreed to the interview. I knew he would anyway when Rambo mentioned my name – 'Johnny Remember Me'.

'He's never heard of you,' Rambo said, when he rang to confirm the interview.

'Oh.'

'But you seemed genuine to me, so I said it might be a good idea if he did it.' What a diamond.

I couldn't have made much of an impression on John all those years ago. Oh, well. Thanks to my cellphone mate Rambo, I was about to interview a punk legend for the first time in a quarter of a century. Snap, crackle and fucking pop.

The morning after I arrived at the 'Pulp Fiction' motel, John rang.

'Mr Cain.'

'Mr Lydon. You don't remember me.'

'Don't take it personally mate. I must've met 50,000 people.'

He was genuine and he was right, unfortunately. John was unique and shone like the sun for a year before doing precisely what he wanted to do for the next 30. The Pistols started it and the Pistols ended it. They defined the year that was 1977. The rest is evolution.

We arranged to meet the following day at noon in a sushi bar by the Pacific Ocean in Marina del Rey. As I waited in the shadows of HBO in my true romance room for the $30 cab ride south, things started to get a little surreal.

I was entering Philip Marlowe territory – hot pavements, palm trees swaying like Hawaiian hookers, summer lawns hissing. I felt more alive, more *satisfied* than I had a right to. I'm married, I've got three boys, for fucksake. What right had I to expect satisfaction?

What can I say? Worlds collide sometimes. They're meant to.

On the freeway to the restaurant two cars collided at a crossroads. Smoke poured out of one engine. 'That's just ruined someone's whole day,' said my Iranian cab driver in the real Motor City.

Marina del Rey is the shyer sister of Venice Beach, which struts its Muscle Beach funky stuff 400 yards further along the coast and pulsates with street theatre, head shops, health-food bars and big fuckers lifting big-fucker weights, and all the while an honest beggar sings, to the tune of 'Jingle Bell Rock':

Jingle bells, jingle bells help me get drunk
Help me get drunk, help me get drunk.

And the freaks come out at night.

Marina Del Rey has one main street where all the bars and restaurants surf, turf and sushi their way down to a beach that makes Camber Sands look like Camber Grain of Sand. LA streets always glow and this one shone like a ruby.

I got out of the cab as John walked out of the front doors of the Mercedes Grill.

'Welcome,' he said. Yellow T-shirt, shorts, strawberry blonde. He looked as healthy as a Californian. The ragamuffin was now an English muffin about to make the most out of a toaster. Easing himself down, coming up brown.

We sat at a table outside the restaurant and I swapped Philip Marlowe for Woody Allen without the wit. I do that sometimes. Fuck.

But it didn't matter. It was Johnny Rotten again on the EMI floor – the speed of his mouth matched only by the clarity of his thoughts. Or should that be vice versa?

LA certainly hasn't dulled any edges. But, whether he likes it or not, sweetness shines silently through the tenacity. It always has. It always will. He is a Finsbury Park boy after all.

I pulled out my digital recorder, put it on the table and switched it on. Suddenly I felt like a Wild West cowboy who has to put his six-shooter on the table in a saloon in order to enter a poker game.

John bent over the table and put his mouth right up to the recorder. 'My name's John and I like to be alive.' He sat down. 'My mum once said to me, 'You were born 50 years-old,' so that makes me 100 now.'

He lit a Marlboro Light but his eyes never left mine. He didn't know me. I was there purely because of Rambo.

'I used to have a beard and long hair,' I said, and dragged heavily on my Camel Light.

'Right.'

'I worked on 'Record Mirror'.' I was willing him to remember. 'The first time we met was the night before the Grundy show.'

Suddenly he looked concerned. 'I only knew we were doing the Grundy interview on the day. It's very important you understand that. I also didn't get a lift home after because Malcolm panicked so much he shot off immediately in the limo and I had to go home on the tube on my own. Nothing on earth looked like me and if I was on my own; I was a target.'

'I saw you in Wolverhampton, I saw you in the States, I went to your place in Gunther Grove, I was the only journalist at the one-off secret gig in Leicester Square.'

'Oh, that was you. I loved that thing you wrote.'

Got it! I registered. I'd lit a match in the cave of his memory. It would soon go out but what the fuck? It was the match of the day.

John didn't take any coaxing. Still the dream interview. The click of the recorder galvanised him. He scrubbed up the chat with the customary heavy-duty bristle brush soaked in bleach and, as the grey skies were starting to clear up, he put on a happy face.

'I was a very moody, contemplative kid, shy as hell, puzzled by life's mysteries. And who wouldn't be in Finsbury Park?'

He laughed. The whole interview, apart from one dodgy moment, was laced with laughter. The image of the bitter, twisted and mysterious Johnny Rotten was always erroneous. The lad likes nothing more than having a fucking good laugh. Lads are like that. I can definitely report that Mr Lydon has not dispensed with that desire, which consequently makes him officially still a lad, thank God.

I explained I'd let him read the interview before publication.

'That's very kind of you, young sir,' he said, in an Irish accent, before proceeding in *that* voice – guttural frenzy infused with wisdom. 'I get promised that a lot but you wouldn't believe how many mean-spirited people there are on this planet.'

He asked if I liked sushi. I said I loved it. He ordered half a dozen dishes and two small bottles of hot saki.

'You look very nervous. You mustn't be like that with me. Relax. Are you all right? Am I all right with you?'

No, you're an absolute bastard.

'Hahaha!'

Do you go home much?

'I travel all the time. I'm back in London every year. I notice the changes in London when I go back – you can't get a view of the river now, you've got to book into a posh hotel for that. That horrible cartwheel thing and that awful tent on the Isle of Dogs that's falling apart. The Isle of Dogs has gone to the dogs. It was all right as Millwall's stomping ground.'

Not a trace of one of those ludicrous US/English accents.

'You stick with your accent. You stick with what you are. I'm too old now to be absorbed into anyone else's culture. I don't really belong to any culture – I suppose I'm one on my own, heaven forbid.

'I don't exactly run to the media and I do keep myself to myself, away from all that pop stuff. I've never been one for the pop icon, swelling my big fat head in the discos or peering out of the pages of *Hello!* magazine, because I actually mean what I say. Those magazines don't like that – 'Say something meaningless, John.' No!'

So you've dropped out?

'I haven't dropped out – I think I was practically run out of the country, wasn't I? I had police raids every bleedin' weekend.'

But you must be living *la vida loca* now, John. House on the beach, house round the corner, house up the road.

'I've got money worries same as everyone else. I live in an average neighbourhood, I don't own a flash car. I feel the same about myself no matter where I hang my hat and I can't help it if people have preconceptions of who I am. I can answer a question truthfully. That's all I can do.

'If people are gonna come with these misconceptions then that's too fucking bad. I think I've spoken enough of the truth over the years. If people want me to be a bad person then yeah, I will be. I can be very bad.'

I remember my misconceptions before I met him for the first time.

'I don't blame you for thinking like that; after all, we did look like a bunch of tramps. At 17 how the hell do you know what you're doing? It doesn't matter that people thought I wasn't honest – I'm always honest with myself and that's good enough. I couldn't put a record out if I didn't believe in it.

'Strangely enough, a lot of it was based on the fact that I had meningitis as a kid and completely lost my memory. It took me years to regain it and every memory since is very precious to me and it's so important that it's accurate and right. I don't alter the past. I don't manipulate according to ego. I'm bad at some things and good at others, but I always tell it like it is.'

So in no way, shape or form were the Pistols a sham?

'No, not from my perspective. There was plenty of sham in it and that was the shame of it. But most of the sham was coming from the management side because Malcolm didn't have a contributing role really, so he had to invent an image for himself as master manipulator. That suited his purpose no end. But Malcolm is still a confused, dithering old twit and he always will be.

'It's a shame I never got on with Malcolm but he never gave me the chance. I suppose I was too far ahead of the game for him. He could manipulate Steve, Paul and Glen because they were impressed by the shock and the T-shirts with 'Cambridge Rapist' on them but to me that was twot, silly stuff, childish but good fun. I hit bigger issues right from the start.'

When I played back the recording of the interview, and slowed Johnny's voice down to 67 per cent, he sounded exactly like McLaren. Spooky. I always thought John and Malcolm were a double act without a straight man – doomed from the start.

'We could be similar, we're both Aquarius. Look, Malcolm is clever and I enjoyed parts of his company very much but I never enjoyed the resentment and laziness. There's no personal animosity, but no, I can't remember the last time I saw him. I read something about him recently – I think he was jealous of me doing the 'I'm A Celebrity' thing. He said it was a cop-out.'

Because Malcolm would love to do it himself?

'No. He would never have been able to survive being that open about himself. When you go into a thing like that, particularly with what I have to lose, it could be sink or swim. But I loved it. I don't mind exposing myself because I don't think there's anything wrong with me. I do the best I can and if that ain't good enough, tough. I'm from the school of hard knocks. Coming from my background you think you're one of the downtrodden until you eventually realise you're not at all.

'Being thrown in with the Pistols so early on and becoming famous, or infamous, you had to deal with it very quickly. I had a lot of, well – shall we call it class? – to back me up. You can't pontificate and lie on TV and be jaunty and jolly and act like some bleedin' fop from the 17th century and then go home to Finsbury Park because there you have to deal with reality. That gave you plenty of common sense – a great advantage.

'You may lack the money but you get the good stuff in bucketloads – quality, value, not morality. You appreciate more – the rows are stronger that's for sure. I grew up not knowing any different. I didn't know people had it any different from me. I thought everybody had a tin bath out in the backyard because there was no indoor toilet. I realised it wasn't like that only when I began secondary school – William of York on the Caledonian Road. That's when I started looking up and out and around.

'From the age of 11 I was brought up in Benwell Road, which now leads right to the heart of the Emirates stadium. From there we moved to Finsbury Park so, all in all, I was born in the centre of the Arsenal universe.

'I've always been good at learning though, exams and stuff. My school was Catholic. It was strict and tortuous, bitter and twisted. Half the kids were in green blazers and half in black because it had just combined with Bishop Gifford and they'd be warring over that.

'I was never one to run with gangs and mobs but I was known by them. I used to stand up the back of the North Bank over the Arsenal and there you had to be known. Everybody knew each other – no Tottenham infiltrations. It was very important stuff. Wars with Islington's lot, wars with all of it. It wasn't one great big lump of happy chaps that the media often portray. There was a bully system that you had to be well aware of. Having wit and wisdom played a great deal in simply surviving.

'There was a power struggle inherent in the working-classes – they all wanted to climb up the social ladder in whatever they did, including being in a firm. The top boys weren't bullies – they'd been through the bully system and they were kinda passive. It was the learners you had to watch out for. I was bullied at primary school. I was absent for a year when I got the meningitis. Must've been around the age of seven, so when I came back I was an alien. 'Dumby-dumb-dumb' was my nickname because I couldn't remember my own name. 'Are you the one who don't know his name?' and I couldn't say, 'Yes' because I didn't know if it was really *me* talking.

'When I went to secondary school the reports said I was a bit soft in the head but I've always been an A-grade student. I did A levels but got kicked out of school before I finished them – English lit, history and geography. I had to go to a day approved school in Hackney. I wanted to do technical drawing but I didn't have the money and there were no grants for our side of town.

'So I had to work on building sites in sewerage farms in Guildford to raise the money. My dad was a crane driver there and, believe me, he wasn't one to mollycoddle or protect me, and that's kind of worse because I had to go and deal with hardcore labourers every day who were in your face, constantly challenging you.'

Did you learn a lot from your dad?

'I learnt to leave home very early. But his attitude was right – when you're a certain age, get out of the nest. Don't be a cuckoo and sit there because that's the road to ruin. Self-reliance and independence, that's what mattered.'

What did you learn from your mum?

'How anybody can die horribly at 49. 'I'm not going to die,' she said to me in the hospital, and I told her she didn't have to lie to me. It's a terrible thing to watch someone you love die like that.

'I've never got over the fact that meningitis robbed me of my memory. I forgot who my own parents were and when, a couple of years later, it dawned on me, the guilt feelings I harboured for what I'd put them through were catastrophic. It was impossible to repair. I couldn't make it up to them.

'The upshot of all that is I can't lie. I don't want to lie. But I was confused about everything and nothing could help me sort myself out, not even drugs. But I hated being stone-cold sober and carrying all that guilt. I forgot my mum and dad and that's the most basic sin for any human being. It was a tragedy, and to this day my brothers don't want to talk about that period of my life with me.

'My mum died over 25 years ago yet I still can't get to grips with it. I couldn't get to grips with it when she was dying. I hadn't sorted it out when she died and I wrote 'Death Disco' as a result. It's is a song of screaming fucking agony, of pure pain, yet, unbelievably, it reached number eight in 'Record Mirror's' disco chart of the year. Is that a compliment? What the hell are they saying? I'm screaming in agony on the record and I'm rewarded for writing the eighth best disco record of the year. How absurd is that?

'That's my life. I write songs about what I feel, I don't know if what I feel is what most human beings feel. I avoid waltzing into self-pity, mate. I'm only raising this at the moment because there's a new DJ compilation out and that song is on it but nobody understands what it's about.

'What was awful at the time for me and, I guess, laughable too, was that my wife Nora – I say 'wife' but we're not combined in that legal way, our way is outside of shitstem – used to run a roller-skating rink in Battersea and 'Death Disco' became a popular song among the punters. It was awful but maybe my mum would have loved the irony that a load of incredibly far-out, gay and wacky girls – fag hags – would be doing wheelies to a song about her death.

'I was crying from the deepest part of my fucking soul. It just proves that the most poignant moment in life is also the most trivial. You realise your own self-pity is selfish. I cry at funerals, I cry at films. I cry at anything. I do. I'm a crier.

'When I was recovering from meningitis there was no system in place to look after you like there is today. No social workers, fuck-all. You were on your own. I had to learn to read and write all over again. My mum reintroduced me to it all and I will adore her for the rest of my life for doing that.

'At the moment some woman is claiming to be my mother's illegitimate daughter from a relationship my mum apparently had before I was born, which has come as some terrible, disgusting shock. It may be the case, I don't know, but the point is it doesn't mean I owe this woman anything. I don't know her.'

More sushi arrived and John moved away from the subject.

'In Japan I was either Johnny Lotten or John Rydon so I booked into a hotel and said, 'I'm Johnny Rydon,' and they said, 'Yes, Mr Lydon.' Aha! I'd found the key. I'd conquered Japanese.

'Japanese is a culture that has absorbed influences in a really nice, neat way and that's what I like about the British too. No matter who goes to live there, they're gonna end up British and I don't think that's a bad thing. Coping with different nationalities is something the working-classes have had to do. It's been ordained by the powers above, and we're presumed to get on living together in one slum. 'Here's a new load, go on, you deal with them. It'll all come good in the end.'

'Oh, it's very nice for the middle-class social-working types to say, 'Ooh, you're all racist.' But we wouldn't be if we'd a decision in the process. The immigrants – and I'm one myself – are in the same melting-pot and we're expected to fight it out for their amusement and judgement. Immigrants don't move straight from Serbia to suburbia, but the powers-that-be ask, 'Why can't you all just get along?' Er, excuse me, you can't 'all just get along' like that. It takes time.

'My old man would always go on about 'the bloody darkies' but his best mate was a Jamaican and they got on like a house on fire.

'My parents were full-on Irish. My dad was from Galway tinkers and they were hated and berated as 'Gyppos'. My parents' marriage was a problem for my mum's family because they thought my dad was low-rental. Not many people know that about the Paddies – their class structure is even worse than the English.'

The Greeks are like that. I speak from experience.

'Don't tell me about the Greeks or the Turks because I was brought up with them – Finsbury Park is the home of the kebab and the rum baba. Green Lanes is great. It's a rocking place and it's all Arsenal.

'Think ladders, and it's all about being one step up so you can look down on the one below you. Now the West Indians have gone one step up and are looking down on the Slavs. In Finsbury Park you just didn't have time to think black, white, this, that or the other. It wasn't relevant.'

I'd written a few quotes down from that first interview in 1976 and thought I'd toss the odd one in over lunch. This seemed like an opportune moment.

There hasn't been a very white thing in dance music music for years. But it's all so easy when the music is done by someone else – and it's done by blacks for whites.

'When did I say that? I was brought up with reggae. I never liked Tamla Motown or the soul-boy nonsense. I didn't like the orchestra in Motown, it just killed it for me. But I guess I was the wrong end of it, just slightly too young. Bits and pieces of Motown were great – Diana Ross's voice I will always love, I could die in it.

'Remember the Average White Band? We never viewed it like that, as black or white. The sound of Philadelphia, what was that? A bunch of white producers for songs with a black message. I think when you declare something is black music you're instantly being hateful and that ain't really acceptable. It doesn't matter about religion or colour.

'I hate disco.'

'True. I liked hard-core reggae, not ska, although when it went into dub, ooh, I could swim in that. It was just a perfect match for the wacky excesses of Jimi Hendrix who, at my early age, I never thought was wacky at all and I couldn't understand the purists of heavy metal at that time thinking that Hendrix wasn't music.

'The only time I took any notice of Bob Dylan was when he played the Albert Hall with an electric band and the purists resented that bitterly, accusing him of selling out, which was ludicrous because some of his best music was amplified. I ain't going to the Albert Hall to hear a bloke strumming his acoustic guitar two and a half miles away!

'My mate Dave's older brother was a mod and that's where I picked up on all that Electric Prunes stuff. That was music I'd never conceived possible and when I heard it I thought, Fuck, that's the business. Iron Butterfly? You can't call yourself fucking Iron Butterfly. Wonderful.'

How important was the influence of American punk on 1977?

'American punk! You're joking. What, Patti Smith coming over and spouting some daft Rimbaud poetry? The Ramones to me were like Status Quo – chugaluglug daddad daddada. Shit. What you were getting then from Manchester to London was already incredibly diverse and utterly devoid of any New York opinion. The only introduction to that would have been Malcolm McLaren's statements later.

'I don't pay homage to very much at all. I love music for what it is and not the you're-a-genius-and-that-came-from-nowhere shit. I think the Sex Pistols practically came from nowhere because there were so many influences involved and at the same time we were all ignorant about the other person's tastes. Malcolm could never quite comprehend our diversity.

'I had some kind of respect for 'You Really Got Me' because they had that guitar hook and I loved the cowbell at the start of 'Honky Tonk Woman'. These were records that my mate Dave's brother would have. I was only eight when 'You Really Got Me' came out but I heard it through the older boys and it was the absurd assault of it that got me.

'The Beatles I got from a very early age. That was the noise my mum and dad would play at weekend parties in between Irish accordion music. Deedoodeediddlydoo – 'She loves you yeah yeah yeah' – deedoodeediddlydoo. I remember thinking, Hullo, I've just come out of meningitis hospital, I've got no memory but I know what I like and it's not that shit.

'It's an odd thing but you do tend to resent what your parents like. I've always found the Beatles a bit twee and a bit fake. They were a rock'n'roll band who found something else to cop on to, but then again, Jimi Hendrix did play on Hughie Greene's 'Opportunity Knocks'!'

Try this for size John.

Groups like The Who and the Stones are revolting. They have nothing to offer the kids anymore. All they're good for is making money. You just read their balance sheets – life's really become safe for them. They're just so pathetic.

'I'll tell you really honestly about Pete Townsend. I think he's a wonderful man but I think he's wonderfully undisciplined.

'Mick Jagger apparently did some great things for Sid. I heard years later from lawyers that when Sid was in prison in New York, Jagger put some money up to help him. I've always said thank you for paying attention.'

And this was after you called Jagger revolting.

'Oh, that's still true. I don't understand why you think that changes anything. Don't be ridiculous. But always respect.

'I don't think the Stones ever had anything to offer the kids. 'Street Fighting Man' was a great record but it was preaching to students. I bought Stones' records years later because there was a record store that was going out of business and it had all the early Decca stuff, which I picked up for 20 pence.

'If you were going to be serious about what music really mattered back then you've got to talk about the Pretty Things. They may not have released much product but their impact is unquestionable. Be aware, The Clash have had how many albums? And the Pistols have had how many albums? But in terms of impact what is the most important? It's not about product it's about achievement.

It only took one album to assure your greatness

'Oh, for fuck sake, stop it. Do you honestly think I did it to be assured of greatness? That's the most absurd statement you could possibly make, you tart.

''Ullo, Barry, you want another pint?' 'Yeah. Cheers John. Tell me something, how you gonna assure your greatness?' Fucking greatness. Hahahahaha!

'People who love rewards hang around rewards and reward each other. They're basically the enemy. When an accolade is thrown your way be very dubious about it and run away from it. Like the nonsense recently when the Pistols were invited into the Hall of Fame. It was quite difficult to convince the rest of the band that it was a bad move, but they finally got it in the end. I mean, 30 years later some self-appointed people are judging us, having the audacity to possess an opinion about us. How dare you? I don't want your reward. I didn't do it for this. I did it to be right and I don't need a silly doorstop trophy.

'My songs weren't nihilistic. I viewed myself as music hall with a bit of burlesque thrown in. It wasn't, 'Haha, kill 'em all.' It was more 'You fuckers are torturing me with your nonsense.'

'However, some awards are nice. The Q award was delicious because it was meaninglessly annoying – an inspiration award, hahahahaha! They wanted to fly me over to London and put me up in a hotel, hahahahaha! I thought, I'll walk down to the lobby to collect that one. Hahahahaha! Yes. Hahahahaha! That makes sense. So what do I do? I turn up on a horse and cart full of old rusty bicycles and toilet seats, hahahahaha!'

Cue 'Steptoe' theme.

'And what does that do? It opens the door for the Sham 69 idiots to say, 'Oh, he's 'Steptoe and Son'.'

'Nah! Really? And what the hell is wrong with 'Steptoe and Son'?'

Cue 'Steptoe' impressions – John made a particularly impressive Wilfred Brambell.

'These awards are ridiculous. I didn't know I was at the forefront of something at the time. It wasn't deliberate. You must understand, there must be no flag-waving. You knew me. I just want to be myself, mate.'

But you were part of the punk pack.

'Hahahahahaha! Punk pack. Hahahahahaha! You look to me as though, ooh, this bloke's famous but... Hullo! I didn't want to run with the pack because the pack was boring and now the pack is dead. It got you nowhere.

'Do you think I ever presented myself as being part of a 'punk pack'? Did I even know or consider these terms? Tough on people who did. You talked to me, you knew me better than most. Where are you from?'

The Angel.

'Now you knew what the Angel used to think of Finsbury Park or Holloway Road. But you knew. But you knew. But you knew a thing or two. And you knew Hornsey. There were limitations, even in your own area. You don't quite understand what I'm saying – these were all Arsenal areas but you couldn't go from one to another without the right passport.'

People from our backgrounds have inferiority complexes that

we bury deep.

'Having an inferiority complex is what makes you. Don't think of it as a negative, you're a silly boy. You're not getting it. Don't think like that. You're not getting it.'

More saki appears but I'm the only one eating the sushi. I realised a long time ago that the best places to conduct interviews over lunch were Oriental establishments where you shared dishes. That way you got to eat twice as much as the interviewee because they're too busy talking to eat – in this case it was 100 per cent more. John loves to chat and I love to listen. And eat.

Tentatively I try another quote.

They try to ruin you from the start. They take away your soul. They destroy you. 'Be a bank clerk' or 'Join the army' is what they give you at school. And if you do what they say you'll end up like the moron they want you to be.

'No, it's not true, many people have gone through the system and have come out to be very good friends of mine. So the system doesn't corrupt you, you corrupt yourself. I may have been poisoned by opportunity but I always remained honest to myself.

'And can you imagine working in a bank as a clerk? All your mates would've come in and asked for money. You'd have been fucked. Anyway, what did the advice of a career's officer mean to me at 15? Fuck-all. I'd been going to clubs like Lacy Lady in Romford since I was 13 and I had to pretend I was 18 to get in. It was places like that where pogoing started.

'I was also a regular at the Roundhouse, which for me was stunning because you'd get in for two shillings after the doorman stamped your hand and you were there all day, from midday to midnight.

'Then you'd go to the all-nighters in King's Cross or the Lyceum. It was an underground thing and it was a secretive little world based around amphetamine sulphate, which we knew all about in Finsbury Park. That was a throwback to the mod days. The mods loved blues and it developed from that.

'King's Cross was a tough-arse place to hang around but that was my world and all worlds are chaos. I'd come straight from the building site on a Friday from Guildford; I had long hair, a sleeveless denim jacket, which I deliberately dyed grey because I fucking resented blue denim. The word 'Hawkwind' was studded on the back and it also had Arsenal written in Hell's Angel-type letters. I'd be out of my mind for the whole weekend snorting in small amounts. One gram of speed would last nearly three days. I never touched cocaine. What is it anyway? A 30-second up, then the flu for three hours. I've never changed my opinion of it.

'As far back as I can remember, the place to get the best drugs was the back of the North Bank over the Arsenal. I think Arsenal was the first serious druggie mob. It was terracing, all standing, and it was so packed the cops couldn't get into it and you'd be in the middle with saucy young women in red and white scarves doing beastly things at early ages. It was uproarious.

'Mods liked their speed but nobody said you had to be on drugs to like mod music. Nobody said you had to be on drugs to like punk. But everyone said you had to be on drugs to like rave and house. Bollocks. I liked the drugs and I liked the music and the two together were stunning. What is wrong with this combination? Who is passing moral judgements on me now?'

I mentioned my toilet dexies days in the dancehalls at, I confess, the then veritably ancient age of 15.

'This is what I thought Dexy's Midnight Runners meant until I heard 'Come On Eileen'.' John started to sing and the other diners turned their heads – 'Oh come on Eileen, come on Eileen, fucking come on Eileen, come on for fucksake, I ain't got all fucking night Eileen.' Hahahahaha!

'I don't believe you can become addicted to speed. I don't even believe you can become addicted to anything. When life's depressing and you feel you haven't got much to offer to *yourself* that's when you're gonna be that way inclined. I know many people who have gone through it and come out the other side and I know many who haven't. Heroin to me has always been the killer one.

It's a sad, sad drug. I took it about three or four times – I chased the dragon – and hated it.

'The Heartbreakers introduced me to heroin. They brought it to the UK in a really big way. But guess what? I introduced them to Dr Collis Brown's and they fucking loved it. 'What, you don't need a prescription? Are you joking?' Thunders said to me in a hotel in Manchester, after I brought four bottles in and they went rampant on the stuff. 'Shit, the cough medicine in England is fucking good.'

'The Heartbreakers were on withdrawal, that's why they took it. And in those days heroin wasn't exactly all over the place. I got them off the heroin and on to the Collis Brown's.

"No, no, Mr Thunders, you're not a heroin addict. You've just got the flu." Hahahahaha!

'I did most of my drugs before the Pistols. I was so worried about getting myself right when I was in the band. I'd been given this opportunity and I really wanted to go for it, and I suppose the *modus operandi* for Malcolm was, like, oh, let's be like a mad Bay City Rollers. But Glen Matlock wanted us to be like a decadent Sixties pimp band, saucy cheeky chappies in white patent-leather sneakers, very much like the way lads in London look like now. Glen was ahead of his time by going backwards.

'I didn't want any of that. I wanted to get on with it and write things I hadn't heard before and say things that should be said. I suppose the closest to a rebellious and pertinent song should have been John Lennon's 'Working Class Hero'. I adored the title and the idea behind it but the lyrics let me down to fuck. They let all my culture down. They just weren't there. Lennon was preaching to university students about something they could imitate but he wasn't talking from the heart, he wasn't saying, 'This is how it is, learn from it.' It was a 'you-too-can-fake-this-image' song and I resented that bitterly.

'When you start analysing, the problems begin. That's what the middle classes like to do. Their education system teaches them to analyse their every thought and motive but it also makes them criminally insane and they end up devaluing people like me and you. They think we're monkeys because we don't go through their system and they like to experiment on us.

'We do things, basically, to attract the opposite sex. Fashion is simply about attracting partners and punk styles are no different in that respect. Nobody around me could understand that about punk straight off – not my family, not my community. They got it eventually, but by then it was too late because it had become fashionable and the 'Sun' started saying this is how to dress like a punk and these are the shops to go to, and when you need to be told that kind of stuff, you're already out of the loop. You're gone.

'The only way you're ever going to get a partner in life is by being yourself and if you step out of that and think you can disguise it by renting a flash car or buying a designer outfit or pretending you're something you're not it doesn't work because it means the partner you've attracted is as fake as you so you haven't got the real deal. They're lying to you just like you're lying to them. Disaster.

'And hullo, I'm 30 years with the same partner because I was aware of that. That's a long time, baby. Nora's led a full life, I've led a full life but we love each other as people and that don't mean we're wrapped around each other's ankles with a chain – 'Where you going now? What are you doing?' Trust. You need someone in your life you can trust. It's a different world otherwise.

'I feel sorry for Malcolm. He has a brilliant mind, but without Vivienne he seemed to lose his premise because I think she was really his mentor and I feel she hated me and does to this bloody day. Malcolm was raised by women and I think he resented it. But that's not a tragedy – you silly punk. Didn't you realise how great that could have been for you? I feel he uses it now as an excuse rather than a wonderful thing. To be brought up around fanny juice is a privilege.

'I saw Vivienne recently in New York at the Metropolitan Museum of Modern Art. There was an exhibition about British fashion from the 17th to the 20th centuries and I wore the original tartan jacket that I designed and Vivienne made for me. I lost the kilt and the pants to moths but I turned up wearing the jacket and gave a speech about being radical and what this means in fashion.

'Me and Rambo were told to leave by a certain exit but I smelled a rat so we sneaked back in just as Vivienne and her entourage were entering. I went straight up to her. 'Hullo, Vivienne.'

'Oh, hullo, John. The last time I met you, you punched me!'

'Did I? Well, it must've been for a good reason.'

'It was at Andrew Logan's Alternative Miss World event.'

'But I remembered I wasn't allowed into that. That's one of the reasons I flamed on Malcolm and Vivienne. There's many, many things that they wouldn't involve me in because they invented this concept of Johnny Rotten the mystery man, shy, taciturn. Fucking hell, did they get that one wrong!

'Yes, I am shy, when it suits me.

'I used to love Vivienne. I worked at her shop in the Kings Road and Chelsea football ground was just round the corner. One particular Saturday Nottingham Forest came down and they were a lethal mob at the time. I knew Forest. Sid knew Forest. He had a cousin who was a Forest fan and he went up there before the Pistols and watched them throw rival fans into the river. It was County one side and Forest the other. The mobs would catch you and throw you in.

'So they all came down to the shop and there I was in winkle-pickers, skintight straight jeans that Sid used later – we all wore each other's clothes – my mum's lilac lace top that I cut so it revealed my nipples, and green hair.

'The Forest boys came running down the street shouting, 'Kill the cockneys!' and Vivienne panicked. 'Quick, close the doors.'

'But I refused and instead just ran into the street and charged at them – and there were hundreds of the fuckers – screaming, 'Arsenal!' Man alive, I fucking single-handedly frightened the living daylights out of them. They couldn't believe what was running at them and they turned away. It was one of the most brilliant moments of my life.

'And guess what? Vivienne sacked me. 'You attracted them,' she said. 'You're the one causing all the trouble.'

'Later, the Pistols played the club right underneath that bridge in Nottingham and, do you know, a guy came up to me after the gig and said, 'You're that mad bastard with the nipples!' Hahahahaha!

'After that the Kings Road riots started between the punks and teddy boys and there were a lot of Clock End Gooners and punks that picked up on it shouting, 'Kill the Teds!' I turned up in a teddy boy outfit once just because I didn't want that.'

He lit another Marlboro and ordered more saki. The sun had enveloped him and started to heat his sushi. But he didn't seek the shade. Instead he raised his cup. 'Cheers. It's good to see you, good to hear a north London accent. Some Brits come over here and they over-English it and it becomes like Spain.

'I know what I come from but I don't yell it from the rooftops. Silence was always the order of the day when you were in a pub. Don't be shouting your fucking head off because someone's gonna knock your teeth in. Pricks. Take all that shit back to Lewisham with you.

'People are pretentious when they should just get to the nitty-gritty. Let me run random for a second because thoughts to me are like that. I like Jonathan Ross. He's a lot of things but he really gets it on a basic level, that man. I can work with him, and I love being on his show and talking to him. And he's got a punk wife. He broke some barriers and now he's the Des O'Connor of our generation. Every generation needs a Des O'Connor. You need the lighter side and the heavier side.'

Who represents the heavier side?

'Steve Jones, have you seen the size of him lately? He spreads around town. He's a DJ here and is getting quite a following.

'I like life – you've always known that about me. Even when I go into dismal mode it's still a form of celebration.

'In 1977 all these bastards were trying to put me down again. I

don't blame anyone and anything other than my own insecurities
but I managed it and I enjoyed it and I thrived on it. Whenever I
walked anywhere it was war – I've still got the scars to show for it.

'When I got attacked in Highbury in 1977 that was West Ham.
Got them, though, got them lovely. What do you fucking think? Do
you think we ran around bragging in the newspapers when we got
them back?

'In '77 I never saw in British society any room made for
intelligence. It was always privilege over intelligence. It goes way
back and I've never seen any good results from posh, rich bastards;
not ever, not in the history of mankind.

'I've got great-grandfathers and uncles who fought in the wars
and the injuries they suffered were appalling – one of them had
his anus blown out, for Chrissake. I was brought up witnessing
this travesty, this mutilation of human beings. I knew I was raised
simply to be cannon fodder for the next bunch of political geniuses
that would get us involved in yet another idiotic war.

'Look, if you're not greedy it's a good start. Making money
shouldn't be a motivation. It ain't the answer.

'But Blair's idea of socialism is ludicrous. He's an absolute
fucker who sidetracked a good principle and turned it into his
own creation, his own I-want-an-original-Georgian-fireplace-
in-Islington socialism, awash with Covent Garden winebarisms
and swiney-arsed youth bands sporting Sixties-imitation hairdos
with a bit of hair gel on the side and the thin look and that whole
Coldplay attitude that is so very weak.

'There doesn't appear to be anything to unite around, no cultural
movement, no respect.

'Blair has completely killed the country. He's sold it down the
river. Crying his eyes out at Princess Di's funeral? What was that
all about? Evil fucking nonsense, if you ask me. Many of my friends
actually said, out loud, 'He really cares,' but I thought there was an
awful lot more important things he should be concerned about than
Princess Di. The Labour Party promised me an understanding, an

inner depth, a wisdom about what was right and wrong. Morality is wrong, values are right. Morality is judgemental and religious. If I work hard and achieve something I should be rewarded for that and not be put down. I will always have respect for people who work hard and do things. Whether they hate me or not or I hate them, there's a bigger world involved.

'I hated Margaret Thatcher but, by God, did I respect her. But I had negative opinions of Blair right from the start. And Harold Wilson wore a wanker's mac and sucked on a pipe. That was back-row-in-Soho stuff. That's why he was bald too.'

He mimicked Harold Wilson in a strip club rubbing his scalp and jerking off. I felt like Billy Crystal in the Meg Ryan restaurant scene from 'When Harry Met Sally'.

'I think the Labour Party is a corrupt party. In one weird way the Tories were right – Labour was block-voting union votes and speaking on behalf of people that had no say. It took away basic rights of freedom and dictated the mandate. Freedom of opinion is essential.

'What we need is 800 different party representatives in a House of Everything. Okay, you won't get union but you would get great couches and boats and furniture and housing like Italy, where nothing is unified but somehow that culture manages to squeeze through without a government dictating. It's very bizarre that Juventus have been demoted. I'm very puzzled that they've done that.

'All I can say is that if you can't beat Arsenal you might as well fuck off.' Hahahahaha!

'I'm asked where my politics lead, left or right. I'm neither. I'm just puzzled that I see more working-class people in the Tory Party than in Labour. You shouldn't just vote Labour because it's indoctrinated into you. These fuckers have cheated us badly over the years and Tony Blair is just about the worst of the lot. He's Mr Bush's lapdog and the president himself can't string a sentence together.

'Apparently the latest excuse for Bush is that he's dyslexic and that's supposed to explain everything. The poor man, let's have another world war. It's unforgivable.

'Arabs are wonderfully friendly people. They're like Paddies when it comes to family celebrations, except they don't fight at their weddings.

'You have to get to them through politeness and accuracy, not through medieval battleaxe tactics. Islam preaches very many things that are very righteous. It is a beautiful religion, utterly true to itself, but, like all religions, its basic premise is 'Please fall for this.' I don't want to. To me all religion is fallacy and mediocrity. One of these days everyone will understand that.

'They are human beings for Chrissake. I come from Finsbury Park, I come from Hebrew, Greek, kebab up the wazoo. I know it. I know it's true. You learn to get on with your mates and you fight the fucking Nazis, right.'

He sang;

We run 'em all
The long and the short and the tall
'Cos we are the Arsenal and we are the best.
We're North Bank so fuck off the rest.

'We ran 'em all and we did that as a mixed breed. Are we dogs? No. We're the future. Your future, no future for you.

'I'm part of a glorious, incredible, wonderful culture called the working-class. We don't have heroes. We don't have victims. Fucking important that.'

If I hadn't joined the Sex Pistols I would have been locked up, put quietly away, classified insane. Difference is, I know I'm not mad. Can you say that?

'Yeah, can you? Can I?

'I thought over the years I must be mental because I feel I'm involved in a constant battle against this tedious tendency human beings have to lie and it really is a problem for me. It means I can't formulate any kind of business concept or learn to make a contribution to society that means something because I always expect to be lied to.

'I know I'm belligerent, I can't help it. I make mistakes, I make enemies when I shouldn't. I don't mean to but I do because of, ha ha, the Mouth. The Mouth from the South.

'I suppose that's a direct result of the old Sex Pistols gigs up north when there wouldn't be a single night without 20 or 40 lads lined up to kick our fucking brains in. And in the middle of all that Malcolm booked us in Barnsley, Bolton, Bradford, all the fucking Bs up there, including a teddy-boy convention starring the Sex Pistols. Every teddy boy in the north of England turned up to kill us. But guess what? They didn't because they liked us.

'We had a splendid row once in a car park in Coventry. The Coventry City lot turned up to do the fucking Cockney bastards and the Coventry Arsenal turned up and I never knew there was such a mob. So there was this fucking war and we were putting our few pieces of stolen equipment in the van in the middle of this pitched battle.

'Scarborough was another one where we had 200 lads who wanted to kill us. I said, 'All right, I'm all alone on this big empty stage and there you are but I've got a mike stand.' And I held it up in a threatening way and it did the trick.

'So I got cocky with that stand over the months – that's how I lost my front teeth. I got used to holding on to the mike stand off-stage and I was at the Screen on the Green when a girl accidentally pushed the bottom of the stand as it was in my hands and it hit me in the mouth and I lost my two front teeth. We had a gig the next night and you didn't cancel gigs then, not like now, especially with American punk bands like the Marilyn Mansons, 'Ooh, I've hurt my ankle – cancel the tour.'

'It was a holiday weekend and Malcolm said we didn't have the money to pay for an emergency dentist so I had to break into a local off-licence and nick a bottle of brandy to keep myself pissed to dull the pain. I eventually had them replaced but three years ago while tucking into a bunch of cherries – I love cherries – a stone broke the steel rod in my tooth and now I can't get it replaced because they would have to remove one on the other side to compensate.

'So, all my photographs from here on in will be negatives! I have such a fear of dentists so I'll never go back. The pain was unbelievable. They put needles in the nerve, and because I've got sinus problems from the meningitis, the pain was terrible. Sorry, mate, I'd rather have the gap.

'It took me a long time even to talk properly after it happened. I hope people don't notice it because it shouldn't be noticed. It's not vanity or a pose, it's just a fucking tooth missing and I can't help it. All right. There it is.

'In certain aspects of the media it's seen as a deliberate image and I don't blame then for thinking that in light of the way that imagery is so important these days. Pete Doherty wouldn't have been allowed to make a fool of himself without the Pistols projecting that imagery. It's the legacy of the Signatures and Courtney Love, and it's the loser end, bum scale of things. To me, honestly, all that shit really hurts.

'That lot didn't understand my mate Sid at all. He was a complicated person but he's become a coat-hanger and that's a tragedy and a joke and a cliché and that wasn't the bollocks at all. Sid had an incredibly tough life – his mother was a registered heroin addict and he really had a lot to fucking put up with. I loved that man but he bought into the Lou-Reed-New-York heroin thing.

'I would never have got into jazz but for Sid. He was jazz through and through and *Bitches Brew* was his favourite album and mine too. It would never have occurred to me to even listen to it but for Sid.

'Sid was a very important person to me simply because he existed. Everybody that exists I love. I don't know you very well but I love the fact that you exist, that you have a spark of life. I don't know what gives that spark to our existence but I'm amazed by it. Amazed.

'When you've forgotten who you are and you get that back

again it's a blessing. Consequently, I guess contracting meningitis was a blessing.'

John ordered more saki. He nibbled some raw eel but decided a fag was more appropriate. So did I, red-hot saki and a Camel Light being one of life's more tantalising combinations.

'We can alter our universe but we decide not to. And that's where God and the Devil come in.'

Didn't you alter something?

'I don't know, that's up to God and the Devil to decide. It might have been just predictable. I don't make any judgement on it. I don't make any judgement on Hitler either. People do things because they think it's for the best. And that's where we get it wrong. It's a tragedy, isn't it?

'I like human beings and that's always been my problem.'

You have no future, nothing. You are made unequal...

'I think that's still true, unfortunately. Now it applies more to, say, Slavs in the UK because lots of English people have now accepted it and work round it. I still think the system ultimately makes people feel subservient despite their educational qualities.

'I don't think I'm a dumb man. I never have, right? I've had a lot of mental problems in my life as a result of meningitis but I've overcome them and I've never been a parasite on the system. That in itself is my own self-achievement, that and making the word 'bollocks' legal, something you could wear on the beach in a fashionable little number. Did you know I went to the court case in Nottingham and Malcolm didn't turn up because he thought we were gonna lose and there might be a problem?

'This is why when he ran for mayor he didn't really run for mayor. Most things he's ever done in his life, he's never really been about commitment. He doesn't follow a thing through. He wants other people to do it for him. But that's what I call an artist. You must understand 'The Rabbit Song' is about such people.'

I don't believe in marriage, mortgage or a house in the country. It's awful. It's disgusting...

'Me and Nora are still not married even though we've been together for nearly 30 years. Oh, my God, I really am consistent. I haven't got a mortgage and never will. I live in Mae West's old house and it's apparently haunted by her.'

Do you go up and see her sometime?

'She was the sexiest woman in the world and she fell madly in love with Rudolph Valentino and bought him the house next door. Naturally, the love was unrequited, old Rudolph was gay. People say she wanders around the house at night, pining for the love she could never have.

'Mae West was the most wonderful woman. I love her films. They were heaven.'

Suddenly he hit me with that stare. I felt my soul was being violated.

'You got a vague bit of Tottenham in ya, might be Chelsea.'

You're joking! I've got two season tickets for the Emirates.

'Do you know who got me two season tickets? Ian Wright Wright Wright. Right right right. I love that man. He could wear a dress on TV and I wouldn't care. He's Arsenal through and through. My brother went to a night game at the Emirates the other night and said after you could grow marijuana plants under those lights. The testing point will be when Tottenham come down to see if they'll do the old spray-paint jealousy act because, let's face it, Arsenal spray-painted Tottenham so many times.

'I got involved in fights at Highbury. You had to – it's your family, it's people you know. But it was always inside the stadium – the stop-it-you-ain't-gonna-shout-that-shit syndrome – not the outside street battles. That was only for the real McCoy.

'Arsenal was a melting-pot. We were the first multi-racial mob. You wouldn't get National Front shit at Arsenal except in a fantastic piss-take way. There was a Jewish guy and he ran as a NF candidate and it was superb.

'Martin Webster was NF leader at the time, leading a bunch of West Ham skinheads who didn't know any better and couldn't suss out what that hierarchy was. Arsenal were a smarter bunch. We asked, 'Why are you the leader and who says so?'

'Finsbury Park was the dead centre of the universe of trouble, especially when Arsenal weren't a particularly good team.

'The Sun once ran this bullshit story that Millwall were gonna come down and steal the clock off the Clock End during a cup game. It's not the power of the press, it's the power of growing up with it.

'One of my all-time best mates is Tottenham. He lives in Whitechapel and the Krays pub was at the end of his road. And here's the joke – half my family are Tottenham. You've got to understand that loads of my mates are Arsenal, another load are Tottenham and another load are Chelsea. We'd meet in the grounds, and these were hard-core fuckers who you'd hate to hell on the day but we were all still friends.'

A hefty guy in shorts who had been dining at a nearby table with his hefty wife and a hefty lobster paid his bill and got up to leave.

'I'm a big fan,' he said to John. 'I love what you've done.'

'Damn,' said John. 'And I'm undercover.'

The guy laughed and waltzed out.

'I don't get that in London too much. You have to be careful where you go. I live in Fulham and they seem to be getting a little firm together – these little Fulham whippersnappers with their Fulham hats and Fulham shirts. It all seems to be coming back. I know it's violent, but it's dealing with the others who are violent too. It was never about beating up women and children.

'I remember Glasgow Rangers coming down in the late Sixties for a night game and they ran along the back of the North Bank throwing beer bottles on the roof so the glass would shatter and rain down on us. It was a real battle but we chased those fuckers right out of the ground.

'That was the time when the Scots claimed they were the toughest bastards on God's earth. I don't know what it is about Scotland but they all look beaten up from an early age.

'All the football books so far, about what it really means, have been bullshit. They've missed the premise that it's not just a culture of yobbism, it's a culture of society based on protecting basically your family and your friends and without people like Rambo, who battled their way through in the early days, none of these new-born Arsenal sods from Tring would be able to go up to Liverpool or Manchester or even get off the train.

'There were thousands of these fuckers out to kill you, and there you are at 16 having to fight your way through it and that's what Rambo did. He's a hero to me, that man.

'We live in a hard-core world, not one of cruelty, one of something else, of value. We could all be incredibly wealthy people driving around in Bentleys, which is the latest LA car, but I'd rather not.'

But could you?

'No. I could see how I *could* sell out, pop trivia.'

But could you afford a Bentley?

'Not mentally. Don't laugh. It would hurt my head to be deceitful. There's been a lot of tosh written and we've deliberately played games over the years about me being a real estate agent. Is it that easy to lie with the worldwide web so dominant?

'The Internet has created a wonderful world of foibles. You can say anything you like. I could propagate many myths about myself but I'd rather not.

'I know a lot of things about a lot of things. No one understood me with Colin Dunne the boxer. But he was the most beautiful boxer, his skill was unbelievable.

'I went to see him box in London on the same bill as Prince Naseem. Frank Warren got someone to come and ask me to his table. But I was there for Colin and with my friends, and I think he had something to do with promoting this Naseem guy so how could I go to his table? Especially when I remembered watching Naseem at the weigh-in – trumpets blaring, flags waving, and in he comes and blows a raspberry. Man, what a cheek. It's unacceptable. The weigh-in was absurd. Everywhere he went there were trumpets.

He didn't box well at all on the night and the crowd booed, but I tell you, that was a fucking great trumpet!'

The laughs were coming thick and fast. John is a natural comedian, when he wants to be. Phantom tape machines are perpetually clicking somewhere in the ether and the thoughts come tumbling down.

'You always try to know people who don't like you, it's the best thing in the world. Top-quality hooligans never lie. It's not about being tough, it's about being real. Real people don't lie, they just tell you what is.

'Two more saki.

'Can I have a wee-wee, Dad?'

As John glided between the tables a couple strolled past the restaurant, the man holding a baby. The woman spotted John and her face lit up. She stood by the entrance and waited – our table was only a few feet away. Cue 'Twilight Zone' theme – she was wearing a black John Lydon T-shirt.

'I can't believe it,' she said when John returned to the table. 'It's like a dream.'

For the next ten minutes John posed for her pictures and played with her baby and toyed with her emotions and she lived the dream. He was her Pop Idol with the 'X Factor'. What more could she want?

And her husband liked him too.

'You got kids?' John asked, after the couple, inflated with dreams, had floated out of the restaurant.

Three boys, 22-year-old identical twins Paul and Andrew, and Elliot who's 11.

'So you understand, you understand what it meant to Nora and me when we were told we couldn't have kids after an abortion went wrong just after my mother's death. It's something I don't talk much about but I want you to understand that kids are very important to me – I used to be a primary-school teacher. I love kids and I lost the very thing, my connection to the world, because Nora couldn't have any more.

'We never wanted to adopt. We don't need to because the children of Nora's daughter Ariana have lived with us since they were young. I bought them a house and one of them even lives next door. My house has always been full of kids. My brother Martin and his kids lived with us for a long time. My whole life is about kids.

'I couldn't live without Nora. She was misguided like me until the two of us joined together. We have a very, very deep love for each other that I've not seen in many other people.'

What does she do?

'Well, she don't cook for a start. What do you mean, 'What does she do?' Nora's like me, she's been confused, confused about where we stand in life and what our social obligations are.'

Do two confusions make a right?

'Yes, they do. What we've done in between is help out everybody who comes into contact with us. What we've done is pay out, and never received one dollar from anybody. That's why I'm fucking broke.

'And how's this for confusing – I just wrote a few pop songs and I'm denied a visa to 32 different countries. Thirty-two! Kissy kissy mate. I don't know what judgement is. And I'm still banned from loads of London nightclubs because they assume, even after all these years, that I'm going to cause trouble. And these are places where Paul Cook gets in! And even he can't get me in!'

At 30 it's too late, most people are clapped out with beer guts – look at Mick Jagger.

'I think it's true. I'm 50, what the fuck do you want from me?'

You're still going strong.

'No. No, I'm not.

'One of the worst periods of my life was when me and Jah Wobble lived in Edmonton just after the demise of the Pistols. He was a Tottenham lad and we rowed all the time. The house we lived in only cost six quid a week because it was supposed to be haunted. It fucking was too – by us! Strummer came over one night.'

He was a lovely bloke Joe. The saki's kicking in. Not only am I interrupting, I'm verging on maudlin.

'Erm, not really. He was all right. I didn't hate him. He was a pub-band bloke. He was older.

'Hot saki please. El quicko hotto, rush back with the hot ones.

'Anyway, Joe came over to see the place, which had been bombed in the war and a woman died in the bathroom. When I took a shower – the first time in my life I'd ever had one and I'm still wary of them, I'm primitive – the soap would move backwards and forwards in its dish

'Wobble got really frightened after seeing something run down the stairs. He thought it was me until he realised I was in the kitchen all the time. There were a couple of hard-core hooligan mates staying with us that night and we all slept in one room because we were shitting ourselves. And the door would swing open and close all night and we were all shaking. One of the blokes was convinced it was my reggae records that were responsible for it all – 'We mustn't be tempting the demons with that mad dark shit.'

'Was it mass psychosis and weakness in us or was it the drugs?

'We refused to pay the rent – we had no money – and the landlord turned up with all these thug guys. We invited them in but they refused because they'd heard about the ghosts. We thought this was wonderful, we're haunted and it's rent-free. We later realised they were more likely scared of us.'

John looked at a diner on a nearby table.

'I ain't done nothing wrong, have I?'

'In my eyes, no,' said the guy.

'You bastard. Cheers.'

The intermission was over.

'I am the International Front. I'm in the union, Jack, in the most accurate, brilliant, beautiful way. Don't you know that? You know it don't you?

'When the Pistols played Crystal Palace a few years back, I became the International Front. Every fucking mob in England was there and the police were stationed on the hill with their batons. They had nothing. We don't row. We don't row among ourselves. We're England. That's what that gig did. If you didn't see it, you missed something special. I love my country. I won't have it fucked up, not by anybody.'

You love your country yet you're in LA.

'This is my country. I'll make a cunt of anything that fucks with me. I'm England.'

I laughed

'You think that's funny? It's the truth. Look around – do you see any animosity? Now why's that? Think about it. It ain't 'cos I'm nice and I sell flowers on the street corner. I sell rebellion.'

What – to families like the ones that just left?

'No, I'm introducing the wonderful concept of the burning Bush. Marijuana is George.

'You are fantastic, you are absurd.

'Next time you walk down Benwell Road you can sing, 'Johnny Rotten's flagellation.' Isn't it unbelievable that they've built that ground in the very area where I said, 'Der, what's my name?' They should have the Johnny Rotten 'Der' entrance at the ground. All together now, der!

'One of my uncles was a Manchester United supporter and he was there the very first time I ever went to Arsenal to see them play United. Georgie Best scored a hat-trick and my uncle's going berserk. It's difficult to explain just how much that hurt, especially when he only supported United because there was an Irish player in the team. Hateful. So I done him, my uncle. I cut his ankle with a Stanley knife.

'Shit, don't tell Rambo that. He'll hate that. He said you were all right. He's got your number, but I don't know what that means. Rambo is top Arsenal. Do you understand that? It's incredible that you're talking to him. He said you were kosher.

'I've never lied to anyone, I don't know what lying is any more. I don't know much about you – don't take this the wrong way –

but I consider all of you, all people, fucking liars until they prove otherwise. And I can't understand why you need to be like that.'

Why would you think everyone's a liar except for yourself?

'Experience.'

But everyone doesn't lie.

'I hope so. Do you know what? I think I'm gonna give up music. I'm just gonna sit on my fat arse with my wife who loves me. Hold on, I want something worse. It wouldn't be worth it unless it was painful.'

You're saying that for effect, John.

'Yeah?'

Yeah.

'Does it work?'

I don't want pain in my life and neither do you.

'I wouldn't want it any other way.'

You can't bullshit a bullshitter.

'Well, we've talked some shit, let's have some serious drinks now. Let's be mates. Can we be mates? Is that all right?'

It would be an honour to be a mate with you. Shit, what an arsehole licking line. Blame the heat of the wine, the blast of the sun, the twist of the rhyme.

'Come on.'

I respect everything you did in 1977. Everything. Fuck, this was embarrassing. Er, what's a typical Sunday John?

'Swimming, ocean, deep-sea diving. I spend most days diving. I've been silly enough to pick that up as my hobby. I love it. I just love getting out in that ocean.'

You're not living a bad life.

'I live the life I want.'

Not many people can say that.

'Maybe. It's fucking expensive, though. I'd like more money.'

You've done exactly what you should have done.

'I don't know what you mean. I don't hurt people.'

You never did. People thought you did.

'Never. It would be nice if I died without hurting anyone. No, wait, Malcolm needs me. Be fair, I've given him a career; I've given you something to talk about. Don't ask me to be negative, I'm not interested. You know the difference. The fact that Paul Cook still exists is a wonderful piece of good news to me.'

Steve was a vastly underrated guitarist.

'Absolutely. I'm ashamed that he hasn't understood how much I love and adore that style. He has created a whole generation of guitarists and he just doesn't understand and that makes him almost a saint in my eyes. You will never say anything bad to me about Steve and Paul. I know what you're trying to do.'

What?

'Can I end with this? Everything in my life that has worked is because of them, because of Steve and Paul.'

Really?

'No. But I do love them.'

I laughed.

'You think that's laughable? They know how much I love them. They know that and what they do with that information is up to them.'

Would you play with them again?

'Every single time they ask me. Steve and Paul matter to me and I respect them. Nothing in my life matters as much as what they want.'

So the chances are you would play again.

'You must understand, it's your first band, it's your people. I don't think you quite grasp how much this means. It's your first people and I'll never let them down. Ever. I don't care about what other bands do.'

You do it for your mates.

'Oh, you do it for your mates, do you? You've reduced it all to that. That's good enough, is it? Yeah, all right, I understand that. Urr-duh, and I needed you to point that out to me.'

True.

'Yeah, now fuck off. You know me, north London, mate. I hope you learned something. Where do you live?'

Muswell Hill.

'You live in Muswell Hill. What's real ale like?'

It's north London.

'Is it, fuck. It's a good war zone.'

I really appreciate you doing this, John.

'Groovy baby.'

I've been looking forward to it.

'I've got some worries about you. Are you borderline Tottenham? I've had to live that shit all my life.'

You're not living it now.

'Are you fucking joking? What? You fucking think it's like going to the local pub here? It's still an Arsenal/Tottenham war. Lovely jubbly. I love it...'

So why are you bringing it up?

'Do you want it? You want a row? You want a row now? 'Cos I don't fucking like it. Order your cab.'

He called the waitress over. 'Hullo, can you order a cab, please?'

It's been a pleasure, John.

'Will you shut the fuck up? I think I may need some blonde dye on my roots.'

You're doing all right.

'Shut up. We've got Manchester United here tomorrow.'

Shall I come down and watch your back?

'No, you won't be good enough.'

I could always use my ladies' steel comb. I don't bother with the packet of three any more. I got fed up with brushing off the cobwebs.

He sang:

You are my Arsenal
My only Arsenal
You make me happy when skies are blue, grey any other colour you care to fucking mention.

But please don't take my Arsenal away...

Back at the ranch I never did get to see the ghost of Mae West in the flesh. But her ex-residence, now haunted by Lydon and Co, is certainly a one-off; a kind of borderline Spurs grey outside (couldn't resist it) and a sexy bric-a-brac explosion inside.

Walking into the lounge was like walking into a fog of faces and glittering conversations and art deco movie-star auras. I had to grope through the Cary Grant smiles and the girlie-Valentino giggles to find a chair and it was only when I sat down that the fog began to clear and I could make out the galleried aspect and the inordinately high ceiling.

This was a house that David Lynch could live in and I envied John his clarity.

Where's Nora?

'She's on the boat.'

You have a boat? Jammy bastard. Shit, anyone from Islington who made it like John made it would like nothing better than to live in California and own a boat. It's Mont de Marsan all over again, but this time round I understand. You only get one or two chances in life and you have to grab them and have unprotected sex with them and have their babies. There is no other way. John was born into nothing but created something and now he lives in Mae West's old house. And who, in their right mind, would deny him that?

I hope I die before I get old?

Fuck off.

What do you think of The Clash now?

'I always thought The Clash were a rip-off of Bernie Rhodes versus Malcolm McLaren and nothing to do with the bands. I loved The Clash as people and I always will. Just wonderful people. But it didn't mean I had to like their music. It was political sloganeering. I thought it was wrong for them.

'Mick Jones was someone I knew anyway from the Roundhouse because he was one of the kids who used to bunk in. Mick was Jimmy Page. He actually tried out to be the Sex Pistols' guitarist.

'Mick Jones was always around. I remember turning up at the Roundhouse when Osibisa were playing and Mick Jones got in because he was part of the Osibisa crowd and I thought, "How the hell did he do that?"

'And Joe had this ridiculous Cockney accent that wasn't quite right. He used to really drive me crazy. What the hell are you talking about Joe?

'This is where Joe Strummer ended up in a house in the country as a lord. He did everything wrong. There's a new documentary coming out about him and they wanted to use the Pistols song 'Problems'. I'm not sure I want them to use it. Do you understand? Joe became the landed gentry and that was irrefutably wrong. It's nice to earn it but it's not nice to buy it.

'Beyond that little world or schism it was really ridiculous because there'd be Joe Strummer running around with all the posh towels, the steel towel-rail people. It was awful trying to get past their middle class sensibilities. We'd still be banned in clubs where the likes of Joe was accepted because he had, what, ambassador credentials?'

The Stranglers?

'The Stranglers were bandwagoneers. They were pub rock at the time and they jumped on it just like Joe Strummer jumped on it. To get understood I had to go on TV and say, 'Hello, my word means...' and I'd have to perfect this language otherwise I was told no-one would listen to me.'

The Jam?

'The Jam hated us because we used the English flag differently to them. They tried to use it to hook into the Chelsea, scooter-mod movement and that was a dead-end so it was about White City and a Who rip-off and it was fake and it was horrible. It was quite grotesque really.

'And at the same time everyone in all these bands was going out with the same girls. Hahahahaha!'

The Damned?

'The Damned were like groupies or road crew, which was nice. I really liked the drummer, Rat, liked him a lot. But then it crept out that his dad was an accountant or something, and it started to look a little bit peculiarly different. He was analysing what they were doing, and analysing it in a way that he copied for his band and it became very corrupt and creepy.

'But I will always like Rat, even though he turned rasty [sic]. I like that man, I don't care, he can hate me, he can say what he likes about me, but I like him. We had good rows, me and him. He never ran from a row.

'I don't run, I'm well known for not running, my whole life. You know me, I'm too lazy to run. I'd rather take a hiding than run, and I have, many a time. Look at this nose. Look at this face. It's been battered, mate. But it's all right. It's all right. Because it's all about meaning what you say...'

After another hour of off-the-record juicy stuff – I'll blackmail him later – my cab pulled up outside.

John walked with me to the car. When I got in he indicated to me to wind the window down.

'What's this book called anyway?'

77 Sulphate Strip.

'What the fuck? Are you joking me? Is my life reduced to a dumb-arse cliché like that?

'Fucking hell, I wish I'd have thought of that.'

2016

PAUL WELLER
WARWICK AVENUE, LONDON

A decade has passed since I first sat down to write this book and those years have brought more than their fair share of turmoil, grief and laughter.

I've come to the conclusion that life is a fucking minestrone after all. Everyone's a tragedy because everyone dies; it really is as simple as that. It's memories that get you through those final years and it's imperative you have more than your fair share at the end if you want to go out in one piece with the semblance of a smile on your face. So they need to be good. Really fucking good.

Music is a mother of a memory; it creates new ones if you let her come inside and implant her magic. Through music you remember feelings and tensions and beautiful faces from worlds you once inhabited. You remember dreams and schemes and singing and dancing and joy. There were times the music was so hot I swear it had fully functional genitals to accompany the pulse. Yeah, you sure need the music in you when you're shaking on your death-bed after all that rattling, all that rolling.

Music geniuses are few and far between, but Paul Weller is a diamond-encrusted one. Let me get that out of the way first. It just needed to be said at this point of the story, before I forget the memories…

It was April '77 and I'd been working on 'Record Mirror' for nearly four months. Life was sweet as.

I'd seen the Stranglers, the Clash, the Damned and the Pistols play in the flesh, watched them cartwheel cross the stage, outta my dreams and into my heart. I'd seen the Feelgoods in Canvey Island, Iggy Pop with David Bowie in Aylesbury, the Buzzcocks in Harlesden, Chicago in Geneva, Nazareth in Hamburg, John Miles in Zurich, Smokie in Bath, Steve Gibbons in Birmingham. I'd interviewed Bert Weedon, Steve Miller, Nils Lofgren, The Rubettes, Mickie Most, David Gates, Bill Nelson, the Chi-Lites, Billy Ocean, Lynsey de Paul, Kiki Dee and, of course, the Pistols, Clash, Stranglers and Damned.

I dined in expensive restaurants with sweet, sweet PR girls who handed me extortionate amounts of records and blinded me with science. They seemed to know so much more about life than me, a bloke who still lived at home with his mum and dad and who had the audacity to sport a Jet Black beard and long hair. But also a bloke without a care in the world. Dina was out of my life for good. Life couldn't get any better.

It did.

At a party in a South London flat a few months earlier three young guys in suits who looked pretty young but were just backdated walked in empty-handed, drank the place dry in an hour, including the bottle of wine I'd brought along, and fucked off again like the oiks from Oiksville they were. Someone told me they were a band who'd just signed for Polydor – the Jam or something. It didn't register – the dope was strong that night in South London.

Later, when I heard about this three-piece punk band called the Jam who wore suits and ties and sang 'Batman' and 'Heatwave', the name rang a bell. But I couldn't put my finger on it. Intrigued, I checked them out at the Hope & Anchor (see p.87).

It was love at first sight.

This really was another music in a different kitchen. Punk slapped in a mohair suit with a razor in one pocket and a condom in the other. The Who kissed by Motown with a dash of Clash. A new kind of soul – modern with the emphasis on mod.

I call it my Salieri moment – y'know, the composer who couldn't believe that Mozart was a genius. How could a bunch of semi-detached, suburban Mr Jones' come up with music like that? It was miraculous – a single guitar, bass and drum hugging each other tight as the songs twisted the night away around them. And you could dance to it. Proper dancing, not frenetic, anarchic pogoing lubricated by cheap lager and speed, although the ground did still shake from the tremor of a plummeting pogo crowd stage front at most Jam gigs – 'Knees Up Mother Brown' for the safety-pin generation.

I was overjoyed to discover the lead singer was just 18. A teenager screaming songs to teenagers in a cellar bar was how I always thought it should be. The Jam just felt so right. And it felt right to write about them. Right on. See, London, indeed, every city in the country in 1977, was pretty much a shithole teeming with a raw, sour, disenfranchised youth whose grandparents were born in the same Victorian slums many families still inhabited two generations' later. Alienated adolescent demi-mondes with no prospect of even a dead-end job. No employment meant a dangerously disproportionate amount of self-analysis. Kings of nothing.

Punk had tapped into that. The music was abrasive and came in tainted spurts. But the Jam injected a sassiness into the bleakness both in terms of melody and lyrics. Their sound was icky-sticky, neat and tricky. They offered a new hope and delivered it while wearing mohair suits. It was a perfect combination; instead of doing everything by the numbers they were away from them, whether it was brandishing Eton rifles, going underground or getting the shit kicked out of them at midnight. They were a soulful Seventies Smiths but with more rings on their fingers and bells on their toes.

A few weeks after that Hope & Anchor gig, Polydor PR Geoff Deane and I organised the infamous photo-shoot featuring the three of them wearing Union Jack jackets and posing outside London landmarks like the Houses of Parliament and Buckingham Palace. We hired the jackets for the day from a swinging boutique in Carnaby Street where I also interviewed the band for the first time. I felt as if I'd been transported back to the fingerlickin' Sixties, enveloped by a purple paisley haze.

Paul was more uncertain about his views back then than his punk contemporaries, his timidity revealed ever-changing moods and a nascent passion. His opinions were still taking shape and he felt uncomfortable with interviews. He once told me he couldn't fill in a tax form when he left school (think he was a little hard on himself there – I can't fill in one now). 'I had to educate myself. I haven't got any special perception. Many of the letters I receive articulate my sentiments better than I do.'

Nobody taught young pop stars how to be good interviewees. They had to wing it until the questions started repeating themselves. Paul would rather listen than talk, always anxious to learn and keen to classify. Unfortunately, as band spokesman he was expected to deliver the hot quote poop like his contemporaries, Johnny Rotten and Joe Strummer. It took him a little while before he began to open like an oyster with pearls of wisdom and a Woking waggishness that belied his years. Earnestness overcame the naivety and that in turn bred confidence. Mind you, selling shitloads of records helped a bit, too.

I saw them whenever I got the opportunity, and not just because of the joyous effect their music had upon me. They were far and away the most down to earth of all the 'punk' bands from that period. Okay, Paul was edgier than Bruce and Rick but his sincerity was disarming. I guess I felt more comfortable with the Jam than any other band I've ever known. Not that we were real bosom buddies or anything but I definitely shared more pints with them. You just never knew where you were with Captain Sensible.

When '77 Sulphate Strip first appeared, I hadn't clapped eyes on Paul Weller for a quarter of a century. After another ten years went up in a weed-stained smoke, I'd resigned myself to the fact that I never would.

It didn't bother me. To be brutally frank, I suspected he'd turned into a complete bastard, based on two experiences I'd had with him ten years apart.

If you've got this far you may recall how I stood outside the Forum in Kentish Town on a bitterly cold night in 2007 waiting in vain for Mr Weller in order to score an interview for '77 *Sulphate Strip*. But it wasn't the first time he'd ignored me.

Back in 1997, one Saturday afternoon just before Christmas, I went down to the Kilburn National where he was playing to say hello and maybe grab a hug. I was trying to get my defunct writing career back on track and Paul Weller interviews were hard to come by. I thought he might be up for a chat with the man whose 'teenage blue' helped inspire 'Life From A Window'. In a review of the band back in 1977 at the Royal College of Art I wrote, 'An artless audience at the RCA show their appreciation of the white-soul boys up there on the stage with the huge Union Jack backdrop depicting the three moods the Jam take you through at a gig – red hot expanding into white heat, contracting into teenage blue.' Paul used the 'teenage blue' line in 'Life From A Window' on the *This Is The Modern World* album and credited me on the back cover. I felt like I'd won an Oscar.

I knocked on the backstage door and asked the guy to tell Paul Weller that Barry Cain was outside and wanted to say hello. I thought I'd catch him right after the sound check and arrange to meet sometime when he wasn't so busy. I didn't want to blag a ticket. Going to gigs was a thing of the past by then and music as a force was out of my mind, out of my soul, out of my life. I soared through the sounds of the Sixties and Seventies and parachuted through the Eighties before crash landing in the Nineties. Music went from overground to underground to background.

I just thought I'd meet and greet a few faces from my, what seemed even then, distant past and well, yeah, accept a ticket, if it was offered. Only polite.

After all, this was someone I connected with, wrote about, drank with, sang to, invited to my wedding. Someone I saw screaming his thoughts and his dreams to other teenagers in bars and clubs that reeked of booze and phlegm. Someone I stood beside as he peered into the gas chambers of Dachau.

Surely an interview wasn't too much to ask.

As the sun set on Kilburn High Road, I waited in vain. I waited in vain long enough to go from smooth-chinned sparky pants to just who is that 5 o' clock shadow. I waited in vain for an acknowledgement, anything, even a simple piss-off.

It hurt. Can't deny it.

I knocked a few more times and got the same negative response. Eventually, I caught sight of Kenny, Paul's long serving road manager, with a bunch of other guys. They were heading to the pub next door for a swift pint before the concert. He wasn't surprised to see me. 'Oh, yeah, we knew you were here. Just wasn't the right time. Sorry.'

I asked immediately if Paul might be up for an interview. It was pretty blunt but I figured I didn't have much to lose.

'Don't know, I'll ask him but I doubt it. Who for?'

I wasn't sure but mentioned the Evening Standard.

'Don't think he'll be interested in doing anything with them, but I'll ask. Enjoy the show.' He handed me a ticket before disappearing into the pub.

I never followed him in, never saw the gig and never asked for an interview again until this book came along ten years later and history, unfortunately, repeated itself. I was a twice-bitten man. I felt like a fool.

I must've offended him in some way. Wasn't he always falling out with people? Miserable sod. But what was it that made him do me over? Twice?

I narrowed it down to a photo we published of him in the penultimate issue of *Flexipop!* in 1983 with his lips round the barrel of a gun, bearing the caption:

WELLER SHOOTS HIS MOUTH OFF FOR THE LAST TIME

It went on:

This is the last dramatic photograph of Paul Weller, taken seconds before he pulled the trigger on his own life on election day. As the first results came in and victory seemed certain for Mrs Thatcher, Weller calmly placed a revolver in the mouth that sang such classics as Beat Surrender and A Town Called Malice and, with a final cry of, 'No Cruise missile is gonna get me,' fired one fatal bullet through his brain. Earlier he had told close friends that if the Tories were going to be allowed to play Russian roulette with his life, he'd rather do the job himself. He added that he had already committed commercial suicide with his last single anyway.

Paul was a staunch supporter of *Flexipop!*, the magazine I launched in 1980, but maybe he thought that was a cheeky bridge too far.

I met up with Rick Buckler recently after a ridiculously long time and he shocked me when he said he hadn't seen Paul in over 30 years. I remembered interviewing them both in a pub just after the announcement of the split in 1982 when Paul turned to Rick and said, 'We are still mates, still close, ain't we?' and Rick replied, 'Yeah and we always will be.'

Rick was one of the most easy going guys I met in the business and I really enjoyed his company. He was genuine and totally accessible but Paul, unsure of himself back then and, shit, five years younger than me, tended to be a little guarded and that could sometimes be mistaken for dismissiveness. It was inconceivable to me that two guys from one of the most popular bands this country has ever produced should completely ignore each other for a lifetime. I assumed it was down to Paul.

But whatever. Not my problem. It was an irrelevance in my life. After all, I was never going to see Paul again. Was I.

I didn't count on one of those '77 *Sulphate Strip* simple twists of fate...

A few years back I met up with *Flexipop!* photographer Neil Matthews and over a boozy lunch – a small glass of wine each and some tap water constitutes that these days – we decided to relaunch the magazine firstly on Facebook, then a website, then a book and finally a theme park. Surprisingly, we did the lot, apart from the theme park.

The *Flexipop!* book and '77 *Sulphate Strip*, found their way into the Somerset House shop during the 'About The Young Idea' Jam exhibition and after two weeks of being on sale, I received a request for more copies as both titles had sold out.

I arranged to meet Neil in the courtyard at Somerset House around 10-30 on a Wednesday morning in July so we could sign the *Flexipop!* books together. I arrived 15 minutes early and while waiting for Neil, I started signing copies of *Sulphate* until something made me look up. Walking towards me out of the glare of the sunshine was Bruce Foxton with his wife, Kate. In 20-odd years I'd seen Bruce once – at the funeral of his first wife Pat.

We gave each other a hug and he introduced me to Kate.

He hadn't lost those boyish good looks. All right, I admit my eyes ain't as good as they used to be, but Bruce still had that sparkle that defies age and the slim physique of a man who's on the road a lot with the hugely successful From The Jam. A dear friend I've seen twice in 20 years. What a shit last sentence that is.

I asked him what he was doing there.

'Just thought we'd check out the exhibition properly while it's quiet.'

He asked why I was there.

'Let's have a coffee and I'll tell you.'

I went into the café while Bruce and Kate stayed outside. It took a while to get served and when I emerged carrying a tray of coffees someone shouted, 'Cainy!'

I turned and saw Paul Weller. I put the tray down on the nearest table and we gave each other a hug (you can probably tell by now that I'm not averse to the odd hug. Better than shaking hands any day, and you can often sense the warmth) and he introduced me to his son.

He still retained that youthful spit and polished elegance he always wore so well and it had continued to hold back the years. Any hint of hesitancy had been replaced by the confidence a lifetime of selling records and concert tickets engenders.

I asked him what he was doing there.

'Just thought we'd check out the exhibition while nobody else is around,' he said and asked why I was there.

'Let's have a coffee and I'll tell you.'

We all sat around a table drinking coffee and I smoked Paul's fags while he took the piss out of my Nike trainers. He remembered, remarkably, the last time we met. He was with Mick Talbot at a record company bash just before the release of 'Speak Like A Child'. I never for the life of me thought it would be 33 years before we'd ever speak again, especially in a courtyard, in Somerset House, in the sweltering July sunshine.

Turned out he'd never heard of '77 *Sulphate Strip*. In fact, nobody who sat around the table that day had ever heard of it. Shit. I told him how I'd waited outside The Forum and Kilburn National. He said he really didn't remember and that he never bore a grudge against me. I wasn't totally convinced.

I guessed I'd been consigned to the Rick Buckler bin in Paul's life, the one marked no animosity intended but *mucho aqua* under the *pont*.

Our lives are strewn with lost friends. We all leave a trail of live bodies in our wake and we're all bodies in other people's trails. I have great friends who I haven't seen in 20 years and it makes me feel ashamed – but hey, they haven't tried to contact me, so fuck them. It's the way of the world.

Obviously, I don't invoke strong emotions, Story of my life. I fret over fuck all and it will be the death of me.

I wandered round the exhibition with the ex-Jam posse who delighted the lucky punters that day, and gave Bruce and Paul copies of *Sulphate* and *Flexipop! The Book* – there goes the profits. We swapped numbers before a few more hugs.

A couple of months later, when it was decided to reprint *Sulphate*,

I took the bull by the horns and texted Paul asking him if he'd like to do an interview for the book. I was in the middle of the Atlantic at the time, on board the Queen Mary 2 and heading for Southampton from New York while reviewing, believe it or not, Crosby Stills & Nash who were playing three shows in the liner's theatre.

Hi Paul

'77 Sulphate Strip is being reprinted again. Don't know if you've had a chance to look at it yet but I was just wondering if you fancied doing an interview for the new edition. Basically, it involves me asking you the same questions I put to you in the first interview we did in that Carnaby Street boutique way back in '77 and seeing how, and if, your attitudes have changed. You'll also get to check it before it's published to ensure you're happy with the end product. It worked really well in the book, especially with John Lydon who said it was the most unique interview he'd ever done. Sulphate has become a bestseller but, for me, your absence in the contemporary interview section meant it wasn't really complete. Anyway Paul, let me leave it with you to mull over. Apologies for the length of this text. Just trying to avoid getting back on the Marrakesh Express...

His reply:

'Yeh mate, I'm up 4 it time permitting. I'm back 11th and away 28th. How's CS&N? They got any blow left? Have fun mate pw x'

It took another three months before we finally decided on a time. My text – the day after David Bowie died:

Hi Paul

Funny, back in '77 I asked you, John Lydon and Joe Strummer what you thought of Bowie. You said, 'He's the most inventive artist of the Seventies.' Just checking re the possible interview. Any time you like.

His reply:

'Sorry mate been caught up in family business. Fri any good? Could meet in Maida Vale? p x shocked about DB mate.'

After a text from me confirming, he replied:

'Warwick Ave tube at 2? I'll be wearing a red carnation and carrying a copy of Sporting Life...'

He was doing neither when I met him in a café in Warwick Avenue that Friday at 2pm on the dot.

'I see you're wearing brogues today,' he said.

We hugged and as my cheek brushed against the fur collar of his jacket, I climbed aboard one of those time machines that pop up unannounced from time to time in different guises – a place, a face, a smell, a sound, a dream – and suddenly I'm sitting opposite the Paul I used to know and he's talking to the guy I used to know – me – and it's magical. He looks 19 again and that makes me feel 24. These are the best kind of people to be with, the ones that make you feel young. That's why a majority of my friends are now over 70...

But this guy's 57 going on 20 and he makes me feel 24.

When I asked him his age, he didn't say 57.

'58 this year'. That one sentence alone sums up Paul Weller. Most people would grudgingly admit to 57, not add a year. Honesty beyond reproach. A man true to his soul. Unaffected. Unfathomable. And unconcerned about growing older.

But had he turned into a complete bastard...?

I was there to find out.

His phone rang the moment we sat at a table outside the café. 'Hi babe, yes babe. Cool babe. I'm with Barry, doing that interview I told you about. Yes, babe.' It was a cosy, loved-up exchange.

I asked if he was talking to his wife, Hannah. It was a wind-up question I couldn't resist.

'Of course.'

I sincerely hope so.

"No mate, those days are long gone.

Too old?

'Too fucking expensive! You've only been married just the once, then.'

Yep.

'You stayed with your missus for 35 years?'

Yep.

'How old are your kids now?'

The twin boys are 31 and Elliot is 20.

'They've left home and all that, yeah?'

No. They're all still living with us.

'Really? Your wife's Greek, isn't she?' Paul had met her a few times.

Yep, Greek women rule the roost. They love their sons and the bigger the boys are, the bigger the love.

'Like the Italians. So just the three boys, then?'

Yep. So just the seven kids, then?

'Yep.'

I remind him of the interview angle.

'Yeah. Good idea. Hannah said she liked the sound of it.'

I explain to Paul that after I've written the article, I'll send it to him to check as I did with the others.

'Don't worry. I trust you,' he said.

That was nice. But I insisted. I just hope he doesn't take too much out – although you'll never know.

So, my opening question to Paul, Bruce and Rick as we squeezed into that Carnaby Street dressing room in April 1977 wasn't exactly dripping with originality…

What are the Jam all about? (For the purpose of this interview, I'm only using Paul's responses).

'The Jam are about rock 'n' roll.'

'Sounds like a good answer to me, although we were a bit more than that,' said Paul, 39 years later in that bitter January sunshine. 'I think we made some kind of cultural dent. When I speak to old Jam fans from that time, I get the feeling it meant so much more to them than just a good record – there was a true cultural connection.

'But on top of that we also possessed the energy and the edginess.

'We caught the mood of the times, I guess, the Zeitgeist or whatever you want to call it. I know it's endured because it still means so much to people now. That wouldn't have happened if we didn't split up when we did – we haven't had nearly 35 years in between of churning out shit records. The Jam ended at exactly the right time and even when I talk to Bruce now, he agrees that it really did make sense to pack it in then. It's a hard thing to try and keep a band going for 40 or 50 years. I take my hat off to the Stones and the Who and bands like that who have kept together.

'It's hard to find all members of a band that think the same way. The Stones was the Mick and Keith show. I don't think Wyman or Watts were really that bothered. The Who were four of the most disparate people you could ever get. It's so hard to find four different people who all think along the same lines.'

I thought this was the perfect opportunity to raise the situation with Rick and read to Paul what Rat Scabies told me in his Sulphate interview...

'The Jam were from Woking and my parents were from Redhill so I knew that Surrey-Belt mentality. The Jam were the classic example of a band formed by geography. I've come up with a theory over the years. A bloke who starts out in suburbia and wants to form a band is very limited to the amount of musicians he can unearth. So if he finds someone who's the same kind of age and who's got a bass or a drum kit then they'll be in the band automatically, even if they don't really cover the same musical ground. That's why a band like the Jam split up. But it's also what makes a band great because they don't have that personal empathy. If you all agree it sucks. Rick Buckler wasn't as interested as Weller was in being a mod, but he went along with it because it was more interesting than being a mini-cab driver or something.'

'In the five or six years the Jam were working and recording, Rick and I probably only exchanged about three conversations and they wouldn't have lasted much longer than a sentence each,' said Paul. 'I never really had much in common with him. The only bond between the three of us was a love of playing music. We were three very different people. It's very true, what Rat said. There was only a three-year age difference between us but when I was 16 they were knocking 20 with a job and a car and girlfriends and I was still fucking about and wanking.'

Things don't change, then.

'Nope, just less of it!

So he's not a bastard – he's a wanker!

'Towards the end of the Jam it was tour, album, single – a conveyor belt that I knew I needed to jump off. That's why it's amazing that bands can go on forever. I thought I just couldn't do it for another ten years. I'd be 34 doing the same thing.

'We did what we needed to do and ended at the right time. I just wanted to change everything and with the Style Council I did. That first year we didn't tour, we didn't want to make an album, just did things at my own pace. It seemed like total freedom compared to being in that very tight-knit band set up. Also, I just wanted to go off and see who else I could be. All I'd ever done from the age of 14 to 24 was be in one band. I just asked myself: "Who the fuck am I? What more can I do?," and started to consciously search for something else.

'The Style Council lasted as long as the Jam. People forget that. We were really successful. The first three years were great and touring became so much more fun. It went off the boil a bit after that.'

If the Jam had stayed together would you have been writing Style Council songs?

'Very difficult to say. It was already going that way a little bit but there were certain things in the Style Council that we just could not have done with the Jam, like the musicianship. The Council songs were all very different from each other – purposely so. Even though I was still the leader if you like, it was very democratic.'

I asked him who he thought were the most musical of those five key bands from '77 – the Pistols, Clash, Stranglers, Damned and Jam.

'What about the Buzzcocks?'

They came at the end of the first wave. Their first hit was in '78.

'Don't know about that. What about 'Spiral Scratch'? That came out at the beginning of '77. Anyway, the most musical were the

Stranglers but they were all old geezers. I'd been playing since 1972 as a semi-pro trying to hone my skills so I came from a different angle.'

My next question in that Carnaby Street clobber shop was:

What do you think of the current state of music?

'Things have been getting out of hand. Instead of writing songs that mean something, all that's dished up is a lot of mindless crap. Now we're getting a natural revolution. It's like going against what your mum and dad say, like at school with all its rules. I'd just like to break down all that. Make your own rules. And it's just the same with the music. Most of the new wave bands are still trying too hard to be stars and get money in their pockets. I don't think they can identify with the kids.'

'Interesting.'

I asked Paul if the astronaut Tim Peake was bigger news to today's young people than David Bowie? Will people still be listening to Bowie in 100 years ... 50 years ... ten years?

'Of course! That's like asking if people will still keep listening to the Beatles.'

Yes, but will they be listening to it in the same way as we did? I remember 'I Heard It Through The Grapevine' blasting out of the speakers for the first time in the Blind Beggar pub when I was 16 followed by 'Where Do You Go To My Lovely?' and I defy any kid of 16 today to experience that same rush without resorting to chemicals. It was all I had. It was everything.

'There are some artists that change the landscape in their time – the Beatles, Bowie. We may never see the likes of them again. They were pioneers but it was probably easier to be a pioneer then because there wasn't any rule book. OK, we had Elvis but he didn't really last a long time – he went into the army and became a clean cut American kid.

'Music definitely hasn't got the same cultural influence and power it once had. There are other things that have taken its place for young people, like social media, like football.'

Do you envy Bowie?

'I don't envy anybody. I'm just appreciative of what he gave to the world. People still listen to Mozart and Beethoven. Bowie and the Beatles? Nah, people will definitely be listening to them.'

But in an entirely different way.

'I used to listen to my mum's Little Richard records.'

And I used to listen to the old songs my dad played on the piano and appreciate them for what they were – songs with heart but no soul. Wonderful melodies and little else. They oiled the memory machine for my parents, not for me.

'You can only have a multitude of memories if you live long enough. I really don't like that whole nostalgia thing which is massive now. There's still a lot of good new music around.'

Coldplay?

'Don't tell me you like them.'

Do I fuck.

'I think they're shocking. It's bed-wetting music. But there's good stuff out there. OK, it hasn't got the same cultural impact and probably won't have again. Music will never die out but its cultural importance has long gone.

'It's also partly to do with the way people listen to it. I've noticed with my kids that they'll play you a track then halfway through they'll stop it and play you another - "Listen to this, too." They never sit down and focus or concentrate on a song like we used to. You'd take the album home, slide it lovingly out of its packaging, put it carefully on the turntable, place the needle on the vinyl, listen to side one while reading the lyrics and then turn it over and listen to side two. You were completely immersed in the experience.'

Now you can have a million love songs on your phone and play them through headphones while you're doing something else. People are hearing music – they're just not listening to it any more.

'But I still think, and I have to say this because I'm a musician, I still think music has a value but I accept it doesn't define people like it used to. There are other things now that do that. Fuck, will rock 'n' roll just roll over and die? I fucking hope not. It hasn't for me but that's because I'm that much older. When was the last musical youth movement? Probably rave and acid house, hip-hop. But with that, the artists weren't as important.'

I tell Paul that the publisher of a brand new hip-hop magazine called *Brick* had contacted me after reading this book. She was convinced there was a connection between hip-hop and punk.

'I can see that connection – especially going back to the late Eighties/early Nineties with acts like Public Enemy. But it was more revolutionary then – now it's all about gangstas and posing and bling and money and all that shite. It doesn't have any real value. It's not spiritual.'

But isn't that the same with all new music?

'No. I meet a lot of young bands and they're really passionate. To them, what they do is important. But what I have noticed, especially at the festivals, is how mainstream everything has become. Using Glastonbury as an example, in the space between 1994 when I first played there and last year when I performed again, you can see how mainstream it is now. In 1994 you could jam, stretch a song out, improvise, and the crowd went with it. Now they're just not interested. They simply want to wave at the camera or wave a flag. I must admit I find that a shame. The crowd just want to hear the hits, the songs they recognise. I guess generally it's because it's a younger crowd.'

Do you think as an artist you can develop so no matter how old you are, your music will appeal across generations?

'I think it does now. A majority of the people who buy my records are my age and grown with me but there are still 16/17 year olds who know the words to some of the oldest songs, probably because their parents played the Jam and Style Council at home when they were growing up.'

We sipped our coffee. The breeze beefed up a bit. It was time for another cigarette.

'Paul McCartney still writes good tunes,' said Paul.' I was a massive Beatles fan and I bought all their solo records until 1974 and then I thought, I can't fucking listen to this anymore. Shocking. I hated *Double Fantasy* when it came out but since then tracks like 'Beautiful Boy' have grown on me, maybe because I'm that much older and it now means something. When you're 21 it's like, "fuck off!". I bought George Harrison's *Living In The Material World* and I thought, no I fucking ain't. He was in that fucking big mansion. I thought it was all bollocks. That's why punk had to happen.

'But I'm still a big Beatles fan, to be honest. If you don't hear their music for a while and then suddenly a song pops up somewhere you think fucking hell, that's amazing. Like the second side of *Hard Day's Night* – there are some wonderful songs on there. When I played their albums for the very first time all the tracks I initially hated I fell in love with a week later.

'The Beatles prove my point. When they split up I was devastated – but it was the right thing to do because we haven't had to put up with 40 years of shit records from them, have we. From start to finish it was simply beautiful.

'When was the last Stones record you bought? It's really just about 'Greatest Hits' for bands like that. First time I saw them was two years ago at the O2 and they were good. Mick was pretty cool. He's 72 now.'

'Do you want to be a star?' His answer back then was unexpected.

'*We're intent on becoming stars. OK, I hate Rod Stewart, I hate Mick Jagger, but I want to be a star. Star is such a horrible word. But look, I took a lot of stick at school from teachers about how thick I was and how I wasn't going to get anywhere. That made me determined to get on. I want to go back and rub it in their faces – "Look what I've become."*'

Paul broke into laughter. 'Fuck. I met both of them the other week. They were very nice as well. I take it all back! We were at Ronnie Wood's wedding anniversary. His missus is a good friend of Hannah's and we had a little dinner. I know Woody a bit anyway.

'What I said is the difference between being 18 and 58. You

develop a different perspective. I take my hat off to the Stones for keeping it going for long. It's not easy to do that. But at that time in the Seventies, they deserved criticism because they had lost touch with reality.'

He asked if I fancied another coffee and insisted on ordering them because he wanted to have a slash. While he was inside I replaced the battery in the recorder. I'd forgotten to change it on the tube and throughout the time we were speaking, I constantly checked the recorder was still working. Doing interviews in shorthand was much less stressful – until you tried to read it back.

'The twin boys were four yesterday,' he said when he returned and, yep, lit another fag. 'They're lovely and I love them to bits but it can be tough. Something you said about your boys being compared to the Krays when they were at school because they were so boisterous reminded me of my boys. But they have got a bit better. One of them is called Bowie. Hannah was a big fan, too.'

Yeah, my kids used to get in a lot of scrapes. I don't know why.

'Must've been the East End in them.'

I told Paul that the first fight I ever had was with Frank Warren who lived on the same council estate as me in Kings Cross. We were both about five years-old. I then mentioned a little adventure Frank and I had with Blondie that will be revealed in a book just up the road from here.

'I saw a documentary about Blondie a while back and it mentioned how some of them got into smack.'

Apparently it keeps you young.

'Yeah, for three months or something!'

The Jam were never a drug band. But you were pissheads.

'We used to smoke a bit of weed, but, yes, we were massive drinkers. It was the culture. Everything revolved around the pub – it was centre of activity, especially for me 'cos I started playing at 14 and worked every week in social clubs.

'I haven't had a drink for six years. I had to stop, I was feeling so rough all the time. I did eventually get into a bit of gear in the

Nineties for a while.'

Was that because you were hanging out with the likes of, ahem, Liam Gallagher? Looking for an Oasis in the desert?

'I didn't need to be influenced by anyone.'

I seem to recall you looked with disdain at rock stars taking drugs.

'I did up until 1994.'

Why?

'It was time for me to be hedonistic. I guess I've got an addictive personality.'

Does that make you a difficult person to live with? You've had quite a few failed relationships and you're the common factor.

'Oh, there's no doubt it's my fault why relationships never worked out for me.'

Rick and Bruce never had that problem. That shows the difference between the three of you.

'What can I say, mate? I don't really want to talk about it.'

Were you a philanderer?

'In my time, yeah. And very much enjoyed philandering as well.'

When you first started touring as the Jam, your first real flame, Jill, used to come on the road with you.

'The last time I saw her was about 15 years ago.'

I liked Jill. She was a really nice girl.

'She was. But she could also be very difficult.'

So why did you take her on the road with you? It's like a Yoko Ono scenario.

'Yeah, it was. We were just deeply in love and wanted to be together all the time. It wasn't easy on the rest of the band 'cos all of a sudden there's this other person which kinda diluted any togetherness I had with Bruce and Rick.

For a philanderer you certainly had long relationships.

'I was married for about eight years, then lived with Dee for a while. I had two kids with my last ex. I dunno why – it's just the way I am. It's a long story and I can't be bothered to go into it.'

What do you mean, a long story?

'It's just too personal. I didn't plan to have kids, they just turned up, do you know what I mean? I'm glad they did. You either stick with them and see it through or you fuck off. I used to fall in love too quickly, just got really infatuated. It got me into a lot of problems. I've changed a lot.'

So it wasn't your dick ruling your head, it was your heart.

'I guess so. I'm too impetuous. I was always waiting to meet the right person.'

But weren't the people you met the right people for you at the time?

'Maybe, but now I know I've definitely met the right person and everything is very different. We've known each other for ten years and been married nearly six. Hannah is lovely and really smart, y'know. When you meet the right person, it changes everything. I've changed as a person because I met Hannah and I've changed for the better. It's through her that I've stopped drinking.'

Doesn't each person we meet change us?

'Yes, but not for very long.'

So Hannah still continues to change you.

'Yes, but there's a different bond between us. She really does complete me.'

Do you still get women throwing themselves at you?

'To be honest, there probably are a few but I really don't notice because I'm simply just not interested. Up until I met Hannah it was still pretty rife.

What sort of ages were they?

'A wonderful array of ages, mate. But I've done with all that. It's funny, once you're married and kids come along, you're both either too tired or too busy to be intimate, y'know, as much as you want to. You have to almost plan when you can get a chance to be with each other with no distractions. I guess it's the same for everybody.'

Nah, me and Dina are at it all the time. We don't stop. Like rabbits.

'Fuck off!'

Sorry Paul, you're wrong there, mate. I guess you've got to face up to the fact that you just ain't got it anymore. Happens to us all, some sooner than later.

'Bollocks! In 20 years' my boys will be 24 and I'll be knocking 80.'

Granddad material. Great Granddad material.

'Yeah, but when you're 80, all your kids will probably still be living with you!'

At that moment a little dog under the next table barked and Paul jumped.

'Oh, I'm sorry about that,' said the dog's elderly female owner.

'No worries,' said Paul. 'What sort of dog is it?'

She said it was a Pomeranian.

'Never heard of that breed, what part of the world do they come from?'

Pomerania, I quipped.

'Do they?'

Great to know our idols are human after all...

(When I wrote those last few lines I was kinda taking the piss – as in "d'uh, Pomerania ... like there's a place called Pomerania". Huh. I found out a week after sending the interview to Paul that it does indeed exist – it's a region split between Germany and Poland that I'd never heard of. And fucking Pomeranian dogs are named after fucking Pomerania. I hoped Paul would think I'd written what I did because it was blatantly obvious to anyone with half a brain they couldn't come from anywhere else but fucking Pomerania with its seven million inhabitants. Okay, it made me look like a cunt but rather that than look like an ignorant cunt. This aside is added to the edited version, by the way, that I'll send to Paul, who never changed one word of the draft. Not one. But he did have a major criticism, as you'll discover...)

Okay, the next question from back then: 'Is youth as important today as it was in the Sixties?' You can add Eighties and Nineties to that question now...

'Kids should make their mark on this generation otherwise it will be

too late. It's a case of every generation having its own cult and refusing what's gone before. Youth was real important in the Fifties and Sixties but now it's not. Maybe the kids have seen all the cults that have come to nothing and ain't particularly bothered. Everything goes in cycles. The present set up won't go on forever. It's like, I can't imagine how anyone can go on stage at the age of 32 and sing 'My Generation' and still be a force. The Sixties were so potent and when they passed it left such a void. Everyone has been out of breath for a long time.

'Christ, it's just that when I was 15 I first saw the Pistols and they blocked my brain. At last, I thought, the whole youth culture has arrived. Before that, the only bands I'd seen were Status Quo and Wings. You could never be them – but you could be a Sex Pistol.

'In places like Birmingham and Glasgow a lot of kids have very little hope of getting a job when they leave school, or even joining a rock band.'

'It probably is to young people. We had less choices then, only football, music, fashion and in some ways it simplified things. Now football is more showbiz than pop music. Those three things defined you. If you wore a certain "uniform" everyone recognised what you were about – what clubs you went to, what music you listened to. Now there are more options but it's not as tribal as it was. That whole tribal thing went up to the mid-Eighties and then faded away.

'The world needed punk. There was a really boring, drab scene at the time and I didn't relate to any bands apart from the Feelgoods. It was all arena rock and Fleetwood Mac and REO Speedwagon. I'd never seen the Who and wasn't into what they were doing in the Seventies. I wasn't into concept records. I liked the short, sharp three-minute stuff. Something like 'Substitute' meant much more to me than any number of *Tommy*s or *Quadrophenia*s or all that concept gear. I just didn't understand it. 'I Can't Explain' was much closer to how I felt at the time.

'When I first saw the Pistols and then later on the Clash, I thought that was the warning shot, the blazing flare announcing to the world it was our time now. We all missed out on the Sixties 'cos we were just too young. OK, I was into the music but not old enough to be involved in the era.

'Then we had Bowie and Bolan in the early Seventies and that was cool but that was followed by a grey numbness until punk happened. It got a lot of kids, me included, back into something, got us out of our bedrooms and into clubs and creating fanzines and seeing bands and making our own clothes. Punk was so much more than just music – it was a cultural revolution. But it became a ridiculous, sad pastiche after a short space of time.

'It was one big explosion and then everyone went off and did their own thing.'

Switch back to Seventies Carnaby Street. 'How do you compare yourself to other bands playing now?'

'We're more musically mature than most of the other bands around now. We don't abide by their stupid little punk rules.'

'We did have tunes. I was into melody, strong melodies, good songs. It wasn't enough just to be shouting, I wasn't having that. We were definitely more musical than a lot of other bands around then. I wanted to be a proper musician – although not a muso. The idea was to try and progress and improve: play and sing better and write better songs.

'And there was a lot of posturing then – loads of bands were writing songs about how bored they were and all that crap. But for a short space of time punk was very important. If nothing else, it activated people and got them up and out, to strive and attempt to achieve something with their lives.

'After that you were on your own; you found what you could take from it, what you needed, what you could use, and off you went.

'That's what we did. I didn't care about punk after that, I was a mod anyway. But in the early days I definitely related to it, especially when I saw the Pistols.'

When was the first time you saw them?

'At a Lyceum all-nighter about three weeks before the 100 Club

Punk Festival in November 1976. They were the last band on at 5am. Supercharge and some hippy band played just before. I was amazed. I remember what I wore; a beige three-button jacket, orange-and -green polkadot tie, a shirt and grey Sta Prest – I'd managed to find old stock – and a pair of loafers. I wasn't into the punk thing. Like I said, I was into being a mod. The rest of the audience were mainly denim-clad hippies apart from the very front of the stage where the Pistols had all their mates.

'It was the same story for many people. We'd seen possibly the first review of the band, the one by Neil Spencer in 'NME', supporting Eddie & The Hot Rods at the Marquee earlier that year. Spencer wrote, "The Sex Pistols are coming" and I'd been talking about it in the pub on our estate and we all said we've gotta go and see this band 'cos everyone had read the same review.

'We'd all been waiting, looking for something, some sort of sign, a movement of some kind. The Seventies were so boring, especially the middle bit – the music was crap, the fashion was crap. We were looking for something that was ours. We'd heard about the Sixties but we were looking for our slice of revolution.

'I also went to the 100 Club Festival and remember walking down the steps and hearing one of the Troggs singles playing. I thought, sarcastically, great. The Clash played, as well as the Pistols, Slaughter and the Dogs, and it was Siouxsie's first gig with Sid on drums.

'That was the most important thing about punk for me – that whole initial rush.'

Cigarette time. Coffee time. Sudden gust of icy wind.

'Why has nostalgia become such big business in recent years?'

Because we're getting older.

'It's not just because of that. Maybe it's an unfair comparison, but when I went to see the Stones a few years ago I was touched to see people of their generation in their Sixties and Seventies still loving it. But what shocked me was the large amount of much younger people that were there. I know they're a legend, a force unto themselves, but I never expected a crowd of such varying ages.'

My next question back then was simple – 'Are you working class?'

'We all come from working-class backgrounds, but to many people, our council houses, surrounded by a few trees and a bit of grass, probably seem like a lower-middle-class set up.'

'When we lived in Stanley Road we had no hot water, no bathroom and no central heating, just a coal fire and an outside toilet. The old man eventually knocked through the wall from the kitchen after he nicked a bathroom suite off the building site he was working on and the outside toilet became an inside one and we had a proper bathroom for the first time. Before that it was a tin bath in front of the fire on a Sunday night. We had this old immersion heater that was like a fucking big kettle that would take forever to heat up after you filled it. Then you'd get a saucepan, dip it into the heater and pour the hot water into the tin bath and it would take another God knows how long to fucking fill it up.

'Then it was the pecking order, with everyone bathing in the same water. It was grey by the time I got in but you didn't give it a second thought because that was the way it was.

'When people started moving out of those slums into decent council estates, the world changed. People became more aspirational. I know it's a cliché but clichés are usually true. Working-class people would compensate for having nothing by trying to dress up to the nines when they went out. Everyone dresses much more casually now. No matter what the venue or occasion people still wear jeans and trainers. It's the universal style. People dress for comfort more than style these days.'

Teenagers were the end product of a council housing system that lifted us from the crumbling Victorian four-families-to-a-house backstreet tenements of pre-rock 'n' roll towns and dropped us onto glistening tower block estates where the kids were all right growing up 'cos they didn't have to share a toilet with twenty other people and had a bathroom they could call home. A bathroom where, thanks to a simple mirror, a guy could see clearly now for the first time, see how good-looking he was and how the way he did his hair made him even better-looking. He now had time to preen himself.

Working-class city kids found their style on those estates. Mod, rocker, skin, greaser, punk, mod, Ted, rude boy, new romantic, they've all walked out of council bathrooms in the sky with fire in their bellies and love in their hearts thanks to a mirror, a comb and lashings of hot water.

The Pomeranian sniffed goodbye and shuffled off onto Warwick Avenue. I wondered if its owner recognised Paul. Fuck, I wondered if the Pomeranian recognised Paul.

I lit a menthol fag; they make the cappuccino taste sweeter. I asked him if he thought, as I did, that people didn't really look terribly attractive back in the day.

'What, in the Seventies?' he asked.

And the Sixties.

'You're having a laugh. We'll beg to differ on that. What about the skinhead girls in the Sixties who wore those tight cropped mohair jumpers and smelled of Brut? Lovely! Something so nice about that. Look at the Eighties, there wasn't much style going on then.'

What about punk girls. Did you find them attractive?

'It wasn't a particularly great-looking style, was it! Listen, I was happy to get anything at that stage. Anyone I could possibly pull at all I was well happy. I didn't think the punk thing was that attractive but look what it became.

'In the early days of punk, people were more individual-looking – you didn't get those ridiculous punk outfits and huge mohicans. There were all sorts of styles around. When I went to the 100 Club festival there were a lot of soul boys in mohair jumpers and pegs and they looked like my mates back in Woking, boys who loved to dance. It was very eclectic then, but devoid of pose. Then I remember a very short time after that walking down the Kings Road seeing so-called punks with stupid, outlandish mohicans.'

Back to '77. 'What do you write about?' It was a fiery response from the recently turned 19 year-old.

'*All I write about is youth and hate. Hatred of teachers who spend all their time telling you how they won the war instead of asking you what you've been doing – I left school with a big chip on my shoulder. I love the English language but when I wanted to read contemporary books at school they insisted on stuffing Dickens down my throat. Same with music. All they played was Beethoven and Tchaikovsky when they should have started from Elvis. Hatred of greedy people – and there are a lot of them around. I suppose I've been cynical since I was fourteen years old, since my teachers kept telling me what I should know when they knew absolutely nothing themselves. All they were good at was tripping out on acid. I could tell them more than they could tell me.*

'*Hatred of people like the National Front – I sincerely hope our dress and national pride doesn't make people think we're involved with them. Bands have got a certain duty to their fans and I hate to see them wearing swastikas on stage. I want to see blacks and whites working together, trying to solve problems instead of creating them. People like that (Bob Geldof), setting themselves up as spokesmen for the kids, make me spew. The young are the strength, the future of this country. I'm still young, I've got time on my side – what have they got?*

'*I'll know when I've got nothing left to say. Then I won't write things down any more -- I'll lose my bottle.*

'*I get a week of sudden inspiration and then don't write another song for a couple of months*'.

'Well, y'know – idealistic youth, 'innit mate!' said Paul when I finished reading his old quote back. 'The one good thing I got out of school was knowing what I didn't want, like a 9-5 job or to be a type of boss, and music was one way of crawling out of that trap. I did write about youth but not sure about the hate thing.'

Still feel like that about Bob Geldof?

'God bless him. He's done some tremendous work, but he ain't a great singer is he. There were so many people that jumped on the bandwagon. Look at Sting and the Police, shocking. I remember appearing at a festival with them in France. They were a four-piece then and they did a bit in the middle where Sting fell to the floor and the others pretended to give him a kicking. Andy Summers had been around for years and played with the likes of Georgie Fame and Zoot Money. I thought at the time that it was just posturing, not what punk was really about. There was a lot of shite around.'

That's why it only lasted two years.

'Went on a bit too long if you ask me. People missed the point and punk never really developed beyond a certain level. The Jam always wanted to develop. With the Beatles, every record took you somewhere else, somewhere further down the road. Same with Bowie. You were on a journey with these people and I thought that's what we should strive to do, move things forward every time and hopefully take our audience along with us. To develop, improve as musicians and writers. Posturing just wasn't enough.'

There was a sincerity about you I didn't find in many other bands.

'Oh, I was serious all right. Probably too serious, but it worked for me. The music I still take seriously. Can't just bang it out and say "fuck it". It's always been very important to me. But it's a wonderful world Barry, ain't it.'

What do you write about now?

'Just whatever comes into my head. I was more on a mission back then, I guess, and I was very inspired by the Clash as well, especially in the early days. The first time I saw them was when they had the paint-splattered clothes. Keith Levine was playing guitar. They really touched me and made me want to say something important, to make some kind of social statement. My early attempts were really naïve and ridiculous but then I was naïve and ridiculous. I soon learned how to approach writing and by *All Mod Cons* I'd hit my stride.'

I told him that 'Down In The Tube Station' was the game-changer for me.

'Thank God we had the chance to make the third album, 'cos

these days we'd have been out on our arses after *This Is The Modern World*. Back then you were still given the chance to develop. After we got really good reviews for *All Mod Cons* the success propelled me to want to be better. The fact that people were taking my songs seriously meant that I took them more seriously. After we made *In The City*, Chris Parry (head of A&R at Polydor at the time) wanted us to get another album out that year. It took me a long time to write the songs for the first album and now I was confronted with a much shorter time to write the second. That obviously had an impact on them. I remember thinking "fuck, I've got to write another load now". 'Setting Sons' was lyrically very strong.'

Was that your favourite Jam album?

'No, that was *Sound Affects*. Musically it really sounded contemporary. We still had our Sixties influences but it sounded more modern than the previous efforts. Our sound had developed and continued to grow.

And what's the best album you've ever done?

'The last one, *Saturns Pattern*.'

I knew you'd say that.

'I wouldn't always say that but most of the time I would.'

I told him I loved the final track, 'These City Streets'.

'Thank you.'

You're still knocking them out, Paul.

'It was such a shame you didn't come to Hammersmith for the last show of the tour in December. Without blowing my own trumpet, it was fucking brilliant. In fact, it was probably the greatest gig I've ever played in my entire fucking life.'

Why?

'We knew it was the last gig we were going to do for at least a year so we said we've really got to turn it on tonight. We played every song we'd rehearsed and performed for two and a half hours. You could feel the surge from the audience just spiralling and spiralling and it lifted the roof off. I thought, "if I die tomorrow, at least I've gone out on a great one". When people ask what your best gig is, a lot of artists say their last – but this truly was. I just hope there are more to come.'

Back to the original interview. 'Are we heading for a police state?'

'The thing that really got to me was when I read about a guy called Liddle Towers who got beaten up outside a disco by six coppers and he eventually died. That's why I wrote Time For Truth. Coppers have now got the right to kill you. We're heading for a police state. More and more laws are being made for the police to carry out. That's what happens when the population increases.'

'I don't know what that means.'

'We like the Queen. I don't see the point of putting her down. And for those that do, it's just their mohair suits – their stab at being fashionable. All the other new bands refuse to talk politics with us 'cos we're always right.

'We're playing three Jubilee shows for nothing. We just wanted to contribute something. Instead of sitting back knocking the country, people should do something constructive'.

'The bit about people should be doing something constructive is all right but the Royal family thing – nah, not at all. The aristocracy is bollocks. The Royal Family is a fucking joke.

'I saw Damon Albarn has been awarded an OBE. I was surprised he accepted it. I got offered one about six years ago and I told them to shove it up their arse. But what was really strange was how many of my family and close friends congratulated me when they heard I'd been awarded one. I told them to fuck off, too.

'I've always hated the upper class and anything to do with aristocracy. I saw how the other half lived from an early age because my mum used to go and clean their houses. I really didn't like the people she worked for – I suppose it was inverted snobbery. It was wrong in some ways but I fucking hated them. I used to go with her sometimes and detested the way they spoke to her. Straight away they put my back up. They walked around like they had fucking sticks shoved up their arses. Horrible bastards.'

'At the time of that interview – it doesn't really apply so much now – a lot of working-class people were quite reactionary. As a kid you believed what you were told and you were told by people who obtained their information from a biased media.

'It was the Alf Garnett syndrome and ignorance was rife, but it wasn't their fault. And ignorance breeds racism. Fortunately, we became more educated and the UK developed a mixed society that makes it all so interesting, so vibrant. In Woking, we had the very first mosque built in the UK. My mum used to work there and I went with her once when I was a toddler and ended up shitting myself after I fell into a pond in the grounds.

'There was a burial ground in Woking honouring Muslims who fought for Britain in the First World War and gave their lives. Tragically, it was defaced with NF slogans in the Sixties and they had to move the bodies. They've just opened a memorial garden in honour of those soldiers on the exact same site.'

Another simple question from back then. 'What is politics?'

'When you've got no money in your pocket and you're out of a job, it's then you know what politics means.'

"Things haven't changed too much. I knew fuck all about politics then and I know fuck all about politics now.

'I like Jeremy Corbyn. Tom Watson seems all right as well. But politics is basically showbiz these days. It's all media-led.

'I now regret doing the Red Wedge thing. I was in Style Council at the time and we were playing more benefits for Red Wedge than concerts for the band. It made me cynical because I thought we were being used, exploited really. We weren't stupid enough to think it was possible to change the world, but after meeting some of the MPs on the road I realised they were just a bunch of fucking careerists and it put me off politics for life. I remember going to a meeting with Red Wedge once in South London and it was all these middle- and upper-class people offering us glasses of champagne and I felt like a fish out of water. Really not my scene and not my people. The artists involved were fine but the people we came into contact with were just wankers. It put me off and I've remained put off ever since.

'Corbyn is the first person in years that has made me interested in politics again, the first person in years that I'd actually vote for. If he was to contact me and ask if I'd like to get involved in some way, I'd definitely consider it.

'Shit, it's cold now mate. Can hardly feel my legs.'

We stubbed out the fags and got a table inside the empty café. Paul ordered two more coffees and I thanked god smoking wasn't allowed because I'd have had another one.

I started telling Paul that I never really hung out with the bands back then as some journalists did. In fact, I didn't even hang out with the other journalists. I guess I felt out of my depth. I was 23 with long hair and a beard. I wasn't a punk.

'A lot of the journos were a bit geeky but even more so now,' he said. 'Today, the music isn't something they really get into. It doesn't possess the glamour it used to have. Last year I went up to the 'NME' offices and there were rows and rows of desks. There was no music playing, no gear going on. It was a far cry from the Carnaby Street days when you could just drop into the office and get on the piss.

'I find it funny, especially with the 'NME' people. They'd write about rock 'n' roll and model themselves on Pete Doherty and they're just not like that now. I remember fondly the A&R departments at record companies. The one at Polydor had a mini-bar that was always stuffed with drink. We just used to hang out with the press officers and get pissed.'

It was time to ask Paul, as I did with Rat, Hugh and John, what he thought of the other bands at the time. Only now, I could also tell him what the other guys thought of the Jam.

John Lydon: '*The Jam hated us because we used the English flag differently to them. They tried to use it to hook into the Chelsea, scooter mod movement and that was a dead end so it was about White City and a Who rip off and it was fake and it was horrible. It was quite grotesque really.*'

'I bumped into him some years back and he was really lovely. I loved the Pistols, they were fucking brilliant, but I didn't really like them when Glen left. They just weren't the same band after that. Sid was a waste of fucking space.

'I saw Steve Jones recently. Shit, when I say recently it was probably 15 fucking years ago. He's a big lad now. He said in *The Filth And The Fury* that he got into punk because he wanted to shag more birds. That's why so many geezers wanted to be in a band then but I suspect it's probably not like that anymore either.'

I asked him what he thought of the Damned, as he'd already heard what Rat had said. 'I loved 'New Rose'. A great record. Loved the first album and the picture on the sleeve. But ultimately, they were a bit too jokey for my liking.'

I reminded Paul that I went to CBGBs with the Damned in '77 – the first time a UK punk band had played in the States.

'The very first US gig I ever played was CBGBs, two shows a night. Funny, I played there recently for John Varvatos, the clothes designer, who has a shop on the original site, although he still has gigs. It's not exactly the same, but they kept the long bar and the stage roughly where they used to be and we played a great little show in there.'

The Stranglers? 'Never my cuppa tea.' I read him Hugh's quote:

'My favourite single of 1977 has gotta be 'In The City'. I remember seeing the Jam perform it on Top Of The Pops and thought, this is amazing. A truly great song that reflected an era.'

Paul looked surprised. Change your mind?

'No. The Stranglers just weren't my kind of music. I couldn't work out what sort of music it was but it definitely wasn't mine.'

The Clash?

'Again, loved the early stuff but once they started to get too stylised they just turned into an ordinary rock band. And once they went to America they turned into an ordinary American rock band. First time I met Joe Strummer was at the 100 Club. He'd been to see us at the Windsor Castle in Harrow Road and he turned to me and said, "You're a mod, ain't ya." He was the first geezer who realized what we were trying to do. He was a nice feller. He didn't exactly take us under his wing but he was that bit older. We stayed in his squat with him one night just chatting and smoking draw and he was really nice.'

The Clash never appeared on *Top Of The Pops*.

'Back then, when you did *Top Of The Pops*, you had to re-record the track and it took us up to three days to do it. It was a real bind. After a while you'd slip the geezer a drink or take him out for one and get him to swap the tapes. I remember re-recording 'Down In The Tube Station' at Wessex studios, where *Never Mind The Bollocks* was recorded. We did the show loads of times because that was all there was. It was crap though.

'The Clash may never have appeared on *Top Of The Pops*, but it didn't stop Legs & Co dancing to 'Bankrobber', did it? Bernie Rhodes was so full of shit. I read a Pistols article recently in *Mojo* that featured a few quotes from Bernie. He said the reason he would never let the Clash do *TOTP* was because they knew about Jimmy Saville. What absolute bollocks.

'Malcolm McLaren was also full of shit. Me and my old man went to see him at the Glitterbest offices in Dryden Chambers. I think we were trying to blag a gig or something and he used to do this really camp performance: "Oh, I haven't got a magic wand to get things, you know". We never got anything out of him.'

I told Paul that McLaren was an interviewer's dream. His answers were invariably epic, dastardly tales of love and hate almost Shakespearian in their intensity.

'Yeah, but it was all bullshit.'

Entertaining bullshit.

Johnny Thunders Heartbreakers?

'I went to see them at Dingwalls with Joe Strummer but I really can't remember what I thought of them. Obviously didn't make a big impression. Wasn't he in the New York Dolls?'

Favourite punk single?

'Gotta be 'Anarchy In The UK', with 'New Rose' a close second. And I also loved '1977', the B-side of 'White Riot'.'

Fave album?

'I really can't think of any favourite album. Punk was all about singles and probably close to the very last shout of singles ruling the record world. Was there a good punk album? I don't know. Not for me. Wasn't even that mad on *Never Mind The Bollocks*. Didn't like the sound on it. I preferred the way the Clash and Pistols sounded live. And I preferred the way the Jam sounded live because there were so many overdubs and our producer, Vic Coppersmith-Heaven, would get me to track all my guitars – three, maybe four tracks of guitar. But I liked just the three of us because it was a much rawer sound.'

Still got the passion?

'Me? Yeah. Do you ever think about getting old, about mortality?'

Me? Yeah. All the fucking time. I've been feeling like shit lately. I went on to tell him about my growing-old ailments and forgot I was supposed to be interviewing, a cardinal sin, but he took a real interest. Amazing how everyone I talk to over the age of 35, without exception, knows that Warfarin is a blood thinner.

He looked so young to me, still hanging onto dreams like that brash, unconfident 18-year-old who caught my imagination all those years ago with some of the finest pop music ever written. The authenticity and grace of youth was intact, the charm impervious to time. He made me feel so young, and it's a wonderful thing to be flung.

'Sometimes I think, how long will it all go on? But if I was a jazz musician or an old blues guy, I wouldn't be having those thoughts. I wouldn't be wondering if I should stop. Because this is what I do. This is all I can do. This is all I'll ever want to do.

'I still love playing live but not so much the touring. All that hanging out is wearying. It really doesn't get any easier, being away from home, away from the kids.'

I nearly said the numbers but bit my tongue.

'But if you want to play to people, that's what you've got to do. The actual playing is a fucking joy; it's just the other bits that go with it I don't always enjoy.

'I never feel that my time is done. When people talk about ambitions, mine is to live long enough so I can do it some more, y'know. Pretty simple really. I want to do this for as long as I can. Beyond that I've no other ambition at all.'

It's keeping you young. You look well.

'Really? Sometimes I catch sight of my reflection in the mirror and it takes me a while to fucking recognise me – oh it's you, you old bastard. I'm 58 this year.'

So, it's official. Paul really is a bastard – he even said so himself.

And he paid for all the coffees. And he laughed at my jokes. And he hasn't changed one bit in 40 years. And his aim was true. Yep, a complete bastard.

They definitely don't make 'em like Paul Weller anymore – great artist, great dad, great man. And I love the talented bastard.

We hugged each other goodbye outside the café. As my cheek touched the fur collar of his jacket, I stepped out of that time machine onto Warwick Avenue and we walked in opposite directions. I wondered, as I did ten years earlier when I watched Rat Scabies wander down Wardour Street, if I'd ever see him again. Then I remembered that five-year age gap and realised there was probably more chance of him attending my funeral. Then I thought it would make up for his no-show at my wedding. Then I heard a screaming siren and wished I was far away. Then I thought, shit, this coffee has made me hyper. Then I looked at my phone and it was 5pm. Shit, we'd talked for three hours. Then I thought about the interview. Then I realized I was a cappuccino kid with a Freedom Pass. Then I searched every pocket for that Freedom Pass. Then I wondered if it was the caffeine or dementia. Then I thought, "who gives a fuck?".

As the coffee rush faded and the solitude became more tranquil, the arthritic twinges returned and my vibrant stride was gradually reduced to a stroll. The cold was infesting my body like a virus.

But my memory was hot as sun...

When I finished writing the article I texted Paul.

Hi Paul

Hope you're well, mate. Ready to send the piece for your perusal. Like I said, nobody has seen this yet and it hasn't been edited. I hope you're not in any way offended by it, 'cos it's a leg pull, but that's why I'm sending it to you, just in case you are! Personally, I fucking love it. But then I would say that. Please feel free to add/subtract, delete, demolish, set light to – it's only words as another Barry once said. I'll send the pic for your approval too, Paul. It's just taking so long in Photoshop to iron out all the wrinkles, mate! (couldn't resist it!) Can't quite remember who was with you at Somerset House, family-wise when we met that morning. Be great if you could let me know their names. Do you still want me to send it to the email address you gave me? This is meant for your eyes only. By the way, it's over 13,000 words and will be the final chapter.

His reply:

OK mate, well as long as there's nothing to offend my missus u can send it to her. If there is, there'll be trouble!! p x

Me: *Can't promise, mate, don't blame me if she wants a divorce! I can send it to another address if you like, just in case...*

Paul: *Only have Hannah's email mate and we don't have secrets. If there's anything that would offend her u better take it out my ol' mate, cos if she's upset, I'm fuckin upset too!!*

Me: *I'll just rewrite the whole thing then!! Will send today next time I'm in front of the computer, Paul. All the best.*

Paul: *What, the whole piece is offensive?!! Ha-ha, me daughter found my email!*

Nine days went by, and the publishers were getting restless

Morning, Paul.

Hope you're well, mate. Just wondered if you'd had a chance to go through the piece I sent.

Paul: *Ello mate, I didn't know u sent it! Ill check this afternoon and have a look! All the georgie p x*

Later that same day...

Very, very nice piece mate. Some nice angles. You keeping on about your age is boring though, mate. Fuck age, fuck death. We're part of the post-war rock'n'roll generations and our lives are touched and altered because of it. Good luck with the book! Footnote: I met you again around 85/86 in a restaurant in Connaught Street and you kinda blanked me, you cheeky fucker! Take care mate, P xx

Me: *Really? Don't remember that! Hope I was with someone important so they could witness I blanked you... Glad you liked it mate and when you get to my age, you young whippersnapper, you'll understand my preoccupation with the years! By the way, here's a pic I took that we could use if you think it's OK.*

Paul: *I hope I don't mate. That pic's rubbish so I'll send u one!*

Me: *Great, as long as it ain't 20 years old!*

Paul: *PS there's a few errors in the piece so u should check it thru.*

Me: *It hasn't been edited yet so they should all be covered. Look forward to getting the pic. Have a great weekend, Paul and thanks again for this. Will let you know when the book's out and you must come to the launch if you're about.*

Paul: *There's a coupla bits that don't make sense so have a look mate.*

Me: *I'll send it to you after it's been edited.*

When Paul sent me the photo of himself that revealed a man working hard at holding back the years – and clearly succeeding – he included the following message:

Here you are mate, use this fucker, not bad for an old cunt

This was obviously a piss-take in light of some of my ageist remarks in the feature and I creased up laughing. But shit, I had to admit, I was shocked at how striking he was in the photo. Totally unexpected. When you look that good, you can afford to take the piss. One thing I always loved about Paul was his innate, incisive humour that helped to take some of the sting out of the bitterness and sadness that permeated much of his music back then and it was a joy to see he hadn't lost touch with it.

Jeez, here's a bloke who drank his way through the Seventies and Eighties, snorted his way through a lot of the Nineties and some of the Noughties before shutting up shop just six years ago. And he has the effrontery to look like that!? What a tremendous incentive for all us middle-aged blokes who've drunk and snorted our way through most of our adult, and not so adult, lives.

Iggy Pop cornered the market in making middle-aged bare torsos cool, but I think we've got a new kid in town.

Who was it who said, 'Fuck age, fuck death'?

Now that's what I call punk.

I texted Paul my response to his photo.

Jesus Paul, very impressive mate. I almost fancy you myself!

Paul: *Don't show it to Dina or ur vibrant love life will be over!!*

Me: *No worries there – she's into old blokes with flabby physiques so I'm on a winner! I knew all those years of eschewing the gym would pay off for me!! Have a cracking weekend and thanks again, you rippling-muscle bastard you.*

Paul: *haha take care mate*

And you, mate. And you